D1751669

THE LAND OF HEART'S DELIGHT

THE LAND OF HEART'S DELIGHT

EARLY MAPS AND CHARTS
OF VANCOUVER ISLAND

MICHAEL LAYLAND

TouchWood
Editions

Copyright © 2013 Michael Layland

All rights reserved. No part of this publication may be reproduced, stored in a retrieval system, or transmitted in any form or by any means—electronic, mechanical, recording, or otherwise—without the prior written consent of the publisher or a licence from The Canadian Copyright Licensing Agency (ACCESS Copyright). For a copyright licence, visit accesscopyright.ca.

TouchWood Editions
touchwoodeditions.com

LIBRARY AND ARCHIVES CANADA CATALOGUING IN PUBLICATION
Layland, Michael, 1938–
The land of heart's delight : early maps and charts of Vancouver Island / Michael Layland.

Includes bibliographical references and index.
Issued also in electronic formats.
ISBN 978-1-77151-015-8

1. Cartography—British Columbia—Vancouver Island—History.
2. Vancouver Island (BC)—Maps. I. Title.

GA475.B7L39 2013   912.711'2   C2013-902078-0

Editor: Marlyn Horsdal
Proofreader: Vivian Sinclair
Design: Pete Kohut
Cover image: *Physical Map of Vancouver Island, B.C., 1913*, from author's collection

We gratefully acknowledge the financial support for our publishing activities from the Government of Canada through the Canada Book Fund, Canada Council for the Arts, and the province of British Columbia through the British Columbia Arts Council and the Book Publishing Tax Credit.

This book was produced using FSC®-certified, acid-free paper, processed chlorine free and printed with soya-based inks.

The information in this book is true and complete to the best of the author's knowledge. All recommendations are made without guarantee on the part of the author. The author disclaims any liability in connection with the use of this information.

1 2 3 4 5   17 16 15 14 13

PRINTED IN CHINA

"Cartography, the most aesthetically pleasing of the sciences, draws its power from the greatest of man's gifts—courage, the spirit of inquiry, artistic skill, man's sense of order and design, his understanding of natural laws, and his capacity for singular journeys to the most distant places. They are the brightest attributes and they have made maps one of the most luminous of man's creations."[1]

—Paul Theroux

❊ ❊ ❊

This book is dedicated to the memory of two stalwarts of the Historical Map Society of British Columbia: R.C. (Bob) Harris and Bruce I. Ward.

Both devoted much of their last years to compiling a list of early maps of the British Columbia area. Without the result of their carto-bibliographic endeavour, this work would scarcely have been possible.

Contents

Foreword by Derek Hayes 1

Introduction 3

CHAPTER ONE: Maps of Speculation and Myth 7

CHAPTER TWO: Maps of Mystery and Intrigue 13

CHAPTER THREE: First European Contact: Spaniards Anchor at San Lorenzo 19

CHAPTER FOUR: *Makook!* With Cook at Nootka 25

CHAPTER FIVE: Soft Gold: Sea Otter Traders 31

CHAPTER SIX: Imperial Flashpoint: Nootka, 1789 39

CHAPTER SEVEN: "Exploration Will Resolve the Doubts" 47

CHAPTER EIGHT: "No Place More Eligible": Anglo-Hispanic Collaboration 54

CHAPTER NINE: "A Perfect 'Eden'": James Douglas Selects a New Fort 63

CHAPTER TEN: Settling into Fort Victoria: Doubts over Tenuous Tenure 71

CHAPTER ELEVEN: "In Free and Common Socage": Colonization by Contract 76

CHAPTER TWELVE: Pemberton and Pearse Survey Vancouver Island's Southeastern Districts 83

CHAPTER THIRTEEN: Explosive Growth: Victoria Feels the Impact of the Gold Rush 99

CHAPTER FOURTEEN: The San Juan Dispute: Cartographic Neglect—and a Pig—Almost Trigger a War 111

CHAPTER FIFTEEN: "Navigating this Boisterous Neighbourhood": George Richards's Hydrography 117

CHAPTER SIXTEEN: "The Back of the World": Vancouver Island under the Crown Colonial 129

CHAPTER SEVENTEEN: The Vancouver Island Exploring Expeditions: Brown, Leech, Meade, and Buttle Head Inland 143

CHAPTER EIGHTEEN: Canada's New Province: To Celebrate, Joseph Trutch Orders a Map 154

CHAPTER NINETEEN: The Two-Million-Acre Dowry: The Esquimalt & Nanaimo Railway's Land Grant 161

CHAPTER TWENTY: "The Most Perfect Map": Tom Kains's Campaigns 173

CHAPTER TWENTY-ONE: "Vancouver Island by Land and Water": Reverend William Bolton and *The Province* Expeditions 187

CHAPTER TWENTY-TWO: The New Century: The Dominion Comes to the Rescue 195

CHAPTER TWENTY-THREE: "A Sea of Mountains": Strathcona Park 207

Afterword 213

Glossary 216
Endnotes 218
Bibliography 221
List of Illustrations 223
Index 228
Acknowledgments 232

Foreword
DEREK HAYES

THE NORTHWEST COAST OF AMERICA was one of the last places in temperate latitudes to be discovered by Europeans. This did not stop many commercial mapmakers' speculating on the geography of the region long before anything was known for sure. Their maps live on to amuse us with their notions of inland seas, magnificent rivers, and straits offering an easy passage to and from Europe. Then, in 1773, the Spanish government suddenly authorized an investigation of foreign intrusions into what it regarded as its territory—the North Pacific Ocean. For it had heard and finally digested knowledge of Vitus Bering and Alexei Chirikov's voyages for Russia from Kamchatka in 1741, when they both made it, independently, to the Alaskan coast. Who knew if they had discovered gold or a secret passage, or set up fur-trade posts?

And so the Spanish dispatched a veteran sailor, Juan Pérez, north from New Spain—today's Mexico—with instructions to sail to 60° north. In July 1774 he reached Langara Island, at the northern tip of those islands we used to call the Queen Charlottes, named after a fur-trade explorer's ship and a British queen, and now called Haida Gwaii. Pérez made the first contact with the Aboriginal peoples of what would one day be British Columbia and incidentally defined a latitude that would one day mark the Canada–United States boundary line—54°40' N. He also produced a map, the first of the British Columbia coast as a result of exploration rather than the rampant speculation and imagination of before. Pérez paused off Vancouver Island near Nootka Sound, but did not land, and his map doesn't even separate Vancouver Island from the mainland; it all looked the same from that early sea.

Pérez was followed in 1778 by Britain's James Cook, searching for a supposed Northwest Passage, and after his crew discovered that they could obtain high prices in China for the fur of the sea otter, for which they had traded on the northwest coast, many returned to search for more, driven by the lure of high profits. But of course, sailing into the unknown required the making of maps, so at least the traders might be able to find their way back to a profitable location, and the knowledge of coastal geography evolved some more.

Later, the Spanish sent out more ships of exploration and survey, as did the British, both being concerned that the other might find and claim a Northwest Passage before they did. In 1792 Britain's George Vancouver began his detailed survey of the intricate coastline. Both British and Spanish that year separated Vancouver Island from the mainland on maps for the first time. Quadra and Vancouver's Island, Vancouver named it, jointly honouring himself and the Spanish commander, Juan Francisco de la Bodega y Quadra. But the Spanish never colonized; it was a later generation of British settlers that effectively withdrew the honour to the Spanish commander by removing his name from that of the island. The victors, as they are wont to do, had rewritten history.

A series of maps drawn by the various expeditions documents this early exploration of the British Columbia coastline, telling us the story in a concise way and letting us see for ourselves how the veil was lifted from the map. Maps are excellent and valuable first-line documents of history, yet they are often overlooked, even by historians. A picture, they say, is worth a thousand words. How many, then, is a map worth, for it often contains far more information?

It is precisely this information that extrudes from the pages of this book, written by Michael Layland, a Victoria resident and the foremost map historian of Vancouver Island. The book has, I know, been many years in the making, and is the product of the most detailed and exhaustive research. This is a history of Vancouver Island from before anyone knew it was here to the creation of Strathcona Park in 1912, and the start of the First World War. On the way we learn of the Spanish, British, and American explorations and exploitations of the maritime fur trade; the establishment and growth of Fort Victoria; the building of the Esquimalt & Nanaimo Railway, with its enormous accompanying land grants; and lots more.

The key, of course, is that all of the stories are illustrated with maps of the period, from hand-drawn expedients to detailed cartographic masterpieces, finely engraved, printed, and coloured. All of this assists us in understanding the state of mind of the participants and their knowledge—or lack thereof— of both land and sea, for it is easy to judge historical events in the light of hindsight, information which, of course, the participants did not have at the time. The maps help us correct that bias. As primary documents they are the very stuff of history.

Derek Hayes, author of
*British Columbia:
A New Historical Atlas*

Introduction

THE *LINGUA FRANCA* OF GEOGRAPHY, maps speak not just about the lay of the land, but also of the state of civilization itself. As artifacts, they help us trace the causes, constraints, and biases—of the nations and of the individuals—under which they were produced.

From the earliest times to the present, mapmakers, or cartographers, have been at the forefront of advances in technology: written language, geometry, paper, printing, astronomy, chronometers, aerial photos, computers, and satellites. Although the first printed books were bibles, "geographies," or atlases, followed very soon afterward.

Archeologists have steadily pushed claims of the "oldest map" backward in time, and contenders for the title are spread over the globe. The oldest map so far discovered dates from the upper Paleolithic era. Twenty-five thousand years ago, a cartographer from the Pavlovian culture in today's Slovak Republic scribed, onto a mammoth's tusk, the meanders of a river and the surrounding hills. This map—if that is what it is—would indicate that cartography predated writing.

Many anthropologists now support the theory that the earliest human arrivals in the Americas came from Asia, but not across the land bridge of Beringia and through a gap in the continental ice sheet. The new theory is that they travelled by sea along the coast, even as far south as Chile.

The topic of early Asiatic voyages—Chinese, Japanese, and Polynesian—to this coast is currently a matter of lively debate by historians of cartography. While there is, as yet, no generally agreed cartographic evidence for such voyages, some intriguing hints of ancient knowledge of this coast are now emerging; these could only have come from reports by ocean-going travellers, possibly even including Marco Polo in the thirteenth century. (See Fig. 1, page 4)

There are Chinese documentary records of journeys to a land far to their east called Fou Sang. Theories as to where that was located have ranged from the Aleutians to Mexico. While Fou Sang remains a mystery, it does seem probable that the Chinese have known about this coast for thousands of years.

Along the Pacific Northwest coast before European

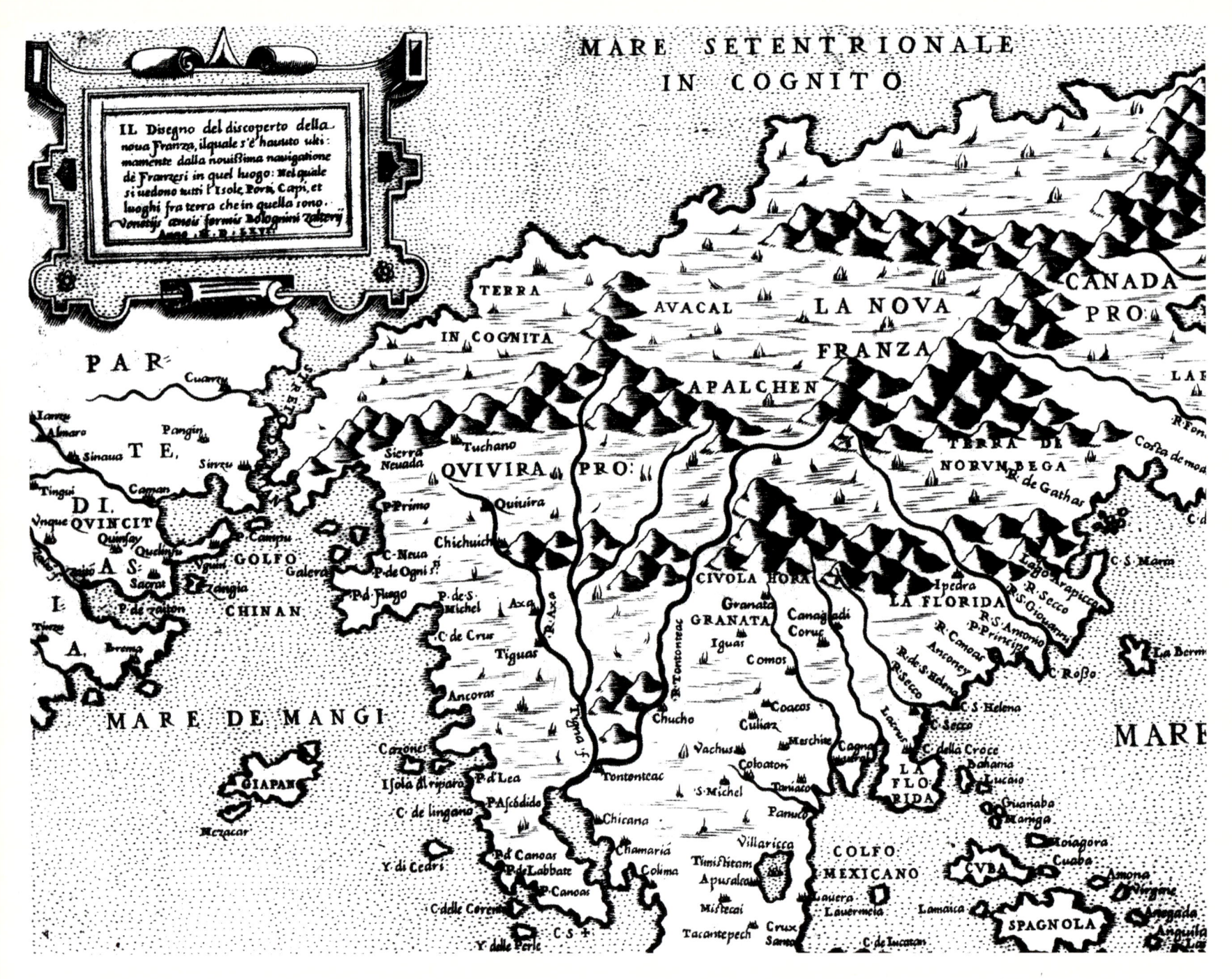

Fig. 1 Attempting to interpret Marco Polo's reports of his travels, the Venetian Bolognini Zaltieri depicted on this 1566 map a narrow Stretto de Anian separating Quivira in western North America from Asia and connecting the Pacific with the unknown Northern Sea. This prescient map was made over two centuries before Cook first transited the Bering Strait.

contact, Aboriginal peoples drew features on rocks that might be interpreted as maps, although none have been definitively identified as such. Some of these pictographs appear to represent either a path or stream between two lakes, or a mystic journey drawn by someone undergoing, perhaps, a rite of passage. It is difficult to date individual rock drawings, but it is reasonable to assume that such artifacts derive from traditions many thousands of years old.

Captain James Cook, exploring what was to European navigators a virtually uncharted Pacific Ocean, found illiterate Polynesian seamen using maps. They navigated enormous distances out of sight of land, accurately finding their way to isolated atolls, using stick charts, constructed from thin canes and cowrie shells, which portrayed patterns of long-period oceanic waves and islands.

In whatever form, and no matter how incomplete or inaccurate, all old maps give us a window into the era in which they were produced, although the glass is always tinted and distorted. All maps will have been generated with intent, bias, and selectivity, and they cannot be separated from those motives. The map reader must consider: Who ordered and who made this map? Why? Who was the intended audience? What was going on at the time? This dimension of intent adds to the value of maps as artifacts by providing evidence and insight about wider issues.

In the era of European discovery, when map-making was driven by the quest for imperial and trade dominance, the prospect of high returns fuelled exploration of land and waters, bestowing of place names, recording in journals and charts, compilation of map and charts from other sources, and publication of the information—all interconnected elements of mapping.

❋ ❋ ❋

The story behind the book's title is this: to entice more settlers from Britain, in 1911 the Vancouver Island Development League published a booklet entitled *The Land of Heart's Delight*. The sentiment echoed Captain George Vancouver's opinion, penned more than a century earlier: ". . . the most lovely country that can be imagined."

❋ ❋ ❋

This book traces the thread of the early maps and charts that were made of Vancouver Island. There are other, related threads completing the fabric of the processes of making those maps—details of what the explorers and surveyors encountered, how they went about recording their findings, how developments in technology assisted their work, and the reasons for them to be there. The constraints of a single volume do not allow telling of the full story, so recounting the exploration aspects must await a "prequel" book. Suggestions for further reading are included in the bibliography, and summaries of relevant technical and political aspects can be found as "extensions" on the website bchistoryonline.com/wiki/The_Land_of_Heart's_Delight.

Fig. 2 Cornelis de Jode of Antwerp added this map when, in 1593, he republished his father's atlas. He attempted to position cartographically the fabled lands of Quivira, Anian, and Bergi, and the supposed Strait of Anian.

INSET
Fig. 3 At about latitude 50° N, de Jode depicted an abrupt change of direction of the coast, creating a bay with two unnamed islands defended by a splendid sea monster.

CHAPTER ONE

Maps of Speculation and Myth

VANCOUVER ISLAND LIES BETWEEN LATITUDES 48°19' and 50°53' north, and is separated from the mainland by the Coastal Trough, which runs from Puget Sound to the channels of the Alaskan Panhandle. Islands large and small, and isolated reefs and rocks above and just below the surface, create a maze of archipelagos and narrow channels full of hazards to shipping. Author Jack Hodgins aptly called this coast "The ragged green edge of the World."[1]

For centuries, the northeastern rim of the Pacific Ocean was a region of speculation, myth, guesswork, and confusion. This was the last temperate coastline in the world to see the sails of European explorers, the last to be displayed with certainty and accuracy upon their charts.

This lack of information did not deter early mapmakers from attempting to include the region on their maps. Separating fact from fiction posed very real dilemmas for those early cartographers. They made valiant efforts to reconcile and incorporate various travellers' tales, myths, and downright guesswork, often getting things wrong.

European cartographers wrestled to solve overlapping puzzles. They were working to reconcile fables, tall tales related by old salts, and disinformation provided out of imperial and commercial rivalry, all compounded by problems over longitude, wishful thinking, and fanciful invention. Just how did the coasts of Asia and North America relate to each other? Maps of this period reflect the various cartographers' solutions.

In most cases they consulted and incorporated earlier maps, adding new information or combining them into new configurations. Maps of the Pacific Northwest drawn between the sixteenth and the latter part of the eighteenth centuries record how geographical knowledge advanced, with a few missteps, immediately prior to the first European voyages of science-based exploration.

Cornelis de Jode published the first printed map focused on the Pacific Northwest in Antwerp, in 1593. He used as the title of the map *Quivirae Regnum* (the Kingdom of Quivira), one of several mythical lands sought by Spanish conquistadores. Centred on the map are two unnamed islands close to the coast between latitudes 49° and 51° north. It might be tempting to speculate that they represent, and indicate knowledge of, Vancouver Island, but this seems improbable: The trend of the coast between Cape Mendocino and those islands is almost ninety degrees in error. (See Fig. 2, page 6)

De Jode seems to have derived the detail and toponyms (place names) from cartography of the period, probably a world map published by Petrus Plancius in 1592. The two islands are also shown on Plancius's map, but they are larger and of different shapes. De Jode adds a decorative element: Just out to sea, near the islands, swims an imposing sea monster, part unicorn, part lion, part fish. (See Fig. 3, page 6)

In 1776, the Venetian cartographer Antonio Zatta published a map of a region that had recently been explored by Russians. Zatta locates "Fou Sang (colony of Chinese)" as an island around 50° north—just where Vancouver Island would later be found. Zatta positions an elephant in the decorative panel, or cartouche, of his map. In the body of the map, he repeats another myth by indicating a navigable channel linking the Pacific with the Atlantic. This was known to the English as the Northwest Passage, elsewhere in Europe as the Strait of Anian. (See Fig. 4)

The version shown by Zatta reflects an apocryphal voyage by a Spaniard, Admiral Bartolome de Fonte, but the idea of such a waterway had been around since the sixth century BCE (Before Common Era). The Greek geographer Anaximander had first proposed it, and it was elaborated two centuries later by the Afro-Roman cosmographer Macrobius. By the sixteenth century, this hypothesis had evolved into a clear passage, called the *fretum arcticum* (the Arctic Strait), between the two oceans.

This concept was most attractive to European merchants. They were eager to learn of an alternative trading route for the spices, silks, porcelain, and perfumes of the Orient. It would release them from both the Arab stranglehold over the western end of the Silk Road and the perils of Cape Horn, and to secure dominion over such a lucrative market corridor would be a prize well worth the cost of discovery. The quest for this passage would lead European ships to the Pacific Northwest, to what would become known as Vancouver Island.

The story of Admiral de Fonte's voyage originated as a 1708 magazine piece purporting to be a letter by de Fonte relating how he had, in 1640, sailed north from Peru to a river mouth about 53° north. There he found an abundance of salmon. Heading inland and upstream, he came upon a vast lake with many islands. This led him through a network of lakes and interconnecting streams trending northeast into Hudson Bay, where he encountered a ship that he claimed had sailed there from Boston.

The article quoting the letter went unnoticed for some thirty years, until Arthur Dobbs, an Irish politician and opponent of the Hudson's Bay Company's exclusive franchise, used it to support his campaign to reopen the search for the Northwest Passage. The Lords of the Admiralty responded by funding a voyage of exploration into the waters north of the Churchill River. A first-hand account from that voyage contained an intriguing map intended to clarify the de Fonte geography. The author of the account was Theodore Drage and the cartographer was Edward Holding. While this map is devoted mainly to the fictitious river system in the interior, the accuracy of some of its local detail hints of a mysterious early voyage to the northwestern end of Vancouver Island.

Fig. 4 Venetian Antonio Zatta attempted to incorporate recent Russian discoveries with several myths and tall tales on this, one of the last maps of the Pacific Northwest published prior to Cook's expedition of 1778.

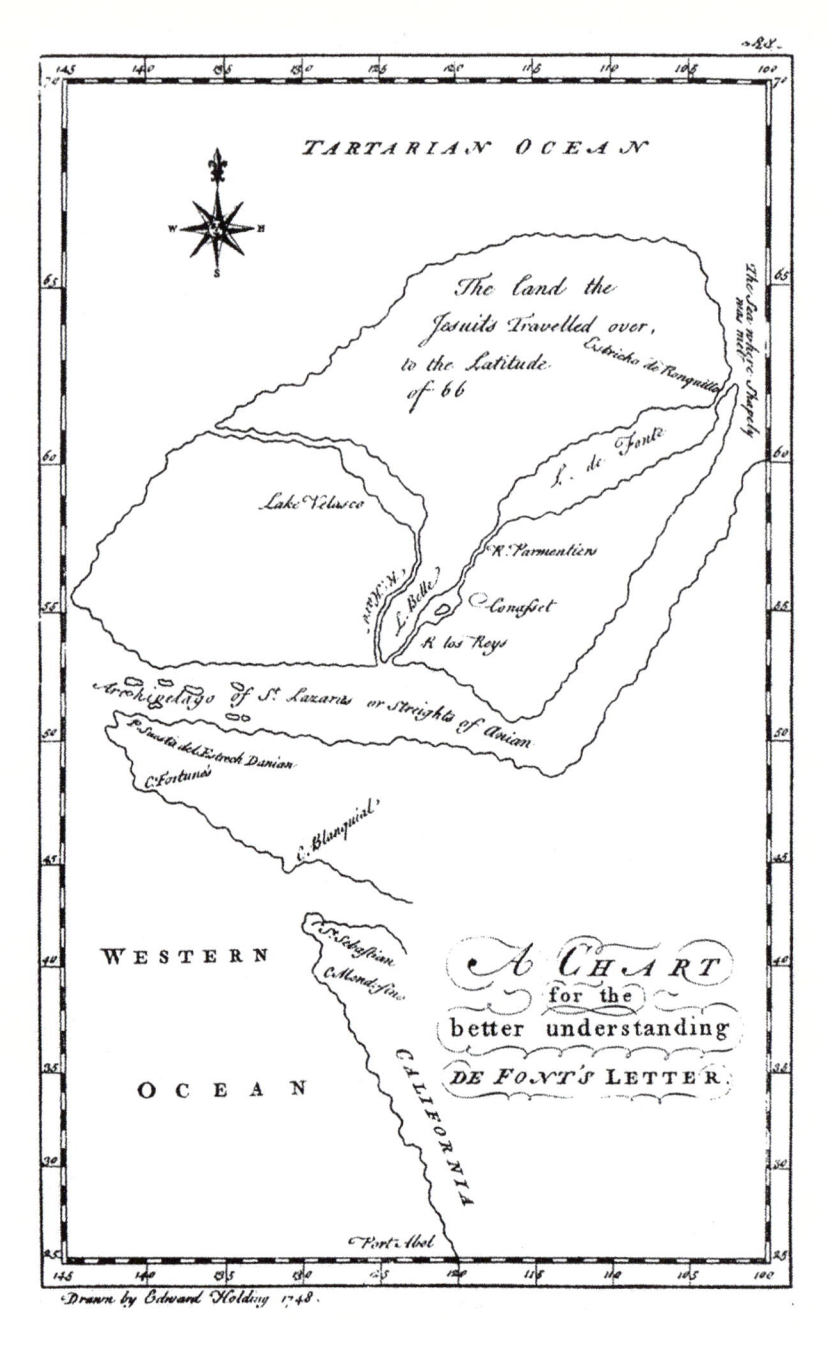

Fig. 5 T.S. Drage published this chart in 1749. Ostensibly about the report of a hoax voyage of de Fonte, it offers intriguing clues to early knowledge of the western end of Vancouver Island and Queen Charlotte Sound.

This information must derive from some time prior to the date of publication, 1749—decades before the documented voyages of the European explorers Pérez, Cook, and La Pérouse. (See Fig. 5)

In Paris, in the 1750s, the brothers Joseph-Nicolas and Guillaume de L'Isle and their brother-in-law, Philippe Buache, were cartographic luminaries of the Enlightenment. They published a series of maps that incorporated versions of the de Fonte route, proudly displaying their credentials as members of the Academy of Science or even Geographers to the King. Their works grew ever more elaborate and fanciful. The large lake became an immense "Mer ou Baie de l'Ouest," but with Juan de Fuca now credited as its discoverer. (See Fig. 6) Other cartographers were drawn in to the inflating fabrication, including Thomas Jefferys, Geographer to King George III. They all vied to interpret the story and to reinforce the idea that a navigable, interoceanic waterway was a reality.

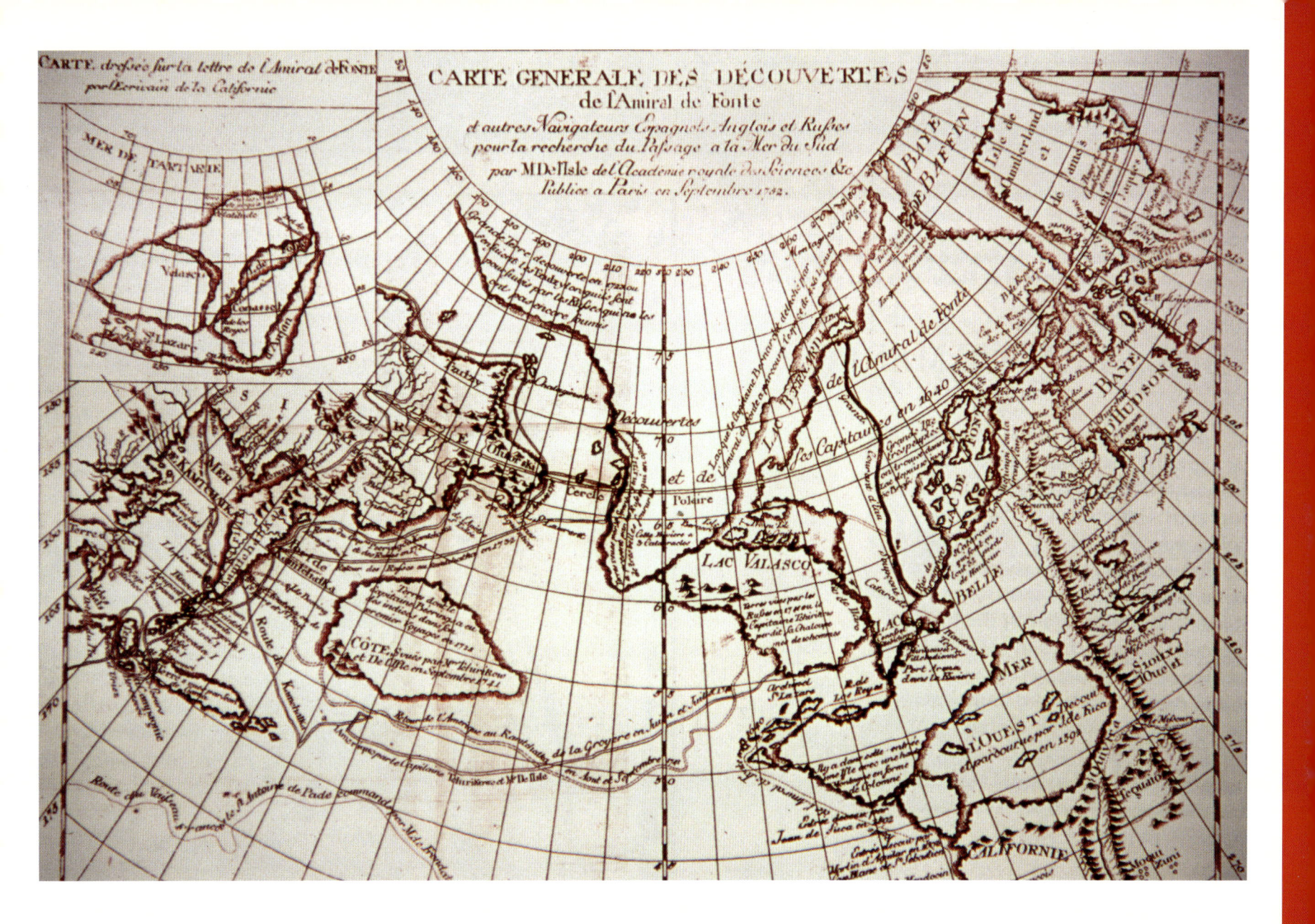

Fig. 6   Three French cartographers collaborated on a series of elaborate maps linked to the report of a hoax voyage by an Admiral de Fonte in 1640, including this one published in 1640.

Fig. 7 The Dutch cartographer Jodocus Hondius, working in London in 1589, published this world map to mark the course of Drake's circumnavigation, including the contentious naming of Nova Albion.

INSET

Fig. 8 Drake's track on Hondius's map appears to hint at an alteration to the copper printing plate, interpreted by some as an attempt to disguise Drake's true landfall at about 49° N. The Latin text next to the * reads: "There, due to intense cold, he [Drake] was forced back southwards. Lat. 42. Date 5 June."

CHAPTER TWO

Maps of Mystery and Intrigue

FRANCIS DRAKE'S VOYAGE, WHICH INCLUDED what is now Vancouver Island, has provoked much debate, as historians have attempted to establish the true itinerary and discoveries of that epic circumnavigation.

Drake embarked in 1577 on the *Golden Hinde*, on a semi-official mission to challenge the Spanish-Portuguese Treaty of Tordesillas, which claimed to divide the as-yet uncolonized parts of the world into their respective realms. England and some other European powers rejected this ruling, and so Drake set out to harass Spanish ports and shipping, including in the "Spanish Lake" that was the Pacific. He was to return home with captured treasure for his monarch, Queen Elizabeth I, who was also one of his investors.

Drake accomplished his mission brilliantly, sacking and looting cities, capturing treasure galleons, and sowing general mayhem throughout the Spanish Empire. He also collected whatever charts and "rutters" (sailing directions) he found on the ships he captured, and interrogated pilots and navigators for their seagoing knowledge. Several of them were taken on board his ships to help guide his further adventures into unknown waters.

The part of the three-year voyage that relates to Vancouver Island concerns a few months during the summer of 1579, after Drake departed from the tiny harbour of Guatulco on the Pacific coast of Mexico and before he set sail westward out across the Pacific, homeward bound.

Surviving details of the voyage are scant, cryptic, and contradictory. Upon Drake's return to England, Queen Elizabeth commanded that all of his journals, logs, charts, and coastline sketches be seized and guarded under the strictest security. Crew members were bound to silence, under pain of death. Recognizing that even this would not prevent leaks, the Queen counselled deception and disinformation, and Richard Hakluyt, her official chronicler, spun a web of conflicting reports to mask the truth and published a heavily edited, first-hand account of the voyage, entitled *The Famous Voyage of Sir Francis Drake*. Drake's manuscripts have never come to light.

Several maps mark Drake's route, including one, dated 1589, by Dutch cartographer Jodocus Hondius, who was based in London at the time. His map showed not only some islands but also evidence that Drake's track, in just the area of Vancouver Island, had been scribed onto a copper printing plate, then altered, seemingly in order to erase the approach to his landfall, which would have been about 49° north. The erased section of the track is still faintly visible. (See Figs. 7 and 8, page 12)

In 1939, BC land surveyor and amateur historian Richard Bishop used modern tables of wind and current patterns to calculate Drake's landfall and first anchorage.[1] Bishop theorized that it must have been at 48° north on the west coast of Vancouver Island, and this corresponds with the latitude admitted by John Drake, Francis's nephew and confidant aboard *Golden Hinde*, under interrogation by the Inquisition. (See Fig. 9)

Another Englishman, Thomas Cavendish, followed Drake's wake into the Pacific in 1587. He too created chaos in Spanish shipping and settlement, capturing a mammoth treasure galleon, the *Santa Ana*. As Drake had done, Cavendish collected any charts, rutters, and navigation instruments he found, along with more tangible booty. He also co-opted any navigators on board, to gain access to their regional knowledge.

Cavendish died at sea a few years after returning from his voyage, and his brother-in-law, Robert Dudley, administered his estate. In this capacity he would have seen Cavendish's collection of journals, logs, and charts. These might have included some of Drake's papers, or clandestine copies of them. In 1647 Dudley published *Dell' Arcano del Mare* (Concerning the Secret of the Sea), the first hydrographic atlas to cover the entire world and the first to use Mercator's projection throughout. It shows coastlines and good anchorages, and adds information crucial to sailing ships—prevailing winds, currents, and magnetic variations. The 146 copperplate charts are scientific as well as elegant, embellished with baroque calligraphy and decorative flourishes. Dudley's text, reflecting his extensive geographical and maritime knowledge, supports the charts.

The atlas's final chart, *D'America XXXIII*, covers the west coast between 37° and 50° north. This chart, known to Drake scholars as the *Carta particolare*, contains information related to Drake's time in these waters and so has been subjected to close scrutiny. (See Fig. 10, page 16)

At its northern edge, close to 50°, Dudley's chart indicates a "C[apo] di Fortuna" with several nearby islets and a coastline continuing northeast, called "Costa Incognita." (See Fig. 11, page 16)

A dramatic headland does thrust into the Pacific at 50° north. Now called Cape Cook, it is notorious among local mariners for dense fogs, fierce currents, and sudden, violent storms. There are several islets in the area and north of the cape, the coast trends northeast. Could this be Dudley's "Capo di Fortuna?" If so, the match could help identify other mysterious names on the chart. Assuming a similar accuracy in latitude, the "Baia Ancon d'Ilhas" (meaning, most probably, "Bay of Islands") could be one of three or four inlets on Vancouver Island, including Cook's Nootka Sound. The "Baia de los Tachaios" could well be Grays Harbor and Willapa Bay, and "Rio de los Tachaios" could represent the mouth of the Columbia River. (See Fig. 12, page 17)

The enigma around this chart does not end there. To produce the *Arcano*, Dudley drew on sheets of paper and passed them on for compiling and engraving onto the copperplates. However, the manuscripts contained considerably

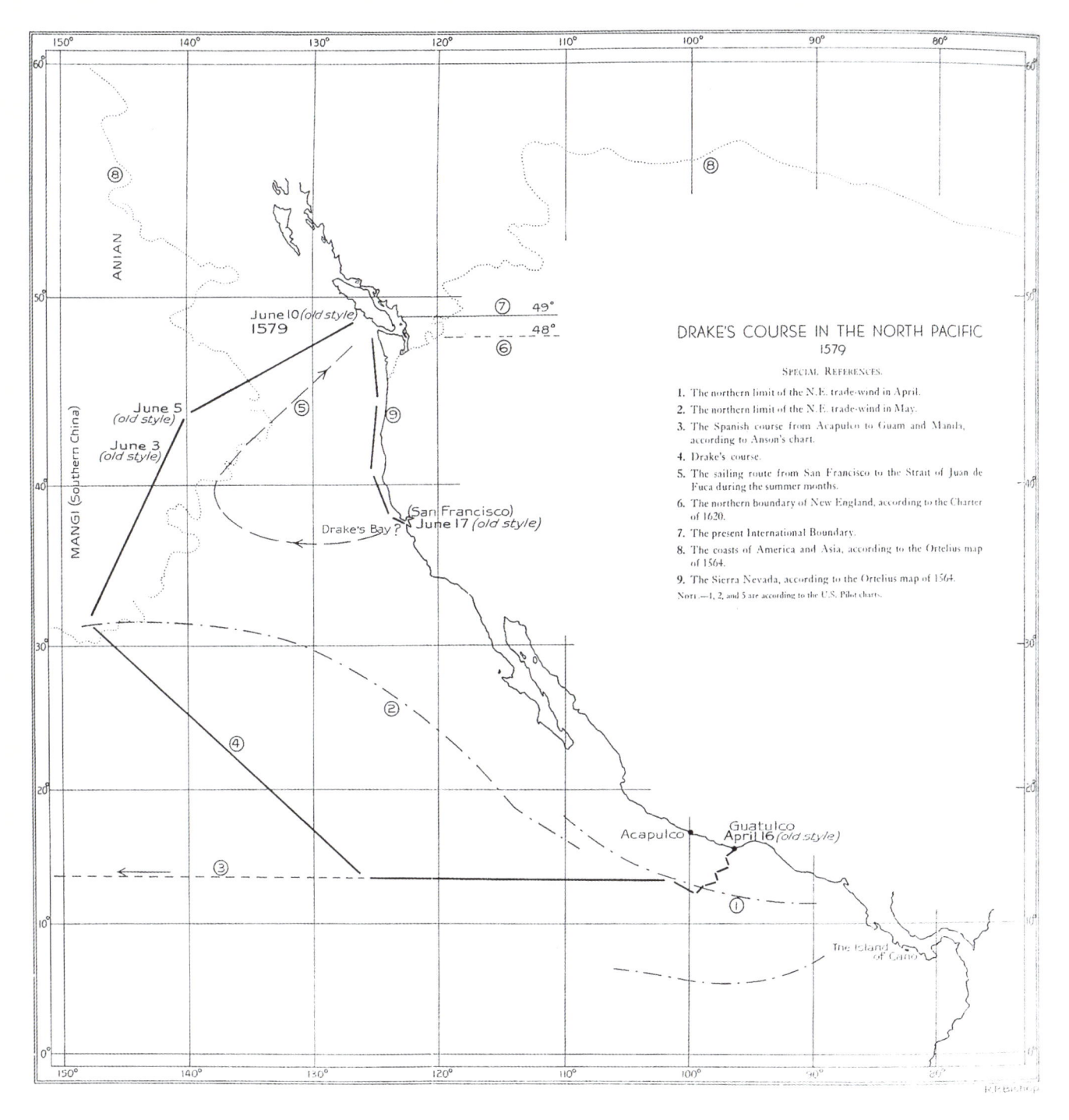

Fig. 9 In 1939, BC land surveyor and keen historian Richard Bishop published his theory and map concerning Drake's landfall on Vancouver Island.

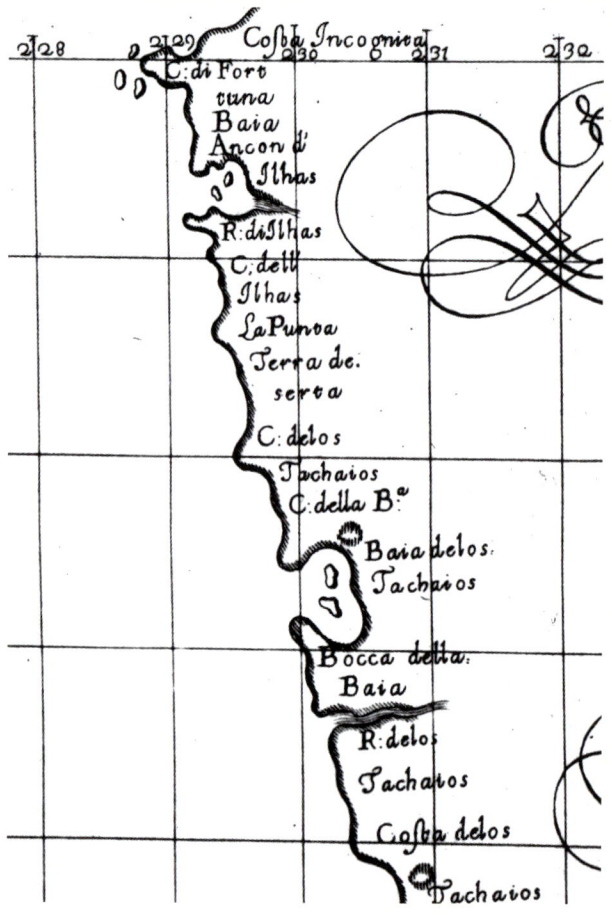

LEFT

Fig. 10 Elizabethan exile Robert Dudley, working for the de Medici family in Florence, published a world hydrographic atlas in 1647. Dudley, who had known Drake and Cavendish, could have had access to secret records of their voyages.

ABOVE

Fig. 11 North of 50°, Dudley's depiction of the western coast of North America peters out as "Costa Incognita." The manuscript original of the northerly continuation of the chart is missing.

more fine detail than what subsequently appeared on the printed charts. Dudley sketched four manuscript charts for *D'America XXXIII*. Three of them, covering the coastline from the southernmost point to latitude 48°, have been housed since 1785 in what was originally the Royal Bavarian Library in Munich. Sadly, the northernmost sheet, detailing the final two degrees of coastline (which must surely have been Dudley's last manuscript for the *Arcano*), is missing from the collection. This is the very sheet that would refer to the west coast of Vancouver Island.

Half a century before Dudley published his atlas, reports of another voyage to this region reached London. In 1596, Michael Lok, an English merchant based in the Levant port of Aleppo, was visiting Venice when a friend introduced him to an old Greek mariner with a tale to tell. Born on the island of Cephalonia, the man had spent his life at sea, including forty years on the Spanish Main and in the Pacific. The old mariner, Ioannis Phokas of Valeriano—in Spanish, Juan de Fuca—claimed that the viceroy in Mexico had sent him on two voyages of exploration from Acapulco north along the coast of the Pacific. The first, with three ships, was to search for the Strait of Anian, but mutiny soon caused it to be aborted. In 1592 the viceroy sent Juan de Fuca, this time in a single ship with a pinnace, to try once more.

The Greek related how, at latitude 47°, he had discovered "a broad inlet of the sea, between 47 and 48." He entered and, for more than twenty days, sailed on a varying course, passing through an inland sea wider than the entrance, and among many islands. Landing several times, he noted the land to be as rich as New Spain, and eventually he emerged into the North Sea, by which name the Atlantic was known in that era.

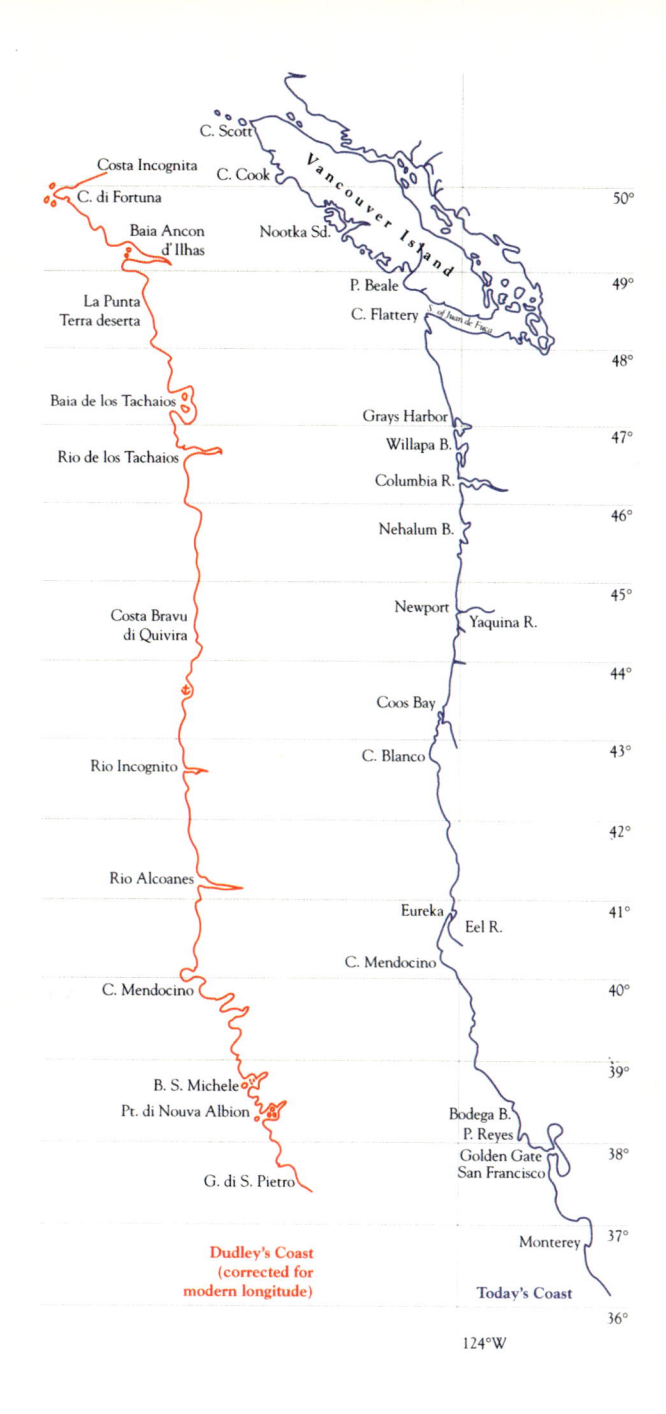

Fig. 12 At the time of Drake's voyage, navigational science did not allow for accurate longitudes, but latitudes were reasonably reliable. Correcting Dudley's coastline for longitude reveals interesting comparisons between Dudley's and present-day toponyms.

CHAPTER TWO 17

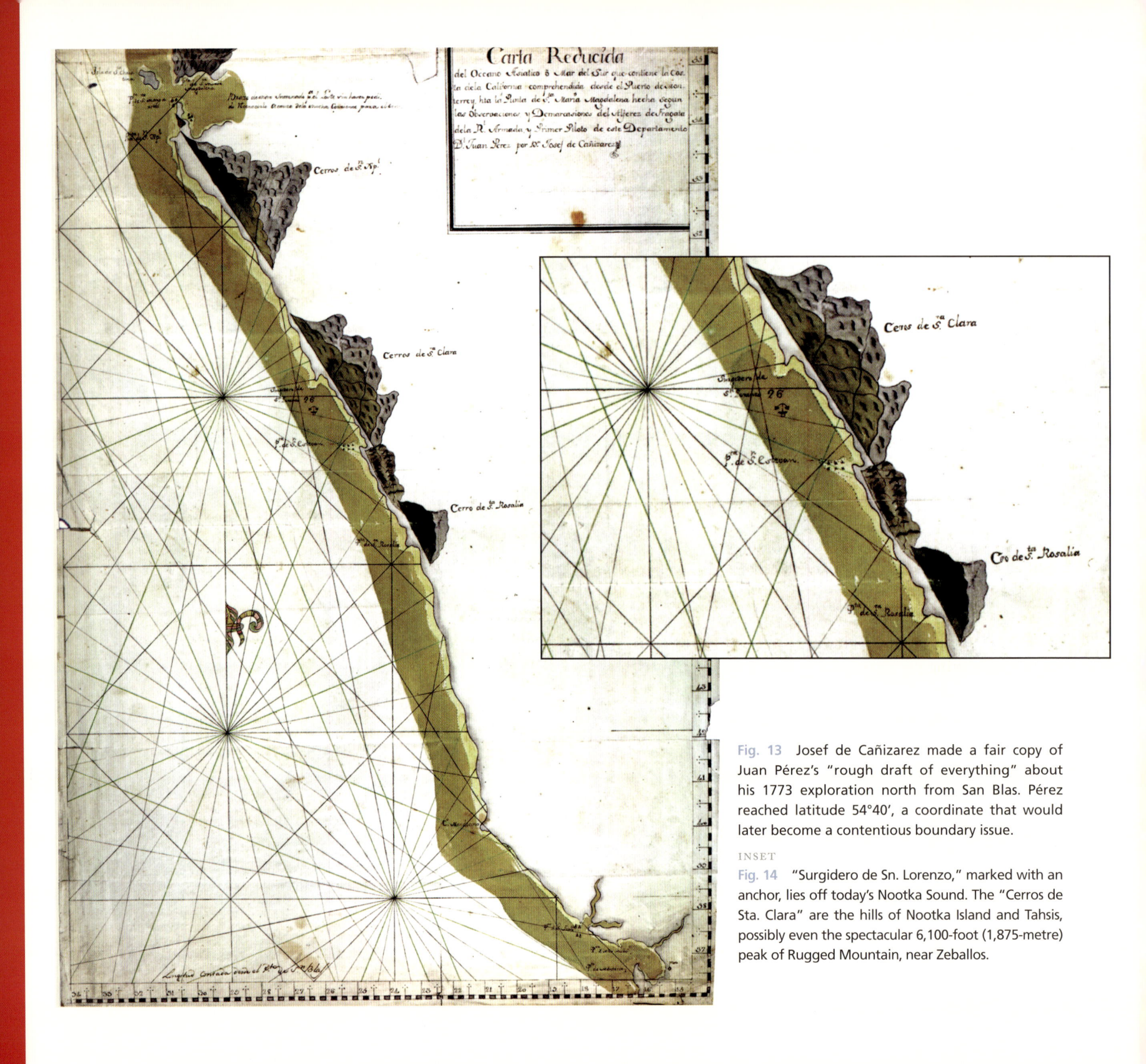

Fig. 13 Josef de Cañizarez made a fair copy of Juan Pérez's "rough draft of everything" about his 1773 exploration north from San Blas. Pérez reached latitude 54°40', a coordinate that would later become a contentious boundary issue.

INSET
Fig. 14 "Surgidero de Sn. Lorenzo," marked with an anchor, lies off today's Nootka Sound. The "Cerros de Sta. Clara" are the hills of Nootka Island and Tahsis, possibly even the spectacular 6,100-foot (1,875-metre) peak of Rugged Mountain, near Zeballos.

CHAPTER THREE

First European Contact: Spaniards Anchor at San Lorenzo

SPAIN'S CONCERN FOR THIS MOST remote and inhospitable corner of its empire resurfaced in the 1740s, after a long hiatus. Spanish ears at the Russian imperial court picked up rumours about three voyages out of Kamchatka, eastbound. Vitus Bering and Alexei Chirikov had reached the coast of North America in 1741. A foreign imperial power established on that coast, within striking distance of Spain's returning, treasure-laden Manila galleons, presented a serious threat to the Spanish economy. King Carlos III of Spain ordered that his viceroy establish a naval base at San Blas, to be home port for a squadron of exploration vessels with a cadre of pilots and naval officers trained in navigation and surveying.

In 1773 the new viceroy, Antonio Bucareli y Ursúa, chose a veteran, Juan Pérez, for a voyage to counter the Russian encroachment. Pérez was to sail to latitude 60° north, make a landing, and perform a formal Act of Possession. From that place, he was to return to Monterey, staying within sight of the coast and keeping a meticulous log. Curiously, Pérez's orders did not specify making maps, but Bucareli did provide him with copies of maps of the Russian voyages.

Pérez, having reached a latitude of about 52°, altered course toward the coast and made landfall off the northwestern tip of the Queen Charlotte Islands. About twenty Haida canoes came out and gifts were exchanged. The local people seemed to be keen, experienced traders as well as skilled canoe handlers. Next morning, Pérez gave orders to turn and sail south. He failed to make the formal Act of Possession spelled out by Bucareli, and no one from his frigate, *Santiago*, set foot onshore.

For two weeks, Pérez kept *Santiago* well offshore, heading generally south-southeast. On August 5, 1773, at around 49° north, Pérez pointed *Santiago*'s bow toward some snow-capped peaks. This was the first recorded sighting of Vancouver Island by any European.

Two days later, a small group of people in canoes paddled out to meet the strange ship. Now taking frequent soundings, *Santiago* edged within six miles (eleven kilometres) of a point of land. As it was evening, they anchored. Bestowing the first European names on any feature on Vancouver Island, Pérez called the anchorage the Surgidero (roadstead) de San Lorenzo, and the nearby headland the Punta de San Estevan. To the northwest he could see another headland, the Punta de Santa Clara. *Santiago* lay off the entrance to what is now called Nootka Sound.

Throughout the calm night, the local Hesquiaht people, keeping a prudent distance, continued to inspect the visitors from their canoes. Some trading took place, crew members exchanging abalone shells for sea otter skins and fresh sardines. At some point, possibly during these trades, the locals acquired two silver spoons of Spanish origin; Spain would later cite these spoons as key evidence in support of its territorial claim to the whole coast, although no Spaniard had actually set foot on shore.

With the dawn, a freshening, westerly breeze developed, exposing *Santiago* to a rocky lee shore, so Pérez hurriedly decided to leave. Over *Santiago*'s stern rail, he took a bearing due north to a significant hill, Loma de San Lorenzo, now Mount Seghers, at the head of Hesquiat Harbour. Pérez noted that "high and snowy peaks" surrounded the place.

In the cover letter to his report to Viceroy Bucareli, Pérez mentions including a "rough draft of everything." He explains that it had been impossible, as they went, "to construct a map of the coast discovered because of the rolling aboard ship."[1]

A document discovered in the US National Archives in 1989 was not that rough draft, but a contemporary fair copy. The legend on the map states that Josef de Cañizarez had drawn it "in accordance with the observations and surveys of [Pérez]." This was the first map to be made using data from a substantiated voyage. American forces had seized the collection during the occupation of Mexico City after the invasion of 1846. (See Fig. 13, page 18)

Based on studies of the various documents associated with the Pérez voyage, including the pilot's own diary and the Cañizarez map, the map was probably drawn at San Blas during the winter between Pérez's two voyages.[2] Cañizarez was a fellow pilot and explorer, junior to Pérez and of known ability as a cartographer. There are some differences in the place names between Pérez's diary and the map. While San Lorenzo, San Estevan, and Santa Rosalía remain the same, for example, the surrounding mountains are indicated as Cerros de Santa Clara. (See Fig. 14, page 18) It is not known if such changes were the result of direction from Pérez or of the cartographer's misreading of the diary. Nor is it known when the map was sent to Mexico City. It was not given to subsequent expeditions nor used in later cartographic compilations of the results from this series of explorations. Both the diary and the map were overlooked, buried among the viceregal papers, for more than two centuries.[3]

Just as Pérez headed north from Monterey, six junior naval officers left Spain, posted to the new department of San Blas. Viceroy Bucareli appointed the senior of them, Bruno de Hezeta, to command the next season's exploration of the Pacific coast northward, with the order that this time they reach latitude 65°. In 1775 the frigate *Santiago* was again the primary vessel, with an aging, 38-foot (10.4-metre) schooner, *Sonora*, serving as tender. A third ship, the frigate *San Carlos*, was to sail with them to resupply the mission at Monterey. Pérez would be aboard *Santiago*, as second in command to Hezeta, with Juan de Ayala commanding *Sonora*. Another of the newly arrived young officers, the Peruvian-born Juan Francisco de la Bodega y Quadra, keen to be part of the action, volunteered to sail as Ayala's deputy.

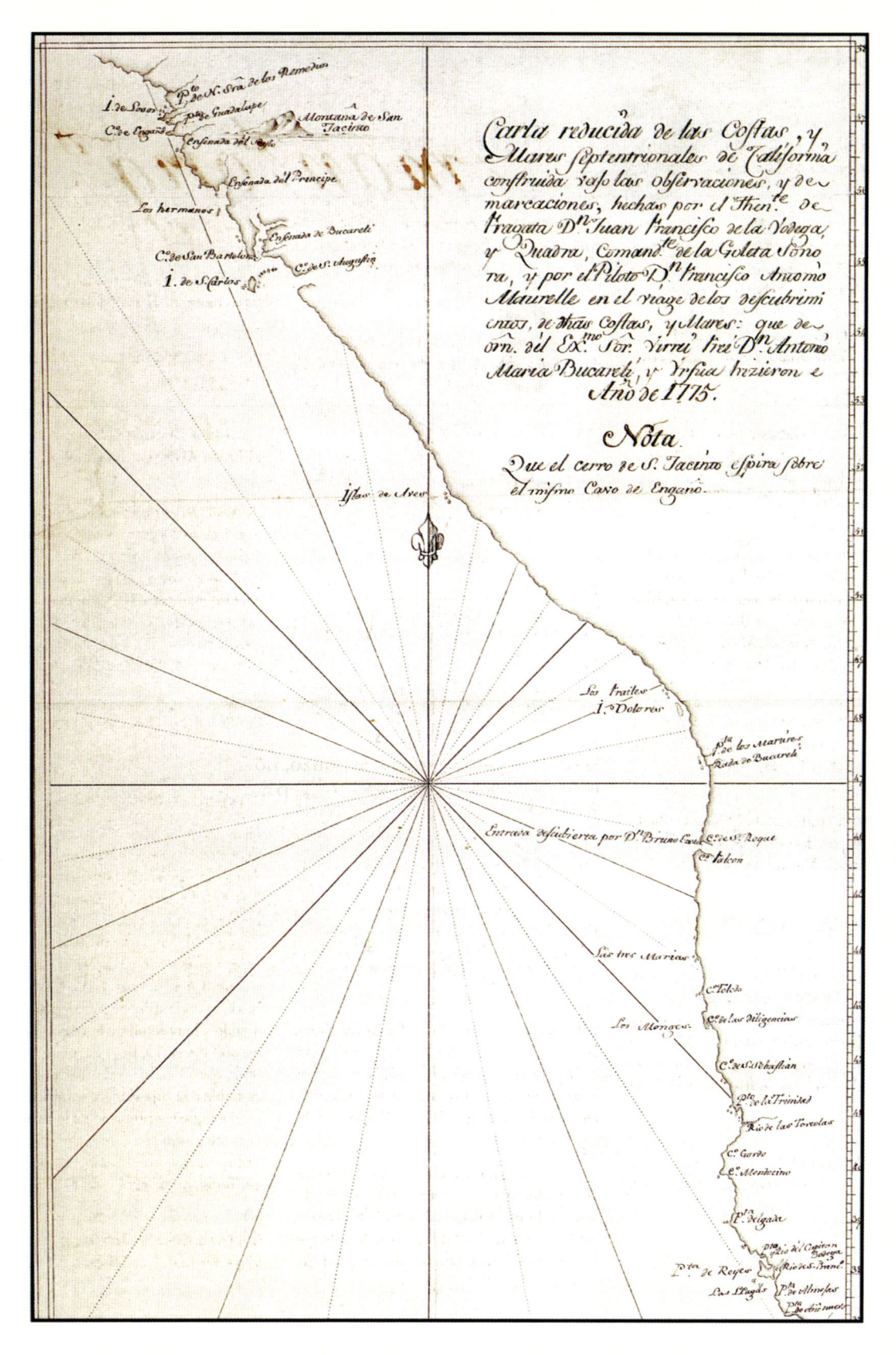

Fig. 15 Bodega y Quadra and his pilot, Mourelle, prepared this record of their 1775 voyage in *Sonora*. They reached as far north as 58°, vainly seeking de Fonte's entrance to the Strait of Anian. The islands indicated between 48° and 49° are probably the Queen Charlottes.

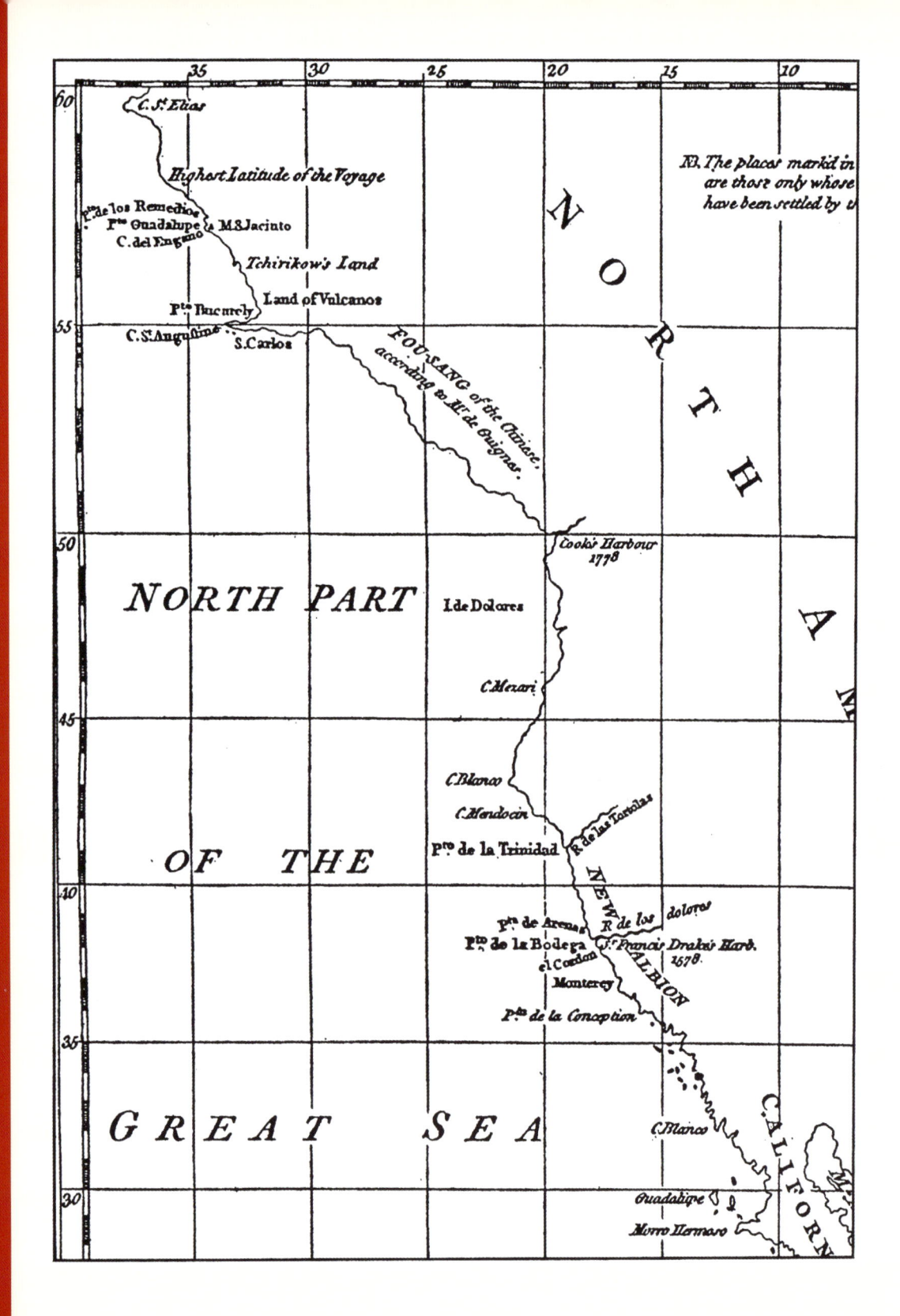

Fig. 16 This chart of the coast, based upon Spanish information about Bodega y Quadra's and Hezeta's voyages of 1775, was published in London in 1781. Could this deliberate leak of cartographic intelligence have been a ploy to pre-empt Cook's expedition or to refute any British claims for priority?

Francisco Mourelle, who had shipped with Pérez the previous year, acted as pilot aboard *Sonora*.

Three days out from San Blas, the captain of *San Carlos* suffered a nervous breakdown and was replaced by Ayala, with Bodega y Quadra assuming command of *Sonora*. A short while later, locals attacked and killed half of *Sonora*'s fourteen crew members as they collected fresh water. To make up *Sonora*'s losses, Hezeta transferred some crew from *Santiago*, but the tragic event created a rift between the two commanders, and soon afterward the ships lost contact with one another.

After the separation, Hezeta in *Santiago* resumed his northbound course, reaching about 49°17' north, and Pérez identified the hills on Vancouver Island that, the previous year, he had named Santa Clara. But again, they had made no landing before Hezeta decided to turn and head south along the coast. They saw no sign of the entrance or strait mentioned by Juan de Fuca, so they dismissed the story.

After the ships parted company, *Sonora* also sailed north. Passing latitude 49°, Bodega y Quadra was able to approach, briefly, to within 1.24 miles (2 kilometres) of the Vancouver Island coast near Nootka before returning to safer waters offshore. The Mowachaht onshore saw *Sonora*'s two masts and, fourteen years later, reported this to the American fur trader Joseph Ingraham.

The voyage established a reputation for Bodega y Quadra as an intrepid and determined explorer. Subsequently he commanded the Naval Department of San Blas and, a few years later, would reappear in the history of Vancouver Island, charged with significant diplomatic responsibility.

Bodega y Quadra and Mourelle attached a number of maps, charts, and tables of readings to their report. Two charts summarized all that had been discovered along the coast up to that time. (See Fig. 15, page 21) The officers do not appear to have known about the Cañizarez map of the Pérez voyage. In Spain, José de Gálvez, the minister responsible for New Spain, studied the report and maps, and arranged promotion for all the officers involved. At that time, other diplomatic intelligence reached the minister: The British Royal Navy had instructed the renowned explorer James Cook to include in his third voyage the search for the western portal of the Northwest Passage.

De Gálvez advised Viceroy Bucareli of this development, strongly recommending that a third expedition be sent from San Blas to monitor both Russian and British encroachments. However, no suitable ships were available until 1779, by which time it was too late. Cook's exploration of the west coast, including his visit to Nootka, had taken place, and without the Spanish knowing it.

In 1781, a London publication, *Miscellanies*, printed a highly edited version of Mourelle's journal of the 1775 voyage of *Sonora* which included a variant of the Bodega-Mourelle chart of their voyage, adding at latitude 50° "Cook's Harbour 1778" (Nootka Sound).[4] (See Fig. 16) By this time, Spanish rivalry with England had escalated into war. The Honourable Daines Barrington had translated the journal, claiming as his motive for publication the geographical knowledge it provided. Since Spain maintained a policy of strict secrecy about the region it considered part of its empire, such information was scarce. It is also possible, however, that Spain had deliberately passed Mourelle's journal to London, to send the message that they had taken formal possession of the coast prior to any visit by Captain Cook.

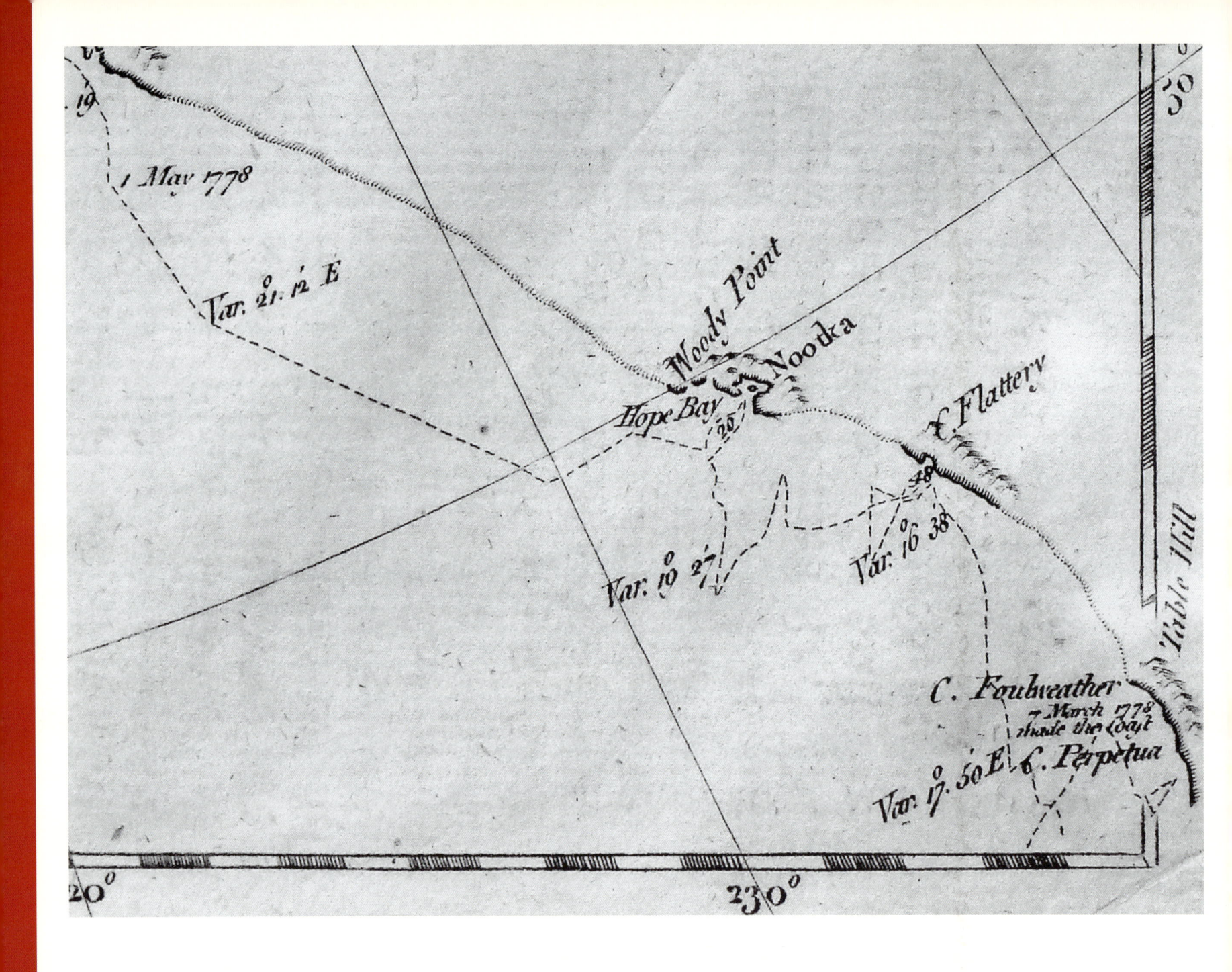

Fig. 17 This is part of James King's chart depicting Cook's track and landfalls at Capes Foulweather and Flattery, and his stopover at Nootka. Published by A. Hogg in London in 1784.

CHAPTER FOUR

Makook! With Cook at Nootka

EARLY IN MARCH 1778, CAPTAIN James Cook, Royal Navy, became the first Englishman since Francis Drake, two hundred years earlier, to see both coasts of North America. Cook, Britain's foremost navigator and hydrographic surveyor, had developed his skills while preparing detailed charts of the St. Lawrence River for General Wolfe's assault and capture of Quebec. Cook's two-ship expedition, the third in his series of great voyages of scientific exploration, had been at sea for nearly two years.

Cook's vessels, the sloops *Resolution* and *Discovery*, made landfall close to 45° north, the latitude the British Admiralty wrongly considered to be the northern limit of Spain's imperial reach. Cook had been instructed not to provoke Spanish ire and risk Spain's siding with the American revolutionaries. For the same reason, the names of both *Resolution* and *Discovery* had been changed—previously, they had been the *Drake* and the *Raleigh* respectively.

Cook had come to this coast on his way to find (or disprove the existence of) the western portal to the Northwest Passage. His orders required him "to proceed northward along the coast as far as latitude 65°, taking care not to lose any time in exploring [other] rivers and inlets, or upon any other account."[1]

Through fog and failing light, around latitude 48°15', Cook sighted a headland, but he needed to regain the safety of the open ocean. Bearing away, he noted beyond the headland "a small opening in the land." Already behind schedule, he had no time to investigate. He knew the story of Apóstolos Valerianos finding a strait—AKA Juan de Fuca—at just this latitude, but, ignoring the possibility, Cook named the headland Cape Flattery. The small opening was probably not the Strait of Juan de Fuca, but Makah Bay, and the headland what is now called Point of the Arches, nine miles (fifteen kilometres) south of today's Cape Flattery, which marks the true entrance to the strait. (See Fig. 17)

A further week passed before the expedition could make another landfall. They had continued to struggle north and, running perilously low on fresh water, approached what

View of the Entrance of NOOTKA Sound when the N...

seemed, from a few leagues distant, to be a wide bay with two inlets. The southeastern limit of the bay was a headland with surf breaking over its rocky foot, which Cook called Point Breakers. This was the same perilous headland that Juan Pérez had, only four years earlier, named Punta San Estevan, and where he had just managed to escape a lee shore.

To the northwest, Cook noted another promontory that he called Woody Point. He was seeing the six-hundred-metre-high spine of the Brooks Peninsula. He chose "woody" for obvious reasons; however, a later hydrographer, George Richards, noting that the whole of this coast could be so described, renamed the feature at the western extremity of the peninsula Cape Cook, to commemorate its discoverer.

Approaching more closely, Cook saw, beyond the rocky shoreline, a land densely forested with a backdrop of rugged, snow-crowned peaks. Reflecting his optimism, he named it Hope Bay. On a light evening breeze they found an entrance, which Cook named King George's Sound, after the monarch. As they arrived, a fleet of some thirty large canoes surrounded the visitors and greeted them with melodious chanting. Musicians on board returned the serenade on flutes and horns, to the evident appreciation of the residents.

Cook and his fellow officers watched the resident people gesticulate and call out, "*Noot'ka! Noot'ka ichim!*" which they interpreted to be the local name of the place. In fact, the paddlers, familiar with the dangers of the exposed coast, had been instructing the ships to "come around, come around the point!" But thereafter, the name Nootka remained. The actual name for the Mowachaht summer encampment was Yuquot, meaning "exposed to the winds." An additional European name was soon bestowed upon the same village, with good reason: Friendly Cove. (See Fig. 18)

On the last day of March 1778, the ships dropped anchor in a small, sheltered bay in the middle of the sound, and parties went ashore. They were the first Europeans on record

Fig. 18 Coastal views were an essential element of marine charts to assist sailors in finding entrances on an unknown shore. The vertical dimension is deliberately exaggerated to aid identification.

to set foot upon what became known as Vancouver Island.

The Mowachaht were eager, experienced, and astute traders. All the sailors quickly learned another word: *Makook?*—"Do you want to do business?" Scorning the glass beads and similar trade trinkets that the visitors first offered, the locals coveted any item of metal: knives, ships' nails, brass buttons, tin cans, and pewter plates. In return, they could supply artifacts and animal pelts, particularly sea otter. For men about to face the rigours of the Arctic, this soft, rich, dense fur promised warmth and comfort. Not only would it make excellent clothing and bedcovers, it also seemed an attractive bargain. In all, the officers and crew of *Resolution* and *Discovery* carried away with them fifteen hundred sea otter pelts, little realizing what they had acquired.

While the vessels were laid up for refit, the expedition's astronomer, William Bayly, determined the latitude and longitude of "Astronomer's Rock," the first accurately coordinated point on America's west coast. Despite the instructions for Cook to not waste time charting the coast south of 65°, some of his officers took the opportunity to circumnavigate nearby Bligh's Island in ships' boats, and made their own sketch maps of the complex inlet. (See Fig. 19, page 28) The two artists aboard, John Webber and William Ellis, also made good use of the time to observe and record the scenery, natural history, people, Aboriginal dwellings and lifestyle, and artifacts. Their work provides an invaluable pictorial record of the Nootka region at the time of first contact by Europeans.

In his voyages of discovery, Cook established the model for how such missions should be undertaken and the findings collated, described, and presented. He also trained a cohort of hydrographic surveyors to serve Britain's expanding global maritime interests.

After exploring the coast of Alaska and into the Bering Sea, Cook decided to return to winter in the balmy Sandwich Isles, where he met his savage demise. The expedition continued after his death, going on to create, unexpectedly, the

Fig. 19 While awaiting ships' repairs at Nootka, Cook's officers explored and prepared individual charts of the inlet. Henry Roberts drew this one. Note that Breakers Point should be on the other side of the entrance.

next stage of international interest in Vancouver Island. In Kamchatka, the crews met Russian fur merchants from whom they learned that the sea otter skins and other pelts that they had acquired in Nootka were valuable. The crews were pleased to sell them, but later, in China, they discovered that they had done so too cheaply.

As their exotic visitors departed, the Mowachaht returned, they probably thought, to the normality of *nuh-chee*, their land. The tranquil haven that had sheltered *Resolution* and *Discovery* for four weeks became, over the next decade, the busiest seaport on the west coast of the Americas.

Cook's expedition returned to England in October 1780. Four years later, and after two unauthorized accounts of the voyage had appeared, the official, three-volume version of Cook's journal, *A Voyage to the Pacific Ocean for Making Discoveries in the Northern Hemisphere*, edited by Lieutenant James King, RN, was published. That same year, Cook's chief cartographer, Lieutenant Henry Rogers, RN, issued an accompanying atlas of charts of the third voyage. His *Chart of the NW Coast of America and the NE Coast of Asia* includes detail of the coastline at the expedition's landfall, then at Cape Flattery, and again at Hope Bay, Nootka, and Woody Point. The chart shows their track well offshore between these points and northwestward until they reached Alaska. The supposed coastline between the identified locations is indicated by a dotted line. This was the first published chart showing data from actual observation of any part of Vancouver Island.

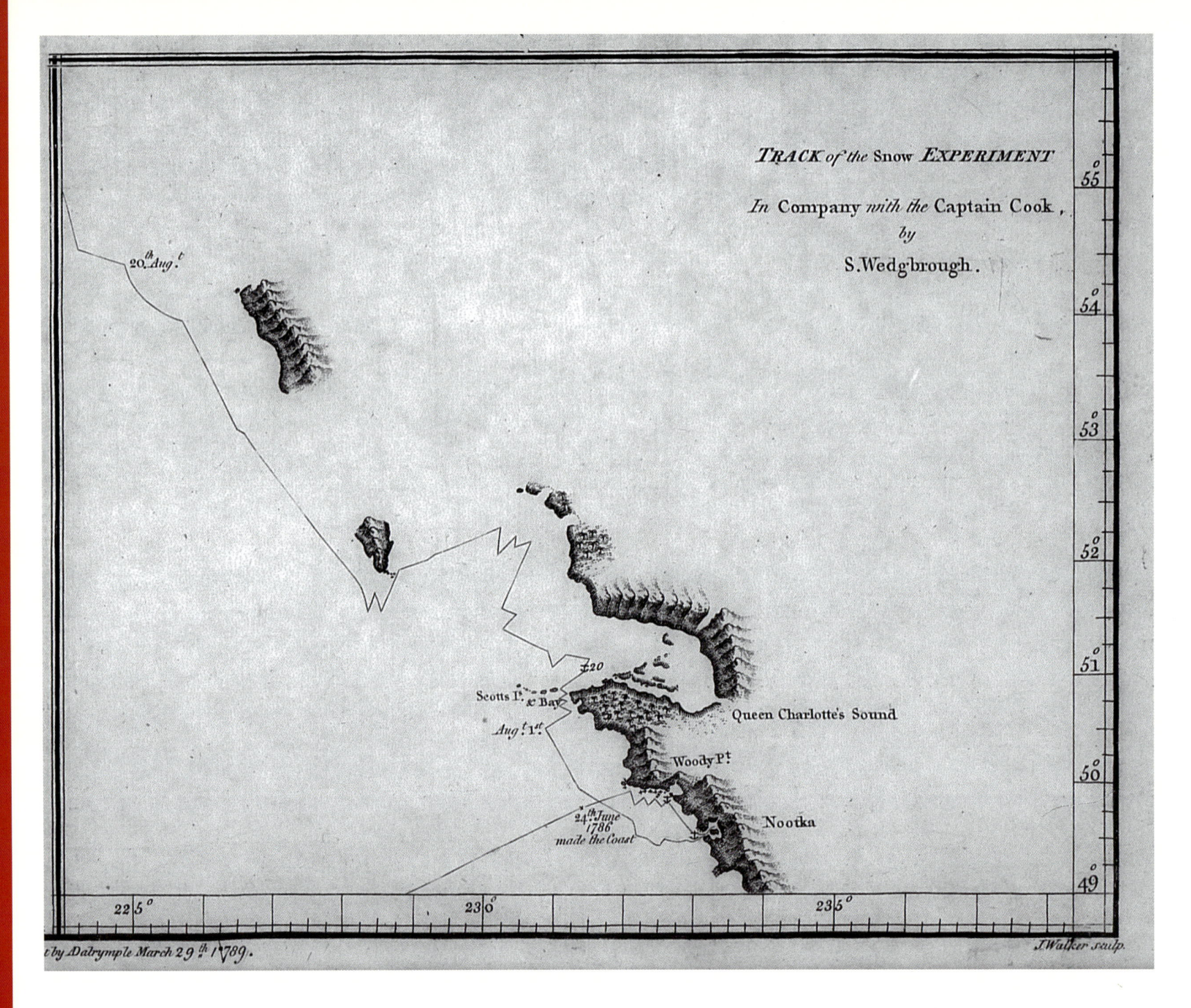

Fig. 20   This chart recorded the voyage commanded by James Strange, who named Cape Scott after his patron before noting a wide entrance to the north that he called Queen Charlotte's Sound. One of his officers, Wedgbrough, drew the chart.

CHAPTER FIVE

Soft Gold: Sea Otter Traders

WHEN NEWS OF THE POTENTIAL for a lucrative trade in sea otter pelts emerged, it sparked an immediate flurry of interest in the northwest coast. James King, in his 1784 introduction to Cook's *Voyage to the Pacific Ocean*, reported the discrepancy between the price of sea otter pelts in Nootka and Alaska and what they fetched in China. He suggested this business opportunity might justify funding a more detailed investigation of the coastline between 50° and 56° north, which adverse winds had prevented on earlier expeditions.

The follow-up voyages were instigated, financed, and carried out mainly by British maritime merchants, some based in London, others dotted along Asia's trade routes. They often involved officers and crew who had sailed with Cook. Some sailed under licence from the two powerful trading organizations granted official monopolies by the British Crown: The Honourable East India Company, which enjoyed exclusive rights over trade with China, and The South Sea Company, which had been granted exclusivity for trade throughout the Pacific Ocean. Other trading ventures circumvented such permission by sailing under flags of convenience—Austria and Portugal were popular—and trading into free ports such as Macao.

Most of these trading voyages, both sanctioned and independent, explored, charted, and added to the list of place names on what was to become Vancouver Island and its surrounding waters. The traders kept careful records of the places they visited, noting the sailing conditions, anchorages, and details of the peoples they met. Such information would be useful for later visits either by themselves or by their business associates and, incidentally, for anyone compiling a composite chart of the region. Such notes and sketch maps also added valuable data about Aboriginal demographics at the critical time of early European contact.

Less than a year after the publication of King's edition of Cook's *Voyage*, the first trading voyages arrived at Friendly Cove, and by 1792, more than twenty vessels were active in the sea otter business. An early arrival was James Strange, with two ships, the *Experiment* and the *Captain Cook*, who bought a house at Yuquot with the intention of establishing a trading "factory." At the close of the season he left his assistant surgeon, John Mackay, with Chief Maquinna to learn the local language and customs, promising to return the following spring.

Mackay unwittingly broke a Native taboo and was ostracized by Maquinna; his possessions and supplies were looted, and he was left to fend for himself. Nevertheless, he fulfilled his part of the bargain. Not only did he learn the language and trading protocols, he explored and acquired geographical knowledge. From the Mowachaht, he learned that Nootka was not part of the continental mainland, but one of a number of islands lying offshore.

After leaving Mackay to his fate, Strange coasted northward. He came upon a group of small, rocky islands and a barren, windswept headland, on which he landed and made an Act of Possession on behalf of Britain. He named the place—the northwestern tip of Vancouver Island—Cape Scott after his merchant patron, David Scott. He also noted that the coastline then trended east and southeast, apparently creating a channel several leagues wide, with strong tidal flows. Strange wondered if this might be Admiral de Fonte's western portal to the Northwest Passage, but he could not spare the time to explore it. He named the entrance Queen Charlotte's Sound, correctly judging that to chart properly such a broken, stormy, and hazardous coastline would require several seasons of fair weather. But one of his officers, S. Wedgbrough, did prepare a chart of their track, showing and naming the sound, and Alexander Dalrymple published it in 1789. *(See Fig. 20, page 30)*

The cartographic clue contained in the Drage/Holding map suggests that Strange was not the first European mariner to venture into this waterway.

The next European ship, Charles Barkley's *Imperial Eagle*, put into Nootka Sound in June 1787. Barkley's wife, Frances, became the first white woman known to have rounded Cape Horn and to have visited Hawaii, Alaska, and the shores of Vancouver Island. The ship had just anchored when a Native canoe came alongside and a dirty figure, clad only in a greasy sea otter skin, climbed aboard. To everyone's astonishment, the figure introduced himself as Dr. John Mackay, late of the brig *Captain Cook*.

Mackay explained that he had been living "as an Indian" at Nootka for the past twelve months and would like, very much, to rejoin a European ship. Not only was he fluent in the local language and trading customs, he knew a lot about the local geography. Despite the unprepossessing look of the visitor, Barkley was quick to see the advantages that such knowledge could bring to his business and welcomed Mackay to join his crew as a trader. That decision was sound: With Mackay's help, Barkley soon acquired all the available sea otter pelts.

Barkley spent a month in Friendly Cove, referred to as King George's Sound by his wife in her journal of the voyages. *Imperial Eagle* then departed, sailing southeast. Two days out, they found and entered another large sound, which Barkley named after the local chief, Wickaninnish. To yet a third broad sound, also containing several coves, bays, and islands, Barkley gave his own name, and he called various features in it after his wife, crew members, and people "familiar to us." While Mackay was away from the ship on a trading foray, Barkley drew detailed charts of his discoveries to date. *(See Fig. 21)*

His next discovery was momentous. Following the coastline, Frances recorded, they "proceeded to the eastward, and

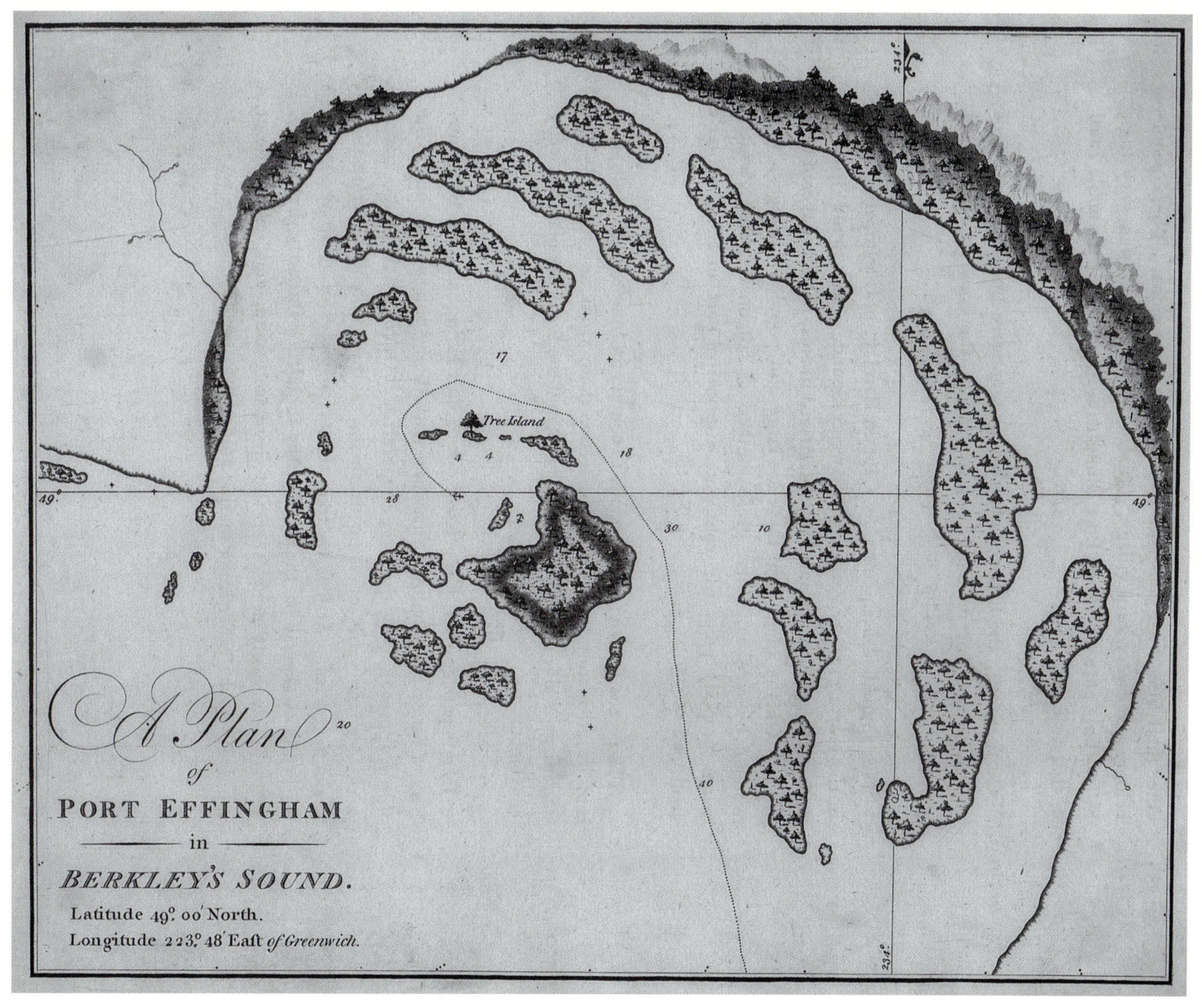

Fig. 21 John Meares acquired the logs and charts of his rival Charles Barkley, including this one of Barkley Sound, and published some of them in his book complaining of his treatment by Spanish officialdom at Nootka.

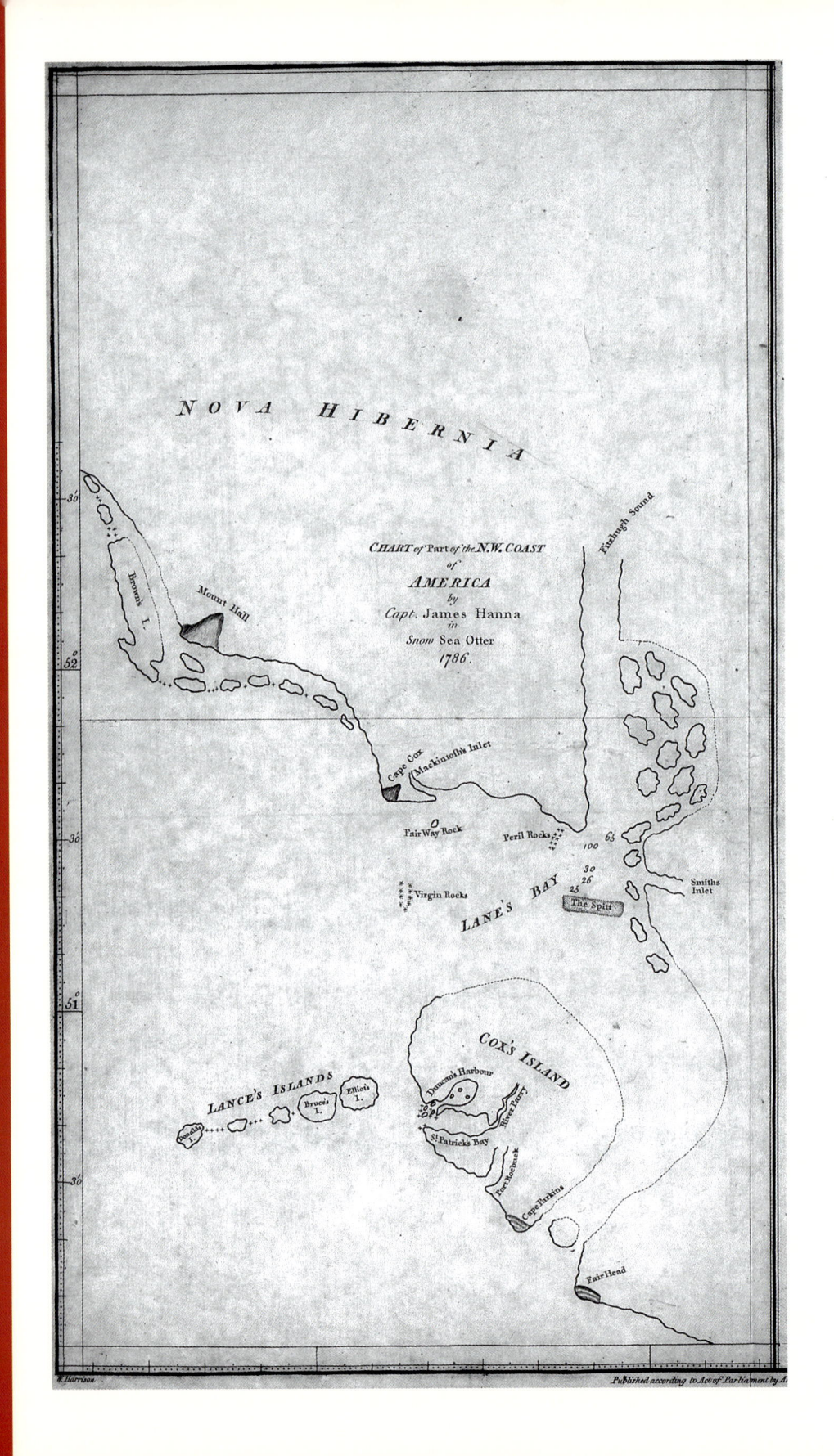

Fig. 22 James Hanna renamed as Lane's Bay the entrance that Strange had called Queen Charlotte's Sound, and there are hints that he might have sighted Hardy Bay and even the Broughton Archipelago.

to the great astonishment of Capt. Barkley and his officers, an opening presented itself, extending miles to the eastward with no land in sight in that direction." The entrance appeared to be about four leagues (twenty-two kilometres) wide as far as the eye could see. Captain Barkley at once identified it as "the long lost strait of Juan de Fuca, which Captain Cook had so emphatically stated did not exist."[1] Barkley did not enter the strait, but turned his bow southward down the western coast of the Olympic Peninsula.

Here, Barkley's fortunes changed. Salish tribesmen from the Makah nation slaughtered a six-man shore party of his crew. Later, he found the market for his pelts had softened, and finally his erstwhile employer, the powerful East India Company, learned of his activities, which caused his backers to fire and virtually disown him. He lost not only his ship, but also his papers, including his logs, notebooks, and charts, and even his navigating instruments, which were impounded in Canton. Those documents—fortunately, with the exception of his wife's personal journals and a sketch map of Barkley Sound—were left in the care of the authorities, and soon fell into the hands of an ambitious schemer, John Meares.

Meares, a former Royal Navy lieutenant, had been a member of the syndicate backing *Imperial Eagle*'s venture and had instigated the move to betray Barkley. He made several trading missions of his own in search of sea otters, using various guises and flags. He negotiated with Maquinna—under contentious terms—for a "spot of ground" on the shore near Yuquot for his Chinese crew to build first a hut, then a forty-ton (thirty-six-tonne) schooner from a kit that he had brought with him. By September the schooner was ready for launching, and Meares named it *Northwest America*. This was the first non-indigenous vessel to be built on Vancouver Island or anywhere on the Pacific coast north of San Blas.

At about this time, the first of a new set of players arrived at Nootka. They were American fur traders out of Boston: John Kendrick, skipper of the *Columbia Rediviva*, and Robert Gray, in command of the *Lady Washington*. They too had read Cook's *Voyage to the Pacific Ocean* and wanted a share of the sea otter market. The Boston vessels had managed to round Cape Horn in a fierce gale and were in miserable condition, their crews suffering terribly from scurvy. The men needed to recuperate and make repairs, wintering over in Friendly Cove.

Before leaving Nootka for Macao at the end of the 1788 season, Meares dismantled the hut he had built. The manager of the syndicate backing Meares, John Henry Cox, had collected, from the various traders who came through Macao, as many charts, sketches, and harbour plans of the Pacific Northwest coast as he could. Meares too had assiduously acquired his own copies of such charts. Cox forwarded the charts to the hydrographer of the East India Company, Alexander Dalrymple, who published them in 1789 and '90. (See Fig. 22) Dalrymple also published a pamphlet proposing cooperation—even a merger—between his company and the Hudson's Bay Company (HBC), to secure for British interests the inland and coastal fur trades.

Dalrymple became the first Hydrographer of the Navy and remained a believer in a Northwest Passage. He urged both the government and the HBC to continue active exploration for a navigable route between Hudson Bay and the Pacific coast. His ideas almost certainly provided the impetus for both Vancouver's voyage of the early 1790s and the simultaneous overland expedition by Alexander Mackenzie.

One of the charts that Dalrymple published was by Charles Duncan, master of another trader, the *Princess*

Royal, showing details of the entrance and the western reach of the Strait of Juan de Fuca. It had been drawn in August 1788, just over a year after Barkley had identified and named the strait. Duncan agreed with Barkley about the name and went even further: From his conversations with the local people at Classet, in Neah Bay, he had learned that the entrance led to a great sea running both north and south, which he took to confirm that this was the portal of the Northwest Passage leading to the Atlantic. (See Fig. 23)

In Macao, at the close of the 1788 season, the fur-trading syndicate backing Meares restructured itself. It now went by the name of Associated Merchants Trading to the Northwest Coast of America, with a licence from the East India Company, and Meares replacing Cox as manager. Their combined fleet of four vessels emboldened them to try to exert a monopoly over the trade in sea otter pelts by establishing a secure, permanent base on the northwest coast. They had not, however, anticipated the Spanish reaction to such a move, nor factored in the entry of Americans into the business.

The two American ships spent a gentle winter at Nootka, making repairs and establishing warm relations with Maquinna and the Mowachaht people. However, Nootka Sound, which had been a haven offering respite to ocean-battered sailors in a remote corner of the world, was about to change, and become the focal point in a crisis of imperial competition. The Spanish Empire had reached its maximum extent and faced both hostility from Britain and a growing assertiveness by the United States. On the sidelines waited Russia and France, watching for opportunities along the northwest coast. Matters were coming to a head.

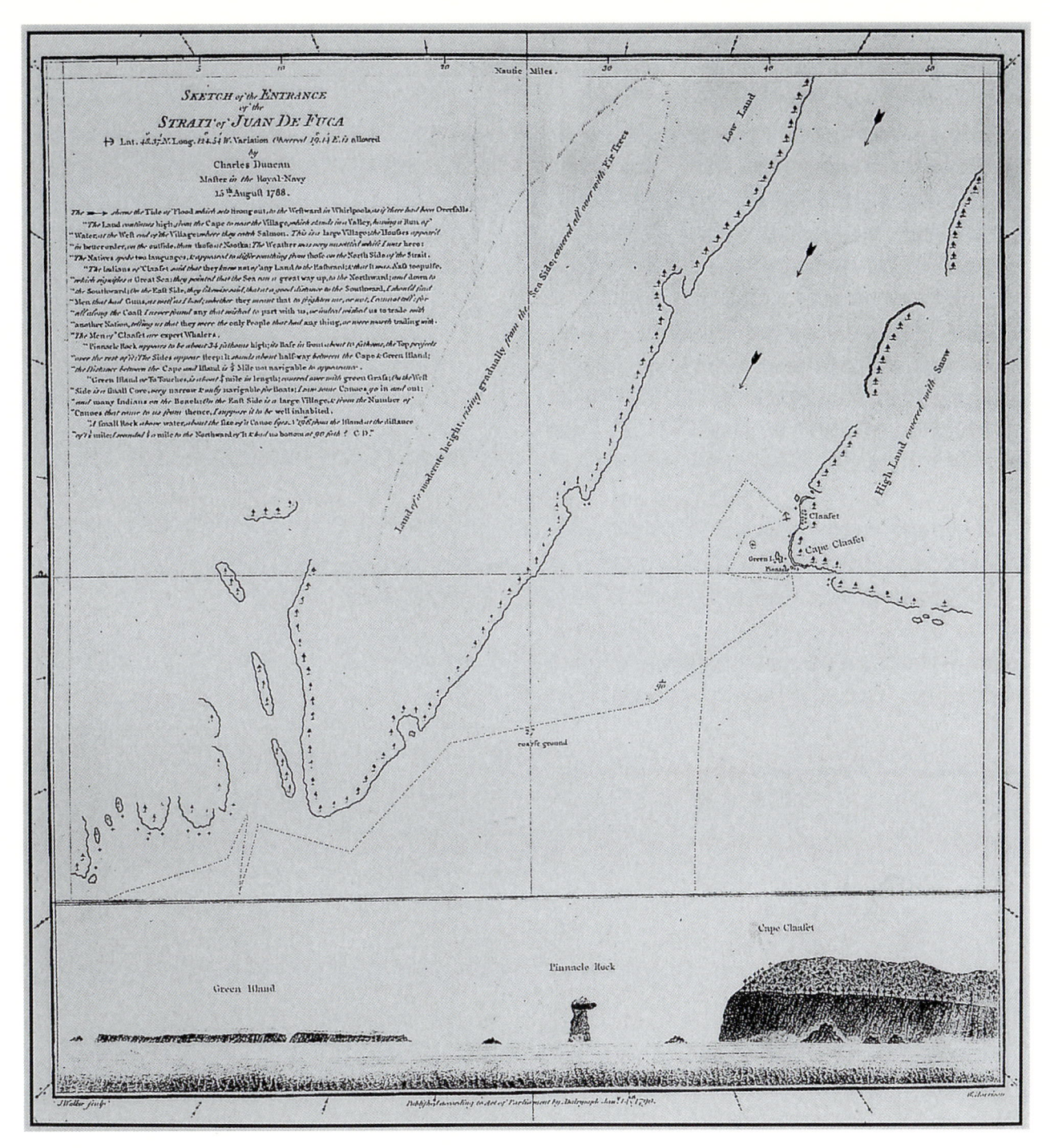

Fig. 23 This chart recorded the second sighting of the entrance to the Strait of Juan de Fuca, by Charles Duncan in 1788. Charles Barkley had sighted the entrance a year earlier.

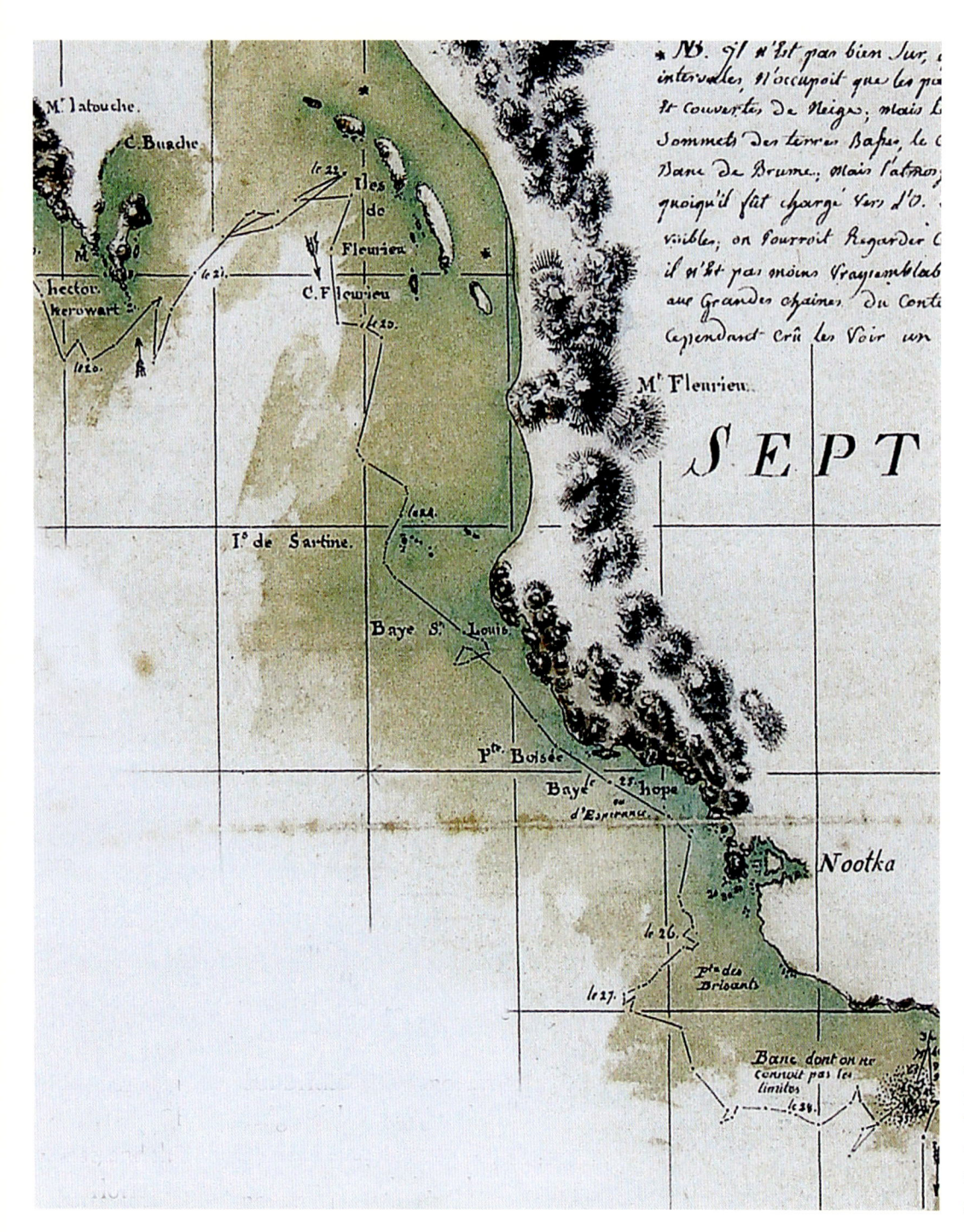

Fig. 24 Scientists with La Pérouse's expedition of 1785–86, using Cook's chart of 1778 for reference, constructed this chart of the coast. This sector shows the southbound track of their two ships as they passed Vancouver Island, without coming ashore but noting a "Banc," the shoal later named Swiftsure.

CHAPTER SIX

Imperial Flashpoint: Nootka, 1789

"THE RUSSIANS ARE COMING!" SINCE the 1740s, this ominous rumour had circulated in Spain and her colony of New Spain. The threat played upon Spanish awareness of their own inadequate knowledge of, and their inability to effectively control, the coast of what they called Alta California, the most remote part of their dominion. Such concerns triggered the creation of the Naval Department of San Blas and the three voyages northward in 1774, '75, and '79.

Meanwhile, in France, the publication of Cook's *Voyage to the Pacific Ocean* aroused a call for a worldwide French voyage of scientific discovery that would include the North Pacific. An experienced navigator, the count of La Pérouse, was instructed to lead a two-ship circumnavigation, taking an eminent team of French scientists and departing in the summer of 1785. After rounding Cape Horn, they stopped in Chile for fresh water. Some of the scientists leaked information to a Spanish official, who saw that their maps showed Russian bases on the northwest coast, even one at Nootka. Viceroy Manuel Antonio de Flores in Mexico City learned of this and passed it on to Spain, and then, on his own initiative, promptly ordered two San Blas vessels north to investigate.

After a year at sea, La Pérouse made landfall on the Alaskan coast at about 60° north and then adverse weather forced him south. He was low on provisions so did not stop on his journey to Monterey, but he did fill in some blanks on the copy of Cook's chart that he carried. He noted a broad inlet north of Nootka—Queen Charlotte Sound and Hecate Strait—and wondered if this hinted that the complex coast might be a chain of islands rather than a continuous mainland. He was, of course, correct in this.

On his chart, south of Nootka, La Pérouse noted a "Banc" of unknown extent. Most likely the shoal, now called Swiftsure, dissuaded him from continuing inshore, thereby depriving him of the discovery of the entrance to the Strait of Juan de Fuca. (See Fig. 24) In Monterey he met the veteran pilot Esteban Martínez and repeated the French understanding that the Russians had established a trading post at Nootka although, not having stopped there, he was unable to confirm this report.

The viceroy gave Martínez command of the expedition to investigate the rumours from Chile, but not until two years later, in 1788, did he and Gonzalo López de Haro set sail for Alaska. There, he discovered that while Russian fur traders had not yet been to Nootka, they expected to get that far the following season. Back in San Blas, Martínez volunteered to lead a follow-up voyage to San Lorenzo de Nuca (Nootka) to pre-empt the Russian plans.

Viceroy Flores instructed Martínez to act as though Spain was there to stay, by erecting buildings and planting crops. On his arrival at Friendly Cove in May 1789, Martínez discovered foreign ships at anchor and learned of the impending arrival of others. He set up San Miguel, a small gun emplacement, on a rocky islet at the entrance to the sound and built a few huts above the nearby beach. He enjoyed good relations with the Mowachaht, at first, and with the American fur traders, who duped him into believing that they were on a scientific and charting mission. The British traders were another matter. With them, the relationship started poorly and then deteriorated.

There followed a complex series of misunderstandings, conflicting agendas, forged papers, and affronted pride that would make a script for the most exaggerated comic opera. Martínez seized three British ships, declaring their officers and crews to be prisoners of war. After stripping the ships of their guns, charts, logs, provisions, cargo, and trade goods, he sent them, with their complements as prisoners, to San Blas.

On new orders from the viceroy, Martínez abandoned Nootka in late October, taking all remaining ships and personnel, and thereby considerably weakening the Spanish case for possession. While preparing for this demobilization, Martínez dispatched the American John Kendrick to Tahsis, Maquinna's winter village, to trade for whale oil.

Under oars, Kendrick's party discovered a narrow side passage leading west toward the ocean northwest of Nootka Sound. Upon returning down the open coast to rejoin Martínez, they discovered that their outpost was on an island, which Martínez called Mazarredo in honour of a famous admiral of the day; he named the newly discovered entrance Bahía de Buena Esperanza.

By the time the Martínez contingent reached San Blas, there had been a change of viceroy, and the new one, the count of Revillagigedo, could see the potentially explosive nature of the summer's events at Nootka. He ordered his new commander at San Blas, Juan Francisco Bodega y Quadra, now with the rank of *capitán de navío* (captain), to make a full investigation, particularly into the actions of Martínez. He also instructed Bodega y Quadra to prepare, with minimal delay, a robust force that could reoccupy Nootka and defend it from attack.

The naval reinforcements sent to San Blas with Bodega y Quadra included six junior officers and, an innovation for the era, two doctors. Bodega y Quadra nominated three of the officers to command the ships that would reoccupy Nootka. In overall command was *teniente de navío* (senior lieutenant) Francisco de Eliza, aboard the huge, thirty-gun frigate *Concepción*. Subordinate were Salvador Fidalgo in the *San Carlos* and Manuel Quimper in *Princesa Real*.

Eliza was a veteran of several naval campaigns, Fidalgo a skilled hydrographer. The experienced pilot López de Haro would buttress Quimper, who was yet to be tested in command. Martínez, since he was under a cloud as a result

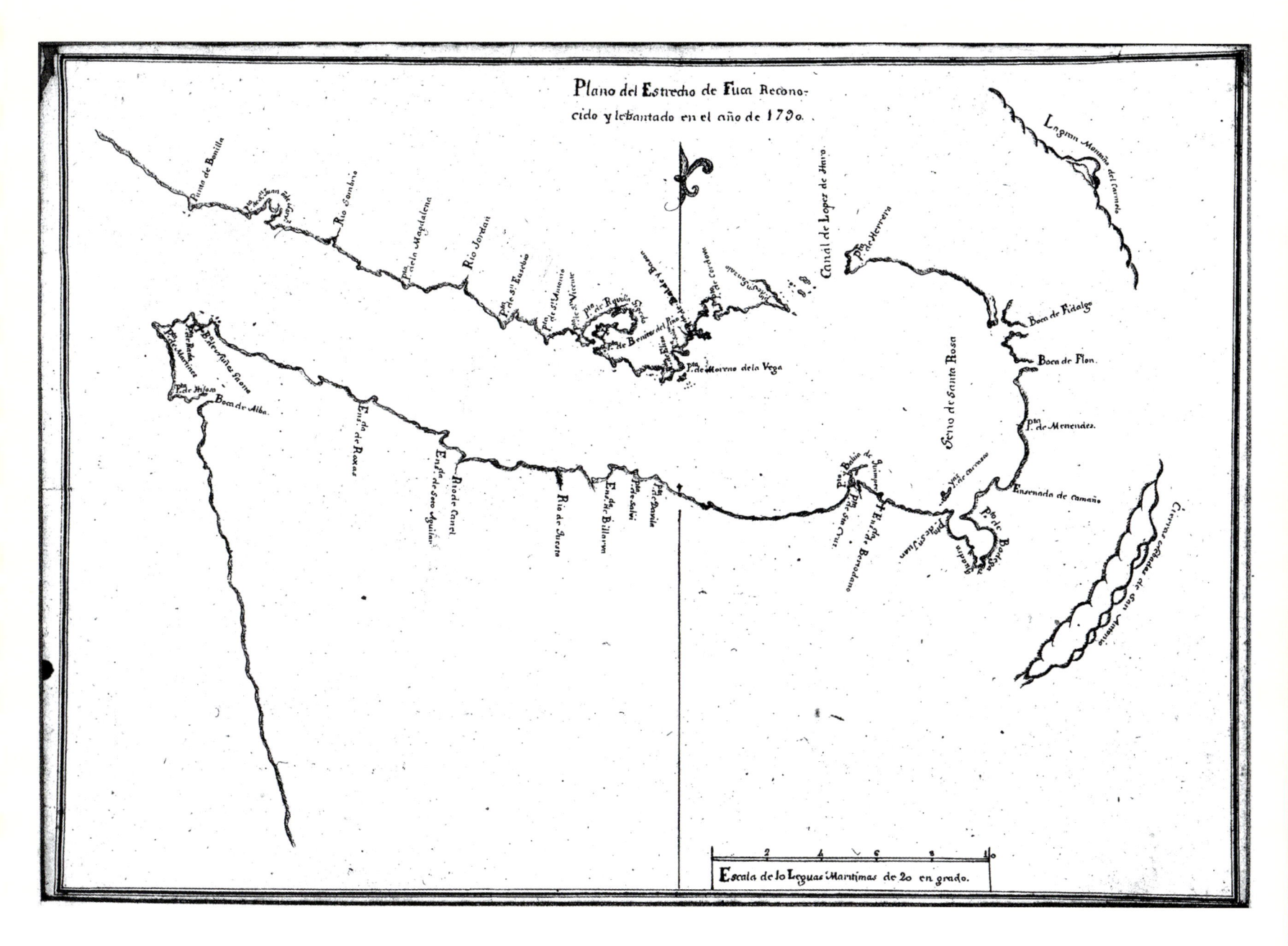

Fig. 25 A major contributor to Spanish exploration, pilot Gonzalo López de Haro had already participated in two voyages to this region before accompanying Manuel Quimper into the Strait of Juan de Fuca in 1790, and he probably constructed this chart.

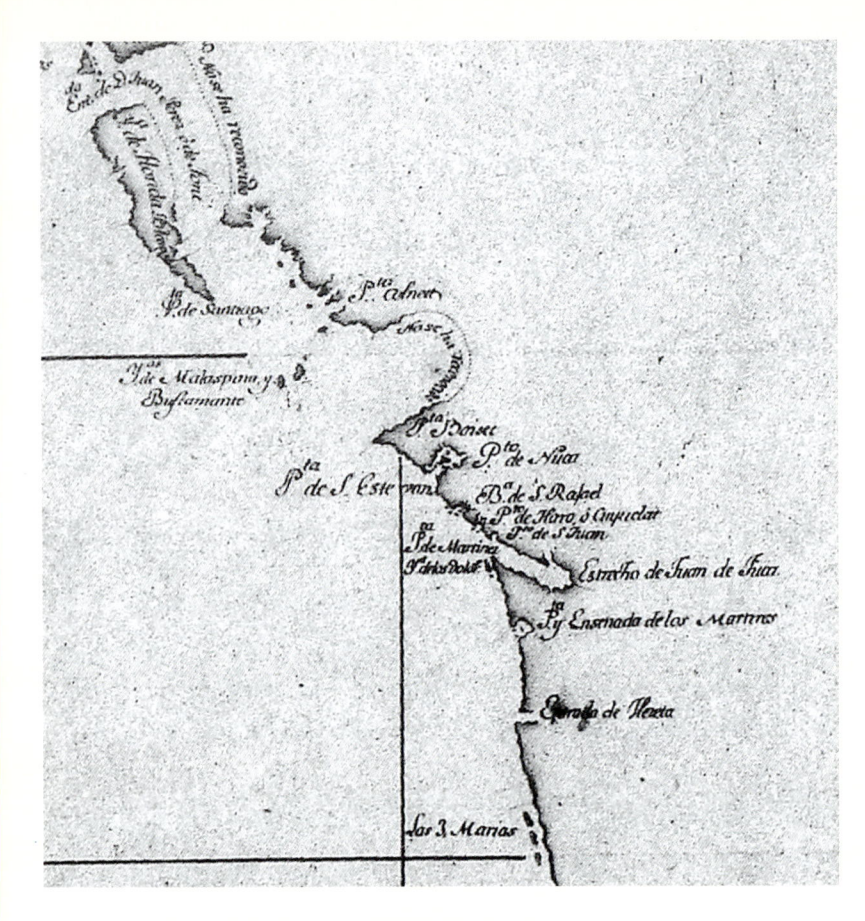

Fig. 26 This is part of a chart compiled in 1791 by Bodega y Quadra of the Pacific coast "discovered and examined up to today by the Spaniards." It includes the findings of the Quimper expedition of 1790. The coast immediately north of "Pta. Boisee" (Cook's Woody Point) is marked "has not been examined."

of his intemperate handling of the previous year's events at Nootka, was included in the expedition against Bodega y Quadra's better judgment. In a humiliating demotion, he was given the responsibility of trading for sea otter pelts.

The three-ship flotilla departed from San Blas in early February 1790, arriving at Nootka at the end of March. With two hundred and fifty men, including a company of militia, this was the strongest and best-equipped contingent yet sent to the northwest coast. Its primary mission was to occupy what they now called Santa Cruz de Nuca. Once the fort was able to withstand an attack, ships were to be sent out exploring, charting, and trading for sea otter pelts. They found Friendly Cove empty, both of foreign vessels and of the Mowachaht. At the end of May, Quimper and López de Haro in *Princesa Real* departed to explore Clayoquot Sound and the Strait of Juan de Fuca.

At Opitsaht, Chief Wickaninnish threw a ceremonial feast for Quimper and warned against venturing with such a small ship into Juan de Fuca because many treacherous tribes lived there. Notwithstanding such warnings, Quimper and López de Haro surveyed almost every significant opening on the northern side of the strait for its potential as a harbour. They visited Puerto San Juan, the rivers Sombrio and Jordan, Revillagigedo (today's Sooke Inlet), and Rada de Valdés y Bazán (Royal Roads) but apparently missed the entrance to what would later be Victoria Harbour. A boat party discovered another large opening on the southern shore: Puerto de la Bodega y Quadra (Port Discovery). Thinking that the strait was closed at its eastern end, they decided to return to Nootka.

Out in the open strait, strong tides and adverse winds drove *Princesa Real* back and forth. Once, nearing the northern shore, they glimpsed a large opening toward the north, which they called Canal de López de Haro; the headland at its portal they named Punta de San Gonzalo. This was the first recorded sighting of Gonzales Point and Haro Strait. They also explored into Puerto de Cordova (Esquimalt Harbour). It was by then mid-August with dense fog, so, unable to get back to base, Quimper was forced to head directly to San Blas. López de Haro's chart of the expedition, *Plano del Estrecho de Fuca*, is a landmark in the cartographic history of Vancouver Island. (See Fig. 25, page 41)

Meanwhile, at Santa Cruz de Nuca, construction had continued in preparation for the coming winter. That season, in 1790–91, Nootka was particularly cold and wet. Scores of men fell sick with scurvy and a variety of fevers, including cholera, from which all who were infected died. To men accustomed to the dry warmth of New Spain, winter in this cove was far from friendly.

That same winter, Bodega y Quadra worked at piecing together a composite map of the entire *Costa Septentrional de California* (north coast of California). In addition to the maps prepared by the earlier Spanish voyagers—with the exception of Cañizarez's map of the Pérez foray, filed and forgotten in the viceroy's archives in Mexico—he had copies of other charts. The collection of fur traders' sketch maps assembled by Meares had been aboard one of the British vessels seized by Martínez. Cook's charts, possibly with additions made by La Pérouse, would also have been available. (See Fig. 26)

Bodega y Quadra's chart covers from just south of Acapulco to Unalaska in the middle of the Aleutian chain of islands. It also marks the Islas de San Duich—an attempt to render into Spanish the name "Sandwich"—the Hawaiian Islands. It was an extension of his own map of 1775, prepared after his voyage in *Sonora*, with updated

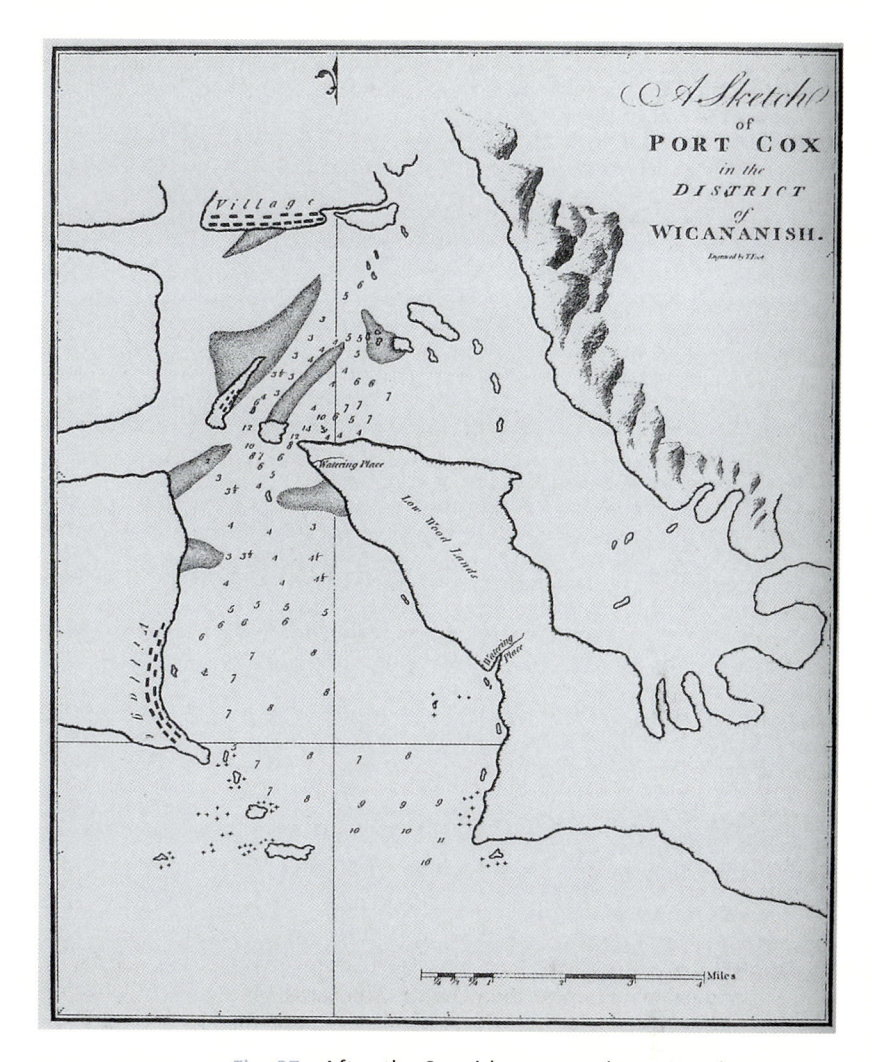

Fig. 27 After the Spanish commander at Nootka arrested Meares's associate James Colnett, Meares published a book seeking official British support for his case against Spain. The book included this, among several maps of the region.

CHAPTER SIX 43

detail, including López de Haro's map of the Strait of Juan de Fuca.

The captured crews of the British vessels, brought to San Blas by Martínez, received better treatment under Bodega y Quadra, but they remained angry. After their release, some sailed for Macao with their covert reports for Meares, relating all that had happened. Meares then carried those reports to London to complain. In 1790 he published a pamphlet, and then a substantial book, *Voyages Made in the Years 1788 and 1789, from China to the North West Coast of America*, recounting his trading voyages and the events at Nootka.[1] He claimed that the Spanish had expropriated his real estate at Friendly Cove and Neah Bay, including substantial buildings, and petitioned the British government to demand that Spain make full restitution and compensation for his loss of business. Despite the fact that much of his testimony was exaggerated or false, influential sponsors still backed him.

Meares included in his *Voyages* several maps that he claimed had been the result of his own explorations but were in fact those of Barkley and others. One of these charts, probably the work of Meares himself, is of a "Port Cox in the District of Wicaninish." Meares so named it to honour his sponsor and predecessor as manager in Macao, John Henry Cox. The chart shows features that are now Clayoquot Sound, the Tofino peninsula, and the shore of Meares Island. (See Fig. 27, page 43)

Another of his maps purported to show a voyage made by the "American Sloop WASHINGTON in the Autumn of 1789" through the "John de Fuca's Straits," then turning northwest around a "Northern Archipelago" to emerge once more into the Pacific around latitude 55°—just north of the Queen Charlotte Islands. The chart plots the track of *Lady Washington* and the eastern shoreline of the "Northern Archipelago" by a curious broken, wavy line. (See Fig. 28) The caption to the map notes that it "demonstrat[ed] the very great probability of an INLAND NAVIGATION from Hudson's Bay to the WEST COAST." Meares also showed an easterly water link from the Strait of Juan de Fuca with a mysterious "River Oregan."

On reading Meares's version of events, with its dubious geography, George Dixon, another ex-naval officer-turned-fur trader, published a scathing counter-broadside. He refuted many of Meares's claims and likened the depiction of a Northern Archipelago to "the mould of a good old housewife's butter pat."[2] Meares responded with a printed rebuttal and Dixon published a second pamphlet.

The British authorities, notwithstanding their full awareness of the unreliability of Meares's character and testimony, and his shady trading under flags of convenience, took up his case. Prime Minister William Pitt seized upon it as a pretext to provoke a confrontation with Spain, Britain's imperial rival. The Nootka Incident—which had happened in such a tiny, remote, and hitherto little-known place—thus became an international cause célèbre.

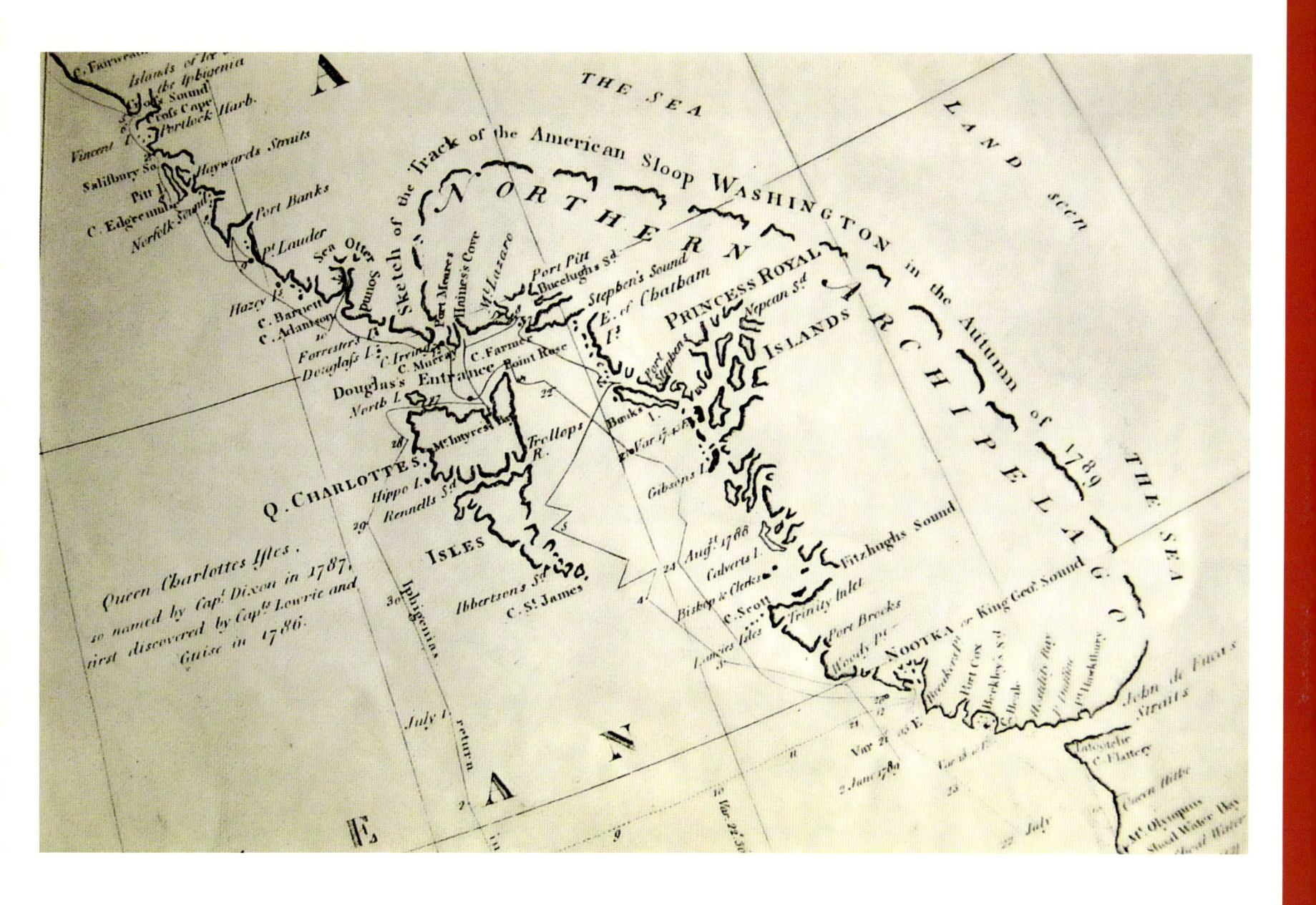

Fig. 28 Meares's "butter-pat" map, the most controversial in his book, depicted a reported voyage made inland between the Strait of Juan de Fuca and Dixon Entrance. This, he claimed, gave strong evidence to confirm the existence of a Northwest Passage from the Atlantic.

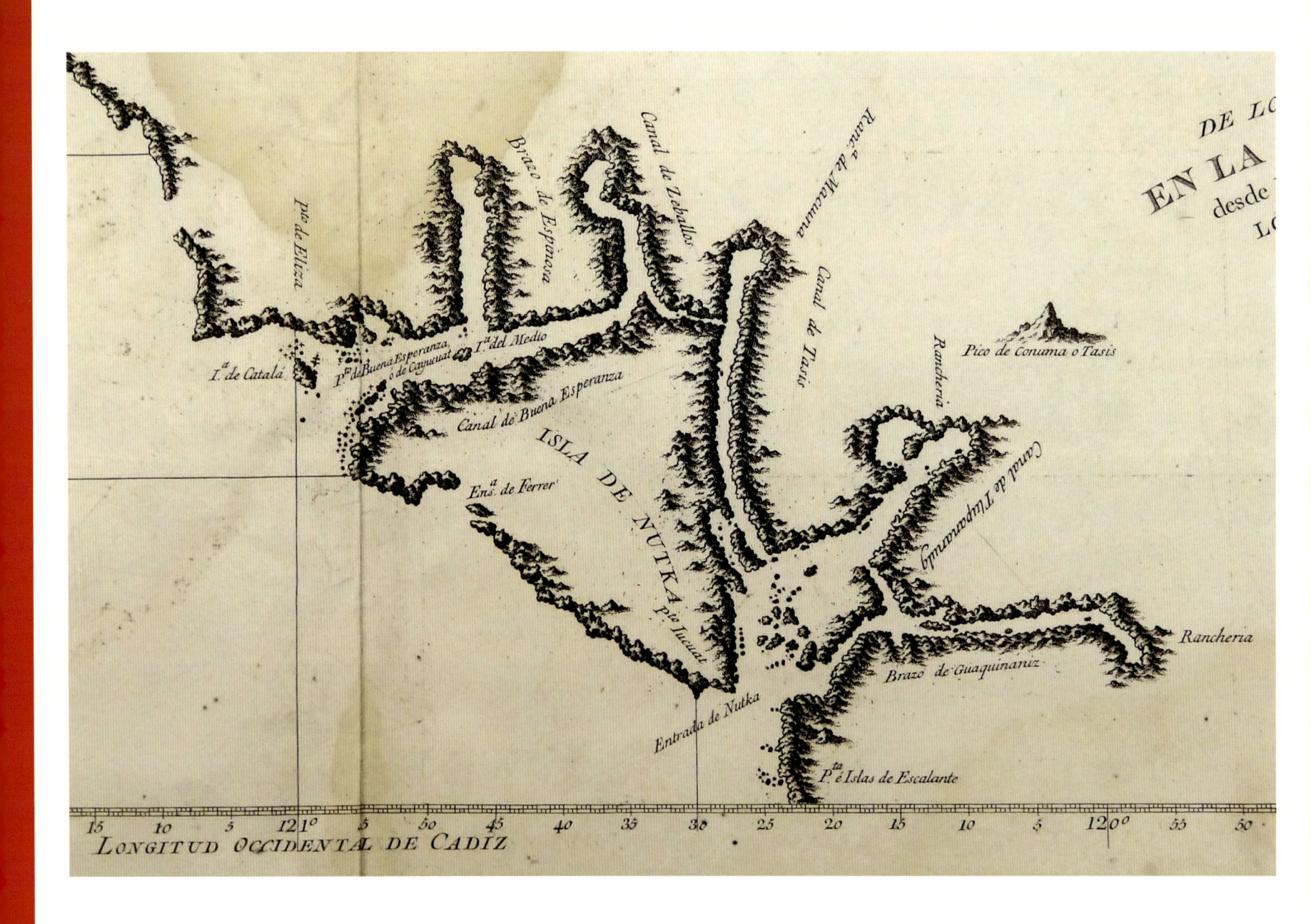

Fig. 29   While the two ships of the Malaspina expedition were anchored off San Miguel in Friendly Cove in 1791, surveying parties in ships' boats explored and charted in detail the complex of channels surrounding Nootka Island.

CHAPTER SEVEN

"Exploration Will Resolve the Doubts"

IN THE PROCESS OF COMPILING his *Costa Septentrional* chart, Bodega y Quadra, now commanding the Naval Department of San Blas, identified several sectors for which he still lacked reliable data. Those gaps included the Strait of de Fonte, the eastern end of the Strait of Juan de Fuca, and the Entrada de Hezeta (the Columbia River). Referring to these sectors, Viceroy Revillagigedo had told Bodega: "Exploration will resolve the doubts."[1]

Bodega y Quadra prepared a set of orders for the coming season, and in February 1791 dispatched a ship to resupply the outpost at Nootka. The intent of the orders, signed by the viceroy, was to provide data to complete Bodega y Quadra's chart of the coast. They instructed Francisco de Eliza, still in command at Santa Cruz at Nootka, to conduct an ambitious season of exploration and included copies of the Bodega y Quadra and López de Haro charts, showing the gaps that needed filling.

Eliza was to personally lead reconnaissance missions, first north to latitude 60° searching for the de Fonte entrance, then south to chart Puerto Clayocuat (Clayoquot Sound) and other inlets. Thereafter he was to explore the eastern parts of the Strait of Juan de Fuca, including the entrance named after López de Haro, and finally the Hezeta entrance. He was to rush the results of all these surveys to San Blas without delay.

Rather than use the frigate *Concepción* as ordered, Eliza chose to take the smaller *San Carlos*. Second Pilot José María Narváez commanded a second vessel, the small schooner *Santa Saturnina*, with a skilled cartographer, Juan Pantoja, also aboard, and an apprentice pilot, Juan Carrasco, who had been with Quimper the previous season. Narváez and Carrasco had sailed with López de Haro in *San Carlos* in 1788 and '89 and the former had overwintered at Nootka. Eliza showed the good sense to delegate the hard work of exploration to his more experienced subordinates.

Narváez, exploring the "Archipielago de Nitinat ó Carrasco" (now the Broken Islands in Barkley Sound), discovered and ventured some fifteen miles (twenty-four kilometres) into a narrow fjord, which he called "Canal de Alberny" in honour of his colleague, the veteran *capitán* Pedro Alberni, who commanded the company of militia at Nootka.

When *Santa Saturnina* rejoined *San Carlos* at Puerto de Córdoba (Esquimalt Harbour), Eliza delegated the next phase of reconnaissance to Narváez.

Narváez's two vessels, *Santa Saturnina* and a longboat, followed the eastern shoreline through Rosario Strait into what became the Strait of Georgia. He gave the name "Isla y Archipielago de San Juan" to the area to the west. As the explorers entered the widening body of water, they became the first Europeans on record to do so. Unless, that is, the voyage in 1592 by Apóstolos Valerianos—a.k.a. Juan de Fuca—is counted.

After passing around Lasqueti and Texada Islands, charting and naming both, Narváez decided it was time to return to *San Carlos*. In the distance, to the northwest, the pilots could just make out two headlands—now called Capes Lazo and Mudge. These, they calculated, must be around latitude 50°, the same as Nootka. Narváez's vessels anchored just off the mouth of today's Little Qualicum River before continuing to follow the coast southeastward. They discovered and explored a significant entrance, naming it the "Boca de Winthuysen" after a senior Spanish naval official.[2] The name was rendered with various spellings over time, but seemed to settle on "Wentuhuysen"; it is today's Nanaimo Harbour.

According to the coastline shown on the chart, Narváez then followed the eastern shores of the chain of islands now named Gabriola, Valdes, Galiano, Mayne, and Saturna. Whether he realized that they were not tracing the eastern shore of the big island is uncertain, given the lack of a journal, but for the next sixty years, the line of the apparent coastline on his chart misled subsequent navigators and cartographers. In 1852, when James Douglas and his surveyor, Joseph Pemberton, made a canoe voyage from Fort Victoria to the newly discovered coal measures at Wentuhuysen, they found that the true coastline of Vancouver Island lay as much as twelve miles (twenty kilometres) to the southwest of where Narváez had shown it.

Narváez was transferred to *San Carlos*, as his cartographic skills were needed to complete the full chart of the expedition, and Carrasco took command of *Santa Saturnina*, returning to San Blas via Monterey.

Back at Friendly Cove, Eliza learned that two ships of a major Spanish scientific exploring mission, under the command of Alejandro Malaspina, had left the anchorage only two days earlier.

Specialists with Malaspina's expedition had set up an observatory at Santa Cruz de Nuca and measured the longitude, and boat parties followed up Kendrick's 1789 circumnavigation of Mazarredo Island and the surrounding channels, to gather more accurate data. Felipe Bauza, the expedition's geographer and director of charts, prepared many small charts from this data, which Narváez and Pantoja incorporated into the chart of their own 1791 expedition, thus combining the results of all the Spanish explorations in the vicinity of the southern end of Vancouver Island. (See Fig. 29, page 46) Within a few years, the toponym Mazarredo became, on Spanish charts, Isla de Nutka. By late October the composite chart, with its supporting smaller charts and survey data, was ready to accompany Eliza's report to Bodega y Quadra and the viceroy.

Eliza's masters, in both New Spain and Madrid, were already acting to follow up the clues in the López de Haro chart by organizing a major expedition to explore the eastern end of the Strait of Juan de Fuca. Eliza's report also speculated that the size of the channel they had discovered (which would become the Strait of Georgia) meant that the land to the west of it, including Nootka and its neighbouring inlets, formed part of a larger group of islands. Within a year, his island hypothesis was proved correct.

At San Blas, Narváez and Pantoja worked with Carrasco to compile a comprehensive chart. They combined the results of their explorations with those of Quimper and López de Haro, the previous season, and the Malaspina survey of the inlets and channels around Nootka. They based their coordinates on the longitude calculated by Malaspina's specialists, and they corrected several place names.

Carrasco drew the resultant *Carta que comprehende* (Chart that includes), which, despite the misleading coastline southeast from Wentuhuysen, stands as the next important milestone of Vancouver Island's cartography. It incorporates five small inset maps of Pto. Clayocuat, Pto. de Nra Señora de los Angeles, Ba. de Buena Esperanza, Pto. de la Sta. Cruz de Nuca, and Pto. de Sn. Rafael (now Hot Springs Cove). The chart also shows important ethnographic information, locating "Rancherías de Yndios" (Native villages) along the coast. (See Fig. 30, page 50)

The *Carta que comprehende* is sometimes erroneously called the Narváez Chart or that of Eliza. Narváez appears to have retained all his own logs and journals and many of his charts; only the journal from his 1788 voyage to Alaska has come to light. A French diplomat, Duflot de Mofras, met the destitute Narváez just before he died in Mexico in 1840 and saw the logs and charts. After he died, Narváez's family attempted to bargain with the Mexican authorities: In return for the back pay they claimed he was owed, they would return the documents. The offer was not accepted, and the paper trail peters out. The manuscript of the 1788 journal appeared in a Philadelphia book dealer's stock in the 1930s. A noted historian of that time, Henry Wagner, acquired, translated, and published it,[3] and there remains a faint hope that the rest of the original documents, or contemporary copies of them, still gather dust in the yet-to-be-catalogued national archives in Mexico and will someday resurface.

By 1790 reports of the events at Friendly Cove, which became known as the Nootka Incident, had reached London and Madrid. An exchange of diplomatic notes, with sabre-rattling escalating nearly to the point of war, ensued until an ambiguous document, the Nootka Convention, averted conflict. Commissioners appointed by both sides were to implement the convention by meeting on site to resolve the matter of the property claimed by John Meares.

Having read the report of the 1790 Quimper expedition, Spanish authorities felt it should be followed up. The viceroy, the count of Revillagigedo, and the commander of the San Blas Naval Department, Bodega y Quadra, had already taken steps to do just that by mounting the Eliza expedition. Orders from Madrid, however, were to be heeded, so they started planning yet another exploratory voyage for 1792.

A new, forty-seven-foot (fourteen-metre) schooner, or *goleta*, called *Mexicana* was built at the San Blas shipyard and ready in December 1791. In the meantime, Eliza's report and charts had reached the viceroy and Malaspina, both of whom appreciated the possibilities that the Narváez findings could hold for the discovery of the elusive waterway across North America.

Malaspina, citing his official mission to investigate the existence of the passage, suggested to the viceroy that two of his officers replace Mourelle, who had been nominated as leader but had fallen ill. One was an expert astronomer

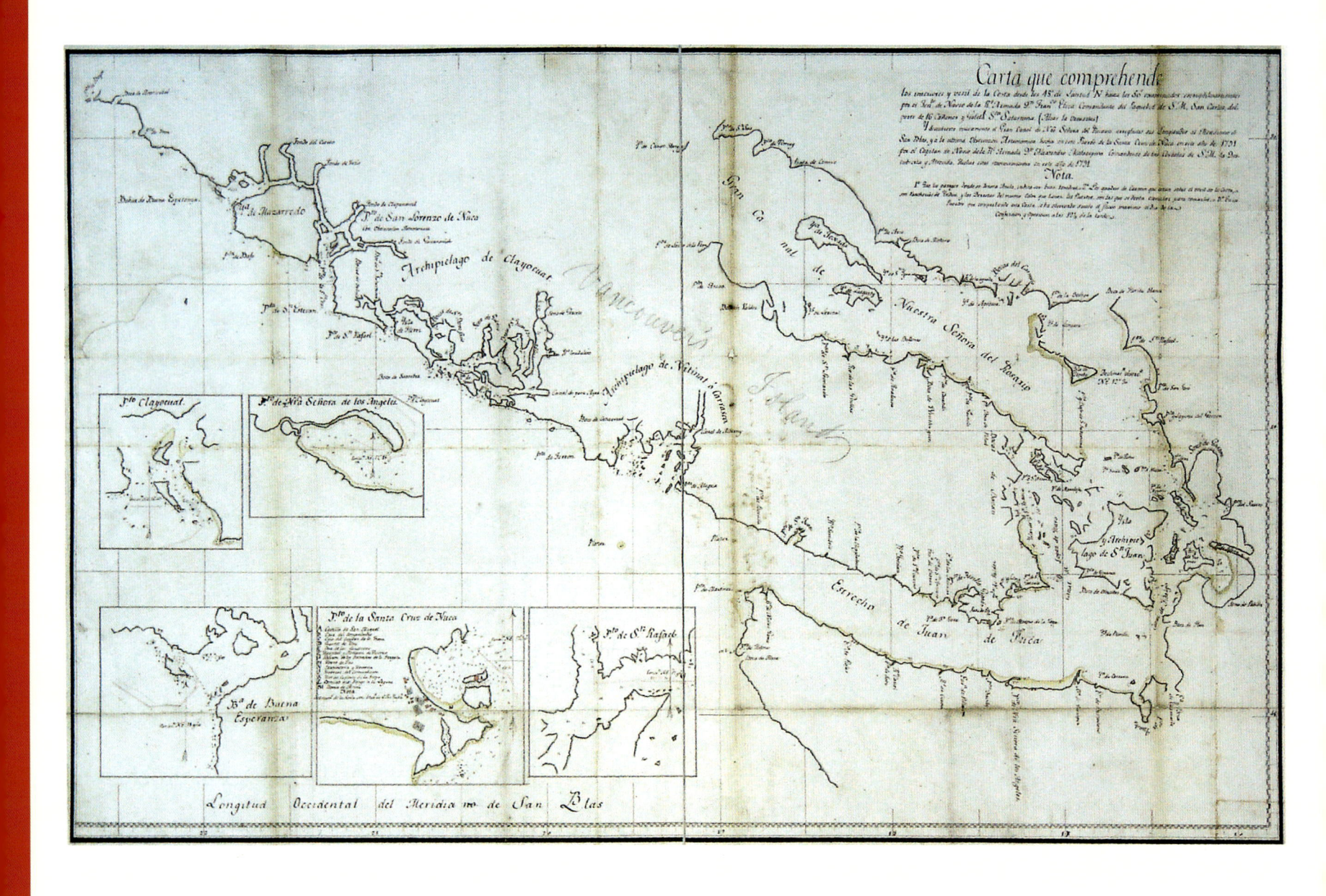

Fig. 30   Spanish knowledge of the coastlines of Vancouver Island and the Strait of Georgia just before the arrival of George Vancouver is shown on this chart. It was the combined work of the three pilots who did the exploring: Narváez, Pantoja, and Carrasco. The inset charts show five harbours in greater detail.

and hydrographer, Dionisio Alcalá Galiano, the other a well-connected and reliable man, Caetano Valdés y Flores. Malaspina also suggested that for safety reasons, *Sútil*, a second goleta, accompany *Mexicana*.

By the time the two goletas reached Nootka, Bodega y Quadra, nominated as the commissioner to represent Spain in implementing the Nootka Convention, had already anchored his ship there. He made sure that Alcalá Galiano and Valdés had copies of all the available charts and journals of earlier expeditions. After two weeks, the goletas left for the Spanish outpost of Núñez Gaona (Neah Bay, just inside Cape Flattery). There they picked up a guide, Tetacus, whom they understood to be a chief from the village of Esquimalt. He was able to recall and name many previous European visitors, including two recent ones: "Wancoober" and "Bolton" (Vancouver and Broughton).

Tetacus showed keen interest in the workings of the vessels. Also, on seeing the navigators' charts, he immediately understood the concept and provided several Salish names for places he could identify. The local name for Córdoba (Esquimalt) was Chachimutupusas; Revillagigedo (Sooke Harbour) was Machimusat; Boca de Caamaño (Admiralty Inlet) was Quechinas. Tetacus called the Boca de Floridablanca (the Fraser River and/or Burrard Inlet) Sasamat. Discussions with him confirmed that this last feature should be given priority for investigation by the expedition.

On June 21, anchored in Boundary Bay, the Spaniards watched a British ship approach. It was HMS *Chatham*, Lieutenant William Broughton, RN, commanding. He came aboard and informed them that Captain George Vancouver, RN, his expedition leader in HMS *Discovery*, was nearby. After a courteous exchange of offers of help, they agreed to rendezvous in a few days off the north side of a headland the Spaniards called Punta de Lángara, in what would one day be named English Bay.

A few days later Captain Vancouver identified himself and requested permission to come aboard. He explained that he was returning from a foray to explore some nearby channels—today's Burrard Inlet, Howe Sound, and Jervis Inlet—and showed his charts to the Spaniards. *Discovery* and *Chatham* joined the goletas and more cartographic consultation ensued. Each team was permitted to copy the other's manuscript charts. Alcalá Galiano informed Vancouver that Bodega y Quadra was awaiting him at Santa Cruz de Nuca for the diplomatic role entrusted to them.

Vancouver proposed that the four vessels proceed together for the next stages of their explorations, to which the Spaniards agreed. Vancouver's work had ruled out the possibility of a navigable water route to the interior and the Atlantic via the inlets examined so far. While Alcalá Galiano was prepared to accept this, the converse was not true. The English captain carried orders to verify, at first hand, the coastline of the mainland; he was required to positively disprove the existence of the Northwest Passage.

While they were anchored in company, Vancouver discussed the question of the land mass to the west. Might it be an island? What did the Spaniards know of channels that connected this stretch of water (the Strait of Georgia) with the ocean farther north? Vancouver's new friends knew little more than he did, showing him a copy of Carrasco's *Carta que comprehende* with the findings of the Eliza-Narváez voyage of the previous season.

The goodwill gesture of attempting to sail together became impracticable, so after Desolation Sound, the expedition leaders agreed to make their way to Nootka separately. The goletas explored and charted, probing into Toba, Bute, Loughborough, and Knight Inlets, although Vancouver bestowed those names later. After sheltering from storms for a few days at the north end of Vancouver Island, in what is now Goletas Channel, the two Spanish vessels managed to make their way to Friendly Cove. The crews of the two tiny, poorly built ships had been out from Santa Cruz de Nuca a little under three months and had made the first recorded continuous circumnavigation of the island.

On their arrival, they found Vancouver already deep in diplomatic discussion with Bodega y Quadra. After only a brief recovery from their arduous expedition, and following the exchange of hydrographic information, Alcalá Galiano and Valdés sailed away from Vancouver Island to return to San Blas and thence Spain, without rejoining Malaspina.

Resting en route in Monterey, they drew the charts of the voyage; cramped conditions aboard the goletas had prevented this while the mission was in progress. (See Fig. 31) The final report of their Vancouver Island voyage was one of the few documents from the Malaspina expedition to be published at the time. On his return to Spain, Malaspina had fallen victim to political intrigue at court and was imprisoned, banished, and declared a non-person. The bulk of the huge volume of scientific data and reports of the Malaspina expedition was consigned to oblivion for almost two centuries.

Alcalá Galiano managed, however, to convince the authorities that his had been an independent commission. The probable author of the report, he included much information about the Nootka area and its inhabitants, regretting that during the voyage, hydrographic work prevented him from learning more about the local people. Drawings by the young pilot, José Cardero, who had shown himself to be a talented artist, supported the report with many illustrations of the people, places, and natural history.

Summarizing the achievements of the goletas' voyage, the report's author wrote: "In the main [it] served only to satisfy curiosity, without being of any benefit to navigators."[4] He was being unduly modest, since the two officers had produced new charts that were published in various forms, and Bodega y Quadra and others, including Vancouver, used the data in later compilations. The Spanish hydrographic office in Cadiz published versions of the expedition's two principal charts of Vancouver Island in the official *Atlas marítimo español* of 1795.

Vancouver incorporated the work of various Spanish expeditions into his chart of the island. From Alcalá Galiano and Valdés, he copied sectors of coastline southeast from Nootka, continuing around Punta de San Gonzalo and then northwest as far as today's Cape Lazo, and from Beaver Harbour around to Cape Scott. Vancouver's charts fully acknowledged the Spaniards' contribution.

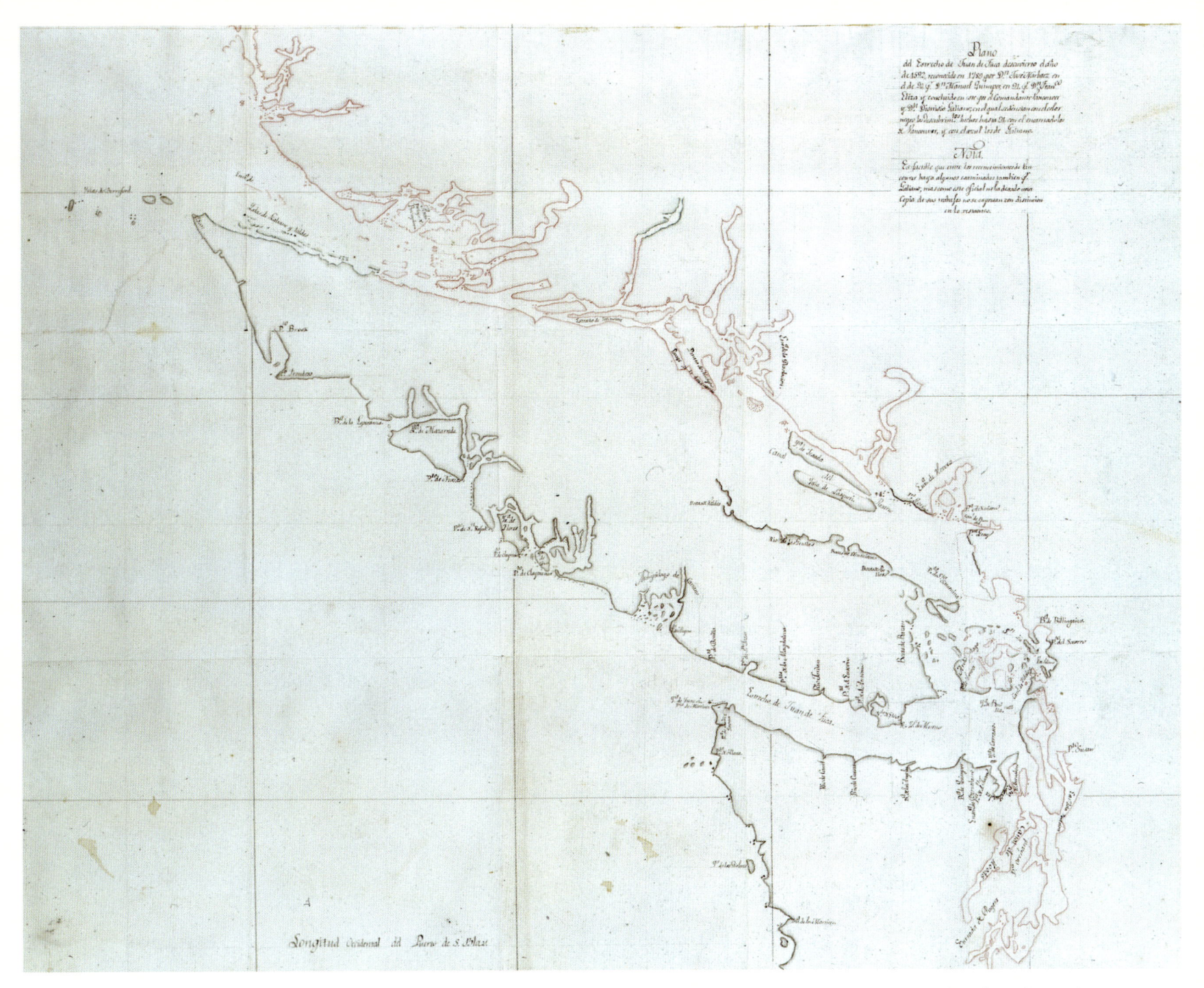

Fig. 31   Bodega y Quadra compiled this composite chart in 1792 to record the cooperation between the simultaneous Spanish and British expeditions that circumnavigated Vancouver Island. Spanish vessels surveyed the detail plotted in dark blue and George Vancouver that in red.

CHAPTER EIGHT

"No Place More Eligible": Anglo-Hispanic Collaboration

GEORGE VANCOUVER HAD BEEN AT sea since the age of fourteen. As a midshipman he had served aboard Captain Cook's *Resolution* and *Discovery* during the great navigator's second and third voyages of oceanic exploration. His shipboard mentors in those years included the astronomer William Wales, the expert navigator William Bligh, and, of course, James Cook himself. Vancouver had been with Cook during the 1778 respite at King George's Sound—later called Nootka—before they sailed north to the coast of Alaska and into the Bering Sea.

Technical aptitude and a disciplined work ethic had gained Vancouver rapid promotion, and he won further recognition for his excellent hydrographic surveys of Kingston and Port Royal Harbours in Jamaica. In the course of these surveys, he assembled a team of competent subordinates and friends whom he would call upon for the great assignment of his life. In 1791, he was given command of the new and sturdy, 330-ton (299-tonne), armed merchantman *Discovery* (not Cook's vessel of the same name) and the much smaller and sluggish armed tender *Chatham*, for a four-year circumnavigation of the globe involving charting and diplomacy.

The stated objectives for his new mission were twofold. The first was to search the northwest coast of America, between latitudes 30° and 60° north to ascertain whether or not a navigable "water communication" with the east coast existed. "Navigable" meant by vessels capable of sailing the open Pacific. The expedition was to chart the coastline of the continental mainland, examining all inlets and large rivers, and paying special attention to the Strait of Juan de Fuca.

The second part of the mission was diplomatic. Vancouver had been nominated commissioner for the purposes of the Nootka Convention. He was to meet with a Spanish counterpart at Nootka and, on behalf of Britain, receive some properties—"lands and buildings"—in the area.

Alexander Dalrymple, the Hydrographer of the Navy, provided Vancouver with copies of all charts then available, including Meares's "butter-pat" map that showed a waterway inland from the Strait of Juan de Fuca. Not included in the collection were charts by López de Haro of the Quimper voyage in 1790 or those by Carrasco of the Eliza–Narváez expedition the following year, because Britain, at the time, did not know of those Spanish voyages out of Santa Cruz de Nuca.

Vancouver's great voyage began in early April 1791, heading "east about," via the Cape of Good Hope, Australia, New Zealand, Tahiti, and the Sandwich Isles. Just over a year after leaving England, they reached the coast of California. After coasting northward for a few days, they met another ship, the Boston fur trader *Columbia Rediviva*, with Robert Gray in command. Here was the very man reported by Meares to have sailed the *Lady Washington* through an inland sea around Nootka.

Lieutenant Peter Puget and the civilian botanist Archibald Menzies went aboard and showed Gray, to his astonishment, Meares's map. Gray acknowledged that he had once entered a wide strait that he supposed must be Juan de Fuca's, but he had only penetrated about fifty miles (eighty kilometres). Finding no otters, he had returned the way he had gone in. The rest of the map seemed, to him, pure speculation.

Gray accompanied Vancouver's vessels almost to Cape Flattery, which they rounded in thick haze and squalls to anchor in the area of Neah Bay. One of the friendly Natives paddling out to see the visitors must have been Tetacus, who later reported their visit to Alcalá Galiano and Valdés. Keeping, as instructed, to the continental shore, the Englishmen continued their survey eastward along the southern shore of the Strait of Juan de Fuca. Lieutenant Joseph Baker was the first to see the spectacular, snowy cone that Vancouver named after him.

They next explored, in ships' boats, into Admiralty Inlet and Puget Sound, and among the islands of the San Juan Archipelago, before anchoring in Birch Bay, where Broughton saw the two Spanish goletas and visited them.

After their rendezvous in English Bay, where they exchanged charting data, the four ships sailed together to anchor in Desolation Sound. No one aboard the British ships knew a word of Spanish. The obvious need for an interpreter for a mission that was partly diplomatic seems to have escaped London's consideration, but fortunately, Alcalá Galiano spoke good English. When the goletas had left Nootka, some seventeen days earlier, HMS *Daedalus* had not arrived. Vancouver, expecting to receive new orders carried by his supply ship, did not want to meet with Captain Bodega y Quadra, his counterpart for the diplomatic aspect of his mission, until he had read them. He decided to continue with his survey until *Daedalus* joined them.

The two expeditions set up a common observatory onshore. The British tended to consider their counterparts' charting work to be less rigorous than their own, but this was mainly a result of the constraints of space aboard the goletas. In fact, Alcalá Galiano's astronomical results were more accurate than those of anyone on the British side. All results from both teams were compared and copied in an atmosphere of cordial cooperation.

Two of the British boat parties explored north from the anchorage, and both made the same key discovery. Johnstone took *Chatham*'s boat through the Arran Rapids to explore Bute and Loughborough Inlets. As he left the latter, about opposite today's Kelsey Bay, he noted that the flooding tide now came from the northwest, not from the south as before. This, he realized, confirmed that, in addition to the Strait of Juan de Fuca, there must be a second opening to the Pacific. There was a passage, possibly

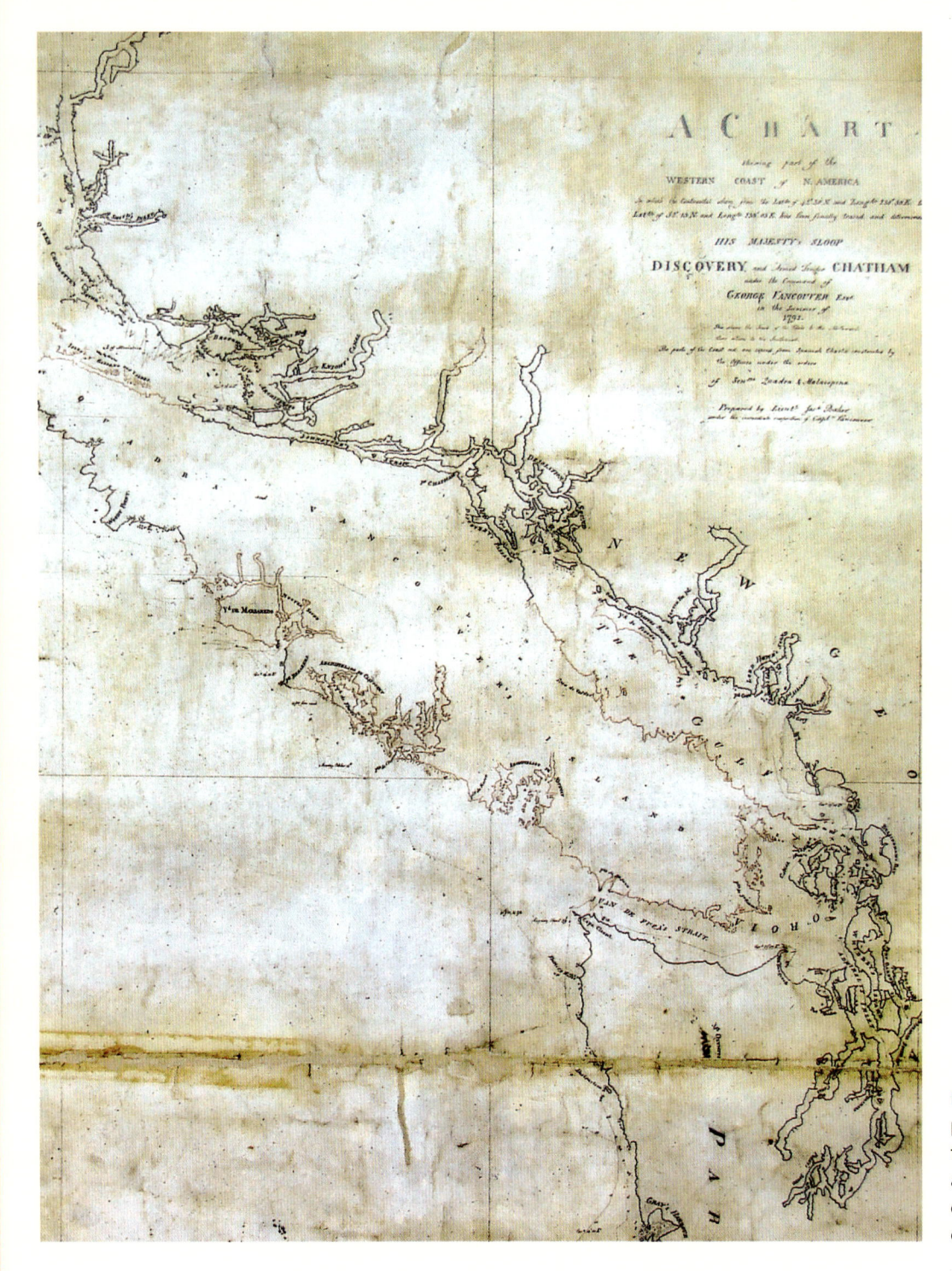

Fig. 32 Joseph Baker, Vancouver's cartographer, prepared this manuscript chart after the expedition's first season. Like their Spanish counterparts, Vancouver and Baker distinguished which parts of the depicted coastline were from their surveys and which from their collaborators'.

navigable, around what must therefore be a large island, or islands, to their west.

Meanwhile, Puget and Joseph Whidbey had been tracing the western shoreline of the "Gulph" and entered Discovery Passage. They too noted the new direction of the tide and drew the same inference about an island before returning to the ships to report their findings. As soon as Johnstone arrived, Vancouver deduced that the two channels merged into one strait, giving access to the ocean to the north. Vancouver elected to continue northward through Discovery Passage, and the Spaniards chose the other, since it seemed to provide better access to the continental shore.

Passing through Johnstone Strait, Vancouver visited an impressive village on its southern shore overlooking a "fine, freshwater rivulet." This was the main encampment of an important chieftain, Cheslakees, at the mouth of the Nimpkish River. They then crossed to the northern shore of Queen Charlotte Sound and rounded Cape Caution into Fitzhugh Sound.

While they lay at anchor, the fur-trading brig *Venus*, flying English colours, joined them. The captain, who had recently called into Nootka, brought a letter from *Daedalus* and also informed Vancouver that "Señor Quadra" was impatiently awaiting his arrival at Nootka. Vancouver decided to now join *Daedalus*.

At the end of August 1792, *Discovery* and *Chatham* arrived in Friendly Cove to find a Spanish naval brig, *Activa*, at anchor, as well as *Daedalus* and a British fur-trading vessel. Vancouver learned that Midshipman Thomas Dobson, aboard *Daedalus*, had some knowledge of Spanish, and he was immediately assigned to *Discovery*. This came at a most opportune time, for a bulky dossier from Bodega y Quadra, all in Spanish, had just arrived, the first of a series of written exchanges between the commissioners.

Accompanying a cover letter by Bodega y Quadra was a detailed history of Spanish activities in exploring and taking formal possession of this coast. He also included full reports into what, exactly, constituted the property used and abandoned by Meares, and the events involving Martínez and the British fur traders. Bodega y Quadra knew far more about this than did Vancouver, who could only go on Meares's version and the resultant, indignant pieces in the London press.

Bodega y Quadra, acting for Revillagigedo, was ready to be accommodating, expecting Vancouver to have a similar mandate for negotiation. The latter, by contrast, considered that neither his original instructions nor the additions brought by *Daedalus* granted him such powers. He was only to take possession "of the buildings, and districts [this was new], or parcels of land occupied by H.M. subjects on April 1789."[1] He did not feel authorized to negotiate the boundary between the two empires.

The courteous exchange of official letters, translated by Dobson, continued, but without agreement. All the while, the personal relationship between the two naval officers—both were explorers and hydrographers—grew in mutual respect and friendship. They combined their surveys and compiled charts of the coast, the inlets of the continental shore, the major, as-yet unnamed island, and the archipelagos that separated them.

The composite charts differed mainly in the toponyms: the Spaniards used their place names, and Vancouver used existing English ones and his own choices. By this time, Alcalá Galiano and Valdés had arrived at Nootka and so had another Spanish exploring expedition, led by Jacinto

Caamaño, which had been investigating the outside coast north of Nootka. All the information obtained was shared freely and after work the exchange of gentlemanly visits and dinners continued. (See Fig. 32, page 56)

Bodega y Quadra indicated to Vancouver that a joint formal visit to Maquinna at his winter village of Tarsheis (now Tahsis) would be appropriate, as it would enhance mutual understanding with the local population, and a large party of British and Spanish officers was assembled to call upon the chief. Returning from the convivial excursion, Bodega y Quadra made a further suggestion, that "to commemorate our meeting and very friendly intercourse" some port or island be named after them both. Vancouver liked the idea, and "conceiving no place more eligible than the land that had first been circumnavigated by us ... I named the island of QUADRA & VANCOUVER ... with which compliment he seemed highly pleased."[2]

Praising the gesture made by Vancouver to honour his Spanish friend, another British naval officer, Henry Trollope of HMS *Herald*, wrote in 1846 that "in distant parts of the world commanders belonging to rival nations joined in acts which tended to benefit mankind; and it is to be hoped that the name given to this island will be maintained, and that Quadra and Vancouver may remind future ages when and how to agree."[3] Sadly, neither the Hudson's Bay Company nor the Lords of the Admiralty shared that sentiment, and British maps of the island soon dropped Quadra's name.

The two commissioners eventually agreed to disagree on the handover of the land and property. Unable to resolve their differences, they referred matters to Madrid and London. This, however, did not impair their friendship. They continued to exchange charts and positional data until Bodega y Quadra left to return to San Blas. The whole diplomatic interchange had taken three weeks.

Vancouver needed to send a summary of his first season's survey work and a report on the diplomatic impasse to the Admiralty in London; Bodega y Quadra agreed to forward a copy of the report to England via Spanish channels. The package, with Lieutenant Mudge acting as courier, included a map of Friendly Cove with Meares's property indicated.

After spending six weeks at Nootka, the three ships of Vancouver's flotilla sailed to Monterey as planned. Bodega y Quadra was already there, having awaited his friend for more than a month. During that time he had received orders that seemed to indicate their two countries had reached a new understanding over Nootka. To Vancouver, this meant even more urgency for his dispatches to get to London, so Bodega y Quadra agreed to convey a second courier, Broughton, to San Blas, and to ensure his safe passage across Mexico. This would be much faster than an earlier plan of sending *Chatham* home around Cape Horn.

Before Broughton left for San Blas, Vancouver and the survey officers prepared fair copies of the charts—British, Spanish, and composite—and a more detailed report. The chart of the region carried by Broughton contained more information about the island's west coast than the versions dispatched previously. It included the fact that Nootka—still called Mazarredo—was an island, and details of the intricate channels nearby. However, the printed version of the chart did not include this new information, and Vancouver himself does not appear to have spotted its omission.

Vancouver and Bodega y Quadra sailed from Monterey together, the good friends bidding farewell at sea, never to meet again.[4]

Fig. 33 Midshipman Henry Humphries, a young artist with Vancouver, sketched this view in 1791, showing, at left, the two-storey house of the Spanish commandant and, at centre, the cemetery. At right, marked A,B,C, is the cove where Meares launched the *Northwest America*.

By the time Mudge and Broughton reached London, European relationships had shifted, and there were matters of state far more urgent than the squabble over Nootka. In France, the anti-monarchist movement had blazed into full revolution, and the new republic had declared war, first on Britain and then upon Spain. These two monarchies, fearful of contagion, signed a mutual defence treaty. They had earlier reached another Nootka-related agreement under which Spain was to compensate British interests—that is, those of Meares and company.

Vancouver's dispatches were read in the light of these changed relationships; the new priorities called for retaining Spain's goodwill while preserving British dignity. Spain's payment of the compensation had been prompt, and despite protests from Meares, the matter was dropped. In January 1794, newly allied, England and Spain signed a third Nootka Convention. Representatives of both nations were to meet on site and Spain would formally hand over to Britain the "buildings and districts of land," interpreted to be just the small plot of land where Meares's boat shed had once been. (See Fig. 33) The ceremonial lowering, raising, and lowering of their respective flags would mark these actions, and then both nations would withdraw. Thereafter, subjects of both nations would be free to make any temporary use of the cove that they wished, but without declaring sovereignty. These developments, however, were not transmitted to Vancouver.

Vancouver continued with his surveying mission for two more seasons, calling into Nootka at the start and close of

CHAPTER EIGHT

Fig. 34   Vancouver's team and the Spanish captains Alcalá Galiano and Valdés together discovered that Vancouver Island was an island by sailing around it.

each season. By mid-August 1794, Vancouver and his team had confirmed that "between the limits of the survey, no navigable communication exists between the waters of the Pacific and Atlantic."[5]

Vancouver's orders were that all journals kept by him and his subordinates belonged to the Admiralty and must be collected and delivered personally. In London, he discovered that Lord Camelford, a vengeful but well-connected junior officer he had disciplined for insubordination at sea, had sullied his reputation.

Vancouver requested access to his own journals in order to prepare them for publication, and this was granted, as well as authority to engage engravers for the charts and plates. He retired to Petersham, a hamlet near Richmond on the Thames, to work on his *A Voyage of Discovery to the North Pacific Ocean and Round the World 1791–1795*. He had completed five of the planned six books before he died on May 12, 1798, two and a half years after returning, and shortly before his forty-first birthday. His brother John ensured that the narrative was completed posthumously and published. It came out later that year as 1,440 pages in three volumes, plus a separate folio atlas of charts and coastal views.[6] (See Fig. 34)

By some mysterious agency, probably the Camelford clique, Vancouver's private notebooks, correspondence, observations, and calculations, as well as several other officers' journals, disappeared from the Admiralty's vault. Also gone missing, soon after the publication of the first edition, were the copperplates for the atlas charts and views. In his scholarly study *Islands of Truth*, Daniel Clayton discussed in depth how agents of the British agenda of colonization quite happily seized on Vancouver's charts to bolster England's claim to the Pacific Northwest coast, despite the official snubbing of the man himself.[7]

George Vancouver was buried in Petersham churchyard beneath a modest headstone. The main finding of his voyage, disproving the existence of the Northwest Passage, meant a subsequent lack of adequate acknowledgment of his achievement, since it was not newsworthy. While important to geographers, it was not the stuff of heroic exploration in the public mind. In more recent years, however, Vancouver's reputation has been vindicated.

His gilded statue stands atop the BC Legislative Buildings in Victoria; another decorates the quay at King's Lynn, his birthplace. In 1999, the lieutenant-governor of the province of British Columbia proclaimed that May 12, in perpetuity, shall be known as "Captain George Vancouver's Day." However, the most fitting monument to this great maritime explorer remains his charts, particularly the one of his first season's work, which boldly identifies the island that he circumnavigated as QUADRA AND VANCOUVER'S ISLAND.

Fig. 35 The HBC commissioned Aaron Arrowsmith in 1795 to produce a map of the territories that interested them. As their traders moved westward, they pasted new information onto the master copy of the map, adding "Frazer's River" in about 1824.

CHAPTER NINE

"A Perfect 'Eden'": James Douglas Selects a New Fort

IN MARCH 1795, BODEGA Y Quadra's replacement, Brigadier José Alava, and Lieutenant Thomas Pierce of the Royal Marines executed the Convention for the Abandonment of Nootka. The Spanish flag was lowered; the Union Jack hoisted, then lowered. Both groups departed, leaving a puzzled Maquinna with documents to produce for any stranger who might come by in the future.

For the next forty years, international awareness of Vancouver Island fell dormant, while the issue of imperial sovereignty over the region known later as the Pacific Northwest simmered. Nevertheless, trading ships, sealers, and whalers continued to visit the western coast of the island and northward. Increasingly, they came from the Yankee ports of the northeastern United States and were known collectively as "Boston Men."

By the early 1820s, the great imperial powers of the day had signed a series of bilateral treaties declaring the region between the Rockies and the Pacific, and between parallels 42° and 54°40' north, to be a zone of interest to just Britain and the United States. Spain and Russia had dropped out of contention, while France continued to watch from the sidelines. Significantly, none of these imperial treaties had involved, consulted, or even acknowledged the indigenous residents.

Those Aboriginal peoples suffered in other ways from the attention of outsiders. It is impossible to estimate accurately their deaths from imported disease, but the numbers were huge. This brought drastic changes to the population of Vancouver Island; to survive, the remnants of whole clans were obliged to relocate and merge with others, abandoning villages large and small. Along with cultural traditions, dialects and even languages were lost, which also affected future place names.

The Anglo-American Convention of 1818 established the forty-ninth parallel as the boundary between the American and British territories westward from the Lake of the Woods, but only to the crest of the Rockies (called, at the time, the Stony Mountains). Jurisdiction over the region to the west of that, known as the Oregon Territory, was left to future negotiation. Under "joint occupancy," citizens of both nations could trade and settle. While Vancouver Island was not specifically mentioned, it fell within this zone of dual interests.

Britain's concerns in this era reflected primarily those of the fur-trading enterprises of the interior. In 1821, the Hudson's Bay Company and the North West Company, hitherto bitter rivals, merged. The British government blessed their union by granting exclusive trading and hunting rights over a vast area, which included the Oregon Territory, although this did not confer any tenure to the land. (See Fig. 35, page 62) Company men became increasingly active in what they called the Columbia Department in the territory of New Caledonia. They established twenty-two fortified trading posts west of the Rockies, including Fort Vancouver on the Columbia River and Fort Langley on the Fraser.

In selecting the sites for these forts, the HBC men sought good agricultural potential, because as well as feeding their own people, they needed to supply the trading outposts along the harsh northern coast. Finding suitable locations involved methodical exploration and mapping, both overland and by water. Three HBC vessels operated in these waters during this period, the brig *William and Mary*, the schooner *Cadboro*, and, later, the sidewheel steamer *Beaver*.

The HBC had an arrangement with the leading London cartographic publisher of the era, Aaron Arrowsmith, whereby he would receive copies of all map manuscripts produced from their operations; in return, he would incorporate the new information into his published maps.[1] Between 1795 and 1850 he issued eighteen updated versions of his *Map Exhibiting All the New Discoveries in the Interior Parts of North America*, which he dedicated to the company. From 1798 on, for the coastline of Vancouver Island, he relied upon Vancouver's published charts, but gave as its primary toponym "Wakash Nation," with "Quadra and Vancouvers Island" as secondary. Also, south of the island, "Classet" was shown as the main title for the entrance to a smaller "supposed Str of Juan de Fuca," hinting at residual doubt. (See Fig. 36)

❊ ❊ ❊

Vancouver Island was never particularly productive for beaver pelts, and by the 1820s, its valuable sea otters had been hunted into virtual extirpation. Initially, apart from its strategic location commanding the access to the Fraser River and thence to the chain of fur-trade forts in the interior, the island held minimal attraction for the company. This changed.

American rhetoric grew increasingly strident following the purchase of Louisiana and the Lewis and Clark overland expedition of 1804–06. The Americans convinced themselves that they enjoyed a God-given "Manifest Destiny" to dominate the hemisphere from sea to sea. In 1823, President Monroe declared his doctrine: "the American continents... are henceforth not to be considered as subjects for future colonization by any European power."[2]

Despite such sabre-rattling, the US government suspected, incorrectly, that its legal claim to Oregon was weaker than Britain's. Officials were not familiar with the details of the third Nootka Convention of 1794, by which Britain had agreed not to claim any sovereignty over the region. In 1819 Spain had sold to the United States, along with title to Florida, her "rights, claims and pretensions" on the west coast north of latitude 42°.[3]

By 1834, the United States Navy felt the need to mount a major voyage of scientific discovery. Under the command of Lieutenant Charles Wilkes, the six-ship United States Exploring Expedition set out, but by 1841 only two of

Fig. 36   In 1846 Edinburgh publisher W. & A.K. Johnston issued a map showing proposed alternatives for the US-British boundary. To the north, James Polk's belligerent "54 40 or fight!" line; at centre, the forty-ninth parallel; to the south, the Columbia River, which Britain had suggested in 1826.

Fig. 37   The United States Exploring Expedition set out in 1838 on a voyage of scientific discovery around the Pacific. Three years later, they arrived in the southern end of the Strait of Georgia, where they charted the "Archipelago of Arro."

Wilkes's flotilla remained to enter the Strait of Juan de Fuca. They surveyed the coast of the Olympic Peninsula, Puget Sound, the southern end of the Strait of Georgia, and the San Juan Islands. Wilkes's multi-volume report supported the policy of taking sole possession of the entire Oregon Territory as far north as 54°40', where the boundary of the Spanish sphere of influence met that of Russia. Governor Simpson of the HBC learned of Wilkes's views and warned the Foreign Office in London. (See Fig. 37)

At the same time, a rising tide of American settlers flooded into the fertile valleys of Oregon, and the HBC, thin on the ground, realized that their monopoly of trade in the region would vanish. Also, the company had lost too many ships and cargo on the treacherous sandbars at the mouth of the Columbia River. They needed a better harbour and felt that their best hope lay at the southern end of Vancouver Island.

Captain William Henry McNeill, skipper of the *Beaver*, reconnoitred several First Nation villages, now known as Sooke, Becher Bay, Metchosin, Esquimalt, and Victoria. McNeill and James Douglas used their versions of the First Nation (Lekwungen) place names. Their name for Victoria Harbour was the Canal of Camosack, and it headed McNeill's shortlist of good harbours.

Accordingly, in early summer 1842, Douglas, with six men and two horses, sailed aboard the company's brigantine *Cadboro* to examine the places McNeill had listed. Douglas agreed with him: "I made choice of a site for the proposed new Establishment in the Port of Camosack which appears to me decidedly the most advantageous situation, for the purpose, within the Straits of De Fuca." He concluded, "I am confident that there is no other sea port north of the Columbia where so many advantages will be found combined."[4]

Having decided on the site for the new establishment,

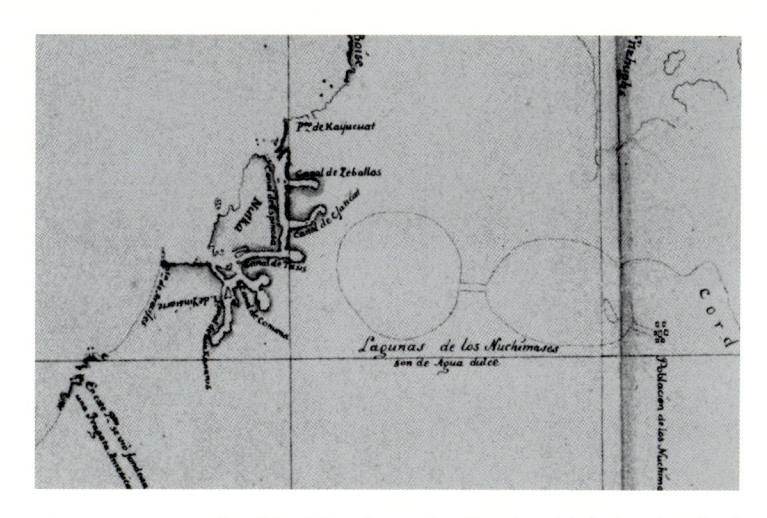

Fig. 38 Maquinna, the Nootka chieftain, sketched onto a Spanish map a route across the island that his men would take to trade with "los Machimusas" (Cheslakees).

Douglas and Adolphus Lee Lewes, a capable cartographic draftsman as well as a field surveyor, set about mapping the agricultural potential of the surrounding land. Lewes, the Métis son of another chief factor, had attended school in England. There, he had "been brought up to ... and [had] served a regular apprenticeship in the land surveying business."[5]

Lewes titled the map he drew to accompany Douglas's report to his superior, Dr. John McLoughlin, *Ground Plan of Portion of Vancouvers Island Selected for New Establishment*. Essentially, the map is thematic, portraying landscapes and terrain. (See Figs. 39 and 40, page 68) Not only was this the first map to be drawn of Victoria, it was the first of any part of the island's interior, except for a sketch drawn by Maquinna in 1793 of his oolichan trail from Yuquot to Cheslakees's village. (See Fig. 38) Earlier cartography had been limited to coastlines, with occasional stylized mountains indicated.

The *Ground Plan*, at a scale of 4 inches to 1 mile (1:15,840), is detailed, but not very accurate. Douglas and Lewes did not establish a network of control points but probably surveyed along Native trails, counting paces to estimate distance and

CHAPTER NINE 67

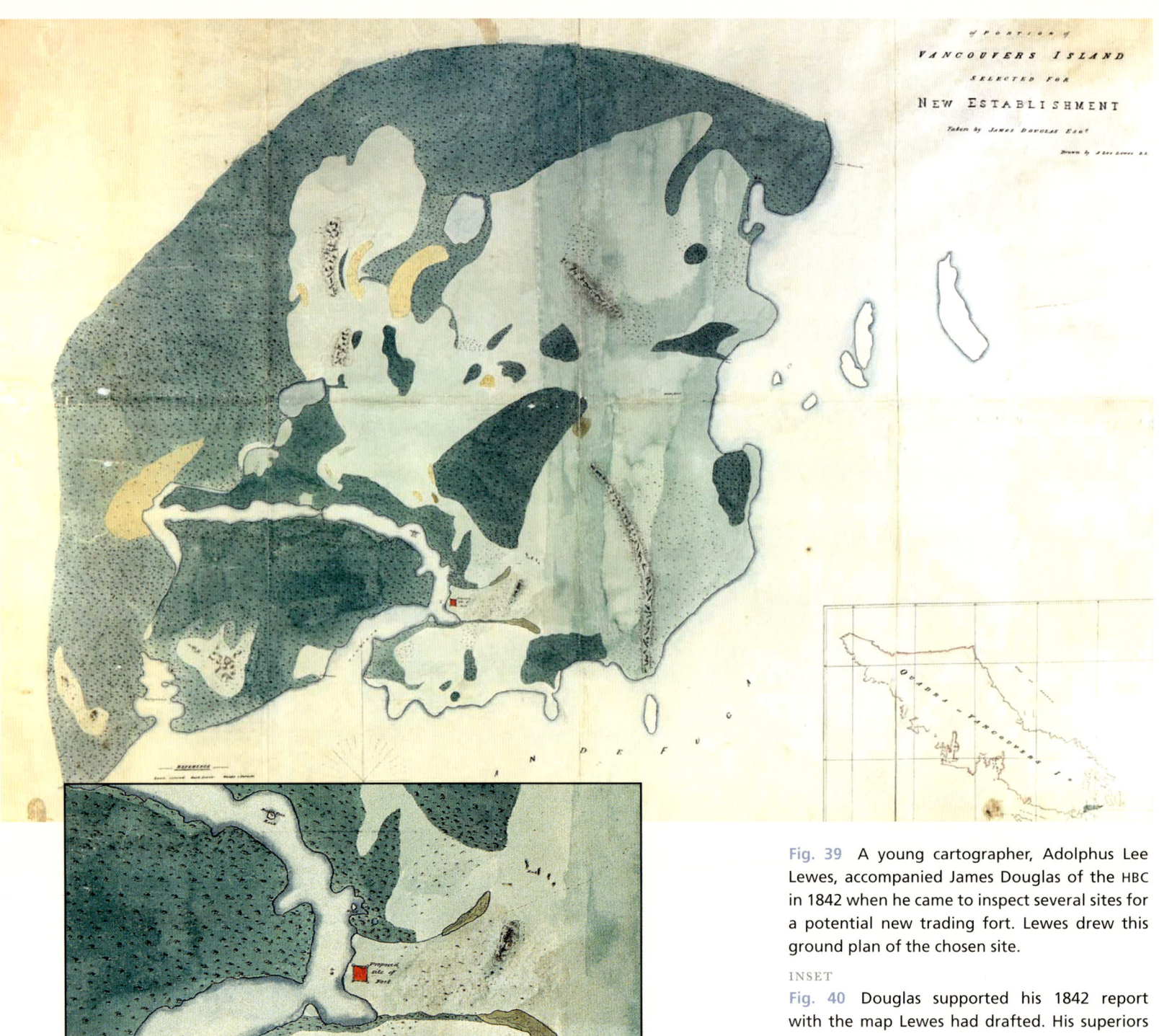

Fig. 39 A young cartographer, Adolphus Lee Lewes, accompanied James Douglas of the HBC in 1842 when he came to inspect several sites for a potential new trading fort. Lewes drew this ground plan of the chosen site.

INSET

Fig. 40 Douglas supported his 1842 report with the map Lewes had drafted. His superiors accepted his recommendation, and he returned the following season to construct Fort Victoria.

using a compass for direction. Nonetheless, there are many features on their map that can be identified today. Evidently, they paid attention to sources of fresh water and to the patterns of local clearing and agriculture. They noted two Native settlements, one at the head of today's Cadboro Bay, the other at Esquimalt.

Lewes provided, as an inset to his *Ground Plan*, a map of "Quadra or Vancouvers Island." Comparison with a modern map shows the limitations of the geographical knowledge at that time. Particularly noticeable are differences in the coastline south of Nanaimo, and the total lack of information about the interior of the island. The detail Lewes used was derived, via Vancouver's chart, from the hasty notes of a weary Narváez in 1791 as he rejoined Eliza after exploring into the Gran Canal (Strait of Georgia). (See Fig. 41)

Their survey complete, Douglas and his team sailed back to Fort Vancouver, and the following spring Douglas returned to Camosack with a construction party. While the building of the new fort was proceeding, the Northern Department of the HBC decided that it would be named, in honour of the young monarch, Fort Victoria.

In a well-known letter to a company colleague, Douglas, the dour Scot, extolled it: "The place itself appears to be a perfect 'Eden,' in the midst of the dreary wilderness of the North west coast, and so different in its general aspect, from the wooded, rugged regions around, that one might be pardoned for supposing it had dropped from the clouds into its present position."[6] The following year, while anchored off Ogden Point, Douglas again waxed poetic: "The view landwards was enchanting... There was something specially charming, bewitching in the place... it was as though nature and art had combined to map and make one of the most pleasing prospects in the world."[7]

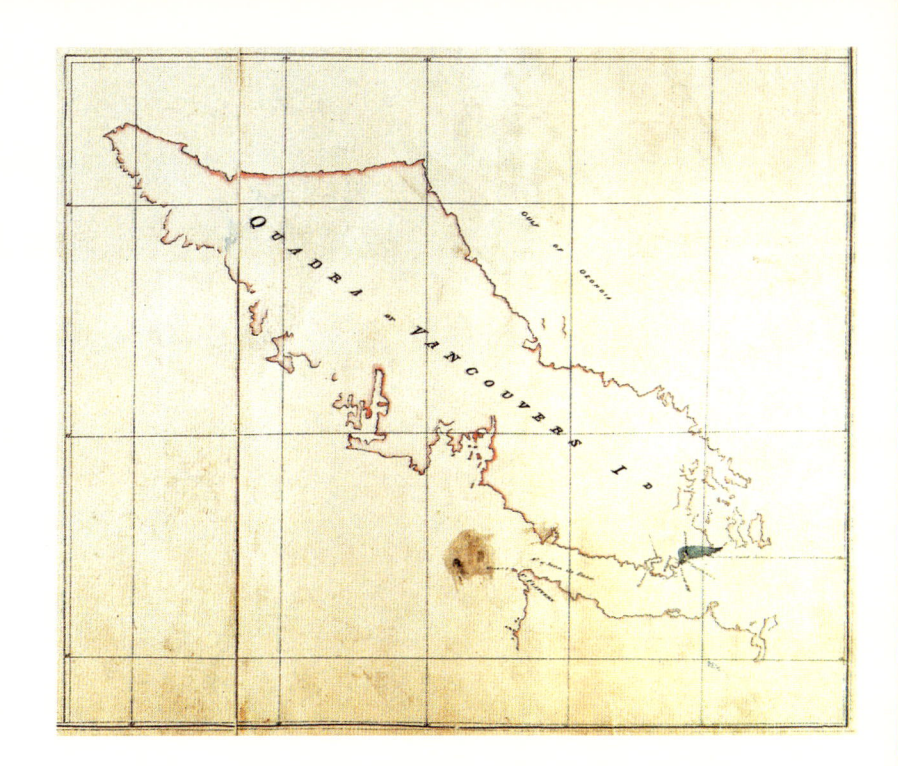

Fig. 41 Lewes's inset map for the ground plan reflects how little the HBC knew of the island's coastline or interior at the time they selected the site of Fort Victoria.

CHAPTER NINE 69

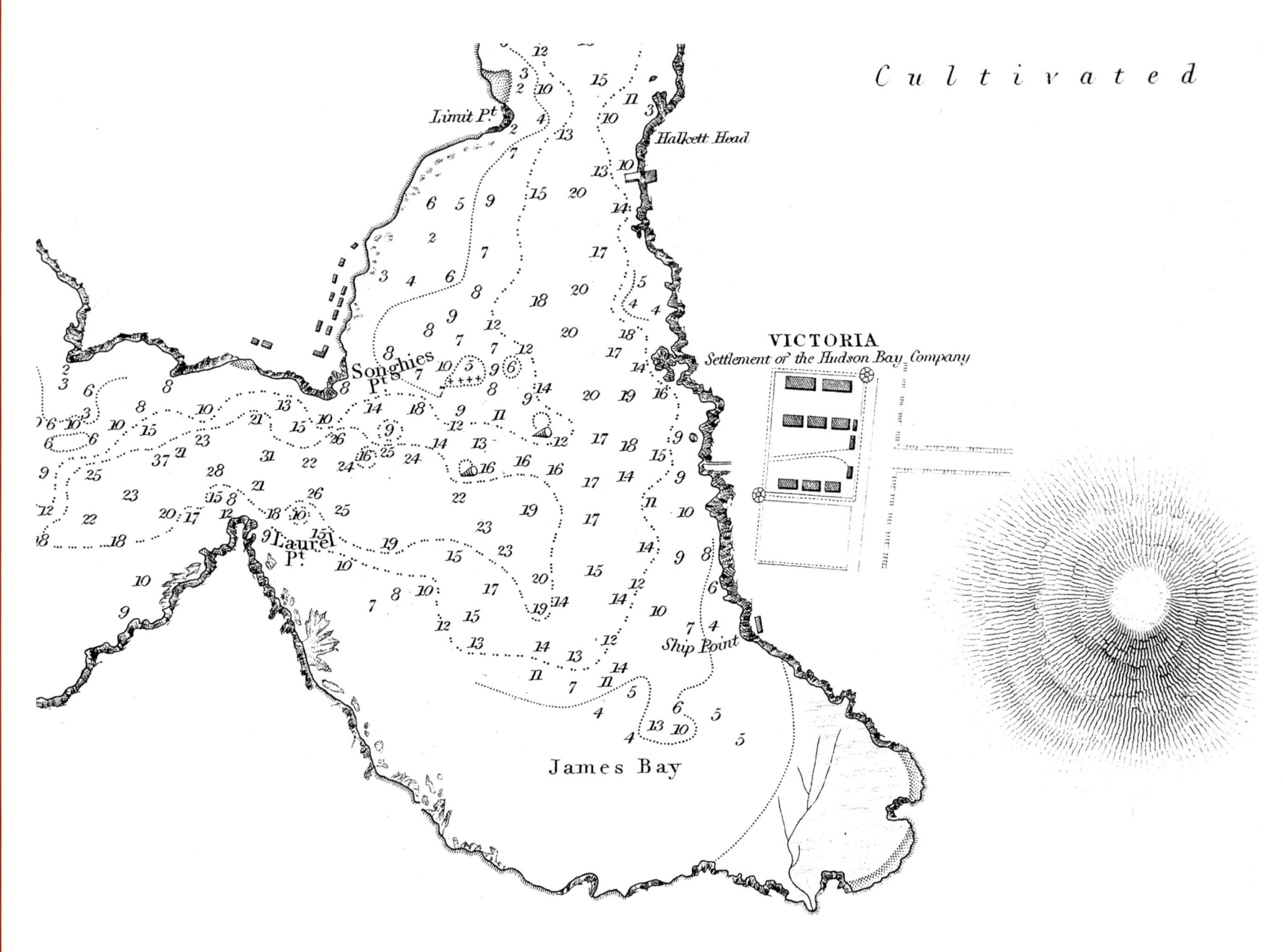

Fig. 42 Threats of conflict with the US over the Oregon question caused Lieutenant James Wood, commanding HMS *Pandora*, to chart Victoria Harbour in 1846, although his superior, Captain Henry Kellett, in HMS *Herald*, received the credit.

CHAPTER TEN

Settling into Fort Victoria: Doubts over Tenuous Tenure

IN 1846, AS ANGLO-AMERICAN TENSION over the Oregon question mounted, Rear Admiral Sir George Seymour, commander-in-chief of Britain's Pacific Fleet, received orders to maintain a strong, visible British presence. Seymour dispatched a squadron to the Juan de Fuca sector on a twofold mission: to show the flag and to evaluate the naval potential of Fort Victoria and nearby harbours.

The squadron consisted of Her Majesty's Ships *Fisgard* (Captain John Duntz), *Cormorant* (Commander George Gordon), *Herald* (Captain Henry Kellett), and *Pandora* (Lieutenant James Wood). Officers and crew from all four vessels participated in preparing the first Admiralty charts of the region since those of George Vancouver, half a century earlier. Later, as Fort Victoria developed into a settlement, the city's street map commemorated all four vessels.

Aboard the forty-six-gun frigate *Fisgard*, Naval Instructor Robert Inskip taught navigation and charting to a class of midshipmen. The class had already made a preliminary survey of Esquimalt Harbour, bestowing many of the place names still used today. Based near Fort Nisqually, Captain Duntz assigned Inskip and his students to the Kellett mission, tasking them with updating and adding detail to Vancouver's chart of Puget Sound.

The paddlewheel sloop first class *Cormorant* was the first Royal Navy steam-powered ship to operate on the west coast; its role was to tow sailing warships when lack of wind or unfavourable tides prevented them from manoeuvring. Taking *Herald* and *Pandora* in tow at Cape Flattery, *Cormorant* headed across the Strait of Juan de Fuca, bound for Fort Victoria. Lacking charts and anyone with local knowledge, the navigators overshot the entrance, and before realizing their mistake reached Cordova Bay. On the beach they found a local who understood their problem and could guide them around to the fort.

Captain Kellett, the senior hydrographer of the squadron, wasted little time on formalities and started his survey work. James Wood in *Pandora* was to chart the approaches and harbours of the southern tip of Vancouver Island: those of

Victoria and Esquimalt, the hazardous Race Rocks, Becher and Pedder Bays, Sooke Inlet, Port San Juan, and Cordova Bay. The packet brig *Pandora*, modified for surveying, was Wood's first command; however, at thirty-two he was already an experienced hydrographer, having spent eighteen years surveying along the west coast of Africa, the Canaries and other Atlantic islands, and in the North Sea.

Kellett in *Herald* headed across to the southern shore of the Strait of Juan de Fuca, intent on charting the harbours of Discovery Bay, Port Angeles, and Neah Bay, and, later, Haro Strait. Severe fogs hindered his work, so he was unable to chart Haro Strait before the surveying season closed. As George Vancouver had not devoted his attention to the eastern shore of Vancouver Island either, this sector was the least known to the British authorities, a cartographic gap that soon placed them at a disadvantage.

At the end of the season, Kellett dispatched to England the charting data—manuscript charts and accompanying notes—and the Admiralty transcribed and published them as a series of seven charts. The first, *Victoria Harbour*, dated September 15, 1848, was attributed to Captain Kellett, although Wood had done all the work. (See Fig. 42, page 70) Wood received due credit for the next chart, *Esquimalt Harbour*. Almost two years elapsed before the survey mission could return to the Juan de Fuca sector, and even then, it was only *Pandora*. Wood was able to spend a further six weeks charting the island's harbours, but again, without investigating and charting Haro Strait.

In February 1849, the Admiralty published a general chart, *Vancouver Island and the Gulf of Georgia*. It was a compilation updating Vancouver's work and even including coastal views from Cook's voyage of 1778. (See Fig. 18, page 27) The chart noted that some information had come from the Spanish expedition of Alcalá Galiano and Valdés. It also included data from the US Exploring Expedition and from the HBC surveys, but without acknowledgment. (See Fig. 43)

The Admiralty, in this 1849 chart, did disservice to Vancouver's friend and generous collaborator, Juan Francisco de la Bodega y Quadra, in two ways: Not only was that gallant officer's name omitted from the island's name, but the Kellett chart also made no mention of his having been a major source for much of the detail on both coasts of the island.

As Kellett's ships departed southbound after the 1846 season, two developments had portents for people watching the boundaries of the United States. The first was an escalation of the war with Mexico that had been waged all summer. A US naval squadron seized San Francisco and the other ports of Mexican California—a prelude to the complete transfer of possession of that territory to the United States.

The second development was an agreement reached suddenly in the US capital. Termed the Treaty of Washington by the British and the Oregon Treaty by the Americans, it defined the unresolved sector of their border, west of the Rockies. The treaty, signed on June 15, 1846, divided the disputed Oregon Territory between those two imperial powers. No other authority, including the resident population of Aboriginal people, was acknowledged. Its effect was to grant ownership of the land to the signatory nations; by this means, the British Crown acquired legal title to Vancouver Island and to what would later become British Columbia.

Article 1 of the treaty read, in part: "The line of the boundary . . . shall be continued westward along the forty-ninth parallel of north latitude, to the middle of the channel which separates the continent from Vancouver's Island; and thence southerly, through the middle of the said channel, and of Fuca's Straits, to the Pacific Ocean."[1]

The resolution of the border was just one element of a complex trade-off between the two parties and, perhaps for that reason, it had a serious shortcoming. It made no mention of the archipelago of dozens of sizable islands that lay across the "channel" referred to so simplistically. More than one channel could be drawn through the islands. Both sides at the table had been able to call upon ample cartography, for both held copies of charts made by Vancouver and the various Spanish expeditions showing the archipelago quite clearly. Lieutenant Wilkes, just five years prior to the treaty, had even added further detail to the configuration of the islands on Vancouver's charts.

HBC officials, as soon as they saw the treaty's wording, pointed out the ambiguity, suggesting it be changed to assert that the line of Vancouver's track through Rosario Strait identified the channel in question. The American side was also concerned, wanting it made clear that the channel for the boundary was Haro Strait. The negotiating diplomats had apparently trusted that their wording would suffice to resolve any future question.

Within a few years, just such questions became the source of growing conflict. In 1848, the British prime minister, Lord Palmerston, requested copies of the best chart available: Vancouver's, updated by Kellett's surveys of 1846, which the Admiralty was about to publish. This chart lacked reliable detail for Haro Strait. Moreover, while it marked Vancouver's track, skirting to the east of the San Juan Islands, there was a highly significant omission: The boundary described in the 1846 treaty was not shown. This could not have been an inadvertent cartographer's error. One plausible explanation is that Palmerston, aware of the treaty's vague wording, deliberately avoided publishing a contentious interpretation of the water boundary so as not to provoke the Americans.

Fig. 43 Kellett's hydrographic mission of 1846 added some reliable navigational data to Vancouver's chart, but, particularly in the boundary area of the San Juan Archipelago, it was still incomplete. This chart does not attempt to indicate the newly negotiated boundary.

CHAPTER TEN 73

Fig. 44 James Wyld, the Queen's geographer, published another updated version of Vancouver's chart in 1848, using information from HBC sources rather than the recent surveys by the Royal Navy. Wyld shows the new water boundary, incorrectly, as starting in Boundary Bay.

The chart detail in the area just north of Nootka—included in the manuscript chart carried by Broughton but omitted in the printed version—had by this time been identified and correctly incorporated, naming the island Nootka, not Mazarredo. The chart portrayed Vancouver Island's mountainous interior in a way somewhat similar, but not identical, to Vancouver's chart as scattered, representative peaks and adding the note "lofty mountains" to the south side of Johnstone Strait.

Perhaps stimulating Palmerston's request for reliable cartography was a map published in 1848 by James Wyld the younger, the grandly styled Geographer to the Queen and HRH Prince Albert. Wyld had an impressive pedigree: He had succeeded his father, who had succeeded Jefferys and Faden, all well-respected London map and atlas publishers. Wyld the elder had pioneered the use of lithography for printing military maps and in 1830 had helped create the Royal Geographical Society.

Wyld had little fresh information for his new map, *Vancouvers Island*. His primary source, from Vancouver's fifty-year-old atlas, was the chart titled . . . *part of the N.W. coast of America*. As well as showing Nootka as an island, Wyld added "Quatsinough Harb." from an unknown source, probably the HBC, since the new Admiralty chart did not name it. As would that new chart, Wyld's map dropped Quadra's name from the island's toponym. (See Fig. 44)

Across the island from Quatsinough, the map included a few more newly named places: "Kellett [Point], Hardy Sd., Beaver Hr., and McNeils Harb.," with the note "Reported Lodes of Rich Copper Ore." Nanaimo was also indicated, as were, across the strait, "Frazers" River and Fort Langley. Around the southern tip of the island, Wyld included a dense array of new HBC names. His map replaced the scattered peaks depicting the mountainous interior of the island with a narrow, unbroken, stylized cordillera running its entire length.

In the area of urgent political concern—the southern end of the "Gulf of Georgia" (later the Strait of Georgia) and the unnamed Haro Strait—the island's coastline shown by Wyld differed little from the erroneous one that Vancouver had copied from Spanish sources. Wyld also showed, with a dotted line, an interpretation of the international water boundary. While the line passed through the archipelago to the east of Orcas and Lopez Islands—Vancouver's route—it joined the forty-ninth parallel in the middle of what is now Boundary Bay, rather than in the middle of the strait.

A handwritten note on a copy of the second edition of Wyld's map stated: "Mr. Bancroft [US ambassador in London] sent a copy of this map to Mr. Buchanan [US secretary of state, later president] on October 19, 1848 remarking 'you will see that this map suggests an encroachment on our rights by adopting a line far to the E. of the Straits of Haro.'"[2] The Admiralty and Palmerston were correct in suspecting that the depiction of the water boundary would prove contentious.

Governor Simpson of the HBC also quickly saw that the boundary through the archipelago in the Strait of Georgia, poorly defined in the treaty, could become a cause for dispute, and proposed that a commission, staffed by experts from both sides, resolve the matter. This idea resulted in a letter from the British ambassador to the US secretary of state, but there the matter stalled for several years. When the question arose again, it had developed into an issue.

At the time of the Treaty of Washington, 1846, the Pacific Northwest no longer held strategic importance for the British government. Far more significant was the overall rapport with the United States.

That same year, Douglas replaced McLoughlin as chief factor of the HBC's Columbia District, and was angered to learn, through naval sources, the terms of the treaty. He felt that the highly productive farmlands around the Columbia and Willamette Rivers and Puget Sound had been surrendered. He then came to realize, however, that he should focus on making optimum use of the territory north of the new border. Simpson ordered him to transfer the company's main west coast shipping terminal or depot from Fort Vancouver to Fort Victoria.

The government did grant one request of the company, that of naval protection for the resources of the island. In the early summer of 1848, the flag-showing, fifty-seven-gun frigate HMS *Constance* arrived at Esquimalt with Captain George Courtenay, RN, in command, bearing orders to secure the recently discovered supply of coal in the region around Beaver Harbour at the northern end of Vancouver Island. The navy expected this to become a vital resource for the new steam-driven naval vessels on the Pacific Station, so it was essential to prevent the coalfields from falling under American control.

Courtenay sent messages to Douglas, who was away trading in the Sandwich Isles. *Constance* immediately departed for Beaver Harbour, where Courtenay took formal possession in the Queen's name. Douglas, on his return, was annoyed, viewing Courtenay's action as an infringement of the company's exclusive right to trade, but Courtenay had justification for his actions: The company held no tenure to the land or to its minerals, just trading rights.

A year later, Douglas received another order, this time to relocate himself and take personal charge of a new company responsibility; he was appointed governor, *pro tempore*, of the new colony of Vancouver Island.

CHAPTER ELEVEN

"In Free and Common Socage": Colonization by Contract

IN JANUARY 1849, THE BRITISH government acknowledged that the mood of expansionism in the United States and the influx of American settlers into the Oregon Territory posed a potential threat to its tenuous authority over Vancouver Island. Soon after the 1846 Washington treaty, James Douglas and his superiors in the Hudson's Bay Company pleaded with the government to endorse the company's claim to tenure. Britain felt prepared to grant the company's request, provided that it did not cost too much, and decided to harden its legal position unilaterally by declaring the island a British colony.

The first step was to issue a Crown grant of proprietorship "in free and common socage"—what would be called today a real-estate transfer "in fee simple"—over "the island called Vancouver's Island." This proclamation of a new colony rested on the understanding that it would be economically self-sufficient. The grant also required the company to ensure that the island be populated by loyal British settlers, from the United Kingdom or other British Dominions. If within five years that had not happened, the contract would lapse.

Upon receiving orders for his new responsibility, the senior company man in the region, James Douglas, relocated his family from the well-appointed comfort of Fort Vancouver to the new and still-spartan outpost on Vancouver Island. His new role as governor *pro tempore* was over and above his duties as agent for the company in that same colony and in the Columbia District and agent for the HBC's subsidiary firm, Puget's Sound Agricultural Company. Thus he would now serve two masters—the Crown and the company.

The 1849 deed of title over the colony—called the "Letters Patent" or the "Charter of Grant"—obliged the company to reinvest 90 percent of all revenues from land titles and mining licences in civic infrastructure such as roads and public institutions. The contract specified the price of land at one pound per acre, a figure calculated according to the Wakefield system, an economic theory espoused by policy-makers in London.

Edward Gibbon Wakefield's theory held that rather than develop a new colony along new lines, it was preferable "to transfer whatever is most valuable and most approved of the institutions of the old ... the same classes, united together by the same ties, and having the same relative duties to perform."[1] In other words, by controlling the availability of land, the colony would mimic the land-holding patterns of the home country—landed gentry buttressed by skilled support staff and workers.

To these ends, the charter specified that land could be sold only in parcels no smaller than twenty acres (eight hectares), at a price of twenty shillings (one pound) per acre, and to be held in free and common socage. The price of one pound per acre was the going rate for good agricultural land in England, not for remote, unbroken, forested wilderness. Moreover, for every 100 acres (40.5 hectares), the purchaser was obliged to recruit and pay the passage of three married couples or five single workers as employees. The stated intention was preventing "the ingress of squatters, paupers and land speculators."[2]

The system was not practical. Douglas, even before he had seen the terms, recommended that, to establish communities, the first settlers should be offered free grants of 200 or 300 acres (81 or 122 hectares). He also suggested that smaller town lots be made available at a nominal price to encourage "the establishment of mechanics and others, whose presence will give enhanced value to the lots in the vicinity."[3]

Six months after granting the charter, the government appointed a lawyer, Richard Blanshard, as "Governor and Commander in Chief in and over our Island of Vancouver and the Islands adjacent between the 49th and 52nd degrees of North Latitude." Twelve days after that, the government yet again changed the description of the area in question. An Imperial Statute for the Administration of Justice stated that "all such islands adjacent to Vancouver's Island or to the Western Coast of North America, and forming part of the Dominions of Her Majesty, as are southward of the fifty-second degree of North latitude, shall be deemed part of Vancouver's Island for the purposes of this Act."[4]

Once again, bureaucrats in London had demonstrated cartographic ineptitude. They had not attached a map, showing the geographical limits of this new imperial domain, to the HBC's Crown grant, nor to Blanshard's orders, nor to the text of the Justice Act, failing to seize these opportunities to remove ambiguity about the channel referred to in the 1846 treaty. They even neglected to correlate the limits of the new colony with the international boundary, thereby creating confusion and dispute about who governed where.

In his 1849 Annual Report to the Governors of the HBC, George Simpson mentioned that he had instructed that the island be traversed "in every direction and noting accurately its features. The attention of the exploring party should be confined to the interior country ... leaving the marine survey (except at the coal mines) to be performed by the steam vessel and sloop of war ... under an officer of scientific attainments." Even earlier, Simpson had invited the governors to recruit and send out a qualified officer who would make a general survey of the island's topography.

The lack of maps was a serious handicap to the task of colonization. If settlers were to be attracted and persuaded to invest, they would want to see detailed descriptions of the lands and resources on offer. The colonial administration also needed a cadastral system—which documents and registers legal boundaries—to indicate what properties were available and to assure potential buyers that a property's legal title was secure.

A surveyor was an urgent requirement. Douglas and his boss, Simpson, suggested a local HBC farm manager, Dr. William Tolmie, a scientist who had done some surveying. However, Sir John Pelly, the new governor in London, had already identified a solution: Captain Walter Colquhoun Grant, a tall, elegant, cultivated fellow who had recently resigned his commission in the Second Dragoons, the Royal Scots Greys, and wanted to acquire a substantial tract of farmland. Grant's pedigree seemed just what the company sought in landowners for the colony. He was an athletic, ambitious Scottish laird from a family of distinguished military men. He also appeared to fulfill their advertised need for a surveyor, enhancing his profile. The arrangement Pelly made with Grant, however, turned into a sorry saga of miscommunication and unrealistic expectation, inevitably doomed to fail.

Captain Grant became the new colony's first settler, and received a two-year appointment as surveyor. He faced two commitments: to select, clear, and establish his farm and, simultaneously, to meet the company's need for maps.

Everyone who met Grant liked the man, including even the dour Douglas, who, while at first doubting Grant's industry, later acknowledged that he had made a reasonable effort and repeatedly extended his credit at the company store. But Grant's affable charm concealed a flaw: He was cavalier where money was concerned, especially that belonging to others. Grant arrived in Victoria, completely destitute, in the summer of 1849. Within a few days, Grant and Douglas, with Joseph McKay, travelled by canoe to inspect potential properties to the west of the settlement.

Against Douglas's advice, Grant selected for his farm a stretch of virgin forest at Sooke harbour, where he had noted a stream that could power the sawmill he had brought.

(See Fig. 57, page 98) Lacking the funds to employ sufficient workers, Grant was obliged to focus all his efforts on establishing his house and farm. Fortunately for him, Douglas and his superiors could not risk having their first settler be seen to fail, so they allowed him to buy food, livestock, and supplies on credit.

However, Douglas immediately realized that it would be impossible for Grant to devote enough time to surveying until he had made progress on his own establishment, and he requested that Adolphus Lee Lewes—the young surveyor who had been with him on the 1842 reconnaissance—be assigned as a full-time company surveyor. This solution would have worked well until a properly qualified and experienced surveyor could be recruited from Britain, but Simpson denied Douglas's request, judging Lewes to be too inexperienced.

Douglas also raised the question of indigenous peoples' property rights on the island. Mention of this issue, now known as "Aboriginal Title," in Douglas's correspondence indicates that senior company officers acknowledged that such rights did exist and needed to be addressed in the colonization process. Over the next few years, Douglas purchased some land occupied, and presumed owned, by local First Nations. Fourteen documents, separate but with similar wording, transferred title over traditional tribal lands surrounding Fort Victoria, Fort Rupert, the Saanich Peninsula, and Nanaimo to the HBC, but acting as agent for the Crown. These deals became known as the Douglas or Fort Victoria Treaties.[5]

The sections of land described in each document, except for occupied villages and enclosed fields under cultivation, became "the Entire property of the White people forever." Each treaty included a written description of the tract of land, referenced to identifiable landmarks or to neighbouring traditional tribal boundaries, followed by the promise that the land would be properly surveyed afterward. (See Fig. 45) This phrase was ambiguous—what land? What form of survey? No such survey seems to have been carried out; the tribal boundaries were not reflected in subsequent cadastral maps and remain contentious.

When describing the property boundaries, Douglas seems to have used Lewes's 1842 *Ground Plan*, extended by later knowledge. Douglas, instructed by his superiors to strike a hard bargain, limited the excepted areas to "fields [the local clans] had cultivated or built houses on by 1846 … All other land was to be regarded as waste and therefore available for colonization."[6]

❈ ❈ ❈

Douglas complained that he had been provided with little detail on Grant's duties as the colony's surveyor. Pelly had been vague in his discussions and negotiation with Grant about this and other aspects of the latter's relationship with the colony. Before leaving London, Grant had presented "certificates of qualification for a survey" and a draft proposal that he reconnoitre and map Vancouver Island, an idea similar to that earlier suggested by Simpson.

Company officials in London, whose priority was to secure the company's legal title to the lands they had already cleared for farming, rejected Grant's proposed plan. Instead, he was "to designate the other areas local company officials considered expedient to reserve for cultivation or otherwise."[7] There was some sense in this. Given the technology available, just the reconnaissance phase of mapping the whole island would have required dozens of man-years.

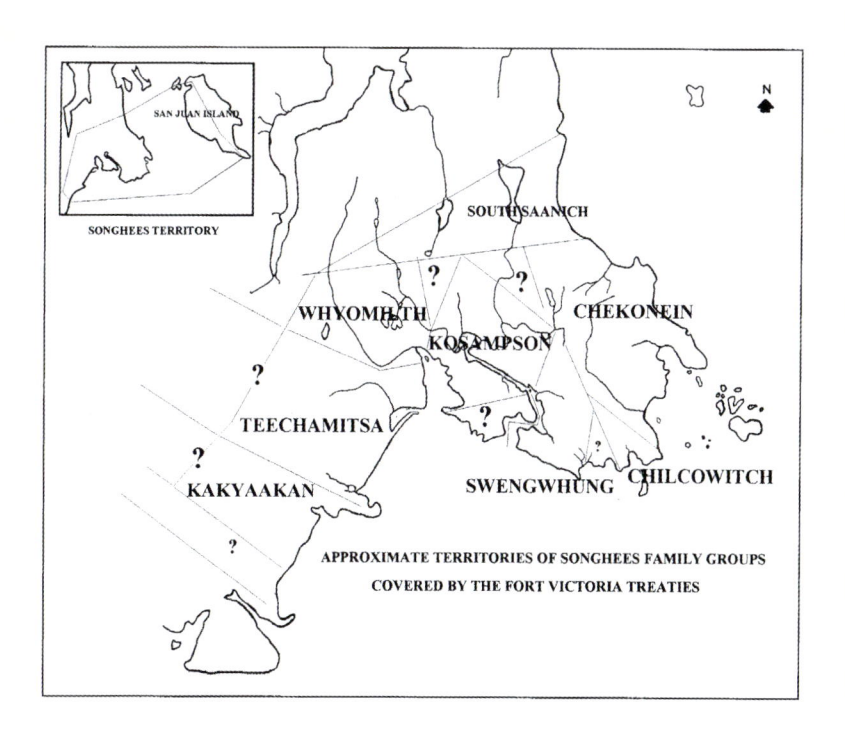

Fig. 45 Archeologist Grant Keddie of the Royal BC Museum drew this cartographic interpretation of the texts of seven of the Fort Victoria Treaties related to the Songhees family groups. He indicates the ambiguities in the texts. The question marks indicate uncertain areas or boundaries.
© Royal BC Museum

ABOVE
Fig. 46 Grant made reasonable efforts, given the circumstances, to comply with his cartographic contract, but Governor Douglas and other HBC officials dismissed the results. His map was a considerable improvement on that made by Douglas and Lewes eight years earlier.

RIGHT
Fig. 47 Grant, and/or his friend Joseph McKay, probably prepared this undated, anonymous cadastral schematic, proposing a grid of square, 640-acre (259-hectare) lots, an approach reluctantly employed later for the colony following the gold rush.

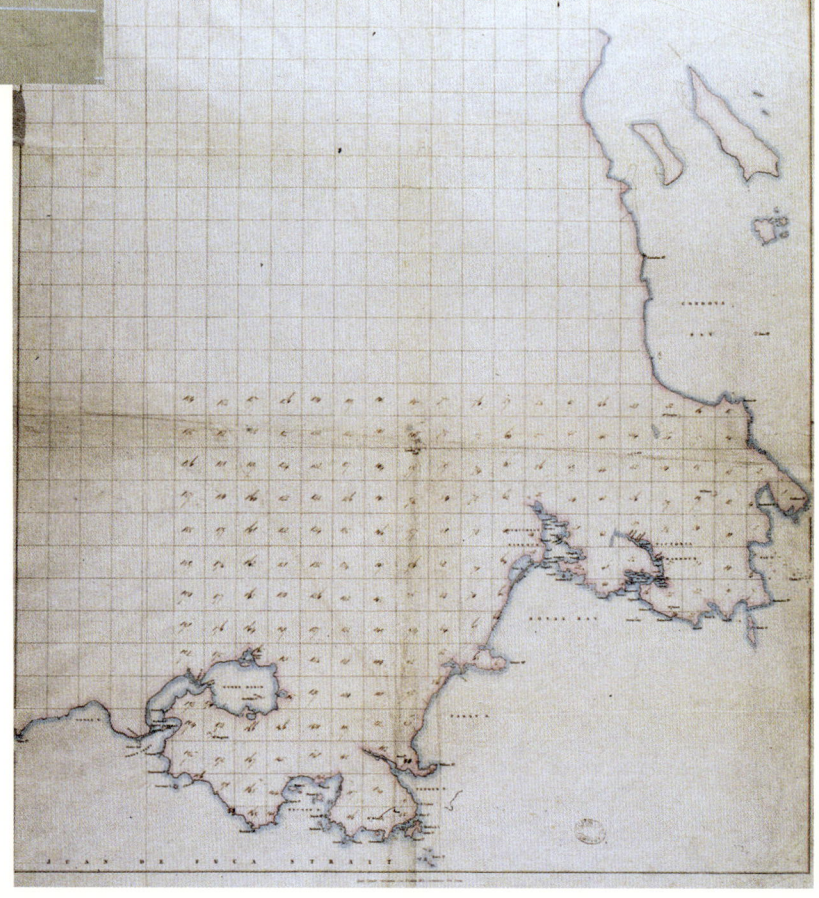

Fig. 48   Captain Grant, Victoria's first settler and surveyor, presented a good summary of the new colony to the Royal Geographical Society in 1856. The society published it in its *Journal*, accompanied by this excellent, up-to-date map by John Arrowsmith.

After a few months, Grant's house, Mullachard, was livable and some crops were planted. Grant did manage to make three sketch maps of the company's properties around Fort Victoria, including a six-sheet enlargement of Lewes's *Ground Plan* of 1842 with trails and outlying settlements added, but still without control points. His friend Joseph McKay had earlier drafted a four-sheet version, which was dispatched to London but has been lost. It seems probable that the two collaborated on Grant's version.

The company dismissed all of Grant's sketches as of little or no use, and by the spring of 1850, Grant had realized that the situation was beyond his capability; he resigned as the colony's surveyor. (See Fig. 46, page 80) Douglas then gave him a contract and five hundred dollars to establish a rudimentary network of control points for the twenty square miles (fifty-two square kilometres) of "Fur Trade Reserve"—the HBC properties. Those control points were Nankuan (Knokkan) Hill, Cedar Hill (Mount Douglas), Mount Tolmie, and Gonzales Hill.

Douglas reported that Grant "worked pretty steadily for about three months, cutting his way through a thickly wooded country."[8] By this time, it was clear to all levels of the company's management that sufficient and reliable maps, as well as a cadastral system, were essential for the new colony. A better solution was required, urgently. (See Fig. 47, page 80)

Grant left the colony in 1853 and rejoined his regiment. In 1857, he presented a paper to the Royal Geographical Society (RGS) in London. His *Description of Vancouver Island by its First Colonist* was a well-written summary of everything known about the island up to that time. The society's cartographer, John Arrowsmith, engraved a detailed map of *Vancouver Island with the Adjacent Coast* to accompany Grant's paper when it was published in the RGS *Journal*. Richard Blanshard was present at the RGS meeting that night in London and contributed to the discussion on the Native population of the island. Grant's paper was well received by the society, which subsequently elected him a Fellow. (See Fig. 48, page 81)

Soon afterward, Grant's regiment left for India to help quell the mutiny. While still in India, Grant submitted a second paper to the RGS, *Remarks on Vancouver Island*, which was read at its meeting in December 1859. It is for these two papers that Grant merits recognition as a significant contributor to the geographical knowledge of the island. Blame for his failure to generate the cadastral maps demanded by the HBC rests just as squarely upon the company, which saddled him with an impossible double responsibility. Company officials did not appreciate the magnitude of the survey task nor provide him with adequate resources to tackle it.

They did, however, learn from their mistakes. For his successor, there were far more generous contract conditions as well as sufficient budget and authority. Grant died of a fever just before he was due to return home from India.

CHAPTER TWELVE

Pemberton and Pearse Survey Vancouver Island's Southeastern Districts

BY LATE 1850, JAMES DOUGLAS, George Simpson, and the board of the Hudson's Bay Company in London all understood the pressing requirement for a qualified and capable surveyor to replace Walter Colquhoun Grant.

In early December, the board received an unsolicited application for a position as surveyor and engineer for the new colony. The applicant seemed ideally suited to their needs on Vancouver Island, and early in the new year, they awarded a three-year contract to twenty-nine-year-old Joseph Despard Pemberton.

Pemberton was well prepared for the multiple tasks ahead. After studying engineering at Trinity College, Dublin, he had worked with a highly experienced topographer and engineer active during the railway construction booms in Ireland and England, gaining a thorough grounding in all aspects of field survey and map-making.

Thus equipped with both theoretical and applied knowledge of the profession, Pemberton took a post as professor of practical surveying and engineering at England's Royal Agricultural College. For two years, he taught students who were destined to manage farms both at home and throughout the fast-growing empire. In the process, he became knowledgeable about the planning of agricultural development and associated cadastral aspects.

In marked contrast to Grant's contract with the HBC, Pemberton's was a clear and detailed document. His was to be a full-time, salaried position, and there was no requirement for him to purchase and develop his own property. The company would provide passages, outward and return, for him and a salaried assistant. Both would live in the bachelors' mess at the fort. Pemberton's salary would be two hundred pounds per year (double Grant's) and he was also promised a discretionary bonus of up to five hundred pounds for satisfactory completion of the contract. There would be a budget for local labour and materials.

The letter accompanying the contract spelled out his duties: "[T]he first objects of survey should be the district round and westward of Fort Victoria. In making

A PLAN OF THE TOWN OF VICTORIA SHEW[ING]

No. 1. Sketch map of the Town of Victoria
to accompany Report to the Hudson's Bay Co.
dated January 20th 1852.
J.D. Pemberton.

ROCK BAY

VICTORIA HARBOUR.

The Hospital
Site of Proposed Reservoir
The Cemetery
Fort Victoria
Garden
Proposed Wharf

Fig. 49 Pemberton and his assistant, Benjamin Pearse, were kept busy both recording real-estate transactions and planning and mapping the growth of settlement around Fort Victoria. This is how it looked in 1851.

your surveys you will keep in view that they will form the materials or ground work out of which an accurate map of the Island is afterwards to be constructed … and as the main object for which these surveys are undertaken is the Colonization of the Island, you will be careful to note the external features and geological formation of the several localities which you examine, mentioning the nature and qualities of the soil and subsoil, the different kinds of timber and other vegetable productions, and in short all such particulars as it may be useful for settlers to be informed of."[1] He would also take responsibility for establishing and maintaining a cadastral system and registry.

Pemberton arrived at Fort Victoria on June 24, 1851. Before leaving London, he had arranged that an experienced engineer and surveyor would help the company recruit a suitable assistant for him.

From the forty responses to a notice in *The Times*, the engineer recommended Benjamin William Pearse. Not yet twenty, and an articled pupil with a civil engineer in London, Pearse turned out to be an unqualified success. The two surveyors worked together productively for many years, remaining lifelong friends, and both became stalwarts of the Victoria community. Between them, Pemberton and Pearse made unequalled contributions to the advancement of geographical knowledge about Vancouver Island and to the infrastructure of the colony in its formative decades.

Pearse took a berth aboard the next sailing of the company's supply vessel, *Norman Morison*, leaving London at the end of May 1851. Survey instruments, mathematical tables, a technical library, drafting materials, and other supplies accompanied him. After a record-breaking passage of 155 days, around Cape Horn, Pearse docked in Victoria Harbour at the end of October. Straightaway he joined Pemberton, then hard at work surveying "the coast of the Canal de Arro, north of Mount Douglas." (See Fig. 49, pages 84–85)

Earlier that month, Douglas had reported that Pemberton "has since his arrival laboured most assiduously at the survey, and required neither prompting nor aid from me." Douglas's letter accompanied Pemberton's report and a new three-sheet map of the *Victoria and Esquimalt Districts*, which appeared to him "to be well executed, and exceedingly accurate." Pemberton himself described the set of tracings as being "unavoidably rough," acknowledging that the map was still a work in progress.[2] The master document, at a scale of 6 inches to 1 mile (1:10,560), was kept at the fort and corrected or added to as new content became available. The maps that Pemberton now started to forward to his employers formed a series of tracings that bear witness to both Victoria's developmental years and his progress in compiling the cartographic record. (See Fig. 50)

Pemberton had brought from London copies of all the maps of the island held by the company, and on his voyage out he had restudied Wakefield's and other texts on colonial development that included land-registration policies. He agreed with the strategy of first establishing a trigonometric framework on which both topographic and cadastral mapping could be superimposed.

Pemberton first reconnoitred the areas of company activity, accompanied by a crew of unskilled day labourers. In the process he soon came to prefer employing Métis, as they were the men best suited to the arduous travel and physical work in the dense forest. These men, usually the sons of fur traders and their Native wives, had come to the west as company employees. Many of them had Iroquois blood and were expert trackers. Douglas had organized the same "Half-whites" into a paramilitary police force called the Voltigeurs.

Fig. 50   By 1852 the area mapped included the complex topography bordering Cordova Bay. At right (south) is Cedar Hill with Tolmie Hill below, while at left are Saanich Hill and Elk Lake. All this land was still covered in first-growth forest.

Fig. 51 Pemberton respectfully gave the number one on the cadastral record to the property, Fairfield, claimed by the governor. The hilly feature to the northeast of the parcel marked A-B-C-D later provided sites for Government House and Craigdarroch Castle.

Pemberton remeasured and completed the triangulation network that Grant had started and extended it to cover Esquimalt, knowing it would have to be measured again once the full set of survey instruments arrived with Pearse. He was able to connect the boundaries of the company reserves and of the few lots already sold to settlers to the triangulation network. They were individually delineated and legally described by a cadastral system called "metes and bounds." By the time of Pemberton's first report, twelve parcels of land had been sold privately to Douglas, Tod, Finlayson, Clinton, Tolmie, Bailey, Dodd, Peers, and Langford. Most of the settlers at that time were serving or recently retired company employees.

Pemberton prepared a three-sheet map covering the reserves claimed by the Fur Trade (HBC) and the Puget's Sound Agricultural Company (PSAC) and the settlers' lots. The map also indicated the roads that were already in use and others proposed to Metchosin and to Sooke. In his report he identified the lack of roads as a key constraint to the progress of settlement. The need for including systematic road planning had been neglected during the early phases of land-title transactions in the colony; not until 1870 did legislation in the form of a Land Ordinance provide allowances for public roads.

The properties reserved for the company farms and the first group of private purchases had all been selected with an eye to agriculture: Boundaries optimized the arable areas, avoiding major rock outcrops and low-lying swamps. (See Fig. 51) Together, the company's and private properties, interspersed with parcels yet to be claimed, formed a haphazard mosaic, and two elements of this land-use mosaic have survived through to the present day. The non-arable land, rejected by the initial purchasers, remained available for civic amenities: Prominent rocky outcrops made attractive locations for churches, and primary schools were often sited on low-value, low-lying plots of land.

No provision had been made for rights-of-way through the large properties, so early routes to and from the fort tended to meander, skirting private and company land. In addition, some Native trails became routes used by settlers, parts of which remain today—for example, Cadboro Bay and Cedar Hill Roads, Quadra Street, and Fairfield Road. Such trails were few, since the local Songhees preferred to make long-distance travel by canoe rather than overland.

Thus took shape the kaleidoscopic pattern of Victoria's street map that frequently causes confusion to recent arrivals. As the larger estates were subdivided, streets were added, often parallel to, or linking with, the existing boundary-related network. (See Fig. 52, page 90)

During the winter of 1851–52, Pemberton studied the technical library brought out by Pearse. Having now examined the southeastern portion of the colony himself, he prepared a report addressing the question of a systematic cadastral scheme. He remained convinced that a triangulation network was an essential basis for the lands of, and surrounding, the Victoria District. The method of straight-line "chaining"—physically measuring distances along the ground—used in flat, open prairie terrain such as South Australia was impracticable on the undulating, heavily timbered, and swampy southern end of Vancouver Island.

His report to the HBC board in January identified and suggested cadastral strategies for three classes of property: rural, town lots, and suburban lots. He also pointed out the need to subdivide the land so that valuable access to roads, rivers, and coastal frontage was distributed fairly. While lots within a class should be, as far as possible, rectangular and of an equal size, the main axis of the subdivision should run parallel to a watercourse or road. He saw little advantage in the system used in the United States, of blindly dividing the land into square sections running with the cardinal points but without consideration of the natural features.

Pemberton also reviewed the question of rights-of-way, supporting the ideas of Captain Edward Frome of the Royal Engineers, surveyor general of South Australia. Frome recommended that the terms of sale of property should include a provision for the issuing authority to reserve "the right of appropriating land for the making of all such roads as may be necessary for the convenience of settlers."[3] Pemberton suggested adding to this the rights to quarry stone for the repair of such roads and to cut timber to repair bridges, provisions he felt would be readily understood and accepted by colonists. These sensible suggestions were not incorporated into law for almost two decades, but Pemberton attempted to implement Frome's other ideas when he came to plan the Sooke, Metchosin, and Lakes (later Saanich) Districts.

The survey work in these southeastern districts of Vancouver Island kept Pemberton and Pearse fully occupied over the next few years. Still to be carried out, however, was Simpson's instruction to traverse the island in every direction. When the British government officials had issued Letters Patent to the HBC commissioning them to colonize Vancouver Island, neither they nor the company had any information about the interior of the island. It had been evident to the Spanish at Nootka and to George Vancouver that the local people did have trading routes, their "grease," or "oolichan," trails that connected the west and east coasts, but their customary form of travel was by canoe. The traverses called for by Simpson would be true exploration of unknown territory.

Fig. 52 Pemberton had been at work for just five months when he drew this map of the area surrounding Fort Victoria, marking the boundaries of the land reserved for a city. Note the area B-C-D (top right), specifically including the critical springs and well near Fernwood.

This task fell, initially, on other company men. Even prior to Simpson's instruction, such exploration had begun. The first recorded crossing of Vancouver Island by a European occurred in February 1849, not at its rapidly developing southern tip, but at the other extremity, inland from the company's second trading establishment on the island, Fort Rupert.

A sixty-year-old company veteran, John Work, explored the twenty-two miles (thirty-five kilometres) of coastline between the fort at Beaver Harbour and "McNeill's" (later Port McNeill), noting the outcrops of coal seams. Then, as Douglas reported, "he also traced them in a westerly direction about 12 miles [19 kilometres] across the Island to the head of the Inlet of Quatsenah . . . This Inlet Communicates with the spacious harbour of Quatsenah, a fine Port for Shipping on the west coast of the Island . . . infinitely more accessible to sailing vessels than Beaver Harbour."[4]

It was probably William McNeill who deduced and appreciated this significant linkage to the complex configuration of the inlet later called Quatsino Sound—years earlier, McNeill had become familiar with the area as a Yankee fur trader seeking sea otter pelts in remote communities along Vancouver Island's west coast. "Quatsenah" and "Quatsino" are both corruptions of the name of an important local clan, Quatse-noch. The eastward extent of the sound as shown on Kellett's version of Vancouver's chart and published the same year as Work's discovery was far less than it really is. The various arms of the inlet would not be thoroughly charted for another twelve years.

Douglas reported in September 1849 that he had learned about the "Cowetchens" or Cowichan people who came, apparently, from about thirty miles (fifty kilometres) up the east coast from Victoria. They lived in a wide, flat, fertile valley that was "traversed by a considerable river of the same name . . . navigable by canoes . . . to a lake of some magnitude which extends to within eight miles [thirteen kilometres] of Nitinat, a spacious harbour and Inlet on the west side of the Island. [The Cowichan Valley] may become a desirable place of settlement when the colony gathers strength and means to push out parties powerful enough to make head against the natives who . . . have lost nothing of their natural savage character."[5]

In late August 1852, Douglas led an expedition to follow up reports of coal at an area marked on maps as "Descanso Creek" or "Bocas de Winthuysen" (soon to be called Nanaimo). In two canoes, probably purchased from the Haida, he travelled with the new surveyor, Joseph Pemberton; his private secretary, Richard Golledge; the mining oversman, John Muir; and "six men and a few Indians," who provided muscle for paddling and defence.

Immediately upon his return, Douglas wrote to the Colonial Office in London, noting the inaccuracy of the maps then available. The line of the coast northward from today's Sidney remained as sketched by Narváez in 1791. The southern part of the eastern shore of Vancouver Island as shown on the map was, in fact, a chain of smaller islands. Bodega y Quadra, Vancouver, and Kellett had all incorporated the same misleading coastline into their charts.

With the barely acknowledged benefit of Pemberton's expertise, Douglas reported that "the true line of the coast ran from 15 to 20 miles [24 to 32 kilometres] W. of its position as laid down on our maps." He "[begged] most earnestly" for a correct survey of the Arro Archipelago and its channels, "as there is a prospect of it's [sic] soon becoming the channel of a very important trade."[6] He was correct, in that a significant dispute with the United States about jurisdiction over the islands and the channels between them was about to arise.

A cartographic mystery connected with the 1852 canoe journey has recently been unearthed by a Gabriola Island resident.[7] Investigating the early mapping of that island, he studied a chart of Quadra and Vancouver's Island from a Russian hydrographic atlas published in 1852. The compiler of both the chart and the atlas, Captain M.D. Teben'kov, had made a more detailed and better depiction of the southeastern coastline of Vancouver Island and the archipelago in the Strait of Georgia (termed the "Gulf") than the Kellett update of Vancouver's chart. Teben'kov's chart is dated 1849—three years prior to Douglas's claimed discovery. (See Fig. 53)

Such knowledge could only have come from HBC sources and been passed to the Russian American Company at Sitka during their business dealings. Reinforcing this deduction was Teben'kov's note that "Cape Flattery and many points of the Strait of Juan de Fuca were reckoned very well by officials of the Hudson Bay Company."[8] Perhaps Douglas and his superiors, anxious that the Royal Navy fulfill the promise of a thorough hydrographic survey of the coast, decided to conceal the HBC's local charting capability while lamenting the lack of a correct survey.

The Colonial Office forwarded Douglas's letter to the Royal Geographical Society (RGS) to be read at its meeting the following February. Later, the society published a map of Douglas's canoe expedition based on surveys by Pemberton and Pearse. (See Fig. 54, page 94) The map indicates a water connection linking the Chemainus and Cowichan Rivers. It also shows the western coast of "Chuan I," a Salish name Pemberton learned from his boatmen. It is now called Saltspring Island, a name that first appeared in 1856 on another map published by the RGS. That map accompanied Walter Colquhoun Grant's paper to the society, *Description of Vancouver Island*.

Douglas instructed Pemberton to return to Wentuhuysen to map the area around where the new bastion and the coal workings would be. Pemberton promptly produced a detailed report and three maps: *The Country around Nanaimo Harbour*, *Chart of Nanaimo Harbour and the Neighbouring Coast*, and a sketch of *Wentuhuysen Inlet*. He opted to use on his maps the anglicized version of the local people's name for the harbour and nearby area, and "Colviletown" for the actual settlement. Pearse returned early the following spring to properly survey and plot a "tolerably correct" outline of the coast between Victoria and today's Nanoose Bay, northwest of Nanaimo.

A few weeks before Douglas's canoe expedition, Hamilton Moffatt, a twenty-year-old clerk-trader at Fort Rupert, made the first major traverse of the island. Moffatt, born on the Isle of Wight, had been in the colony barely two years when he set out to cross the island by a known oolichan trail that connected the Nimpkish clan of the Kwakwa̱ka'wakw with the Nootka people. In 1792 Vancouver had noted that Cheslakees and his clansmen possessed guns and other European trade goods, which must have been obtained from Maquinna. The following year, Maquinna told Peter Puget and the Spanish commandant at Nootka, Salvador Fidalgo, of this traditional link and drew them a map.

Moffatt started from a fishing village (Vancouver's "Cheslakee's") at the mouth of the Nimpkish River and in a hired canoe paddled up the river and along Nimpkish and Woss Lakes toward a spectacular peak he named Ben Lomond. He portaged across the divide to the Tahsis River and paddled down Tahsis Inlet as far as Friendly Cove. His

Fig. 53   This map, dated 1849, is from a Russian atlas. Of particular interest is the coastline north from Victoria. Although it predates Douglas's canoe journey by three years, it shows more detail than did Vancouver's chart, information that most likely came from HBC sources.

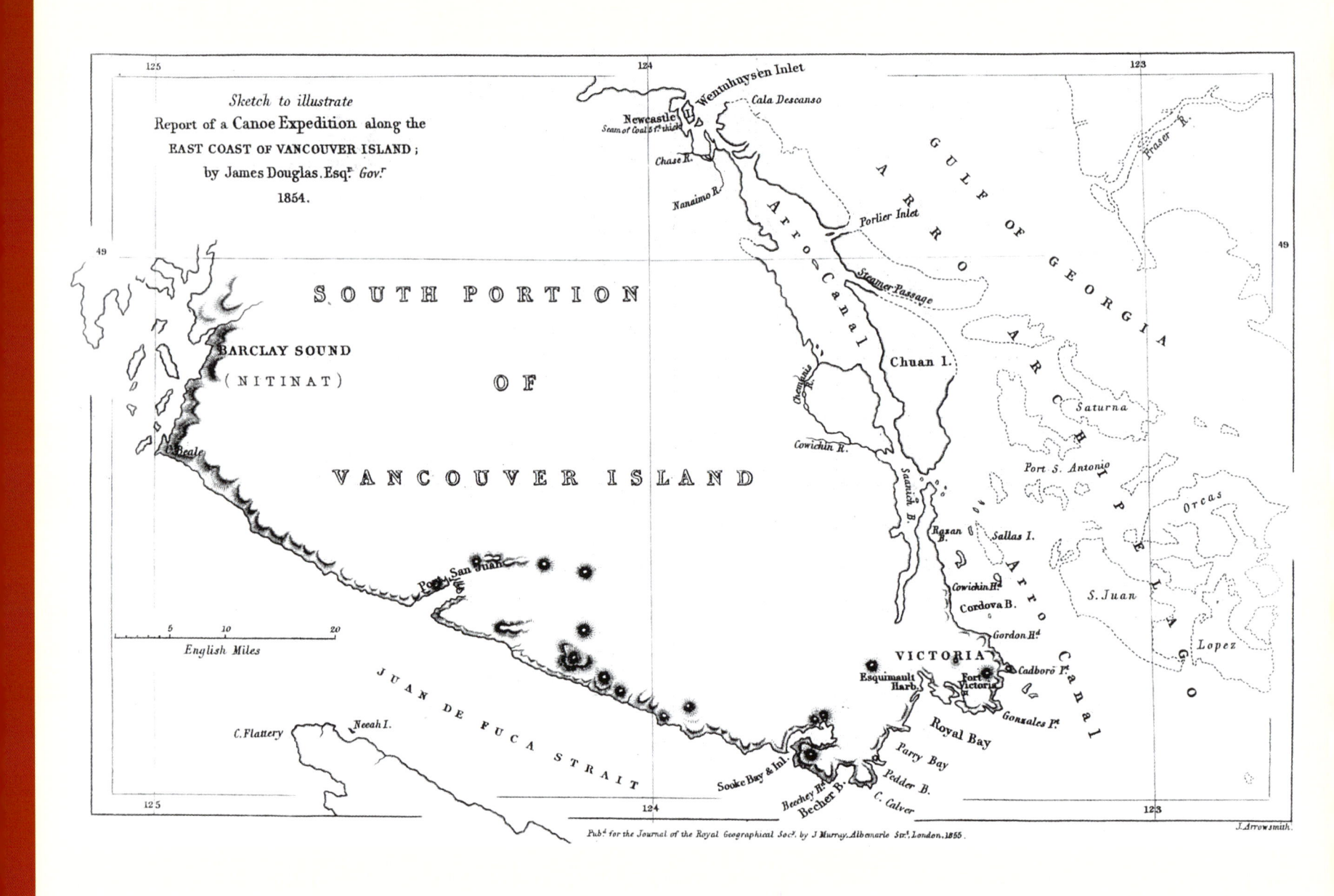

Fig. 54 Douglas claimed, in his paper to the RGS, that his canoe journey to Wentuhuysen had discovered a completely different coastline from that shown on existing maps. This map also indicates that information about the home of the Nitinat people was faulty.

journey had taken five days. Moffatt did not send his report to Pemberton until seven years later, in 1859, accompanied by "a chart, unfinished, but pretty correct of the Koskimo Inlet, Portage and coast of Vancouver Island as far as the Nimpkish River."9 Pemberton included "Moffatt's Track" on his map in a publication dated 1860, *Facts and Figures relating to Vancouver Island and British Columbia*. The detail Pemberton showed, however, did not correspond with the description in Moffatt's journal. Nor was any detail shown of Koskimo Inlet, which Moffatt mentioned in his covering letter as having been explored on his return journey. (See Fig. 55, page 96)

Within the map drawn for Pemberton's book *Facts and Figures*, the cartographer Edward Weller inserted a larger-scale map, *Diagram of Victoria and Esquimalt Harbours*, indicating the road from the naval wharf at Duntz Head through the PSAC farms to "Songes" and across the first of the Johnson Street bridges. It also showed a proposed alternative route and a new bridge at Ellice Point, which Pemberton discussed in his text. (See Fig. 56, page 97) In 1850, a naval party from HMS *Thetis* had cut the first trail linking Esquimalt and Victoria, but in the decade that followed, the heavy traffic of the gold rushes caused much damage. When thrown from his mount on this same road in 1864, Pemberton suffered injuries that triggered his resignation as surveyor general.

Another twenty-year-old was in charge of the HBC store at Colviletown, the strapping and fearless, Edinburgh-born Adam Horne. In May 1855, Chief Factor Roderick Finlayson sent for Horne to brief him for an important but perilous mission. As they pored over a map of the island, Finlayson pointed to a creek north of Nanaimo. At its mouth there was a village of the Qualicum people, thought to be related to the larger settlement at Cape Mudge. Not much was known about the Qualicum, but the Cape Mudge clan had a warlike reputation. Finlayson suspected that the Qualicum village was at the end of another oolichan trail that led from the Alberni Canal, and Horne's mission was to verify this and explore the route.

Horne's original sketch map has been lost, but late the following year Pemberton retraced his journey in a hasty reconnaissance and also included "Horne's route" on the map that accompanied *Facts and Figures*. From the highest point of the trek, Pemberton saw that the middle of the island was "a ridge of mountains (some with snow on them) but not unbroken." After reaching the Somass River, Pemberton carried on down the Alberni Canal and into Barkley Sound. He could see its potential as a harbour for many large ships, but it would need to be "properly examined and surveyed."10

CHAPTER TWELVE   95

Fig. 55   Pemberton published *Facts and Figures* in 1860, accompanied by a map of Vancouver Island by Edward Weller. It showed the earliest explorations into the interior of the island, including two of his own journeys.

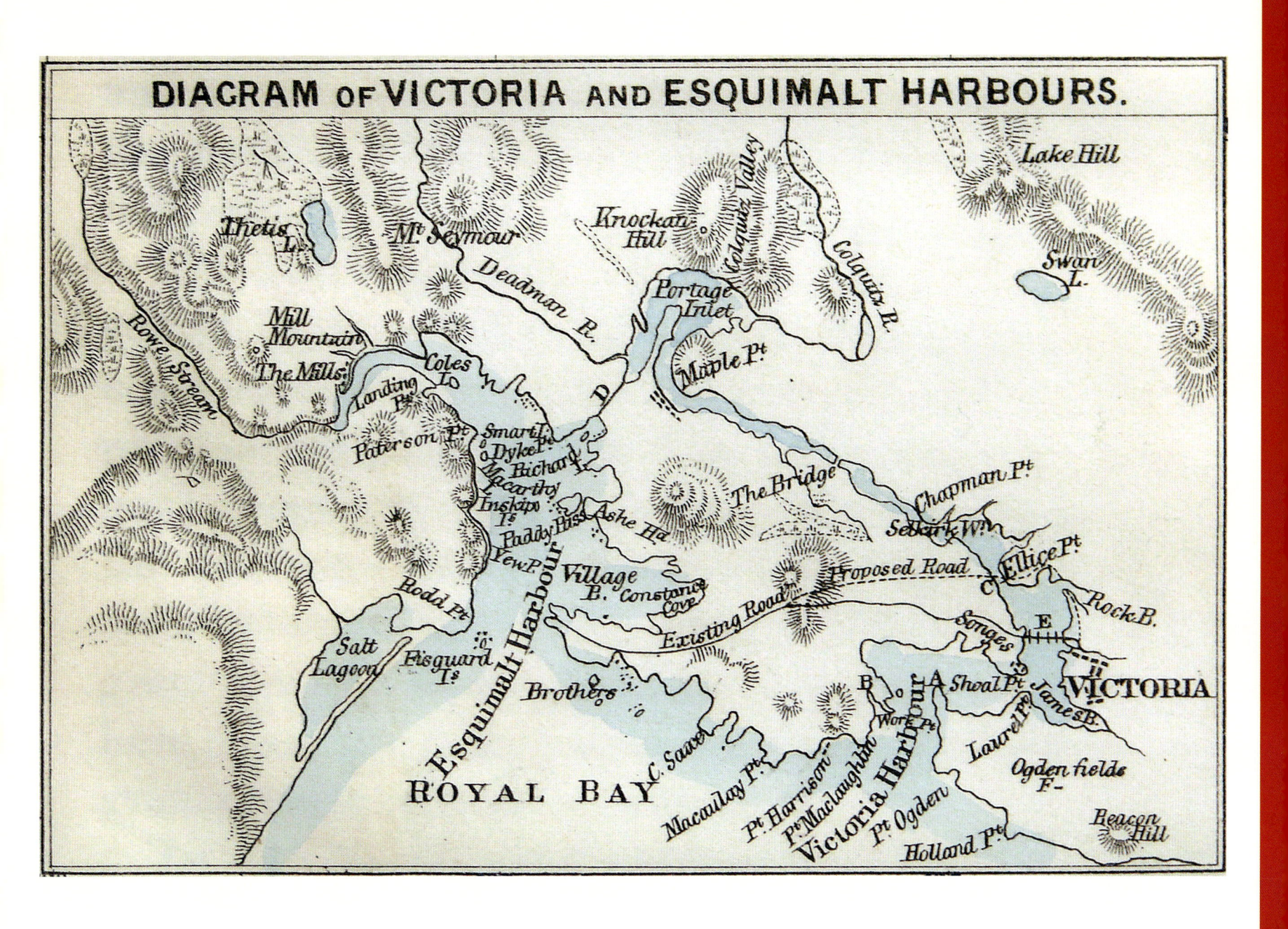

Fig. 56 Pemberton and Weller provided an inset map for *Facts and Figures*, detailing Victoria and Esquimalt Harbours. It also showed the road between them, with the first Johnson Street bridge.

Fig. 57 A westward extension of the printed one-inch map of Victoria and Esquimalt Districts included Langford's farm, Pedder and Beecher Bays, and Sooke harbour. Although Captain Grant had left the colony, his property was indicated to the west of Sooke inlet.

CHAPTER THIRTEEN

Explosive Growth: Victoria Feels the Impact of the Gold Rush

BACK AT THE SURVEY OFFICE in Fort Victoria, Joseph Pemberton and Benjamin Pearse continued with their heavy workload. In addition to extending the network of triangulation control points along the coast, both northward and to the west, they explored inland. (See Fig. 57) They also faced the mounting task of preparing land titles for the agricultural properties of the two companies, Hudson's Bay Company and Puget's Sound Agricultural Company, the public reserves for churches, schools, and parks, and lots for individual settlers.

Between his arrival in the summer of 1851 and his departure in 1855, when he went on leave to England, Pemberton and his small team generated an astonishing volume of map sheets—both originals and updates—and cadastral plats, a type of map used in registering property rights. (See Fig. 58, page 100) In the single year of 1853, Pemberton produced a dozen maps, including five topographic sheets showing several types of information, supported by Pearse and William Newton, a skilled and industrious draftsman. He brought a systematic approach to scales for this mapping: six, four, two, and one inches to the mile. Sheets with greater relevance for early settlement were plotted at a larger scale than those covering areas that were yet to be developed. By the end of that year, the team had completed a four-sheet project: *Map of the S.E. Corner of Vancouver's Island ... at a scale of 2 inches to 1 mile* (1:31,680). It covered the eight land districts from Sooke to Cowichan Bay. That version has been lost, but its update of two years later remains.

The onerous requirements of the Wakefield system acted as barriers to settlement. Officers in the field perceived that the system would not work and gradually devised ways to circumvent the protocol, for which they found growing support from their superiors in London.

Company officials and employees were the people most interested in settling on Vancouver Island. For them, and any others already resident in the territory, the company waived the need to provide farm workers. Although they adhered to the mandated price of one pound per acre, they included

Fig. 58   The most remote farm operated by the HBC on Vancouver Island was at Cadboro Bay, near Sungayka, an important village of the Chekonein branch of the Songhees people. By 1852, most of the inhabitants had moved to be near Fort Victoria.

only arable land in the calculation and did not charge for pockets of rocks, water, or swamp. The creation of far smaller town and suburban lots avoided the minimum parcel size of twenty acres (eight hectares). The requirement for money up front was eased, allowing payment by installments. Together, these stratagems to elude Wakefield succeeded: By 1858, 180 private landowners held over 17,500 acres (7,100 hectares) and 150 smaller lots. More than 90 percent of these landowners worked, or had worked, for the HBC or PSAC.

Pemberton's first contract expired in June 1854, and Douglas reported that "[Pemberton] has given perfect satisfaction... I think it will be difficult to find a person so well adapted for the situation he now so creditably fills, or who will discharge its duties with equal zeal and untiring energy."[1] In London the HBC secretary, Dr. Archibald Barclay, agreed. He wrote to Pemberton "to inform you that [the governor and committee] are much satisfied with the zeal and talent which you have shown... they will be happy to retain your services."[2] Barclay added that Pearse and Newton would be offered renewal of their contracts.

Barclay also authorized Pemberton to come to London to discuss the terms of a new contract, which he did a year later. The new terms included payment, in full, of the five-hundred-pound bonus for the first contract, and doubling Pemberton's salary for a further three years. He would also receive an annual allowance of one hundred pounds in lieu of accommodation at the fort. As he was considered to be in London on company business, his new salary was paid for the time he was away from the island.

Upon receiving Barclay's letter assuring him of a continuing engagement, and before he travelled to London, Pemberton reciprocated the confidence placed in him: Encouraged by Douglas, he invested in a sizeable property a few miles east of the fort. Pearse followed suit, acquiring an adjoining parcel. These investments eventually made both men wealthy. They were able to take advantage of the easing of the Wakefield protocol, Pemberton paying just £196 for his 533 acres (216 hectares), the rest being viewed as rocks and swamp. He called the whole estate Gonzales, as it included the headland named for an earlier explorer-surveyor, Gonzalo López de Haro. The rocks discounted in the pricing calculation became known as Rockland, now some of the most valuable real estate in Canada. Pearse acquired much of what would later be known as Fernwood, which was the name of his residence. (See Fig. 59, page 102)

While he was in London, Pemberton arranged with John Arrowsmith, the company's official cartographic publisher, to print a map, *The South-eastern Districts of Vancouver Island*, based on a manuscript he had brought with him. The printed map, at a scale of 1 inch to 1 mile (1:63,360), covers an area similar to the four-sheet manuscript (at 2 inches to 1 mile) that Pemberton had described as having "cost a greater expenditure of time and labour" than any of the earlier maps he had sent to London. The new map provides a clear indication of the remarkable topographical accomplishments of Pemberton's team during his first four years. It shows the extensions to the trigonometric network, including a hill in Central Saanich named Mount Newton, commemorating the new cartographer. Part of the print run was mounted on linen so that the map could be folded and kept in a slipcase for conservation, and several of these still exist. (See Fig. 60, page 103)

An inset map shows the southern end of the island with the "Gulf of Georgia," the Strait of Juan de Fuca, and the adjoining shores of the United States. While there is

CHAPTER THIRTEEN 101

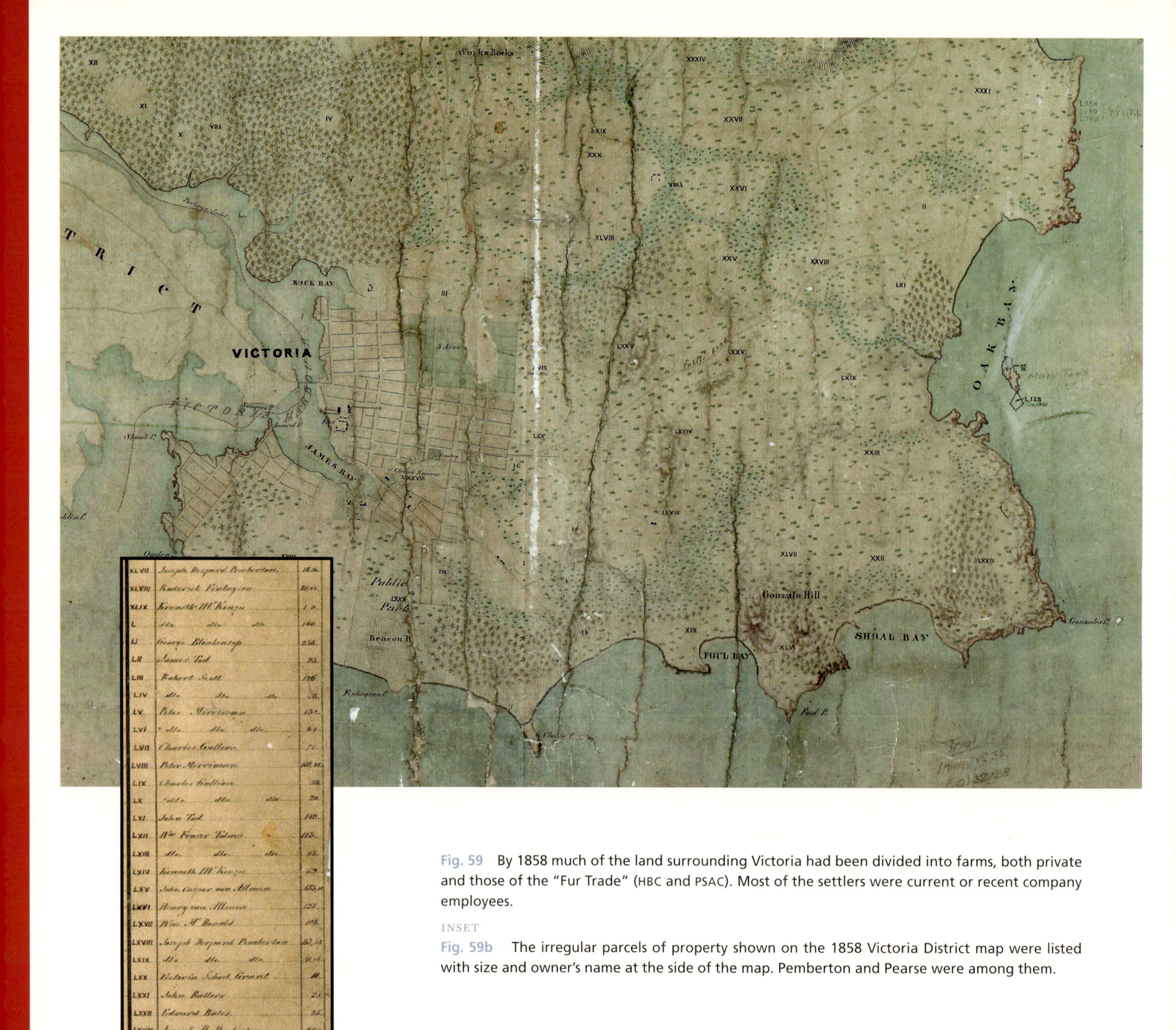

Fig. 59 By 1858 much of the land surrounding Victoria had been divided into farms, both private and those of the "Fur Trade" (HBC and PSAC). Most of the settlers were current or recent company employees.

INSET

Fig. 59b The irregular parcels of property shown on the 1858 Victoria District map were listed with size and owner's name at the side of the map. Pemberton and Pearse were among them.

Fig. 60 As the pace of settlement increased, a map of the area was needed for public distribution. In 1858 Pemberton took a manuscript to London for lithographic printing by Arrowsmith. The significance of the later pink colouring is not explained.

no indication of the international boundary, a dotted line threads through Juan de Fuca and "Vancouver's Strait" (otherwise called Rosario Strait). This marks the line of Vancouver's 1792 track and implies the British interpretation of the water boundary. Haro Strait is clearly shown, as is a good rendering of the various islands of the San Juan Archipelago, both confirming that by this time, Pemberton and Douglas were fully aware that there was more than one channel through the archipelago.

The covering letter for Pemberton's second contract stressed an early priority. He was urged "to examine other parts of the Island beyond those now in course of survey more particularly the harbours on the West Coast, and the country between these and the settlements on the east Coast, and ascertain the practicability and probable cost of making a road across the Island."[3] He returned from London late in 1855 and set off immediately to retrace Adam Horne's route from Qualicum to Alberni Inlet and Barkley Sound, the supposed home of another west coast community, the Nitinat people.

Pemberton's third expedition across the island was in 1857, and he wrote a brief report to Douglas, outlining his three-week journey overland from the estuary of the Cowichan River. The party explored upstream, rafting a series of interconnected bodies of water, which now form Cowichan Lake. Then they descended a fast, southwest-flowing river to the long lake and village of the Nitinat people. He learned that this was their actual home territory, not Barkley Sound, which became known for a while as "False Nitinat."

Pemberton's party returned to Victoria around the island's southwest shoreline in a Nitinat canoe, which they had obtained in trade. Already well accustomed to travel through Vancouver Island's forests, Pemberton omitted all but the briefest detail of the rigours of the journey.

Pemberton appended his report to Douglas to his 1860 publication, *Facts and Figures*, indicating "Pemberton's Track" on the accompanying map drawn by Edward Weller, cartographer to the Royal Geographical Society. In his book, Pemberton compliments the local peoples' ability to understand maps. He wrote: "Give a pencil and a sheet of paper to an Indian, and he can quickly make a rude map of a country he has travelled through."[4]

At the end of December 1857, quite exceeding his authority to do so, Douglas proclaimed that all gold deposits in the valleys of the Fraser and Thompson Rivers were the property of the Crown. He also declared that mining permits, obtainable only in Victoria, would be required at a fee of one guinea per month. His declaration came just in time: The following spring, news of rich placer discoveries in the Fraser River reached San Francisco, and on April 25, the first 450 of 30,000 prospectors and associated service providers arrived in Victoria, doubling its population overnight.

Fortunately for Douglas, the new colonial secretary in London, Sir Edward Bulwer Lytton, supported his preemptive action, reinforcing the proclamation by creating a second British colony on the North Pacific coast. Initially it was called New Caledonia, but by the time the Act of Parliament was passed, on August 2, 1858, the name had been changed to British Columbia.

News of the creation of the second colony was included in a new atlas, published later that month. *The Weekly Dispatch* of London brought out its *World Atlas* as a supplement, negotiating with Edward Weller for the cartographic design and engraving of all the maps. On one plate Weller drew half-page maps of British Columbia and of Vancouver

Island. A colourist added watercolour emphasis to the supposed borders, in, of course, imperial pink. Upon whose information the depiction of the border was based is not clear, but Weller himself was well connected, enjoying access to the map library of the Royal Geographical Society. (See Fig. 61, page 106)

On the Vancouver Island map, the pink line included the whole of the San Juan Archipelago lying west of Vancouver's track, but excluded all the islands from Cape Mudge to Goletas Channel, thereby implying that those lay within the new colony of British Columbia. The coastline between Victoria and Nanaimo reflected the knowledge gained on Douglas and Pemberton's canoe journey of 1852. Nitinat and Cowichan Lakes were shown, as well as Central and another (Sproat) lake, but otherwise, interior detail was restricted to a few prominent peaks. (See Fig. 62, page 107) The accompanying text reported: "The interior [of Vancouver Island] has been little visited by the white man." And it described Victoria as "the village, for it is really nothing more, consists of some 70 log huts."

❧ ❧ ❧

Bulwer Lytton also arranged for a 164-man contingent from the British Army, called the Columbia Detachment, to be dispatched to the new colony. Six officers under Colonel Richard Clement Moody of the Royal Engineers, along with NCOs and sappers, volunteers all, set sail in three groups.[5] They were specialist technicians and tradesmen whose skills included road construction, bridge building, carpentry, blacksmithing, and, importantly, surveying, mapping, and even printing.

Some of these Royal Engineers had arrived at Fort Langley when, on November 19, 1858, Douglas was sworn in as governor of the Crown colony of British Columbia. He retained the equivalent title for Vancouver Island, but the new dual appointment was conditional on his cutting all ties with the HBC and PSAC. Strictly speaking, these were not "Crown colonies" since that designation should refer only to territories acquired through military conquest. Nonetheless, it became the popular term for both British Columbia and Vancouver Island. Douglas appointed Pemberton as official surveyor for the new colony in addition to his existing duties.

Meanwhile, back in Victoria, new settlers, merchants, and other businesses swamped the survey office with a flood of applications for lots. To cope, Pemberton recruited five more surveyors. The market value of real estate now significantly exceeded just its agricultural potential, so in order to speed up the registry process, Douglas instructed Pemberton to rescind the arrangement for omitting rock and swamp areas in calculating the price of land to settlers. This later caused resentment toward the beneficiaries of the short-lived dispensation, particularly Pemberton and Pearse. An official inquiry, however, exonerated the two surveyors.

Well before this frenzy of activity, the British government had decided to sever its arrangement with the HBC for the governance of Vancouver Island, and on January 20, 1858, gave official notice of intent to repurchase the colony, effective May 30, 1859. Pemberton received similar notification that his contract would not be renewed for a third term. It was due to expire in late 1858, but his offer to stay on until the date of repurchase was accepted. He and his team were encouraged to apply for the equivalent posts under the new regime—Pemberton would still report to Douglas, but both would be government, not company, officials.

CHAPTER THIRTEEN

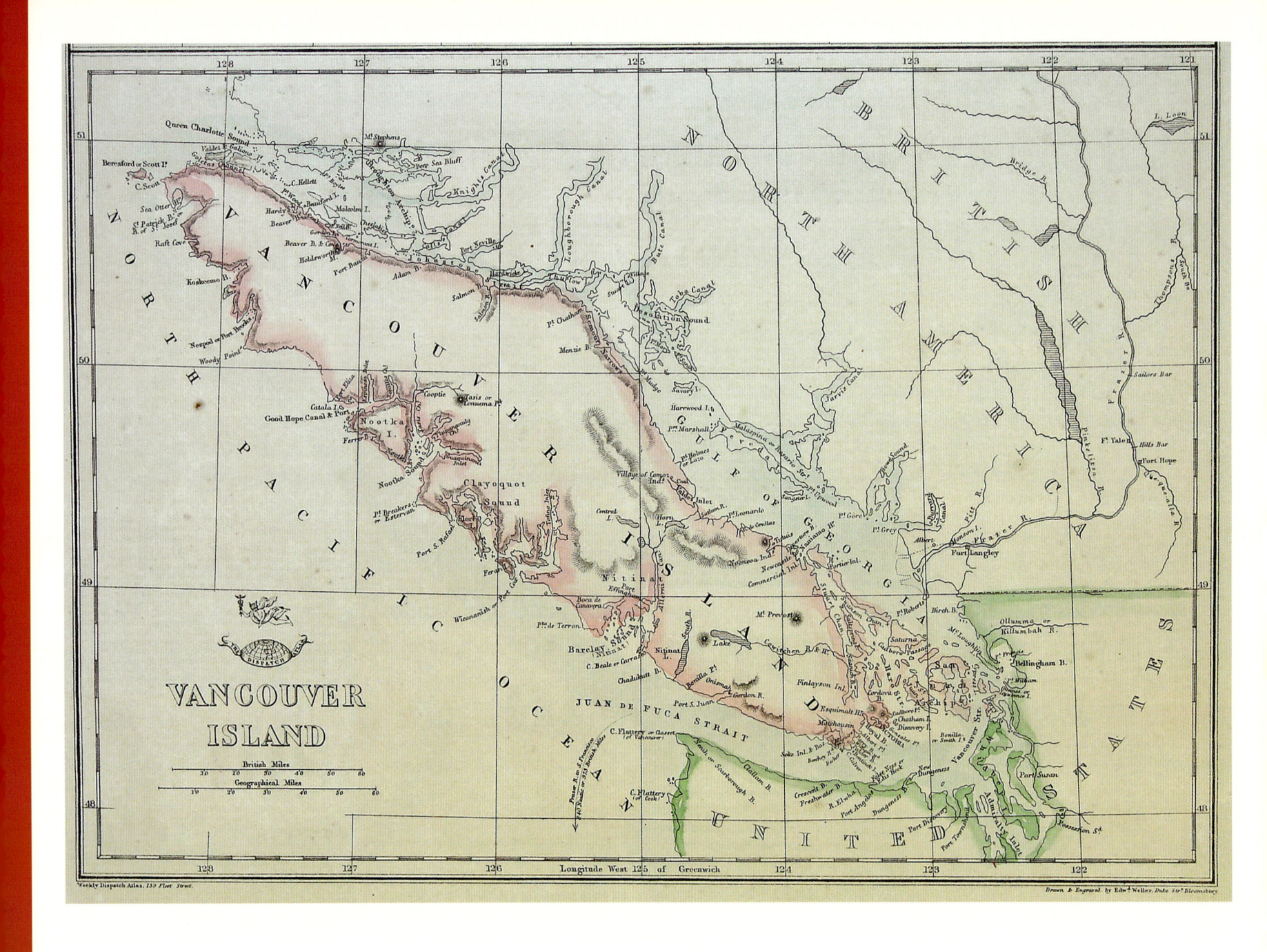

Fig. 61 Weller's 1858 map of the colony of Vancouver Island implies, with a pink-wash margin, that the territory included the San Juan Archipelago but not the islands east of Seymour Narrows or north of Johnstone Strait and Goletas Channel.

Fig. 62   The pink washes on this 1858 map by Weller indicate that the islands excluded on the map of Vancouver Island were part of the new, and distinct, colony of British Columbia.

News of the Fraser River gold rush, emphasized by the proclamation of the new colony of British Columbia, stimulated popular demand for information about this remote place. In response, the London publisher G. Routledge issued in 1858 a pocket-sized book, *British Columbia and Vancouver Island*, by William Carew Hazlitt. It was a compendium of geographical, historical, and even linguistic information, and included the 1857 RGS article by Walter Colquhoun Grant and a series of articles by *The Times*' correspondent in San Francisco, replete with details of the conditions encountered by the earliest prospectors at the Fraser diggings.

Hazlitt included a folding map of the two colonies drawn by Francis Young. Although Hazlitt expressed gratitude for permission to reproduce the Arrowsmith map that accompanied Grant's article, the map in the book differed in coverage, scale, and detail. It seems probable that the RGS allowed Young to consult the latest material in its map room. His depiction of the interior of the island resembled, but not exactly, those of Arrowsmith and Weller. The sources would have been open to interpretation. In his title block, Young called the island "Vancouvers"; Hazlitt's book uses "Vancouver's" on its jaunty cover and just "Vancouver" in the text. (See Figs. 63 and 64)

The Act of Parliament creating British Columbia established its geographical borders but once again skirted the contentious international issue. It stated, "[It] shall include Queen Charlotte's Island and all other islands adjacent to the said territories except . . . No part of the Colony of Vancouver's Island, as present established, shall be comprised within British Columbia for the purposes of this Act."[6] The question of the line through the San Juan Archipelago, in accordance with the 1846 Treaty of Washington, remained unresolved.

A naval officer, Captain James Prevost, was the British nominee for the joint commission to survey and record that water boundary. Unlike the British, the Americans nominated one official, Archibald Campbell, as their commissioner for both the land and the water boundaries. Prevost and Lieutenant-Colonel John Hawkins, RE, chief of the British Boundary Commission and responsible for the land portion of the new border, found it difficult to negotiate with Campbell.

London had given Prevost secret orders for that negotiation. He was to press for acceptance that Rosario Strait was the channel described in the treaty, and failing that, he was to make the utmost effort to ensure that another channel be defined, one that "must contribute very much to the quiet possession of Vancouver's Island."[7] This Prevost interpreted as meaning that San Juan Island was to remain within British jurisdiction. He viewed it as strategically vital for the security of Victoria, the naval anchorage at Esquimalt, and the mouth of the Fraser River. It was also critical to marine communication between the two British west coast colonies. However, Campbell would accept nothing but that the line pass through Haro Strait, and he remained obdurate throughout six meetings with Prevost in 1857.

Meanwhile, Douglas was equally insistent that San Juan Island formed part of "Vancouver and the islands adjacent," as stated in Blanshard's appointment, and that therefore, jurisdiction over this piece of real estate lay in Victoria. Thus was the scene set; all that was needed was a spark to ignite a major showdown.

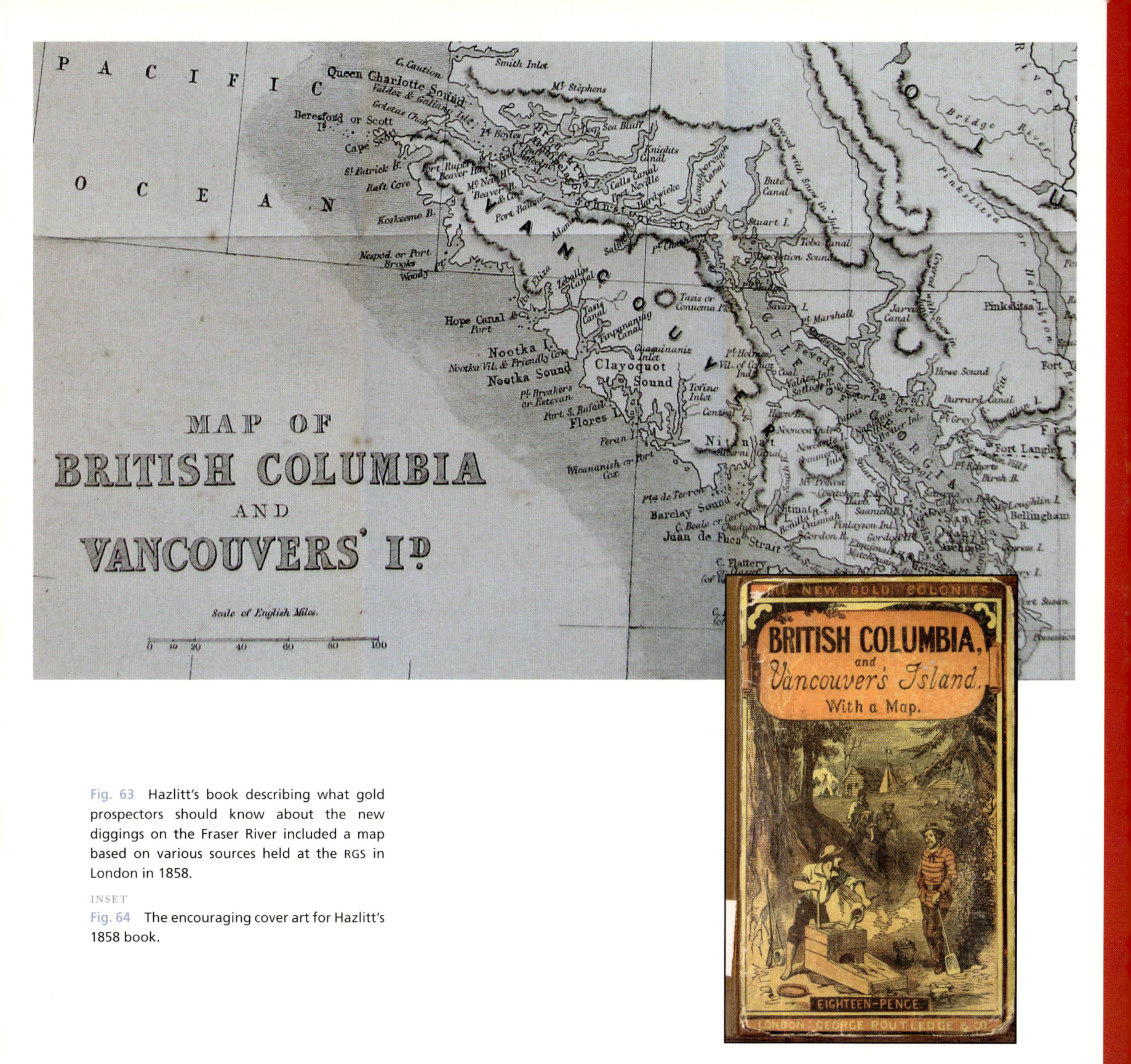

Fig. 63 Hazlitt's book describing what gold prospectors should know about the new diggings on the Fraser River included a map based on various sources held at the RGS in London in 1858.

INSET
Fig. 64 The encouraging cover art for Hazlitt's 1858 book.

Fig. 65 During and following the negotiation of the new boundary, the US Coast Survey established triangulation networks in Puget Sound in preparation for a hydrographic survey. Stations on Gordon Head and Darcy and Discovery Islands were key elements.

CHAPTER FOURTEEN

The San Juan Dispute: Cartographic Neglect—and a Pig— Almost Trigger a War

IN 1853 THE HUDSON'S BAY Company's farm subsidiary, Puget's Sound Agricultural Company, cleared a flat part of San Juan Island and established "Belle Vue," a sheep farm. They had tried raising sheep around Victoria but, according to Captain Duntz, had given up because "there was no keeping them on account of the wolves which infest the adjacent woods."[1]

That same year, the United States divided the region south of 49° north into Oregon and a new Washington Territory; the administrators of the new territory interpreted the treaty of 1846 as giving them jurisdiction over San Juan Island. This, they felt, not only permitted their citizens to homestead there, but authorized them to levy taxes on residents, which included the PSAC farm. In lieu of unpaid taxes, they seized some sheep. Arguments about jurisdiction over the island smouldered for a few years.

Between 1850 and 1857 the American authorities demonstrated continuing interest in the archipelago and its surrounding waters. The USS *Active* of the US Coast Survey was on station, preparing for a detailed hydrographic survey by establishing chains of astronomy and triangulation stations covering Admiralty Inlet, and from Discovery Island and Gordon Head to Saturna Island, tied into Point Roberts and Birch Bay. In 1857 the agency published a sketch "showing the progress of the survey" at a scale of 1:600,000. Both Haro and Rosario Straits were thoroughly provided with control points. While the forty-ninth parallel is included, there is no indication of the international water boundary on the chart. (See Fig. 65)

Most of the thirty thousand prospectors and hangers-on who had come from San Francisco and elsewhere for the Fraser River gold rush of 1858 failed to find their fortune. Unable to subsist in the cold and expensive environment of the diggings, many retraced their steps to start afresh at homesteading, heading for the kindlier country of the coastal plain of the new Washington Territory. By the summer of 1859, about a dozen of these had found their way to San Juan Island.

A minor incident between one of those American homesteaders, or squatters, and the PSAC farm manager flared into an armed standoff. The homesteader, Lyman Cutlar, shot a company pig that had been rooting up his potato crop, and the parties could not agree on compensation. This incident and its aftermath became known popularly as the "Pig War." A headstrong American brigadier-general, William S. Harney, became involved, sending a military force to occupy the island and to resist any attempted landing. More than four hundred infantrymen with field artillery dug in. (See Fig. 67)

Douglas, strong-willed and just as hot-tempered as Harney, was only two weeks into his new role as governor of both Vancouver Island and British Columbia, although now without any formal connection to the HBC or PSAC. Highly concerned by the growing American encroachment into what he considered British, and therefore "his," territory, Douglas ordered three well-armed warships of the Royal Navy, based in Esquimalt, to make ready for action. They were to mount a blockade and remove the Americans militarily.

Fortunately, and before a second shot could be fired, two veterans of the war of 1812 arrived on the scene. Both Rear Admiral R. Lambert Baynes, RN, and General Winfield Scott, the head of the US Army, had seen at first hand the bloody reality of war, and both knew that further conflict must be averted. Scott countermanded Harney's orders and Baynes diplomatically declined to acknowledge Douglas's authority. Between them they reached an amicable and pacific solution: Both sides would limit their force to just one hundred men and establish camps at opposite ends of the island until such time as their diplomats could resolve the question of jurisdiction.

In 1859, Colonel Moody of the Royal Engineers, serving also as lieutenant-governor of the new colony of British Columbia, had suggested another interpretation for the word "channel" in the treaty. In a private letter to an influential friend in London, Moody wrote that he took the wording to refer "to the whole width...between the mainland and Vancouver's Island, & having within it sundry islands." He calculated that a line drawn down the middle of this channel would pass through Orcas Island. He went on: "I wd. propose to give up our share of Orcas for Pt. Roberts."[2] Point Roberts was an anomaly that had been left isolated on the US side of the border. However, the British government failed to heed Moody's pragmatic suggestion for a compromise.

Additional chorographic information about the two new colonies trickled into London through various channels: the Colonial Office, the HBC, the army, and the navy. There, commercial cartographers such as Arrowsmith, Weller, and Wyld endeavoured to compile the new data, at times contradictory, into their existing maps for revised versions.

The second edition of Wyld's *Vancouvers Island*, published in 1861, attempted to reconcile the detail of "Barclay or NITINAT SOUND," derived from Narváez by way of Vancouver's chart, with the new information on Pemberton's explorations reported in his *Facts and Figures* booklet. Wyld was also able to revise the southeast coastline of Vancouver Island and the archipelago now called the Gulf Islands, using the wealth of detailed information acquired by Captain George Richards, RN, in HMS *Plumper*. Wyld retained the narrow cordillera from his first edition, but showed it as cut by Pemberton's traverses and the "Cowitchen R." He also depicted, unaltered, the water boundary as meeting the forty-ninth parallel in the middle of Boundary Bay. (See Fig. 66)

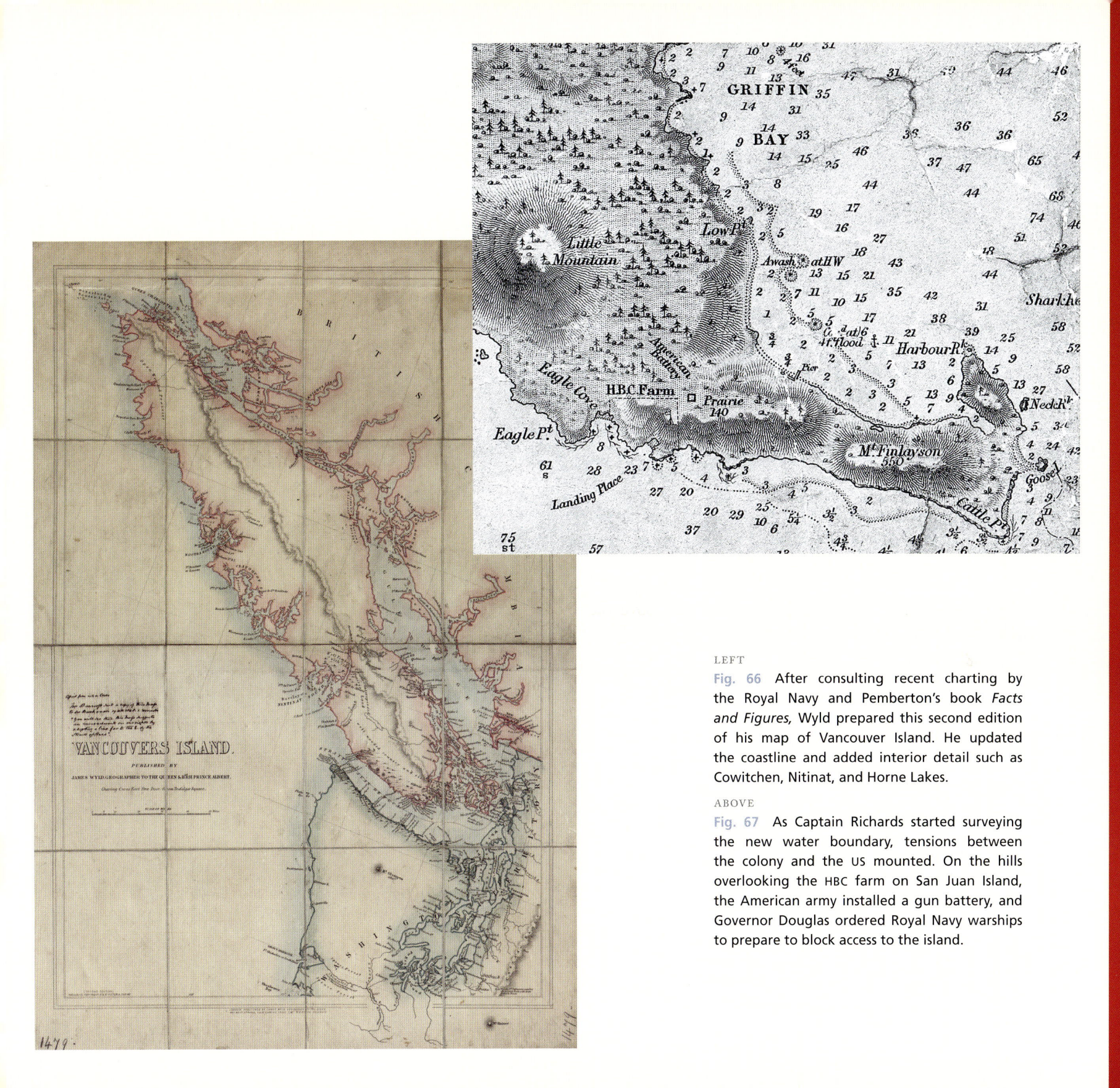

LEFT

Fig. 66 After consulting recent charting by the Royal Navy and Pemberton's book *Facts and Figures,* Wyld prepared this second edition of his map of Vancouver Island. He updated the coastline and added interior detail such as Cowitchen, Nitinat, and Horne Lakes.

ABOVE

Fig. 67 As Captain Richards started surveying the new water boundary, tensions between the colony and the US mounted. On the hills overlooking the HBC farm on San Juan Island, the American army installed a gun battery, and Governor Douglas ordered Royal Navy warships to prepare to block access to the island.

Fig. 68 In 1872, Kaiser Wilhelm I ended the long-standing dispute between Britain and the US over the water boundary, deciding in favour of the American case.

While the two military contingents were amicably camped at either end of San Juan Island, the American Civil War intervened, so it was not until 1868 that the United States and Britain reopened the question of the boundary through the San Juan Archipelago. By then, Britain had decreed that her two colonies on the Pacific were to be united as British Columbia, with responsibility for foreign relations retained in London. After three years' negotiation, the sides were still unable to agree on the boundary.

In 1871, within a new multi-part Treaty of Washington, the parties referred the San Juan question to binding arbitration by the new Kaiser Wilhelm I of the German Empire, specifying that only Rosario and Haro channels were to be considered. The kaiser appointed three eminent commissioners: a geographer, a high court judge, and an expert on commercial law.

In Berlin, both the British and Americans prepared and presented detailed cases, and this time both buttressed their reasoning with extensive portfolios of maps and charts. James Prevost, now a vice-admiral, presented the British case, supported by twenty-six maps—Spanish, British, and American. The US case, presented by diplomat George Bancroft, included eight maps. Both sides then issued replies to the other's claim. Britain included twenty-two more maps and the US added a further seven.[3] At long last, the parties had appreciated, and deployed, the invaluable tool of cartography in boundary negotiation.

After a year's deliberation, at times heated, the commission voted two to one for the Haro Strait channel. It seemed that, for two of the commissioners, the phrase in the treaty "and thence southerly" carried more weight than the phrase that followed: "through the middle of the said channel." A line drawn due south from the mid-channel point on parallel 49° north passes through Haro Strait. However, the open sector of the Strait of Georgia at that midpoint trended southeasterly. The dissenting opinion was that of the commercial expert. He wrote that the treaty should be amended to specify the middle channel, but the US secretary of state, Hamilton Fish, dug in his heels. The middle channel was neither within the scope of the arbitration nor would it be considered. End of story.

The kaiser endorsed the majority verdict and, on October 21, 1872, issued his ruling, which is still reflected on modern maps. The German journal *Petermann's Geographischer Mittheilungen* published a map illustrating the kaiser's decision, with both the British and American lines indicated and the latter highlighted as decided upon. (See Fig. 68)

One month after the ruling, the British contingent on San Juan Island marched smartly out of its well-kept camp and sailed away. For the second time in the history of Vancouver Island, an officer of the Royal Marines saluted as the Union Jack was hauled down on a remote island outpost of the empire.

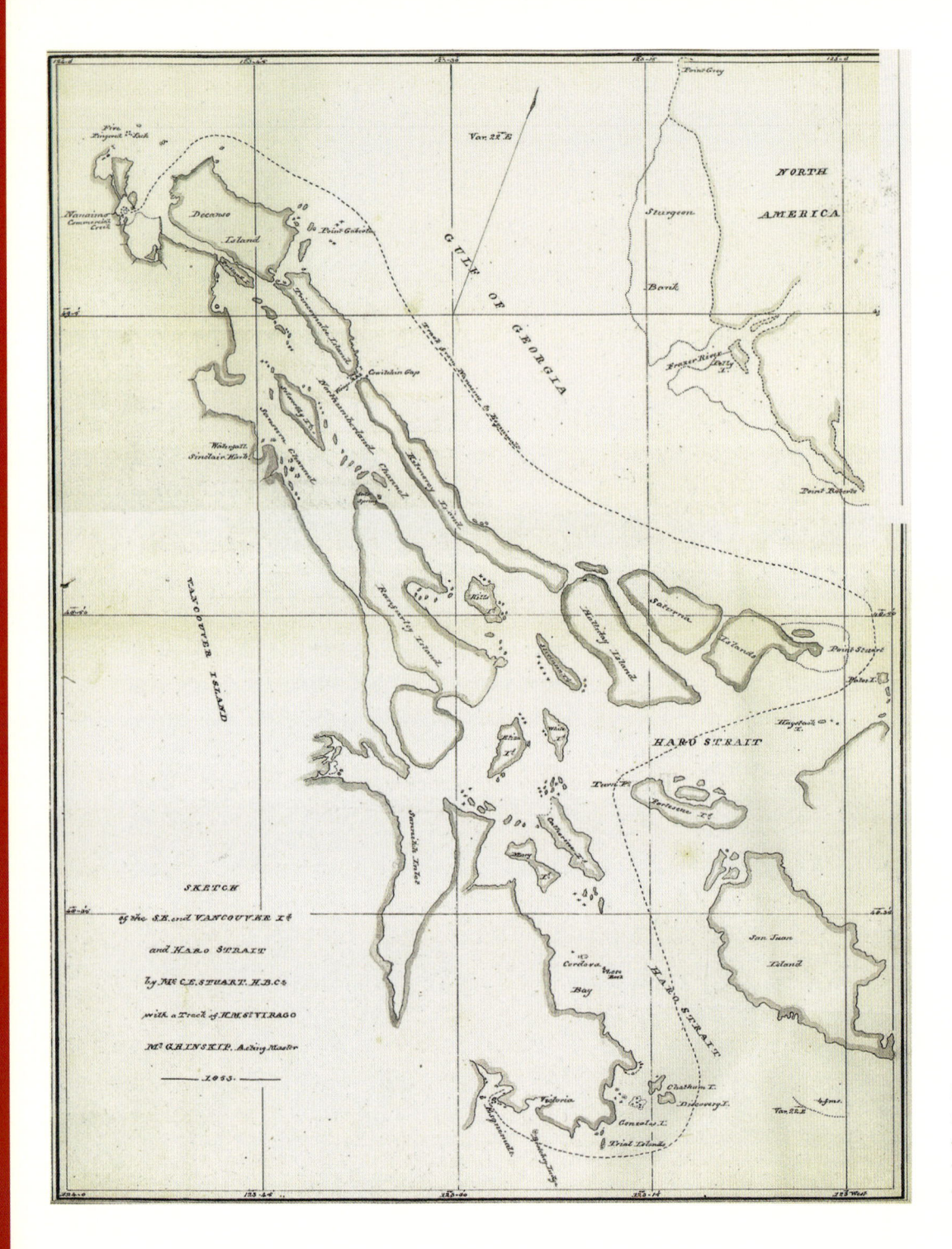

Fig. 69 In response to Douglas's call for better maps when reporting his canoe journey of 1852, the Royal Navy worked with the HBC on this chart. The delineation of the islands is far better than on Teben'kov's, but many of the toponyms coincide.

CHAPTER FIFTEEN

"Navigating this Boisterous Neighbourhood": George Richards's Hydrography

IN MARCH 1857, REAR ADMIRAL John Washington, Hydrographer of the Navy, wrote his last-minute "Instructions for a Surveying Voyage to Vancouver's Island," to update and emphasize the specific tasks entrusted to Captain George Henry Richards, RN, newly in command of HMS *Plumper*.[1]

Immediately upon arrival on Vancouver Island, Richards was to consult with Captain James Prevost, RN, the senior British boundary commissioner. His first task would be to "make an accurate nautical survey of such portions of the channel islands" intended to support and inform the negotiation of the international water boundary. As part of this survey, and based upon an astro-trigonometric network, he was to determine, agree with his US counterpart, and mark where the land boundary—latitude 49° north—crossed the mainland coast (at Semiahmoo Bay and Point Roberts).

When this was done, Richards was to chart the channels, islands, and coasts of Vancouver Island at his own discretion "according to their importance." He was to maintain friendly relations with the local staff of the Hudson's Bay Company, particularly their surveyors, with whom he was to share information. *Plumper* carried a scientific library of reference works on botany and natural history, and the ship's surgeon was equipped for collecting and preserving specimens.

There was no more experienced, capable, and vigorous hydrographic surveying officer than Richards, whose chartmaking experience, ability, energy, and tact came at a crucial period in Vancouver Island's history. Over the next seven years he fulfilled every requirement placed upon him.

Supporting Richards, in addition to the normal complement of ship's officers aboard *Plumper*, was a team of "masters," navigation and surveying specialists. The senior of these was John Bull; the others were Daniel Pender and Edward Bedwell. The second mate, Lieutenant Richard Mayne, RN, also participated in surveying operations and undertook several overland expeditions, both on the island and into the interior of British Columbia.

Richards assisted Prevost in the frustrating wrangling over the water boundary. He also worked with Joseph Pemberton, exchanging topographic and chart data for the combined maps of Esquimalt, Victoria, and Nanaimo Harbours. Prevost had navigated in these waters for a few years, initially aboard HMS *Virago*, when he and the master, George Inskip, RN, added much hydrographic information about the Inside Passage and the Strait of Georgia to Vancouver's charts.

In 1853, the year following Douglas and Pemberton's canoe journey, Prevost and Inskip had worked with Captain Charles Stuart, the HBC factor at Nanaimo, to produce a new sketch chart of the offshore islands between Esquimalt and Nanaimo, giving them names, most of which were never adopted. (See Fig. 69, page 116) Several of the HBC toponyms on the Stuart chart had been used in Teben'kov's chart of 1849—for example, Cowichan River, Point Stuart, and Arro Canal—another important clue reinforcing the idea that HBC officers were the source for the Russian's chart.

The sketch marked *Virago*'s track through Haro Strait, rounding "Point Stuart," the eastern tip of Saturna Island. This was where Juan Pantoja had first seen the Gran Canal de Rosario (the Strait of Georgia) in 1791. Ironically, the plotted line of *Virago*'s course closely matched the line of the kaiser's arbitration of the water boundary almost two decades later.

Richards's instructions from Admiral Washington included a paragraph referring to place names. After deploring the practice of renaming toponyms already in use, as seen in the American Wilkes's charts, he exhorted Richards to respect the right of "discoverers or first explorers to give the names & once given & established by use it must be held sacred." Specifically, he was not to "allow the names given by the Spaniards Galiano & Valdés in 1792 and Vancouver in 1793 to be altered. And in all cases if possible add the native name with its meaning if it have any."[2]

Richards mostly complied with this instruction, using a few Spanish place names, but in doing so he created some ambiguities. He needed names for the chain of four "new" islands southeast from Nanaimo. For the northernmost one he chose Gabriola, a corrupted Spanish toponym from Narváez via Vancouver's and Kellett's charts. For the next two, Valdes and Galiano, he demonstrated his familiarity with the details of the 1792 voyage of the Spanish captains, but Vancouver's chart had already used their names for other islands off the northern tip, so they needed changing. Richards renamed the northern Valdes Bute Island but ambiguously retained Galiano for two distinct islands. To the southernmost island of the chain he gave the name of his subordinate, Mayne.

The HBC and colonial administrators had already given several place names, most of which Richards respected. He followed another time-honoured Royal Navy custom of naming places after shipmates (Pender, Bull, Hankin), officer friends (Prevost, Fulford, De Courcy), sister ships (*Trincomalie* [sic], *Thetis*, *Ganges*), and, of course, his superiors (Baynes, Washington, Beaufort). Increasingly, as he continued in his surveys, local guides/interpreters helped him adopt local place names, or English approximations thereof (Shushartie, Nahwitti, and Hesquiat).

Richards faced an interesting toponymic dilemma in his chart of *Haro and Rosario Straits*: that of the name of Mount Douglas. Originally, HBC people had called this prominent knoll on the Victoria skyline "Cedar Hill," since this was where, in 1843, the pickets for the fort had been harvested, but more recently the popular name had changed. The Admiralty's standard hydrographic instructions decreed that no topographic feature less than 1,000 feet (304 metres) high could be called a mountain, and Mount Douglas measured only 696 feet (211.6 metres). Rather than give offence to the governor—"the father of British Columbia"—by demoting the feature to "Douglas Hill," Richards bent the rule to retain the local usage. More compliantly, Richards reduced a neighbouring feature to "Tolmie Hill," but later this too regained its "Mount" status. (See Fig. 70, page 120)

One of the islands off the Saanich Peninsula was named on the same chart "Sidney Is." by Lieutenant Pender, probably after an old comrade of Richards's. Later, the first settlers on the peninsula opposite the island adopted that name. When the settlement became the Town of Sidney, it repaid the compliment by incorporating into its coat of arms the image of HMS *Plumper* surmounted by a heraldic signal beacon, in recognition of Richards's later work with lighthouses.

Because of the pressing diplomatic need for charting related to the contentious water boundary, the Admiralty rushed into print two charts of *Plumper*'s early surveys. In 1859, it published *Haro and Rosario Straits* and, two years later, *Haro Strait and Middle Channel*. Publication of the former did not await the results of Richards's detailed survey of the Fraser River from Fort Langley downstream, then under way. The depiction of the southern end of San Juan Island on the latter showed both the "HBC Farm" and, close by, "American Battery."

Northward from Willow Point opposite Cape Mudge, Richards recharted the coast of Vancouver Island already surveyed by Vancouver; however, their objectives differed. The earlier navigator's primary task had been a restricted one, to record just the configuration of the saltwater boundary of the continental mainland, not islands. The latter's concern specifically included Vancouver Island; he was to construct a more complete hydrographic chart of the seabed and the depth of water over it, paying particular attention to harbours and anchorages. He also included land features important to mariners, and navigational factors such as tides and currents. Richards collected data not just for publication in the Admiralty's charts, but also for their *Sailing Directions*, tide and current tables, and for meteorological publications. Vancouver had been sailing unknown waters; Richards benefited from his predecessor's exploratory charts and journals.

Richards, following Vancouver's place names, referred to the eastern shore of Discovery Passage as Valdes Island. A later survey team discovered that this was, in fact, three islands, separated by narrow, winding passages. In 1903, to remove confusion over the name Valdes Island, the Geographic Board of Canada named these Quadra, Maurelle [*sic*], and Sonora Islands, belatedly redressing the Admiralty's decision to omit the Spanish element from Vancouver's 1792 gesture of friendship and collaboration. Francisco Mourelle was Bodega y Quadra's pilot and *Sonora* was the tiny schooner on their 1775 voyage of exploration. Richards had named a prominence on Galiano Island "Quadra Hill."

A few days later, *Plumper*'s survey parties progressed northward, transiting Seymour Narrows. Although acknowledging that the tide rips were "excessively dangerous for boats," no one aboard voiced the suspicion that beneath the turbulence there lurked an even greater hazard, later known as Ripple Rock.

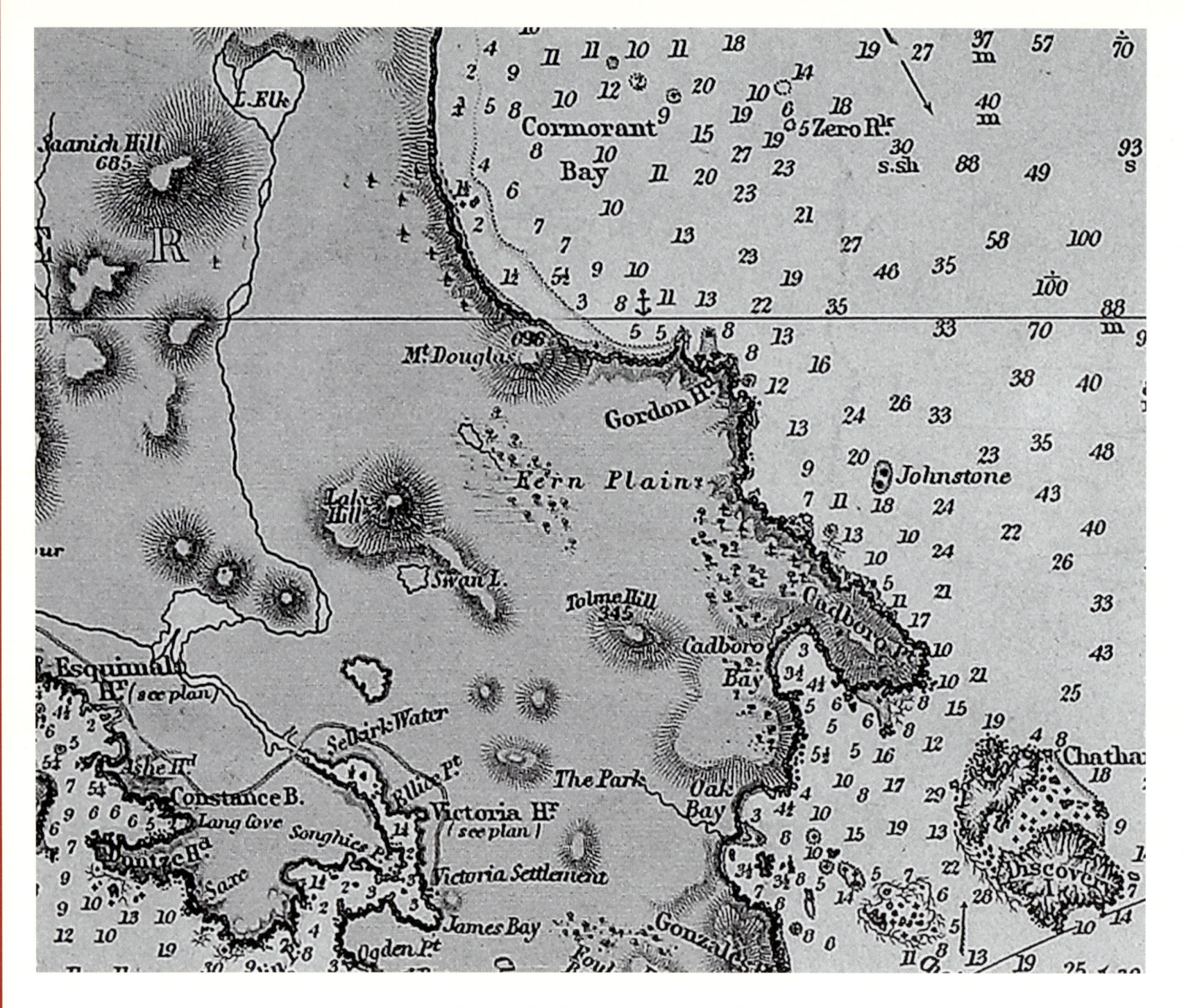

Fig. 70 Richards went against his standing instructions in allowing the below-minimum-height "Mount" Douglas to retain its topographic descriptor.

Fig. 71 Richards and Pemberton collaborated on this chart of Victoria to combine marine soundings with onshore detail of the growing community of Victoria.

By early November, *Plumper* had been refuelled with coal and was back in Esquimalt, the surveyors to spend the winter ashore working on their charts. The only charts of their work published by the Admiralty in 1860 were those surveyed the previous year: *Nanaimo Harbour and Departure Bay* and *Fraser River and Burrard Inlet*. The large volume of work carried out in 1860 was published over the following three years. Two harbour charts, *Esquimalt* and *Victoria*, were also reissued in 1861, incorporating land detail provided by Pemberton. (See Fig. 71, page 121)

HMS *Plumper*'s replacement vessel was the paddle-wheel sloop HMS *Hecate*. Ten years older but powered by steam-driven sidewheels, *Hecate* had 25 percent greater endurance under power, although she did not sail as well as *Plumper*. Lieutenant Mayne commented, "We were greatly delighted with the change, for though possessing no external beauty *Hecate* was very roomy and comfortable, my new cabin alone being nearly as large as the messroom of the *Plumper*."[3]

Richards noted in his journal that Mayne, after an overland trek, had "perfectly succeeded & made a good sketch of the country between Alberni and Nanaimo." The detailed map that Mayne prepared showed his routes and as much topography as he could, as well as recommendations for a road. He gave two alternatives for the eastern portion of the road, with reasons for both, and his suggestion for linking the coastal road with Alberni was followed, more or less, by the eventual route through Coombs, by the Little Qualicum River, and along the southern shore of Cameron Lake. The railway took the north shore route. The Admiralty transmitted Mayne's formal report and map to the Royal Geographical Society to be read at its meeting on May 12, 1862.

The winter of 1861–62 was one of the most bitter on record, with temperatures, even on the coast, falling to -12°C. at night. The Fraser River below New Westminster froze over, as did Victoria Harbour, with *Hecate* locked in the ice for several days. Obtaining fresh water became a problem for both ships and citizens. Not until mid-March could *Hecate* depart on survey duty, and even then, Richards recorded, at Nanaimo they found "snow covering the ground and everything very wintry." With difficulty, *Hecate* reached Sapperton, to deliver three manuscript charts of Barkley Sound and one of Nanaimo Harbour to the Royal Engineers for printing on their new lithographic press. This made the charts available locally, many months earlier than if Richards had followed the normal course of shipping the manuscripts to England. (See Figs. 72 and 73)

Richards invited another of his officers, Lieutenant Philip Hankin, RN, to make an overland expedition to cross Vancouver Island from Kyuquot Sound to the east coast. Surgeon Lieutenant Charles Wood accompanied him, to investigate the botany of the area, and they rejoined *Hecate* at Fort Rupert three weeks later. Richards's covering letter to Douglas in June 1862, enclosing Hankin's report, concluded, "The survey of the greater part of the Western Coast has been completed and several new harbours and anchorages discovered, which when published for general information, will lessen the frequency of disasters which have annually befallen vessels navigating this boisterous neighbourhood."[4] (See Fig. 74, page 124)

Having fulfilled his mission to chart the coasts of Vancouver Island and the adjacent mainland, Richards prepared to return to Britain. He knew, however, that there was important work still to be done in British Columbia's coastal waters north of the island, so he chartered the local vessel

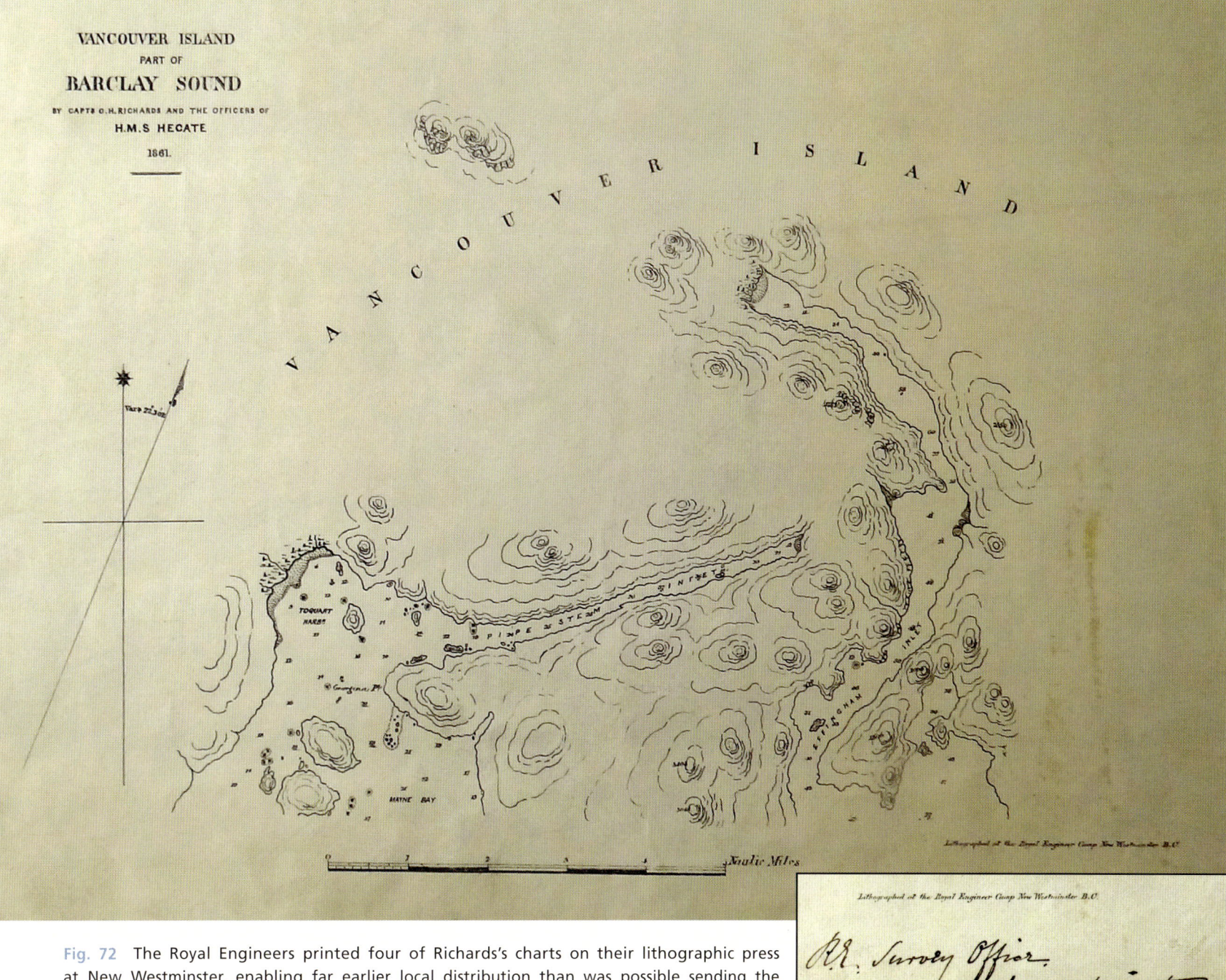

Fig. 72 The Royal Engineers printed four of Richards's charts on their lithographic press at New Westminster, enabling far earlier local distribution than was possible sending the manuscripts to England.

INSET
Fig. 73 This copy of the chart of Pipestem Inlet shows manuscript authentication by an RE officer.

Fig. 74 The northwest end of Vancouver Island on the summary chart of Richards's three-year hydrographic survey shows, for the first time, the complexity of Quatsino Sound and the Hankin-Wood overland expedition from Kyuquot to the Nimpkish River.

most suited to hydrography, the aging HBC paddlewheeler *Beaver*. It had plied these waters for twenty-six years. Master Daniel Pender, RN, with Second Master Edward Blunden, RN, six petty officers, and two dozen seamen were transferred from *Hecate* to the vessel, now modified for surveying and recommissioned as HMS *Beaver*, to continue the work. Governor Douglas, despite budgetary difficulties, agreed to contribute to the costs of the charter.

At the end of December 1862, on the eve of *Hecate*'s departure from Esquimalt homeward bound for England, the Legislative Assembly of Vancouver Island passed a formal vote of thanks to Captain Richards and his officers for services rendered to the colony in the survey and exploration of its coasts.

Richards was appointed Hydrographer of the Navy and served for eleven years, thoroughly revising and supervising the expansion of this specialized department of the Admiralty. He issued the directive that any British survey vessel, on passage anywhere in the world, was to make soundings and, if necessary, detour to investigate "vigias"—reported hazards to navigation, such as submerged rocks and reefs. Richards introduced another policy: to provide all of Her Majesty's ships with atlases of charts and to send them regular bulletins for updating those charts.

Daniel Pender continued Richards's work in the Strait of Georgia, Johnstone Strait, and Queen Charlotte Sound. During the next seven years, aboard the tiny HMS *Beaver*, Pender and his team surveyed the mainland inlets, the channels of the Inside Passage, and the offshore islands as far north as the Alaskan boundary and Observatory Inlet, a total of 994 miles (1,600 kilometres) of coastline.

Perhaps the most dramatic episode of the Pender–*Beaver* phase of the survey was the discovery and charting of Ripple Rock. Captains Vancouver, Gordon and Richards, as well as many others, had all passed through the turbulent tidal races of Seymour Narrows without suspecting their hidden danger. Arrowsmith's published version of the 1849 Admiralty chart of *Vancouver Island and the Gulf of Georgia* indicated that there was a clearance of fifty fathoms (ninety-one metres) for the length of Discovery Passage, the waterway between Cape Mudge and Chatham Point. In 1860, *Plumper*'s work had recorded seventeen fathoms (thirty-one metres) at the narrows.

Six years later, the skipper of a trading schooner informed Pender that there was a dangerous submerged rock in the middle of the channel. Pender investigated the vigia at the next opportunity, discovering, to his astonishment, a pinnacle with barely three and a half fathoms (six and a half metres) of clearance at low water. He sent an urgent letter to Richards, who, recognizing the threat, distributed an immediate notice to mariners. He even felt that the danger justified a separate chart, giving it the name Ripple Rock. Pender's subsequent soundings over the menace decreased the clearance further, and Richards issued a series of amended versions of the *Seymour Narrows* chart. (See Figs. 75, 76, and 77, page 127) Despite these warnings, Ripple Rock continued to present a deadly threat to navigators of the Inside Passage until 1958, when mining engineers blew off the peak with a huge explosion from below.

On completing his survey work at the end of the 1870 season, Pender handed *Beaver* back to the HBC and returned to Britain. He worked under his old mentor, Richards, to supervise the publication of seventeen major charts, the many harbour surveys, and the associated *Sailing Directions*, based upon his field work. Eventually, Pender was appointed assistant hydrographer and retired with the rank of captain.[5]

By the time Pender's work was concluded in 1879, the Admiralty had published a further twenty-nine charts and seventeen insets showing detail of harbours or channels related to Vancouver Island and the surrounding waters. These were in addition to Richards's earlier charts, associated with the international boundary questions. Also, there were charts of the Fraser River, the Queen Charlotte Islands, the northwestern shore of the Olympic Peninsula, and Admiralty Inlet, all derived from the work done aboard *Plumper*, *Hecate*, and *Beaver*. At the time, few coasts in the world were charted as thoroughly and accurately.

Richards's charting of the coasts of Vancouver Island and British Columbia, seventy-five charts in total, was considered sufficient for navigational purposes until the turn of the century; Britain deployed no further hydrographic vessels on the station until HMS *Egeria*, in 1898.

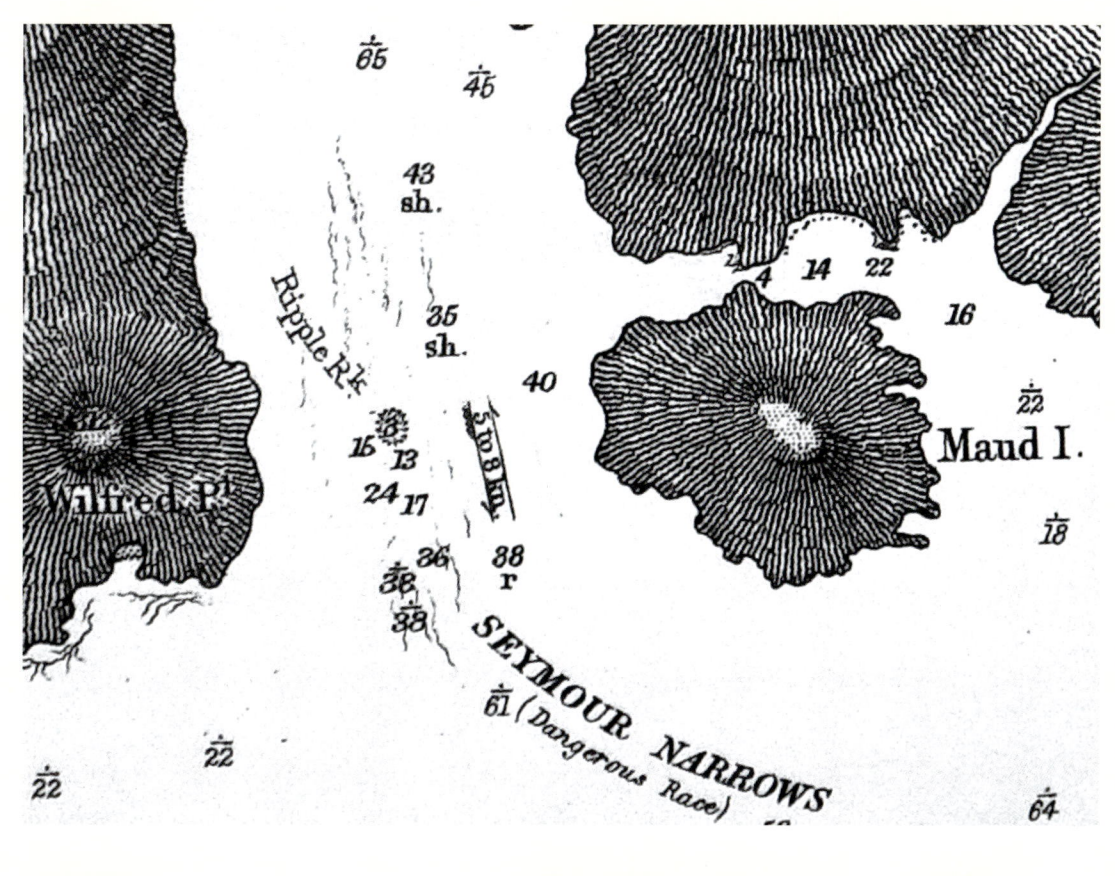

Fig. 75 Richards published three versions of the new chart #538 in quick succession, in response to Pender's reports of the perilous Ripple Rock. Each new version showed increased severity of the hazard to vessels travelling through Seymour Narrows.

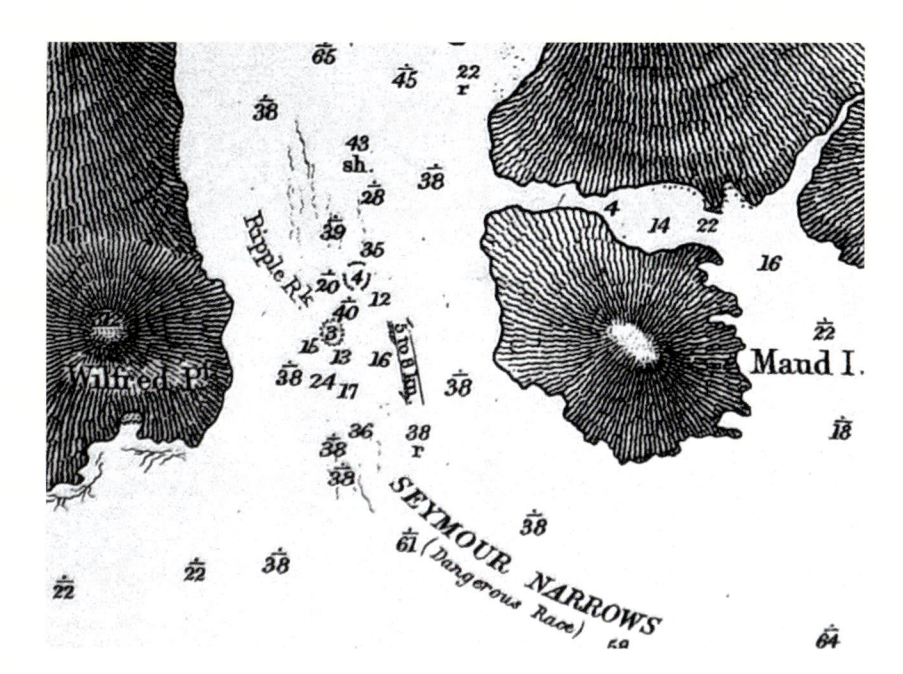

Fig. 76 Chart #538, version two

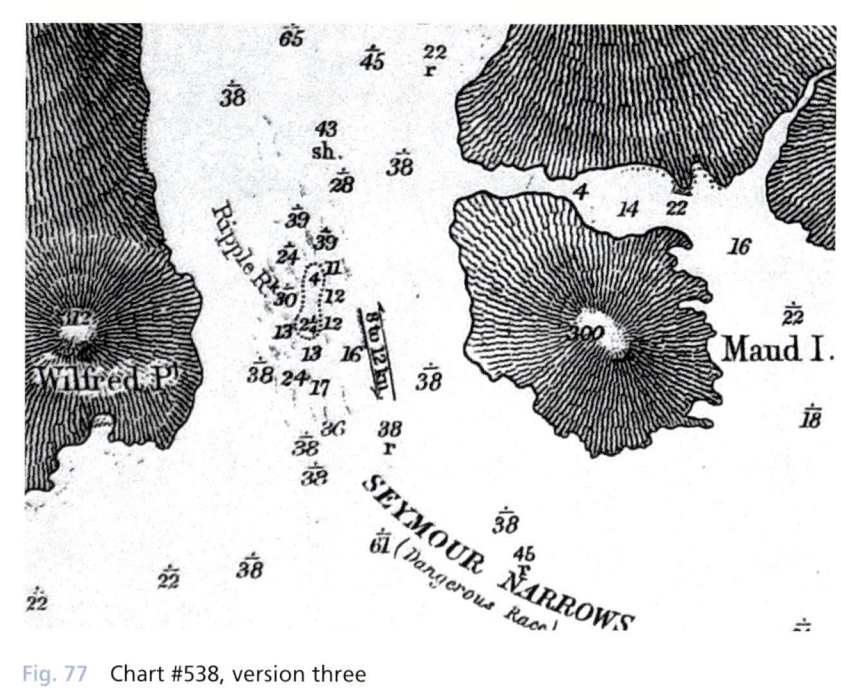

Fig. 77 Chart #538, version three

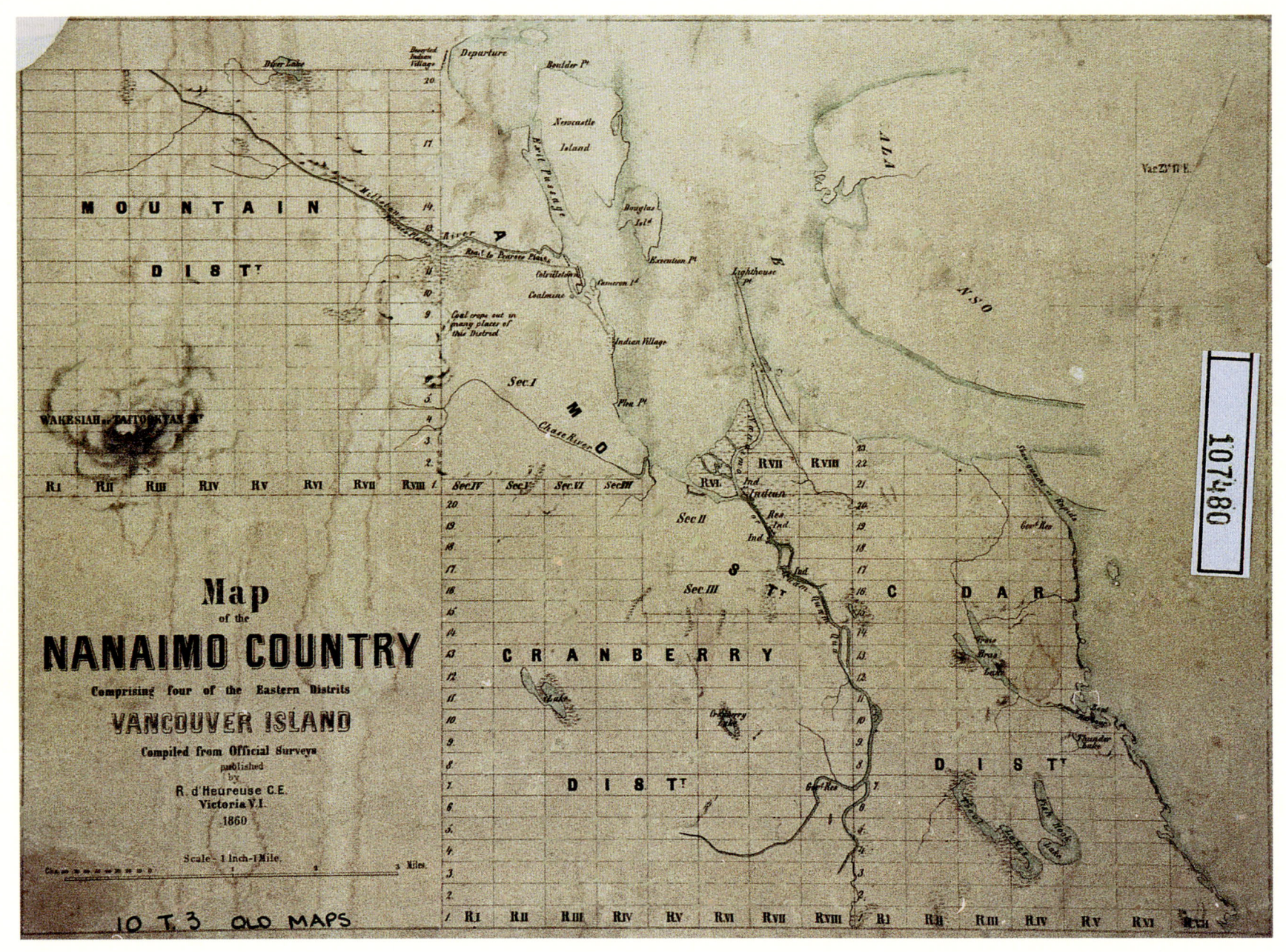

Fig. 78 Rudolph d'Heureuse had almost completed this general map of the districts surrounding Nanaimo by 1860. Although he provided two local toponyms for the significant peak at left, Robert Brown named it Mount De Cosmos, after a politician of the time.

CHAPTER SIXTEEN

"The Back of the World": Vancouver Island under the Crown Colonial

SOME SCOTTISH WRITERS DISPARAGED THE two British colonies on the Pacific coast of North America as being "the back of the world." This referred more to their remoteness than the quality of the land itself, which was considerably more fertile than the highlands and islands of the critics' homeland.

By the mid-1850s, a trickle of informal homesteaders had appeared on the Saanich Peninsula and in the Cowichan Valley. They sought land but lacked the capital to afford it under the Wakefield System. At first, Governor James Douglas and his colonial surveyor, Joseph Pemberton, turned a blind eye to such activity, hoping that a sorely needed supply of farm produce would result. Following the 1858 gold rush, that trickle grew in volume.

Douglas instructed Pemberton that "the whole country be immediately thrown open for settlement, the lands surveyed and sold."[1] The surveyor and his superior understood that the land-registry methods used thus far would not be able to cope, but by then Pemberton's *ad hoc* cadastral system for the area surrounding Victoria was in place and too entrenched to be changed. For the remainder of the colony of Vancouver Island, apart from a few isolated areas already settled, a different method of land-title registration was needed, one that allowed settlers to occupy the land prior to a survey and full payment.

Over the next few years a new cadastral system evolved for the rest of Vancouver Island: Maps now showed a grid of parcels that could be pre-empted—claimed, occupied, and "improved"—with full title being granted upon survey, payment, and formal registration. A complex series of laws, ordinances, and proclamations supported this evolution. By 1862 a single man (British only) could pre-empt 100 acres (40.5 hectares); a married-and-accompanied man might claim 150 acres. Lands specifically excluded from pre-emption were communities already established and Aboriginal settlements. The price was reduced to fifty pence per acre, equivalent to one US dollar. All lots were to be rectangular, aligned with an axis that might be tied either to true north or to a natural boundary such as water frontage. Road allowances were provided. (See Fig. 78, page 128)

Under this system for Vancouver Island, Pemberton's surveyors first marked out a grid of "sections and ranges" and recorded major topographic features, Native villages, and arable land. They gave each parcel a unique reference designation on the resultant plan, such as "Section 2, Range 2, Somenos District." These new districts were square, with five-mile (eight-kilometre) sides, unlike the randomly shaped and sized districts surrounding Victoria, whose limits were natural boundaries or lines between stations of the trigonometric network. In this way, the lands office could keep better track of which parcels had been pre-empted, which were registered, and which remained available. The registration process included the formal survey and marking of the corners of the parcel.

Colonel Moody of the Royal Engineers, commissioner of lands as well as lieutenant-governor for the new colony of British Columbia, devised a separate cadastral system for the mainland, based, to Douglas's displeasure, on an American model.

Douglas asked his superiors to send out several more trained surveyors to meet the increased workload in both colonies. Fortunately, the flood of prospectors, merchants, tradesmen, and gold-rush opportunists arriving in Victoria included a few qualified civil engineers and land surveyors seeking employment. Pemberton employed some and gave seasonal contracts to others. Significant among them were John Trutch, the younger of two brothers, both engineers, and Hermann Otto Tiedemann, a Berlin-educated engineer and architect who accepted the position of chief draftsman and town planner for Vancouver Island.

In Victoria, Trutch established on the ground the cadastral grids for the districts of North and South Saanich, starting at the summit of Mount Newton. Tiedemann worked initially on two projects. The first was the new, four-sheet plan of the Victoria District, complete with street names hurriedly devised by Pemberton.

The second was to design the new lighthouses for Race Rocks and Fisgard Island. He also designed the first legislative buildings, soon nicknamed "The Birdcages" because of their pagoda-style rooflines. His artistic skills were amply demonstrated by a superb, full-colour panorama, *View of Victoria*. Pemberton took Tiedemann's manuscript to London to be printed by the firm Day & Son, Lithographers to The Queen. The view showed the palisade and bastion of the HBC fort and the new Birdcages, the harbour crowded with shipping, both sailboats and steamers, and a small flotilla of Native canoes. In the foreground, he drew the longhouses of the "Indian Village (Songhees)." The following year, 1861, the same printers produced a new map based on Tiedemann's work, the latest cadastral configuration of *Victoria and Part of Esquimalt Districts*, indicating the highly significant HBC reserves and sites of government buildings. (See Fig. 79)

A separate, private venture published an edition of another Tiedemann manuscript map of Victoria. Attempting to counter the exodus of disappointed miners from the diggings, entrepreneur and businessman Alfred Waddington published two documents: *The Fraser Mines Vindicated*, the first book privately published on Vancouver Island; and a lithographic map of the burgeoning town where he had already become a significant speculator in real estate. (See Fig. 80, page 132)

Involving himself in local politics, Waddington served for a year as an elected member of the Legislative Assembly,

Fig. 79 In 1861 Pemberton commissioned another London lithographer, Day & Son, to publish a map showing numbered rural real-estate lots and reserves for church, HBC, and First Nations. Printers of the era loved ornate type fonts.

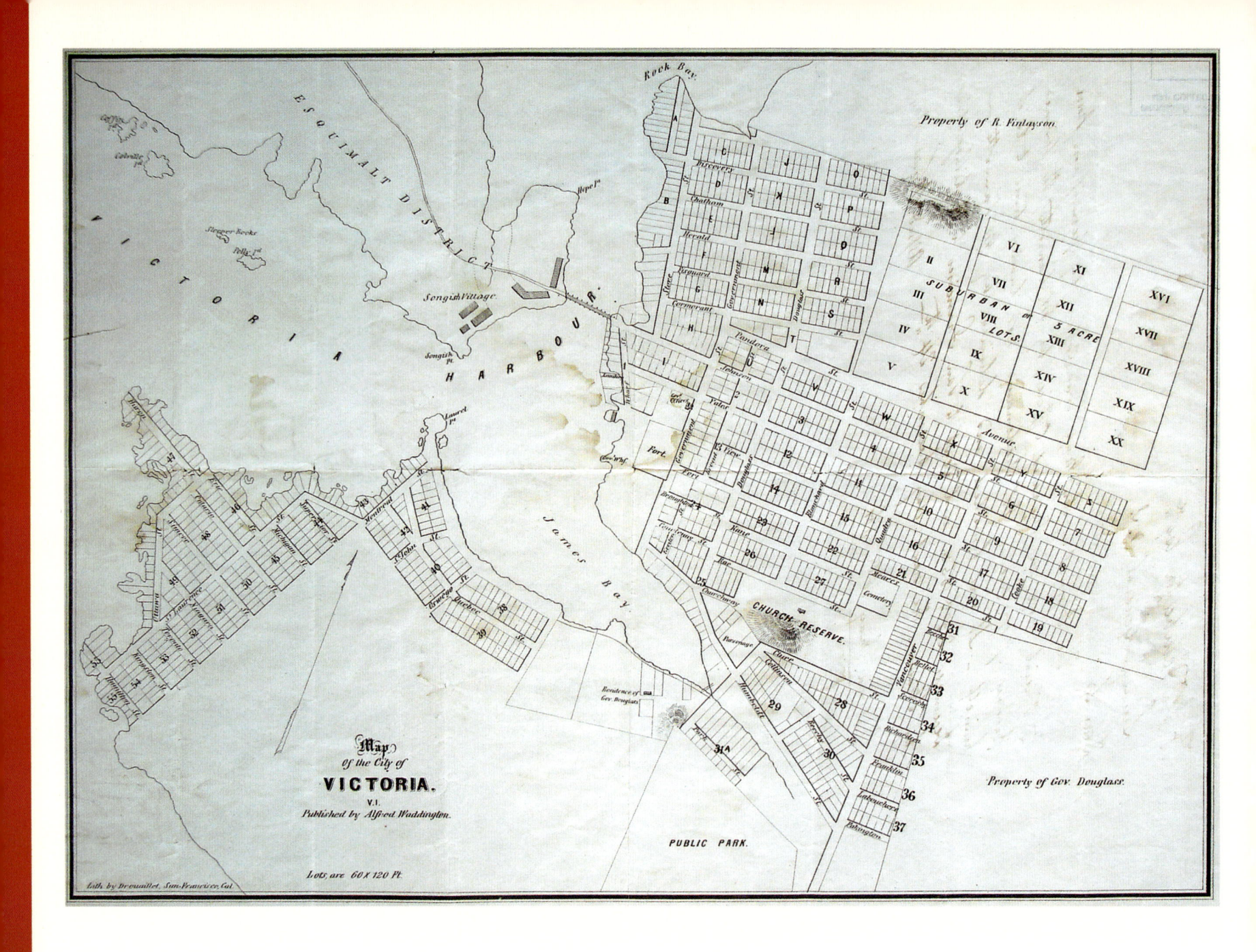

Fig. 80 The energetic entrepreneur Alfred Waddington, keen to nurture his investments in Victoria real estate, sponsored the printing of a map of the community to encourage further development. It denotes Victoria as a city, although officially it was still a town.

Fig. 81 Waddington, by 1863 a member of the Legislative Assembly, helped draft the new city's charter of incorporation and financed a second printed map, covering an area larger than the previous one.

usually in opposition to Governor Douglas and the "fur trade elite." He also participated in the drafting of the charter of incorporation of Victoria as a city. Associated with this campaign, he arranged for the private publication of an updated map of the city in 1862. (See Fig. 81, page 133) He sent both maps, published in 1859 and 1863, to be lithographed in San Francisco.

In 1860, a civil engineer, Rudolph d'Heureuse, published yet another lithographed version of Tiedemann's fine cartography. His elegant *Map of the South-eastern Districts of Vancouver Island* covered the region from the tip of the Saanich Peninsula around the coast to Sooke Harbour, and included an inset town plan of Victoria as it was in 1858. (See Fig. 82) Not much is known about d'Heureuse, but he soon joined Pemberton's drafting team. He had sent the map to Berlin for printing, which hints at Tiedemann's involvement in the publication.

❖ ❖ ❖

With the creation of British Columbia in 1858 as the second British colony on the west coast, various administrative departments of the colony of Vancouver Island saw changes and now reported to London. Some senior colonial officials arrived, including a judge, attorney general, treasurer, chief constable, and customs collector. While most of these were specifically designated for British Columbia, after June 1859 they also acted for Vancouver Island. Pemberton was confirmed as surveyor general for Vancouver Island, with Benjamin Pearse as his assistant.

One man's influence increased during those early years of the colonial era: Captain William Young, RN, who arrived in 1857 as secretary to the British delegation of the Boundary Commission. A dashing, decorated naval administrator, he was quickly accepted into the governor's social circle. After marrying Douglas's niece, he became his trusted aide and was seconded from the commission to be the colonial secretary for British Columbia. He acted in the same role in the administration of Vancouver Island, and as such, he provided the formal channel of communication between the governor and the surveyor general.

Another new development was the involvement of the Emigration Commission, also called the "Land Board," an imperial government office based in London. Its purpose was to promote settlement of the colonies by suitable British people, and to do this, they needed two things from Victoria: detailed maps of the land that was available, and reliable descriptions of the conditions that potential immigrants could expect. Pemberton addressed the first request straightaway. In March 1859 he sent Pearse, with a party of assistants, to the area around Nanaimo to prepare preliminary maps and cadastral grids for the districts of Mountain, Cedar, and Chemainus—all previously identified as having good potential for agriculture. (See Fig. 83, page 136)

Pemberton accompanied another new surveyor, Oliver Wells, to a second prime prospect for a farming settlement, the Cowichan Valley. After a brief reconnaissance, Pemberton left Wells to map the districts of Shawnigan, Cowichan, Comiaken, Quamichan, and Somenos, a daunting task for a new employee. Wells responded to the challenge and by the end of September had completed the five maps. Rudolph d'Heureuse fair-drew (carefully copied) the manuscripts prepared by Pearse, Trutch, and Wells.

Governor Douglas forwarded the manuscripts to Sir Edward Bulwer Lytton, the colonial secretary in London, commenting that the maps formed "interesting additions to the topography of the Colony" and suggesting that

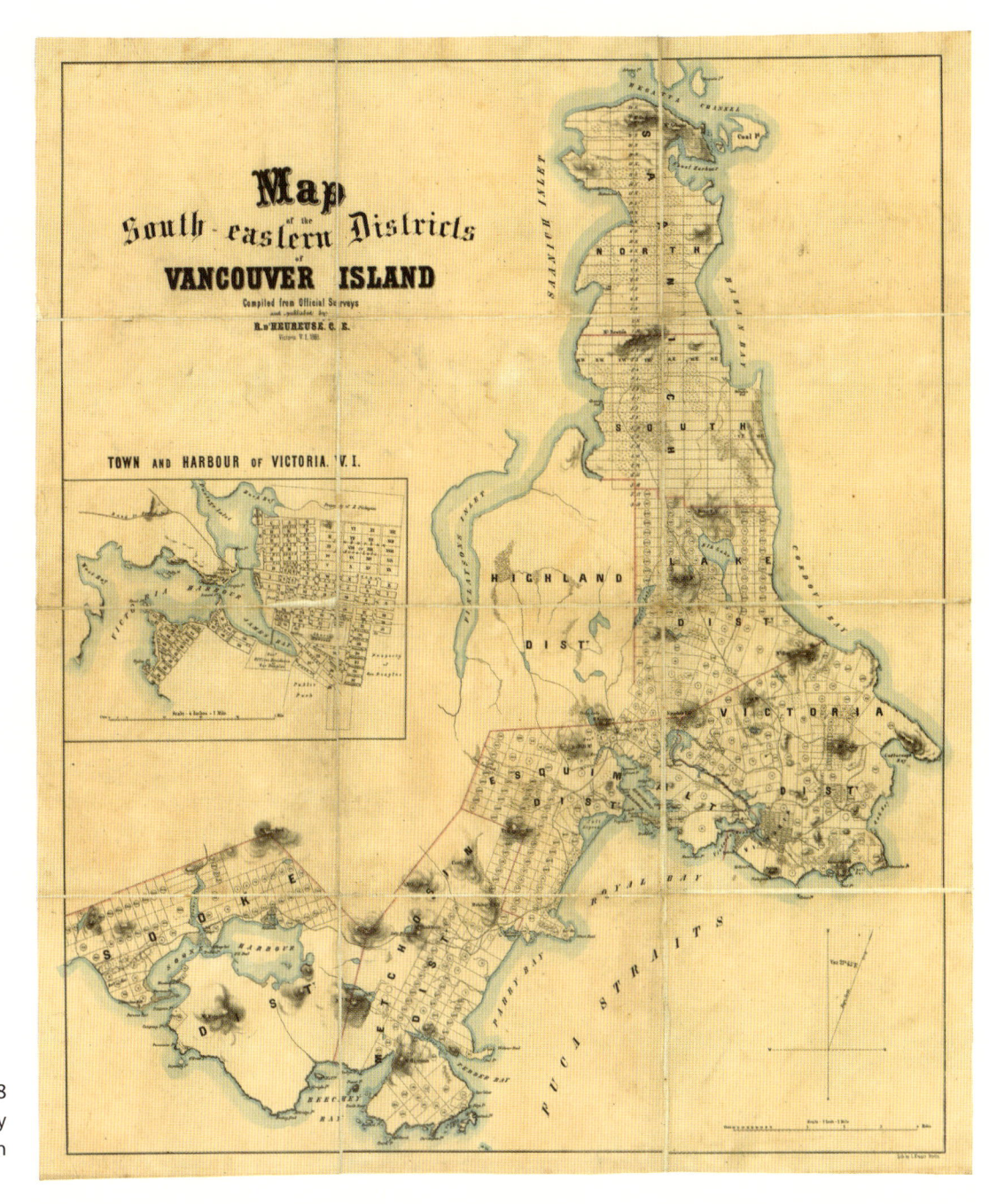

Fig. 82 Another version of Tiedemann's 1858 map was drawn and published in 1860 by Rudolph d'Heureuse, who sent it to the Berlin lithographer Leopold Kaatz for printing.

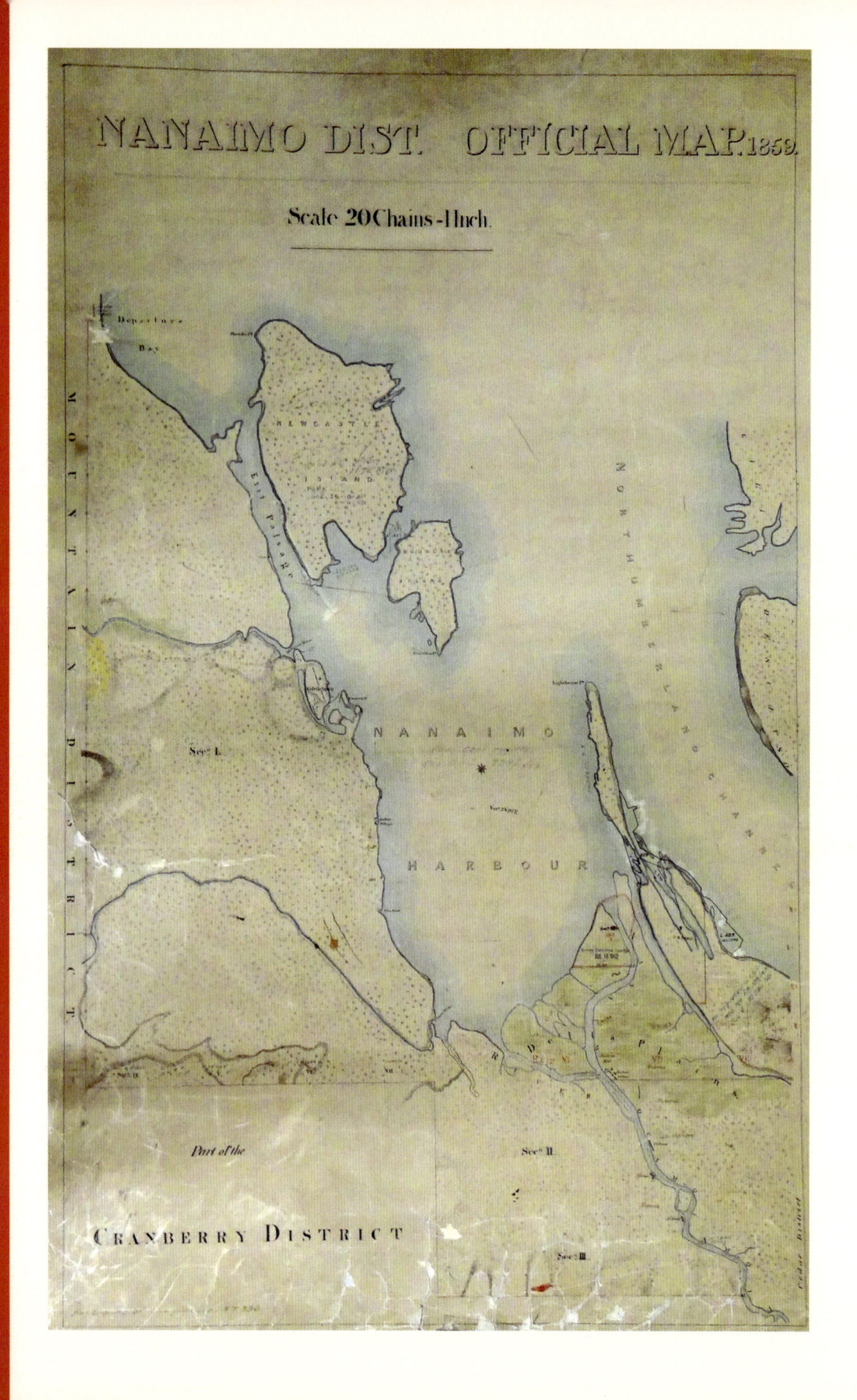

Fig. 83 In 1859 Pemberton and his team worked on several maps simultaneously, adding information as it came in. This draft-in-progress shows the island's second-largest community, Colviletown, in the early stages of its development.

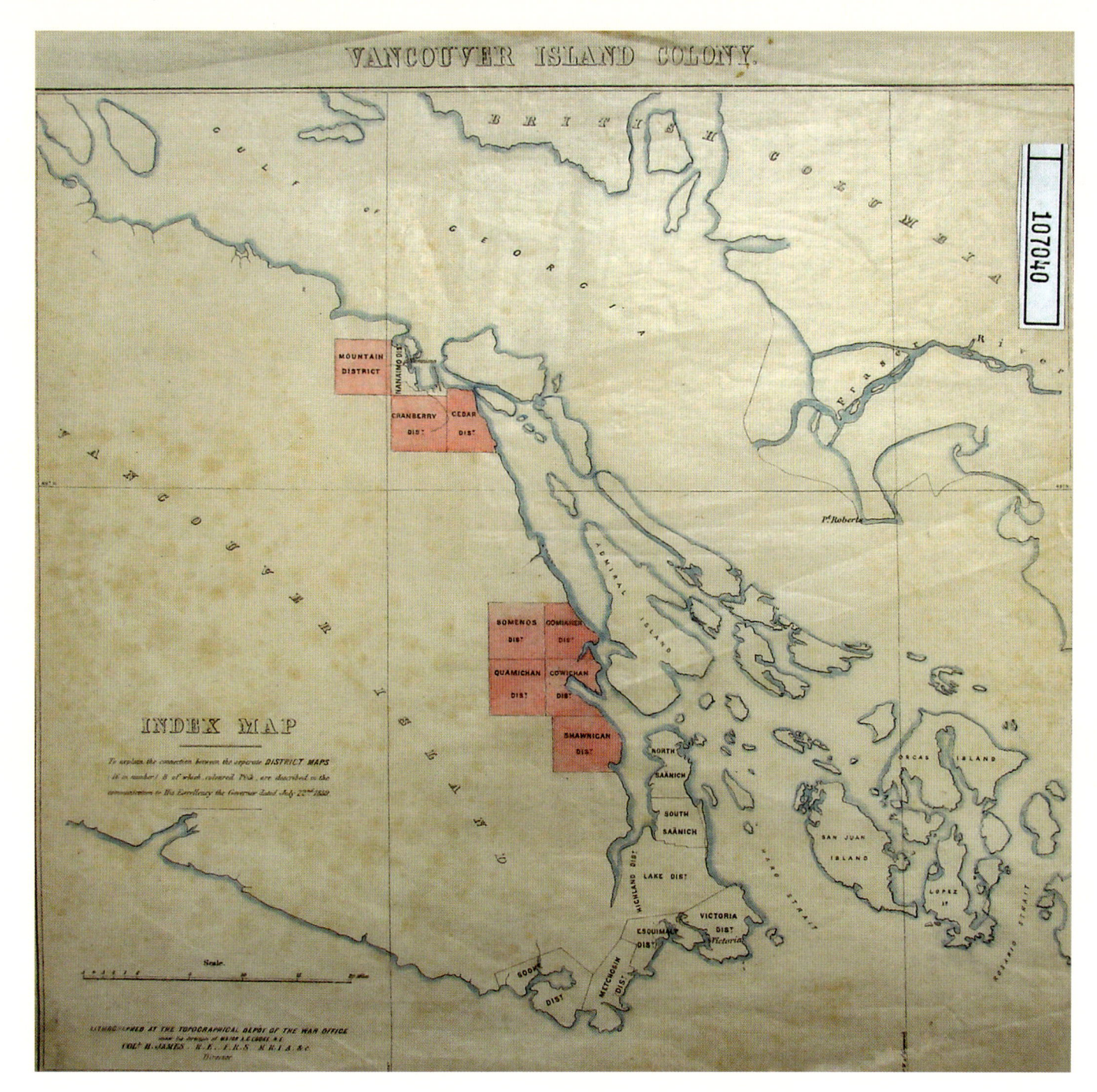

Fig. 84 Supporting official efforts to promote farming on Vancouver Island, Pemberton's surveyors made eight maps of the Cowichan Valley and the area around Nanaimo. The Royal Engineers printed these maps in England; this is their index to the map sheets.

they be lithographed and made available to potential settlers. Bulwer Lytton agreed and arranged with the War Office for printing by Royal Engineers lithographers at their Topographic Depot. Copies were provided to the Emigration Commission and to the Royal Geographical Society as well as shipped to Victoria for local distribution. (See Fig. 84, page 139)

Young, the colonial secretary in Victoria, published a two-page report on the Cowichan Valley by Wells, who wrote: "I am firmly persuaded that under a common, judicious system of farming as good returns can be obtained from these lands as in any part of the Continent of America."[2] The commissioners in London also published a *Survey of the Districts of Nanaimo and Cowichan Valley* based on the reports by Pearse and Wells.

Wells's report and the new district maps helped trigger another flurry of land speculation in the Cowichan Valley. Nineteen people paid the first installment on a total of nearly ten thousand acres (four thousand hectares)—20 percent of what Pemberton estimated to be the best land on Vancouver Island. These investors included several from London and San Francisco, and even Lieutenant Mayne and Master Bedwell of HMS *Plumper*. They purchased "Cowichan Scrip"—options to take up parcels at the Wakefield rate of one pound per acre. Except for one case, this was a pure gamble.

Douglas was concerned that Native title to the Cowichan lands had not been resolved. Suspecting that this issue could return, he wrote to the Colonial Office in London, proposing that the estimated one thousand Native families be paid for their lands at the same rate as his purchases of title for the area around Victoria in 1850, a total of three thousand pounds. To do this, he would require an advance from colonial funds against revenues from land sales. Lord Newcastle, secretary of state for the colonies, acknowledged the logic in Douglas's idea, but declined to authorize the advance.

Wells's survey posts were "removed by Indians" within three years, although there appears to have been little overt hostility toward the settlers themselves, and brush fires obliterated his cutlines, further complicating the process of pre-emption.

At the close of 1859 Pemberton departed on a year's leave, with full confidence in Pearse's competence to run the land office. In the spring, a new task was assigned to the team, that of laying down the principal roads through the districts of Victoria, Esquimalt, Metchosin, Saanich, and Lakes (the area around Elk, Beaver, and Prospect Lakes.) The acting surveyor general was to consult with committees made up of three local landowners as to the positioning of the roads. Sooke was soon added to the list. Supervising the layout and construction of the road network became a major element of the surveyor general's responsibilities.

Another major task at the office was helping to unscramble the complex web of real-estate transactions between the HBC (including its subsidiary, the Puget's Sound Agricultural Company) and the Crown, both before and after the contract for colonization. (See Fig. 85) This was needed for calculating the financial settlement between the parties upon reconveyance of the colony back to the Crown. What was the price payable to the company? They did not resolve this until April 3, 1867, some eight years after the colonial secretary in London took over responsibility for the colony from the company. The figure eventually arrived at was £57,500, with the company retaining title to several blocks of land in and around Victoria. During the company's tenure, 162,505 acres (65,800 hectares) of Vancouver Island, from a total of some 7.5 million, had been sold or pre-empted.

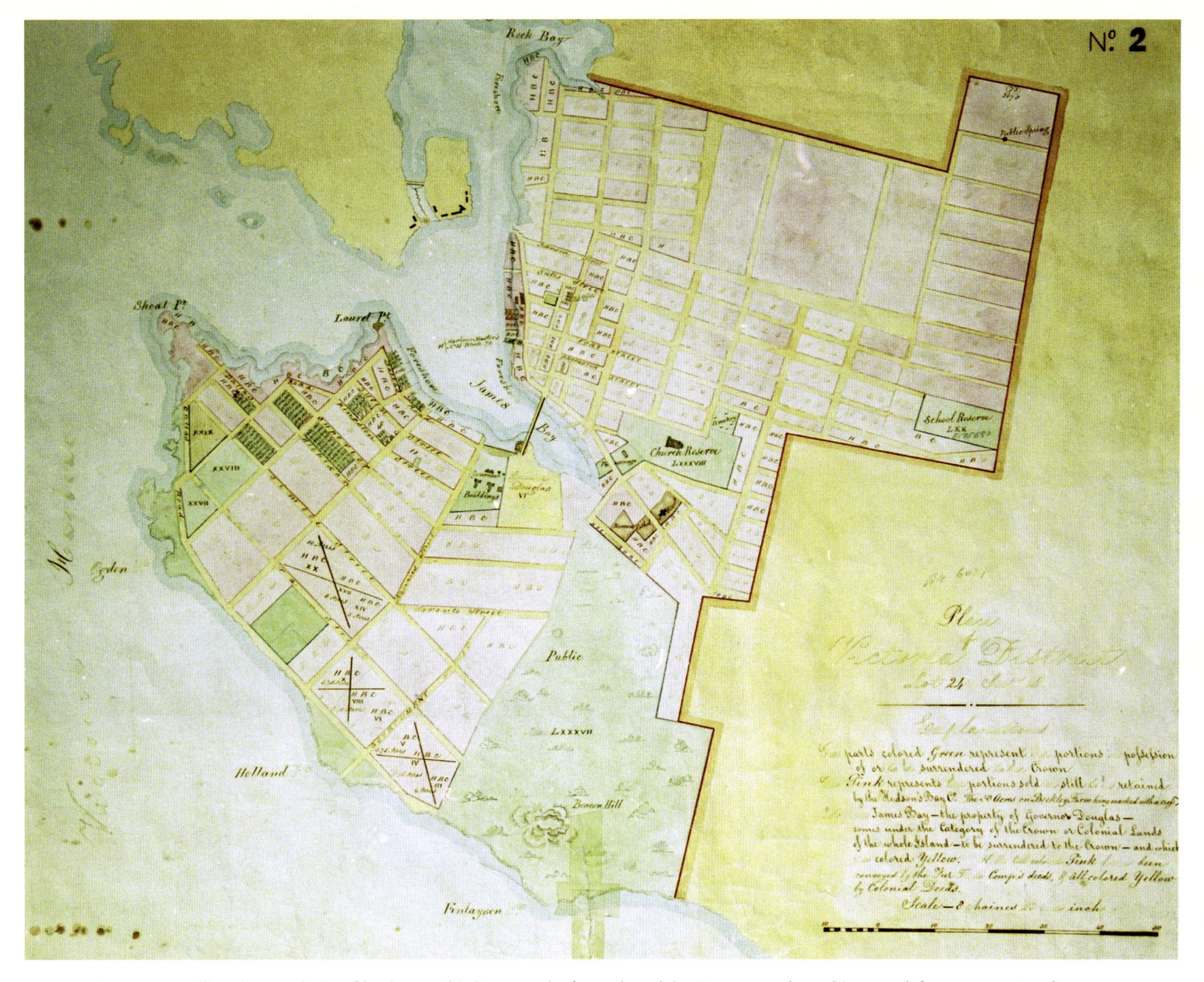

Fig. 85   Unravelling the complexity of land ownership between the fur trade and the Crown proved a multi-year task for surveyors. As a first step, this 1862 map summarized the holdings according to the HBC.

In London, Pemberton addressed the second of the emigration commissioners' requests for details about the two colonies and their potential. By August, he had written and had published a book, *Facts and Figures relating to Vancouver Island and British Columbia Showing What to Expect and How to Get There*.

Pemberton included, as the first four of fourteen appendices, explorers' reports on the interior of Vancouver Island: his own overland expeditions from Nanaimo to Alberni and from Cowichan Bay to Nitinat; Moffatt's exploration from Nimpkish to Nootka; and Vancouver's notes *On the Country in the Neighbourhood of Point Breakers* (Estevan Point). He also furnished four useful maps drawn by Edward Weller, the Royal Geographical Society's cartographer.

In 1861, when Pemberton returned from his year's leave in England, Pearse reported to him that the sets of results from the trigonometric surveys along the coast, by themselves and by Richards, had been compared. Between the two sets, they found a difference of only 60 feet (18 metres) for the distance between Sooke and Nanaimo, about 70 miles (113 kilometres). Pemberton's two-man team, with just a canoe and five voltigeurs, having to climb giant trees in order to take angles with a sextant, had come up with a measurement close to that made by a much larger team of well-equipped surveyors and two hundred sailors. This was cause for satisfaction.

In a letter written by Young, the Legislative Assembly put a formal question to the surveyor general concerning the progress of inland exploration of the island. Pemberton responded that budget constraints had made such exploring activity impossible because he had given priority to cadastral work and the design of the road network. Young replied to confirm that the governor concurred with this response.

For a few years Pemberton had been suggesting to Douglas that Victoria be incorporated as a city, and in the summer of 1862, the assembly passed a bill to this effect. (See Fig. 86) As a result, Pemberton and Pearse saw their real estate holdings take another jump in value, and they were now both financially comfortable.

Lord Newcastle warned Douglas, privately and well in advance, that his dual governorships were coming to an end. The formal public announcement came later that year, 1863, accompanied by the governor's elevation to the peerage. Henceforth, he was addressed as Sir James Douglas, KCB (Knight Commander of the Order of the Bath). Disagreements with Colonel Moody marred the last few years of the Douglas governorship, although the timely arrival and visible presence of the Royal Engineers' Columbia Detachment had ensured that the fledgling colony of British Columbia, and probably Vancouver Island as well, remained within Queen Victoria's empire.

Early the following spring, Pemberton went again to London on a special mission to acquire dredging equipment for Victoria Harbour. Fellow passengers on Pemberton's return voyage included another distinguished Irishman: Arthur Edward Kennedy was on his way to be sworn in as the new governor of the colony of Vancouver Island, replacing Douglas.

Fig. 86 In 1862 Victoria was incorporated as a city, and Pemberton prepared an official map to accompany the formal document, the Victoria Incorporation Act 1862.

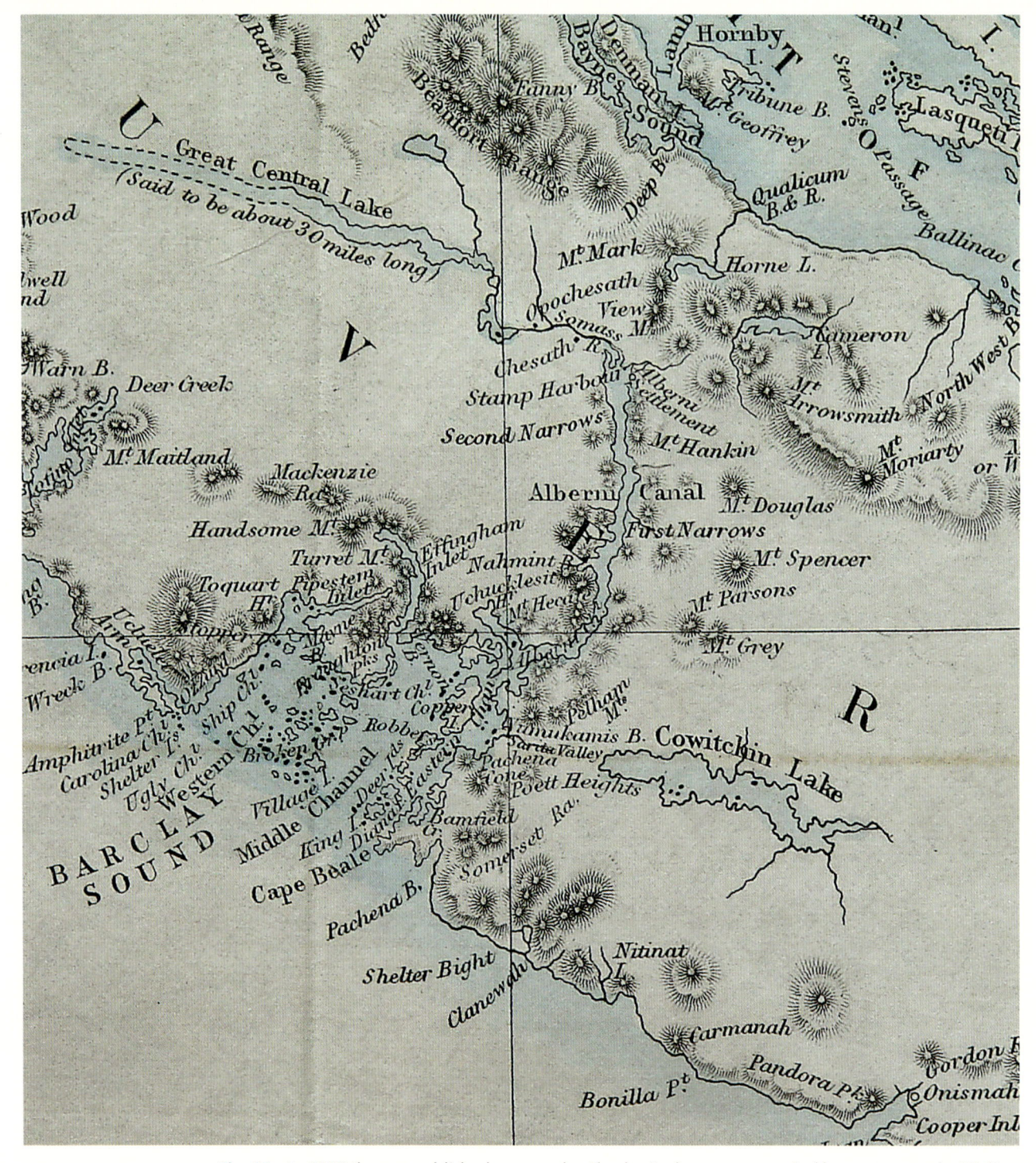

Fig. 87   In 1865 the RGS published an essay by Charles Forbes, accompanied by a new map by Weller.

CHAPTER SEVENTEEN

The Vancouver Island Exploring Expeditions: Brown, Leech, Meade, and Buttle Head Inland

THE MAN WHO STEPPED ASHORE at Victoria on Good Friday, March 25, 1864, carried himself with a distinguished military bearing. Seventeen years' service as an officer in the British Army, followed by eight as a colonial governor, had given Arthur Edward Kennedy confidence. He knew that he could, once again, bring administrative order to an imperial outpost that had not been running well.

Across the Strait of Georgia, Kennedy's counterpart in British Columbia was another experienced colonial governor, Frederick Seymour. The British government had instructed both of them to bring about the union of the two colonies. This aroused bitter opposition from the Vancouver Island Legislative Assembly, because it posed a threat to its senior status. There was one matter, however, upon which Kennedy and everyone in Victoria—including Sir James Douglas himself—could agree: the need for a thorough reconnaissance of the island's interior, in particular to find economically viable mineral deposits, preferably gold.

In 1865 the Royal Geographical Society published the paper by Dr. Charles Forbes, *Notes on the Physical Geography of Vancouver Island*, that had been read at its meeting of March 14 the previous year. One of Edward Weller's maps supported the 1865 article, but it showed little topographic detail in the interior: just a few peaks, a supposed "Great Central Lake said to be about 30 miles [48 kilometres] long," and elements drawn from Hankin's 1862 traverse from Tahsish to the Nimpkish River, with the village of Cheslakees indicated at its mouth. Weller also drew "Cowitchin Lake" at about the right size, shape, and orientation, but misplaced it to the west by some twenty-five miles (forty kilometres). (See Fig. 87)

Also in 1862, another naval surgeon based in Esquimalt, Alexander Rattray, published *Vancouver Island and British Columbia; Where they are; what they are; and what they may become*. His book included a small outline sketch map, three scenic engravings, and two meteorological diagrams. The author addressed what was then becoming an issue: "Our unhappily imperfect knowledge of the greater part of

Vancouver Island necessarily renders any inquiry respecting it both incomplete and unsatisfactory. A large part of it remains to be explored. An urgent necessity exists for a complete survey of the interior of the island."[1]

On both the island and the mainland, settlers had been experiencing violent opposition to their presence from the indigenous population. Fatal incidents had occurred at Bamfield, in the Gulf Islands, in Bute Inlet—in a massacre triggering the so-called Chilcotin War—and in Clayoquot Sound. Kennedy immediately identified the root cause of the trouble—failure to negotiate with Native people for access by European settlers to their traditional lands—but could obtain no promise of financial support for treaties from the Colonial Office in London.

At the first opportunity, while visiting exciting new diggings on the outskirts of Victoria, at the optimistically named Goldstream, Kennedy issued a challenge: If a privately organized and funded expedition of exploration were to be mounted, he would officially sponsor it with a matching contribution of two dollars for every one raised from the public. This struck a receptive chord. Local businessmen formed a committee to set about the twin tasks of raising the funds and recruiting suitably qualified personnel for the expedition itself.

A week later, the local paper carried a two-part letter addressed to the editors; entitled "The Land We Live In," it was signed with the pseudonym "Geographicus." The letter concerned the scope of the exploring expedition, pointing out that the interior of the island was not totally unknown and listing the earlier reconnaissances made by Pemberton, Mayne, Horne, and Moffatt. The thrust of the letter was the common knowledge that in the interior of the island there were several areas "worthy of renewed and thorough examination." The writer concluded by offering his services to the expedition "as a volunteer and not as a salaried servant."[2]

Geographicus turned out to be a botanical collector, Robert Brown, who was working on a meagre contract to an Edinburgh group. He had already made brief visits to Alberni and some west coast villages, and at Alberni he had examined two nearby lakes, Sproat and Great Central. He had been well received in Victoria but was neglecting his responsibilities toward his sponsors in Scotland: almost a year had elapsed and they had yet to receive a single seed from him.

This self-assured and plausible young man, who could count just a few weeks of experience in the mountainous forests of Vancouver Island, hard up financially and with a dissatisfied sponsor, had offered his services free to the Exploration Committee. He asserted his entitlement to the designation "doctor"—of medicine or philosophy, he was not specific. Despite his limited credentials, the committee was persuaded, and at their next public meeting they appointed Dr. Robert Brown "Commander and (Acting) Government Agent for the Vancouver Island Exploring Expedition."

As his deputy, termed "lieutenant," they nominated a recent member of the Royal Engineers' Columbia Detachment who had opted to remain when it was disbanded. Dublin-born Second Corporal Peter Leech was a trained survey technician, specializing in astronomical observation and computation of latitude and longitude.

Two more ex-sapper NCOs were selected for the team. Corporal John Buttle, who had been with the Boundary Commission, had trained at Britain's Ordnance Survey for four years as a surveyor and cartographic draftsman. Since he had also received instruction at the Royal Botanic Gardens at Kew in the collection and preservation of botanical specimens, his title on the team was "naturalist." The other ex-sapper was Lance Corporal John Meade, who had served with the Columbia Detachment and showed excellent cartographic ability on the expedition.

Another interesting team member carried the title of "artist," but Frederick Whymper contributed far more to the expedition than illustrations. His father and brother were both famous mountaineers, and he too was a rugged outdoorsman.

Brown set strict rules for the expedition's operations. Each member was required to keep a daily journal, which would belong to the expedition, as would any maps they drew.

One more member, termed "hunter," would join them at Cowichan. Known throughout the region as Tomo Antoine, he was a small, scruffy character with one arm. Tomo was the son of an Iroquois voyageur, who had come out west with the fur trade, and a Chinook woman from the Columbia River. He had arrived with Douglas at the founding of Fort Victoria twenty years earlier and had already accompanied several journeys of exploration across the island. Once they were under way, Brown soon realized that Tomo's "single arm was worth more than most men's two, and without [his] help the map of Vancouver [Island] would have been but a sorry blank yet, and the first exploring expedition a forgotten affair."[3] Tomo spoke good French and English, as well as several local languages, and he had drawn two sketch maps of the lakes and rivers of the Cowichan region.

Brown was also delighted to discover through his new interpreter that "every bend has a name, every hill a story, every dark pool a tradition." Each night around the campfire, Kakalatza, a local chief recruited as their guide, became an enthralling teller of traditional tales.

At each base camp, clouds permitting, Leech found their geodetic position by astro-observation using a sextant and chronometer, and he and the other surveyors climbed peaks to take bearings to surrounding landmarks. These results were the first reliable measurements obtained in the interior of Vancouver Island and a major achievement of the exploring expedition. Whymper, too, made effective use of his time in camp to sketch and paint scenery, people, camp life, and incidents from their journey, a further valuable legacy of the expedition.

The first phase of the trek started from Cowichan Bay, where they benefited from the printed district maps by Oliver Wells. (See Fig. 88, page 146) Midway along Cowichan Lake, the team divided into two. One party, under Leech, went south, heading for Port San Juan. Brown led the others westward on foot down the Nitinat River and Nitinat Lake and then by canoe to rendezvous with Leech's group at Port San Juan. There, Brown decided he needed a meeting with the committee, so, leaving Leech to ascend the Sooke River with the main party, he departed for Victoria. After Brown's departure, Leech discovered promising signs of placer gold on a tributary later named the Leech River.

In Victoria, Brown learned that his view of the objectives for the expedition differed from that of the committee. They did not see it as broad-spectrum, scientific fieldwork, or even a mapping reconnaissance, but as a mission to prospect for gold. He had also fallen into disfavour with his original sponsors in Scotland.

❊ ❊ ❊

The Reverend Matthew Macfie, FRGS, had arrived in Victoria in 1859 and spent the next five years tending a motley flock, observing their quirks and learning much about the two colonies. During his time in Canada and following his return to Britain, he gave a series of lectures on what he had seen and learned. He compiled those lecture notes into a book, *Vancouver Island and British Columbia: their history, resources, and prospects*, intended "chiefly for

Fig. 88   Robert Brown's exploring expedition annotated this copy of the Cowichan Bay sheet, one of Oliver Wells's maps for the Emigration Commission. A note off the south shore of the estuary indicates the position of their supply vessel.

the perusal of merchants, statesmen and intending emigrants." It was published by Longman, Green, Longman, Roberts & Green of London in 1865.

While acknowledging that his book was not the first to address the topics, Macfie felt that the changes he had witnessed rendered previous titles outdated and confusing. His publisher commissioned two folding maps from Edward Weller to be bound into the text. The book provided interesting lists and statistics as well as perceptive, amusing vignettes, and anecdotes of life, society, and characters, pulling no punches when commenting on the influence of the HBC and James Douglas himself. Macfie applauded the exploration initiative of the new governor, Kennedy, and the early bulletins from Robert Brown.

One of Weller's maps showed British Columbia and Vancouver Island (See Fig. 89, page 149), the other the proposed route of a "Transcontinental Waggon Road & Telegraph." Macfie strongly advocated building such a route.

Richards's charts, and explorations by Pemberton and other HBC employees, added to the cartographic detail of Vancouver Island; however, the map was at half the scale of Weller's map of the same year in Charles Forbes's paper for the RGS *Journal*, and it contained far less detail. It did indicate the gold found near Sooke and three possibilities for the boundary through the San Juan Archipelago.

After briefly reuniting at Cowichan, the Vancouver Island Exploring Expedition again divided, with Leech leading an exploration inland from Nanaimo, while Brown investigated the Comox Valley. Leech's party arrived at the rendezvous of Port Alberni first, joined by the others two weeks later. During his wait, Meade sketched maps of their various journeys into eighteen pages of his journal, recording the discoveries of both parties.

Having been in the field for twenty weeks, the expedition members returned to Victoria to learn that they had become celebrities. Several hundred miners had established a community called Leechtown at the junction of the Leech and Sooke Rivers, and were actively working the rivers; rumour had it that more than a hundred thousand dollars in gold had been extracted so far, doing wonders for the local economy and morale. A delighted Governor Kennedy invited Brown to give him a personal briefing.

Brown hoped that a follow-up expedition would be organized, and although he would not be available for it because of other commitments, he offered the benefit of his experience to the organizers. The government authorized publication of Brown's summary report, to praise by the local press.

Out of funds and feeling unable to mollify his Edinburgh sponsors, Brown offered them his resignation; they declined it but did not renew his contract. His plans for the future were to publish a popular version of his expedition, accompanied by Whymper's illustrations and Buttle's maps. The government of the colony allocated fifteen hundred dollars as a reward to the explorers, and Brown's share, four hundred dollars, enabled him to settle his debts.

He sent a summary of his expedition to the RGS, which published it in the society's *Journal* in 1865, and in 1866 returned to Britain with a collection of notes and maps, intending further research and publication.

In early October 1864, after serving as Vancouver Island's senior surveyor for thirteen years, Joseph Pemberton resigned as surveyor general. This also meant stepping down from membership on the Executive Council. His long-time deputy and close friend, Benjamin Pearse, replaced him in both roles. Curiously, Pearse and his staff at the lands office appear to have had little connection with the exploring expedition beyond preparing a plan of Leechtown and designing an access road from Sooke.

The overall economic situation of Vancouver Island continued to deteriorate, and severe depression loomed. Kennedy agreed with London that the only solution was to unite the two colonies, despite vociferous opposition from both populations. In the meantime, however, for the island, there remained the possibility of another Leech River. The governor took personal command of the search for it, as the previous year's Exploration Committee had been quietly disbanded. He heeded the advice of Robert Brown that the best candidate to lead the next mission would be John Buttle; in early June, Kennedy announced that Buttle was to lead the 1865 exploring expedition with six companions.

They started at Tofino in Clayoquot Sound. Since this inlet had been the scene of conflict between the Royal Navy and the Ahousaht people, the gunboat HMS *Forward* carried them. From the eastern side of the inlet, the team ascended a stream to find a large body of fresh water. Buttle recorded: "I resolved to call the whole sheet of water Lake Kennedy—the largest fresh water lake yet discovered on the Island."[4] He constructed an excellent sketch map of the lake and its feeder streams.

After meeting their supply ship, Buttle and his team continued exploring up Bedwell Arm and the Bear (now Bedwell) River. He divided the group; one party continued to prospect up the main stream while he ascended a tributary, now called Ursus Creek. He climbed a one-mile (eighteen-hundred-metre) snow-covered peak to find that he was surrounded by dramatic scenery.

Toward Comox Buttle could see what appeared to be "a beautiful sheet of water at least twenty miles [thirty-two kilometres] long ... either a chain of lakes or a large lake with islands in it,"[5] and he drafted a clear sketch map of where he had been and what he had discovered. Subsequent explorers, surveyors, and mountaineers have puzzled over which lake Buttle saw. With higher mountains intervening, it would not have been possible for him to see the lake that was later named Buttle.

In the Bear River his other party discovered traces of gold that offered "profitable and paying diggings." When this news reached Victoria, another gold rush ensued. This time, no gold was extracted and the angry prospectors returned to voice unjustified complaints over Buttle's "misleading" report. Meanwhile, the expedition continued investigating Hesquiat and Nootka Sounds. Buttle's last foray, before winter set in, was up Tahsis Inlet and the Tahsis River, across the divide and onto Conuma Lake, now Woss Lake.

The 1865 exploring expedition returned to Victoria, but, unlike the previous year, not to a heroes' welcome. Buttle found that his reputation had been badly tarnished; mortified, he fled with his family for San Francisco.

On his return to Britain, Robert Brown worked at getting his many articles, both learned and popular, published but was unable to find a serious British publisher for his *Memoir on the Geography of the Interior of Vancouver Island*. Beginning in 1869, H.W. Bates, secretary to the RGS and editor of a multi-volume *Illustrated Travels*, published Brown's four-part account of the Vancouver Island expedition, but without including a map.[6]

Also in 1869, the prestigious German journal *Geographischer Mittheilungen*, edited by Augustus Petermann (who had worked for several years in London), did accept Brown's memoir. It published a twenty-page German translation accompanied by a detailed map. The renowned cartographic publisher Justus Perthes of Gotha produced the two-colour, steel-engraved, and

Fig. 89 The Reverend Macfie's 1865 book included two maps by Weller. He shows, in a cartographic first, the discovery of gold near Sooke.

Fig. 90 The minute cartographic detail made possible by steel engraving could sometimes render maps illegible at published scale. The density of information provided here by Brown would have been far clearer if printed at 2x or even 3x.

lithographed map, based on materials assembled and provided by Brown. (See Fig. 90)

Admiralty charts incorporating Captain George Richards's surveys were probably the primary cartographic source, and Brown included one feature, Snowsaddle Mountain, reported by Lieutenant Philip Hankin as lying to the west of the upper valley of the Tahsish Arm of Kyuquot Sound. Richards had incorporated it into his charts, even giving its elevation: 4,151 feet (1,262 metres). This peak was in an area beyond that explored by either Brown's or Buttle's teams.

Other additions to the interior topography of the island were derived from the sketch maps made by members of Brown's team, particularly Meade and Buttle, from the Buttle expedition, and from Brown's own later enquiries. The toponymy of the map was rendered in a mixture of German and English. "Vancouver I." lay between "Grosser Ocean" and the "Strait of Georgia," next to "Britisch Columbia." Coastal and interior place names were in English.

The scale of the printed map, 1:1.3 million, reflected the limitations imposed by the format of the journal and, unfortunately, rendered the wealth of relief and drainage detail and the toponymy difficult to read.

The topographic detail was dense in the region covered by Brown's expedition and by Buttle's. The lakes and rivers actually explored by the expeditions were plotted with reasonable accuracy. Brown included the detail from Buttle's reconnaissance maps of Kennedy Lake; the shape and position shown were remarkably good, to Buttle's credit, but the size was somewhat enlarged. Brown (or his German cartographic compiler) also did a fair job of presenting the Tahsis-Nimpkish trail, combining Buttle's Conuma Lake with Moffatt's report of a Lake Kanus. The axis of Nimpkish Lake, however, was shown about thirty degrees too far southwest. Nitinat Lake was also skewed, running east-west instead of northeast-southwest, and the lake was shown much wider than it really is.

Brown's map also included several significant errors. The "beautiful stretch of water" that Buttle thought he had seen from the mountain at the head of Ursus Creek was depicted as and named "Buttle Lake." Also shown as possible features, by barely discernible pecked lines, were the nonexistent "Chemainos Lake" and a large, unnamed lake at the headwaters of the Salmon River. This latter, Brown explained in his *Memoir*, derived from "a family of Nuchultaws, whom I met on the river in 1866." There was an exaggerated and malpositioned "Muchalat Lake," possibly confused with reports of the lake later named Vernon. Sooke and Shawnigan Lakes were similarly exaggerated in extent.

Despite such examples of cartographic guesswork, the map recorded the important findings of the Brown and Buttle expeditions, and two years later it provided valuable source material for the so-called "Trutch Map."

No English version of Brown's *Memoir* ever appeared in print, although there is an original manuscript in the BC Archives—sadly, without Brown's manuscript map.[7] The RGS did, however, publish a paper by Brown in its 1869 *Journal*: "On the Formation of Fjords, Cañons, Benches, Prairies and Intermittent Rivers," in which he theorized on the glacial cause of the Norwegian fjords and the inlets of the BC coast. Weller contributed a map of Vancouver Island for that article, essentially a reduced version of the map that had accompanied the German version of the *Memoir*. (See Figs. 91 and 92)

On the strength of the article in Petermann's *Mittheilungen* and its map, the German University of Rostock granted the author an honorary doctorate; Robert Brown was, at last, entitled to put "Dr." before his name.

CHAPTER SEVENTEEN   151

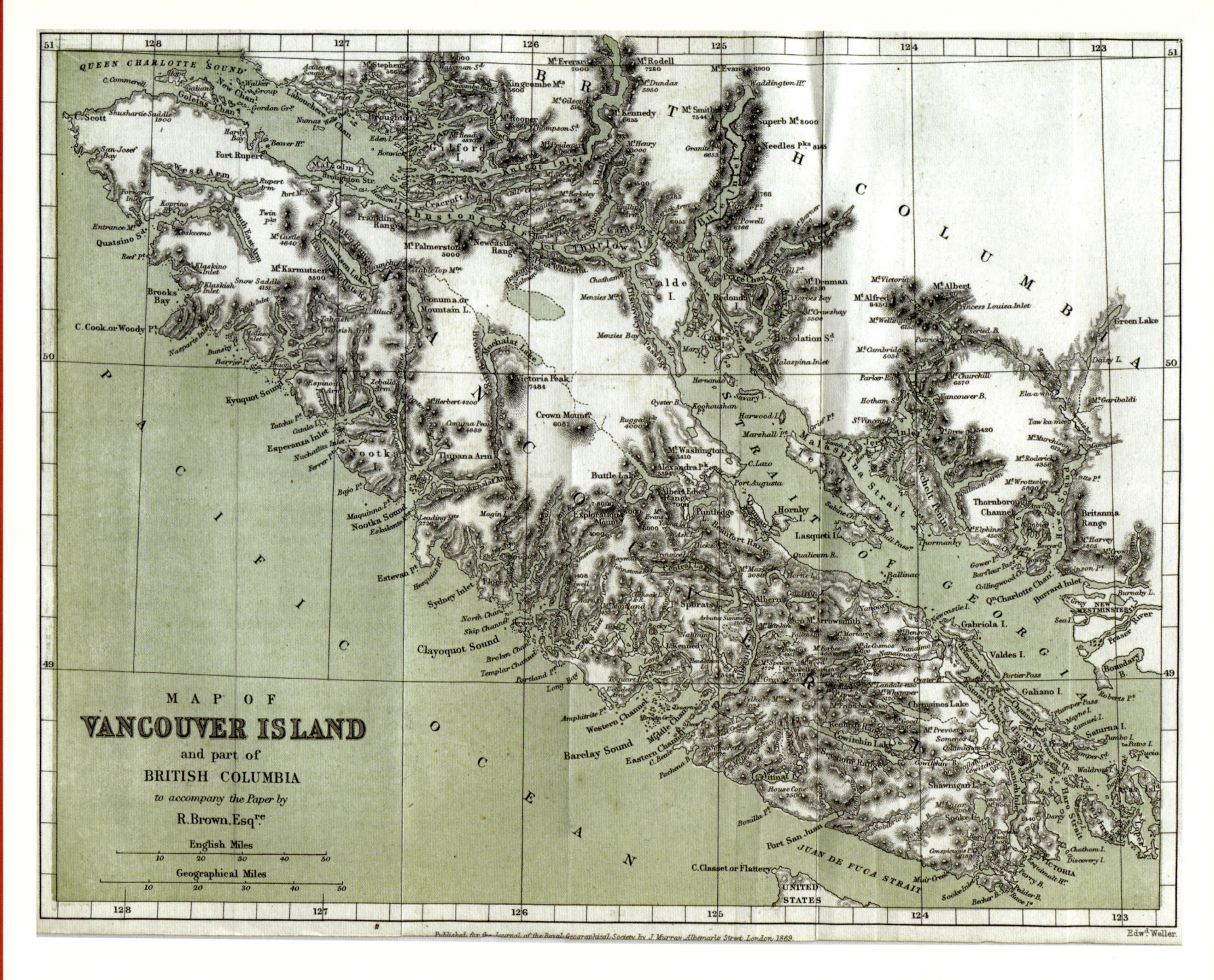

Fig. 91 Weller drew heavily on Petermann's map of the discoveries of the Vancouver Island Exploring Expedition to illustrate an unrelated paper by Brown.

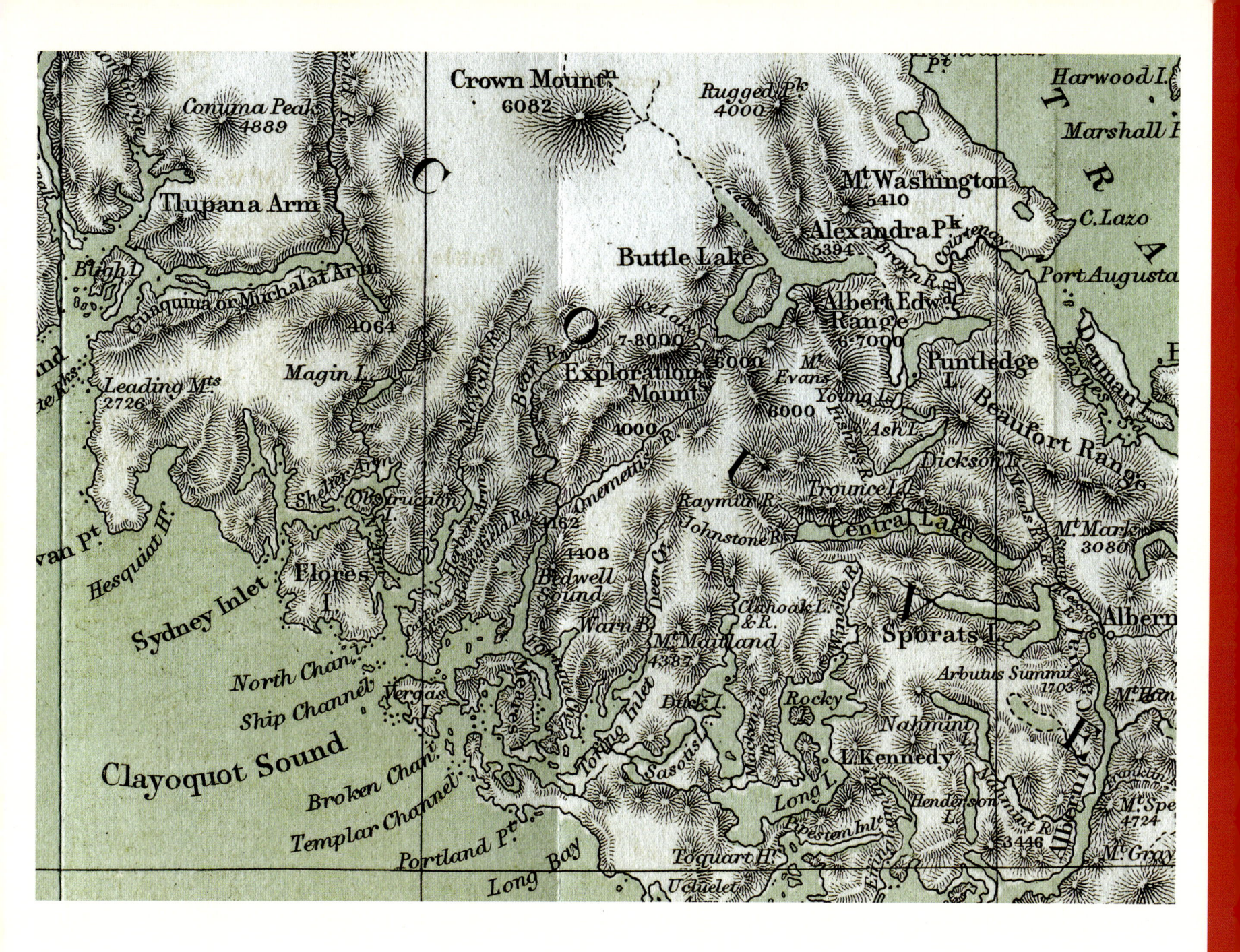

Fig. 92 The body of water seen by Buttle, named by Brown and depicted here, did not exist. It was probably a low-lying, dense bank of fog. Another major lake, discovered later, was given Buttle's name.

CHAPTER EIGHTEEN

Canada's New Province: To Celebrate, Joseph Trutch Orders a Map

DURING THE MID-1860S, THE ALREADY dire economic situation of both British colonies on the west coast continued to deteriorate. Vancouver Island, refused further credit, faced imminent bankruptcy, and London mandated the union of the colonies. Under that Act, Arthur Kennedy was to hand the governorship of Vancouver Island to Frederick Seymour.

For a while, the capital of the united colony was New Westminster, but through trickery in a contentious vote, the Victoria faction managed to change that. The formal transfer of the seat of government took place in May 1868, with much of the combined civil service relocating. Among the technicians in the lands and works department transferring from New Westminster to Victoria was a talented cartographic draftsman, James Benjamin Launders. He had arrived as a second corporal with the Royal Engineers' Columbia Detachment and, when it disbanded in November 1863, stayed on to continue mapping the interior of British Columbia.

Between field survey assignments, Launders worked on compiling a multi-sheet map of British Columbia at the scale of 10 miles to 1 inch (1:633,600). This was a project that had been started under Colonel Richard Moody, RE. It incorporated the work of the Royal Engineers with that of later explorers—government, naval, and private—and township mapping associated with the gold rushes. Launders brought the project with him to Victoria.

Joseph Trutch, the commissioner of Lands and Works, was familiar with Launders and his cartographic expertise. Before being appointed commissioner, Trutch had been a surveyor and an engineering contractor, designing and building major sections of the Cariboo highway. He had also built and operated the Alexandra toll bridge over the Fraser River, profiting handsomely on the contract. While he was on survey projects, he had looked out for and acquired extensive real-estate holdings on the mainland and around Victoria.

Trutch also knew the importance that a complete, up-to-date, topographic map of the province would hold for effective governance; he arranged that Launders would produce a single-sheet, reduced-scale map to be printed and distributed. The cartographer started on this new map at the scale of 25 miles to 1 inch (1:1.6 million approximately), while his superior arranged funding for its publication.

Governor Seymour did nothing to address the $1.3-million debt he had inherited. Late in 1867, he even requested a further loan of fifty thousand dollars from London and his plea was answered with silence. Two new political factions emerged: the Annexationists, advocating that the colony apply to join the United States—which had just acquired Alaska—and the Confederationists, who proposed a similar arrangement with the new Dominion of Canada. Joseph Pemberton came out in favour of the Annexationists, unless a railway were built to connect BC with the settled regions of the Dominion. Sir James Douglas, watching from the sidelines, called the whole situation "a strange, incomprehensible muddle."

Robert Brown had concluded his 1869 *Memoir* with the comment: "With these and other elements of prosperity [lumber, coal, and salmon], notwithstanding the present state of affairs, I see no reason to doubt the ultimate success of the English Pacific Colony more especially since Vancouver Island and British Columbia are united under one government and the people seem inclined to have a little more work and a little less politics."[1]

During the American Civil War, the question of jurisdiction over San Juan Island had remained quiet, the island's mixed population and twin military establishments co-existing in reasonable harmony. Following the war, American politicians, both federal and local, attempted to fan the embers of the old dispute. In 1869, the colonial secretary in London and the American ambassador there agreed to reopen the issue of the Strait of Georgia water boundary.

The man who, in 1869, replaced Seymour as governor was Anthony Musgrave, an able administrator and shrewd politician. Aided by Trutch, he skilfully orchestrated the union of British Columbia into confederation with Canada. A three-man delegation, with Trutch its de facto leader, went to Ottawa in June 1870 to negotiate the proposed terms. The delegates achieved all that they sought.

The resulting agreement included the construction of a transcontinental railway; also, Ottawa was to undertake a systematic geological survey of British Columbia. This latter provision was later interpreted to include geodesy and topography, and both of these provisions had significant impacts upon the mapping of the new province.

Trutch continued on to London in order to brief officials in the Colonial Office. He carried Launders's recently completed manuscript of the 25 miles to 1 inch map of the province, and negotiated with Edward Stanford, a cartographic publisher, to lithograph and print five hundred copies. Stanford had acquired the Arrowsmith firm's assets, including presses, plates, and stock of maps, including more than a dozen associated with Vancouver Island. Under the deal with Trutch, Stanford would own the copperplates and be able to sell copies of the new map of BC. The company also undertook to update those plates for a few years as new data came in, and provide copies of the new versions.

Early in 1871 the new, largely elected Legislative Council of BC voted to accept the terms of union. Governor Musgrave entrusted the negotiation of the entry into the Dominion to Trutch, who shuttled among Victoria, Ottawa, and London. He carried additions to Launders's map for Stanford to incorporate into the plate, then about to be printed. These corrections delayed publication, and the maps, usually dissected and mounted onto linen for protection, were available for distribution in the spring of 1872.

Fig. 93 Although often called "the Trutch Map," this masterwork of BC cartography was the single-handed product of the gifted but unfortunate James Launders. Shown here is just the portion covering Vancouver Island and the adjacent mainland.

The result was a cartographic masterwork. Launders's map of *British Columbia to the 56th parallel, north latitude* was a true snapshot of the state of the topographic knowledge at that time. The coastline reflected the work done by Captain Richards and continued by Pender. The detail combined the results of actual surveys with the best speculation available. The impact that the various gold rushes had had on the geographical knowledge of the region was graphic. Launders had spent a dozen years keeping track of exploration reports and reconnaissances across the mountainous vastness of the mainland and compiling them into a single map. (See Fig. 93)

Launders's knowledge of the geography of Vancouver Island was more limited. After moving to Victoria, he had access to the maps and records of Pemberton and Pearse, but had done no direct fieldwork there. Evidently, he consulted a copy of the Brown-Petermann "German" map of 1869, because he repeated many of its speculative or erroneous features. This rendered the map, a cartographic landmark of major value for British Columbia, less so for Vancouver Island.

There were no apparent changes to the terrain detail of the island between Launders's original of May 9, 1870, and the amended, printed version, so it seems that Pemberton did not review the work in progress. Had he done so, he might have corrected several errors in features that he had explored.

The map is often referred to as "the Trutch Map" and Launders, its single-handed creator, has been forgotten. Recent neglect, however, pales when compared to the lack of compassion or gratitude Launders received from his various superiors.

In 1869 Trutch had felt it necessary to report Launders's absenteeism, due to an addiction to alcohol, to the colonial secretary, and the response was that Launders should be formally warned that repetition could cause dismissal. Three years later, in one of his last acts as surveyor general, Pearse also complained to a new chief commissioner about Launders's "continued intemperate habits."[2] This time the report triggered Launders's letter of resignation. He received perfunctory acceptance and the rejection of his respectful plea that, in view of his twenty years of loyal but poorly rewarded service to the Crown, he be granted the fare home to England.

After BC joined the Canadian Confederation, Trutch returned to Ottawa, where Sir John A. Macdonald invited him to serve as lieutenant-governor. On August 14, 1871, Joseph Trutch was ceremonially sworn in.

❖ ❖ ❖

In 1873, just a year after publication of the Launders–Trutch map, a smaller, simpler version, printed in four colours, appeared in London. The agent-general for the new province, Gilbert Sproat, had commissioned the map from the cartographer James Wyld for inclusion in a handbook, *British Columbia Information for Emigrants*, which contained statistical tables and practical recommendations for would-be settlers and miners.

Wyld's map, at a scale of 47 miles to 1 inch (1:3 million), included Sproat's Lake, named by Robert Brown in recognition of a friendship formed when the latter was botanizing in the Alberni region prior to the Vancouver Island Exploring Expedition. The map also showed, clearly and correctly, the arbitrated water boundary through Haro Strait, and a dotted line marked "Projected Canadian Pacific Railroad" running down Bute Inlet, across Valdes Island—as the group of Quadra, Sonora, and Maurelle was known at that time—to Vancouver Island and down to Esquimalt, with a branch line to Alberni.

❖ ❖ ❖

In 1874, Launders attempted to show that, despite his alcoholism, his draftsmanship remained acute. He drew an ornate, cartographic north point that he left on the desk of A.S. Farwell, the new surveyor general. (See Fig. 94) The 3-inch (7.5-centimetre) arrow was made up of sixteen arms, each drawn with up to nine parallel lines of varied weights. At its centre, within a circle less than half an inch (a centimetre) in diameter, and in concentric circles, is printed the entire Lord's Prayer and the date—so finely that it can be deciphered only with a 3x magnifier. (See Fig. 95) Farwell curtly rejected Launders's accompanying request for reinstatement on the grounds that his "habits were insufficiently steady."³

Launders tried to earn a living as an engraver, first in Victoria and then in Nanaimo. He died in 1878 in that city, an alcoholic pauper. A brief announcement in the *Daily British Colonist* recorded his passing as that of "a surveyor and draftsman of no mean ability."⁴ He lies in an unmarked grave in the cemetery that, ironically, he had laid out as his ultimate survey project.

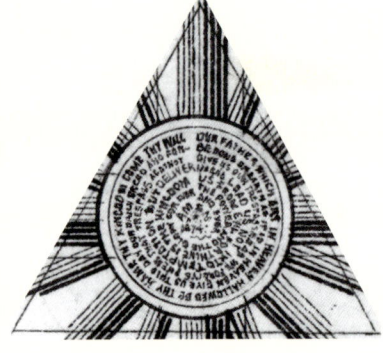

The year that Launders died, another talented draftsman was at work in Victoria. Eli Glover, an itinerant American cartographer who specialized in creating perspective or bird's-eye views of urban centres, spent four months working on the view of Victoria. Onto his perspective rendition of the latest town map available he drew twenty-five hundred buildings, shorelines, stands of trees, and skyline prominences, as if seen from a hypothetical height over Brotchie Ledge, near Ogden Point at the southwestern end of what is now James Bay, and looking northeast toward Mount Baker on the far horizon. Finally, he enlivened the scene by adding ships and sailboats on the water and carriages passing along Dallas Road.

Prominent among the houses Glover depicted was the residence of a notable merchant, Richard Carr, and his family. His second daughter, Emily, was then seven years old and later wrote her memories of the town at just that time in *The Book of Small* and *A Little Town and a Little Girl*. She concluded the former book with "Victoria's inner land being higher than her shore, every aspect is lovely... So stands tranquil Victoria in her island setting—Western as West can be before Earth's gentle rounding pulls West east again."⁵

Glover captured this mood well in his perspective view. The results of his work were printed lithographically in San Francisco and sold by Glover's local collaborator, stationers M.W. Waitt & Co. (See Figs. 96 and 97)

LEFT
Fig. 94   Ex-Royal Engineers cartographic draftsman Launders created this elaborate north point in a unsuccessful attempt to gain reinstatement with the lands office.

ABOVE
Fig. 95   The hub of Launders's north point, with the Lord's Prayer and the date (1874) inscribed, is shown here at 8x magnification. It failed to convince the authorities of the steadiness of Launders's hand.

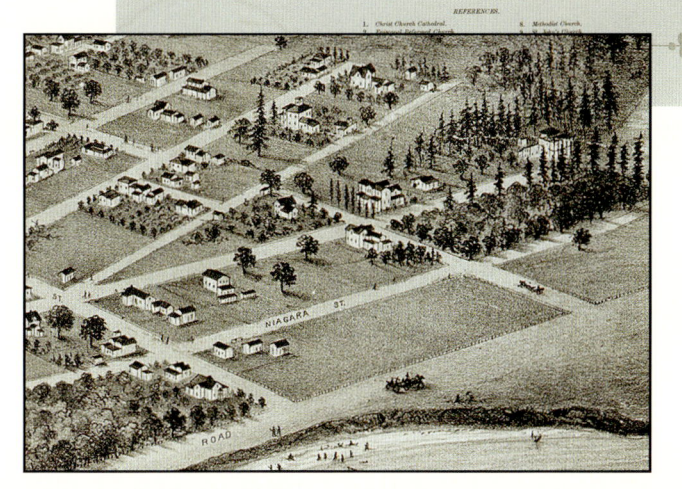

Fig. 96 A specialist in perspective cartography, Eli Glover compiled this artistic and accurate view of Victoria, based on the most recent version of the city's street plan, superimposing buildings and treed areas.

INSET
Fig. 97 Glover depicted James Bay at the time Emily Carr wrote about in *The Book of Small*. In the centre of this portion, just to the right of the triangular block, he showed Carr House.

Fig. 98   Sandford Fleming's surveyors explored various routes to bring the CPR to the Pacific. Route four came down Bute Inlet and crossed to Vancouver Island.

CHAPTER NINETEEN

The Two-Million-Acre Dowry: The Esquimalt & Nanaimo Railway's Land Grant

THE 1871 TERMS OF UNION of British Columbia into the Dominion of Canada included the construction of a railway "to connect the seaboard of British Columbia with the railway system of Canada." Construction was to start within two years and be completed within ten years of the date of the union. The Dominion would arrange and pay for the construction, and the new province would convey, in trust, title to a strip of land "not to exceed...twenty (20) miles [thirty-two kilometres] on each side of the said [railway] line."

British Columbia, in its official *Gazette*, interpreted the description of the island grant as being "a strip of land twenty miles [thirty-two kilometres] in width along the Eastern Coast of Vancouver Island between Seymour Narrows and the Harbour of Esquimalt." Vancouver Islanders hoped this wording strengthened their case that "seaboard of British Columbia" meant the railway, instead of terminating somewhere on the mainland, would reach the west coast of the island, at Alberni or Esquimalt.

The question of routing was key, and depended on better topographic information than was currently available. On July 20, 1871—the formal entry of BC into the Dominion—Canadian Pacific Railway (CPR) surveyors, under engineer-in-chief Sandford Fleming, started examining routes and evaluating potential termini. The CPR published a preliminary report, with maps, on the results of these explorations up to January 1874. Route option number four came across the Chilcotin plateau, down the Homathko canyon and Bute Inlet and over Valdes Island before descending the east coast of Vancouver Island as far as Esquimalt. (See Fig. 98)

The surveyor for the potential crossing at Seymour Narrows, between Valdes and Vancouver Islands, was a trained and seasoned professional from Scotland, Joseph Hunter. He had also worked on contract to the federal government, making reconnaissance surveys for the right-of-way for the section of the island railway between Nanaimo and Mill Bay.

Sputtering on for nearly fifty years, a squabble between the provincial and Dominion governments concerned the extent and content of the railway land grant on Vancouver Island. In Victoria, the perception that Ottawa was cooling on the commitment to provide a rail link even led to a vote in the legislature supporting secession. The associated petition, although "mislaid" in London, persuaded the colonial secretary to arbitrate between the two administrations a set of compromises called the "Carnarvon Terms." These included a key provision that the section of the route between Nanaimo and Esquimalt was part of the overall rail system. The prime minister, Sir John A. Macdonald, who had just been elected as MP for Victoria, gave high priority to construction of both the transcontinental line and the Vancouver Island railway.

Credit goes to the new premier, William Smithe, for breaking the 1884 political dispute between the fractious provincial legislature and Ottawa over the railway. Immediately prior to taking office, Smithe had served, briefly, as chief commissioner of Lands and Works, and during that time, emulating Trutch, he ordered a new map of the province.

Smithe contracted a civil engineer, Edward Mohun, to update Launders's map of 1871. Mohun had been chief surveyor for the Dominion and Provincial Joint Indian Commission for eight years and had surveyed in many parts of the province, including much of Vancouver Island. In 1873 he explored the still-almost-unknown interior of the island that lay between Fort Rupert and Menzies Bay "with a view to ascertaining whether there was any land suitable for settlement and in what quantities."[1] He explored up the Nimpkish Valley to well beyond today's village of Woss, as well as the Salmon and other rivers flowing into Johnstone Strait.

Vancouver Island, as drawn on Mohun's map of 1884, was essentially as shown on the Launders's version of the Brown-Petermann's map, but with a few corrections. Mohun drew Sooke and Shawnigan Lakes as much closer to their true scale and direction. He altered Karmutzen Lake to "Nimkish [sic] L.," improving its orientation but retaining its exaggerated width. The most significant change was in the area of the Salmon River. Here he depicted the tributary pattern of the major river system that he had investigated and added a "Mohun L." with a dotted shoreline. He also marked the Beaver (Kokish) and Adams Rivers.

Mohun did reproduce many of the features erroneously shown on the earlier publication, with the lakes Buttle, "Chemanis," and "Niteenaht," remaining as before. However, his map added a few important elements to the interior of the northern part of the island. The two narrow channels dividing Valdes Island into three, discovered a little earlier by the CPR's Joseph Hunter, were shown on the new map, but the islands were not yet named.

The map was prepared in Montreal to be printed in Edinburgh by J. Bartholomew in 1884. The final scale was 25 miles to 1 inch (1:1.6 million approximately), the same as Launders's map. Mohun was credited with compiling and drawing the map under the direction of the Honourable William Smithe. By the time it was published, Smithe had become the provincial premier, but the map gave his previous title of chief commissioner of Lands and Works. Also in 1884, the *Encyclopedia Britannica* republished, with a few minor changes, the Vancouver Island portion of Mohun's map as Plate III in volume XXIV of the ninth edition. (See Fig. 99) The Professional Association of BC Land Surveyors elected Mohun as their first president.

❈ ❈ ❈

Fig. 99   The ninth edition of the *Encyclopedia Britannica* was published in Edinburgh and Philadelphia between 1875 and '89. From 1884, volume XXIV, the atlas included this map using detail almost identical to Edward Mohun's of the same year.

Fig. 100 An early version of the cadastral map showed districts and parcels located in the nearly two million acres of the E&N land grant. Note that, big as it was, the grant did not reach Esquimalt, the planned rail terminus.

Another legal wrangle concerned the extent of the rights of the settlers who had occupied and improved the plots of land that later fell within the E&N strip. The provincial Settlement Act of 1884 had given them only the surface rights, and these did not include coal, timber, or base metals. In 1904 a Settlers' Rights Act reversed this, confirming that such parcels had been granted "in fee simple"—in other words, with full title to the timber, non-precious metals, and coal. The government published a revised version of the medium-scale map showing the E&N land grant and the relevant pre-empted parcels within it. (See Fig. 100)

As of 1885, although the boundaries of the land grant had been described in broad terms, they had not been accurately surveyed or marked on the ground. A potential source of dispute was whether pre-empted parcels close to the boundary fell within the area. This was addressed in an Act of 1905, by which time the government had surveyed and marked the southern and western boundaries.

Most of the country through which the landward boundaries of the land grant passed was remote and mountainous, holding limited attraction for settlement. In a few places, however, it did cut through areas suitable for pre-emption, or already claimed. Such areas of interest were given priority—for example, along the southern boundary between Goldstream at the head of Saanich Inlet and the mouth of Muir Creek on the shore of the Strait of Juan de Fuca.

The surveyor general at the time, William Gore, was a man of wide experience in the field in western Canada and the United States. To undertake the important survey of the E&N boundaries, he selected another experienced professional engineer, William Ralph. In 1885 Gore instructed Ralph to cut, survey, and mark the line of the southern boundary, a distance of just over sixteen miles (twenty-six kilometres), which passed through rough, unknown country, difficult to access.

Huge though the grant was, its southern boundary did not provide access for the E&N to the naval dockyard at Esquimalt. The last eleven miles (eighteen kilometres) of track before Russell Station, the initial terminus in Victoria West, and the eventual continuation to Victoria lay outside the grant, so the railway's management needed to negotiate with the various owners along the route. At times, these negotiations turned acrimonious.

❖ ❖ ❖

In 1886, the new British Commanding Royal Engineer in Canada, Lieutenant-Colonel Edmund O'Brien, came to Victoria to follow up on his predecessor J.W. Lovell's reconnaissance report concerning how to protect Esquimalt and Victoria from potential Russian threats. Strategists perceived the threat of an attack by the Russian navy on Esquimalt or against British mercantile shipping in the North Pacific.

Colonel O'Brien brought Company Sergeant Major E. Hopkins, and two junior surveyors with him, Royal Engineers all. Later, a specialist survey officer sent out from England, Lieutenant John I. Lang, RE, joined them. This was the first party of Royal Engineers surveyors to serve on the British Pacific coast since Colonel Moody's Columbia Detachment had been disbanded twenty years earlier.

The colonel came to evaluate the various opinions and alternative proposals triggered by the earlier reports, and to survey and select permanent gun emplacements to defend Esquimalt dockyard and Victoria. He attached a set of panorama sketches of "fields of fire"—the arcs that would be covered by the guns.

Hopkins, Lang, and the other surveyors had come for

CHAPTER NINETEEN 165

what was termed the "Frontier Surveys"—the topographic mapping of the area surrounding the strategic targets. Their fieldwork took two seasons. Time, the rough terrain, and dense forests did not permit a survey based on a triangulation network, so the best they could achieve were separate site surveys connected by traverses along roads. The network of control points previously established by the HBC surveyor Joseph Pemberton was apparently by then not usable. Those points would have provided data valuable for overall accuracy, and saved time. There was, however, a reliably charted coastline, thanks to Captain George Richards's work in HMS *Plumper* in 1860.

The resultant maps, marked "For War Department purposes only," were intended for use by the military garrison in defence of the planned gun emplacements. The six sheets, printed at a scale of 6 inches to 1 mile (1:10,560), covered the area bounded by Albert Head, Thetis Lake, Royal Oak, Mount Douglas, Cadboro Point, and Discovery and Trial Islands. They depicted the topography with contours at 25-foot (7.6-metre) intervals, spot heights, benchmarks, and marine soundings. Cartographic detail shown included water features, vegetation, roads, trails, streets, bridges, buildings, and Native villages. Names of some landowners were also indicated.

The skilled cartographer Hopkins drew the six maps and, most likely, the lithographers at the RE Topographical Depot in Southampton printed them. The Frontier Survey maps of 1888 have been considered the finest cartography to depict any part of the province of BC up to that time and for long afterward. (See Fig. 101)

While the Russians had been seen as a potential threat to the dockyard, another was closer at hand—the neighbour to the south. Although relations seemed friendly enough, the US Army kept a watchful eye on the new fortifications. In 1897, First Lieutenant Andrew Rowan, Nineteenth Infantry, arrived incognito in Victoria. Dressed and equipped as an artistic gentleman tourist, Rowan chatted with the proprietor of the Dallas Hotel, a fellow American. He then hiked overland as close as he could get to Rodd Hill (probably at the location of the historic site's current administration building) and set up his easel to paint "the view." He also hired a dinghy, complete with a garrulous boatman, for an excursion that just happened to pass close by the other fortification sites under construction around the harbour.

Rowan's intelligence report included drawings, maps, charts, and photographs of the Esquimalt defences. The text of his report was discovered recently but without the accompanying maps. He noted: "Great secrecy is observed... three forts... although well located and splendidly constructed, do not form extremely formidable works... they would not be a match for the larger guns of such vessels as the [USS] *Oregon*."[2]

Rowan's appraisal was never put to the test, and the defensive emplacements protecting Esquimalt and Victoria were never called upon to fire a shot in anger.

❋ ❋ ❋

Following BC's entry into the Dominion in 1871, the pace of immigration increased. Farming, settlement, and mining put pressure on the surveyor general's department to maintain the cadastral record of pre-emptions and mining licences; limited budgets and technical resources meant that mapping and other forms of survey had to be curtailed.

In 1880, however, Gore, the surveyor general, and his superior, Commissioner George Walkem, were able to order

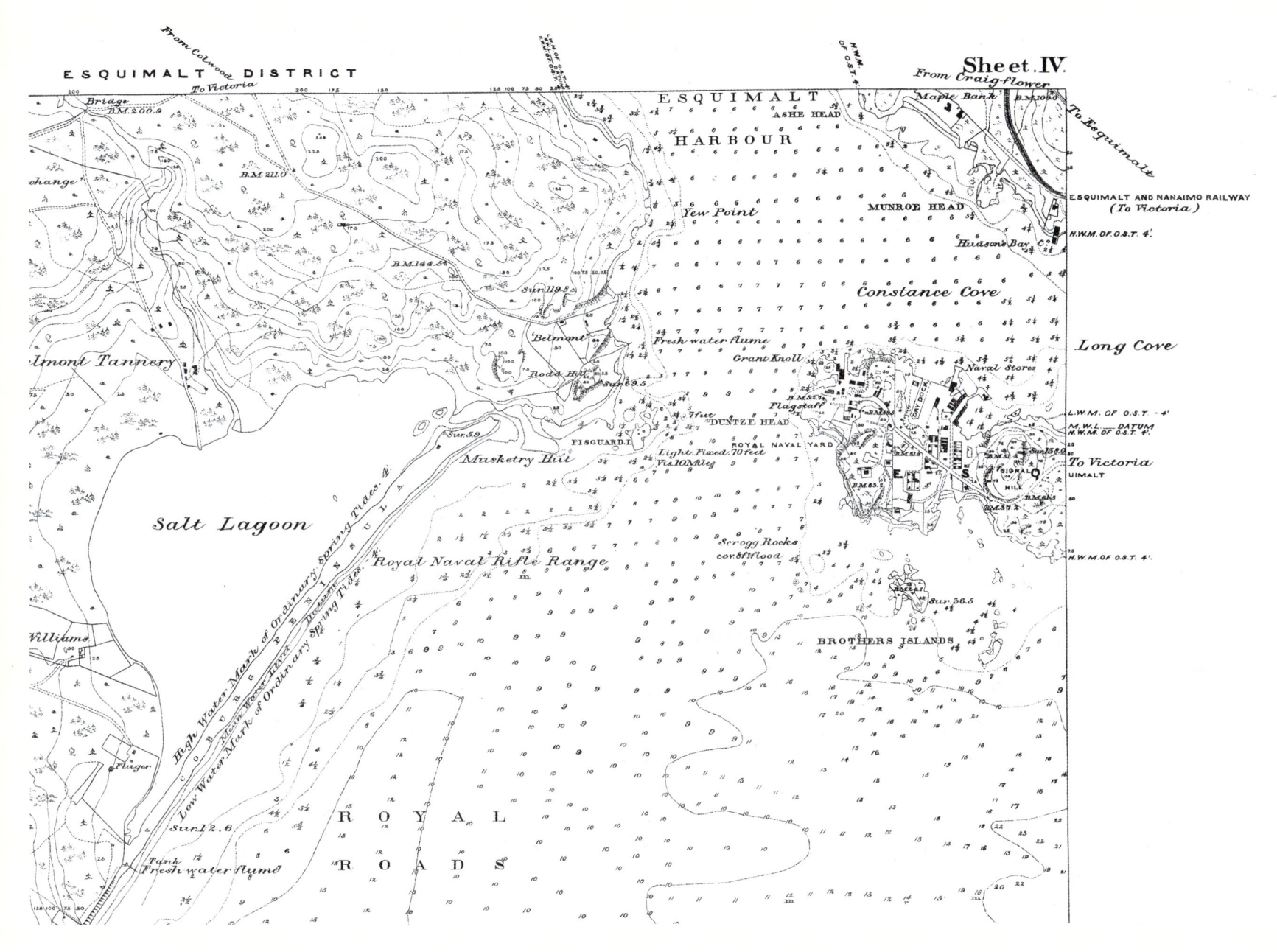

Fig. 101 During 1886 and '87, in the "Frontier Surveys," a small team led by Lieutenant John Lang, RE, surveyed the area surrounding Esquimalt and Victoria. The block of six map sheets was intended for the garrison defending the two strategic harbours.

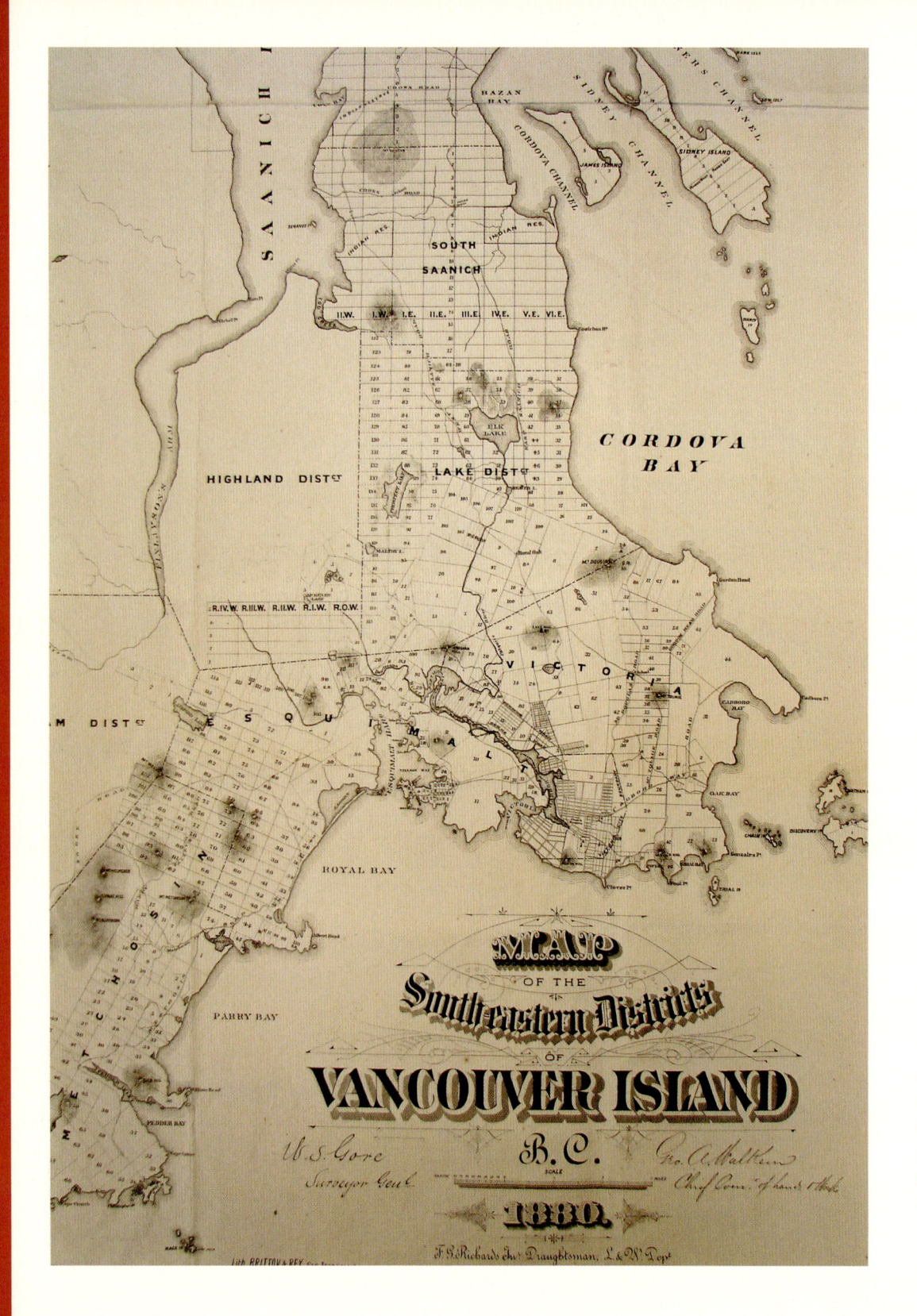

Fig. 102   The surveyor general ordered this map in 1880. The excellent draftsmanship of Francis Richards was sent to San Francisco for lithographic printing. The short-lived gold-rush community of Leechtown, shown outside the main area, was important information at the time.

the printing of a new *Map of the South-eastern Districts of Vancouver Island B.C.* From a manuscript by draftsman Francis G. Richards, lithographers Britton & Rey of San Francisco engraved and produced a high-quality, single-colour map at a scale of 1 inch to 1 mile (1:63,360). It showed district boundaries, which were often linked to the lines of the trigonometric network that ran between hilltops, finely depicted with hachures (symbols indicating slope), and cadastral information. As an evidently late addition, and outside the boundary, the map showed the short-lived gold-rush community of Leechtown with access by the Sooke and Leech Rivers. Both Gore and Walkem appended their signatures to the printing plate. (See Fig. 102)

From the late 1880s on, the economic picture improved. Incoming settlers were diversifying into new ventures, not just agriculture and mining, but logging, milling, commercial fishing, and canning. As government revenues grew, Gore was able to commission reconnaissance surveys of gaps in the maps, areas that had remained unknown or little explored. After 1887, he contracted with independent surveyors and engineers to visit and prepare reports on such locations across the province, including Vancouver Island.

Gore gave priority to areas that offered good potential for agriculture but were outside the E&N's land grant. The reports were to describe the terrain and its principal topographic features such as rivers and lakes as well as forests, soils, signs of exploitable minerals such as copper, iron, coal, limestone or clay visible on the surface, fish and game, Native villages, and settlements. He selected surveyors with an all-round knowledge of land use and resources, as well as technical competence and the ability to operate in the wilderness.

In the late summer of 1887, Gore sent out two men to add detail to the discoveries made fourteen years earlier, by Edward Mohun, in the valleys of the Nimpkish and Salmon Rivers. John Gray and Henry Fry were both trained and experienced railway engineers who were also skilled land surveyors. In addition, they were to scout for possible extension routes northward for the E&N Railway. They made reconnaissance surveys of the area around Karmutzen, Anutz, Hustan, Woss, Vernon, Muchalat, Gold, and Klaklakama Lakes, and also investigated the Salmon and White River Valleys.

The surveyor general included abstracts of Gray and Fry's findings in his annual report. At the end of each field season, draftsmen in the lands office incorporated the surveyors' maps onto their ongoing master sheets, thereby maintaining them as up-to-date records of the state of provincial chorography (geographical knowledge). Periodically, funds were made available for publishing versions of the general map for distribution to other government offices and the public. In 1929, the Department of Lands published, in book form, all such abstracts to date for areas on Vancouver Island. These surveyors' reports provide a series of snapshots in time of the progress of learning about the more remote areas of the island.[3]

On August 4, 1890, William Ralph again set up his theodolite, an optical instrument for measuring angles, over the mark at Muir Creek and pointed the telescope in the direction of Crown Mountain to begin the survey of the western boundary of the E&N land grant. The task was daunting; he had to cut, survey, and mark a straight line up the very backbone of Vancouver Island. It was a distance of 138.5 miles (223 kilometres), so the Earth's curvature would be significant. Ralph needed to employ geodesy in measuring the true shortest distance between the Muir and Crown survey stations, and he had to get the line along the spine right, first time.

CHAPTER NINETEEN 169

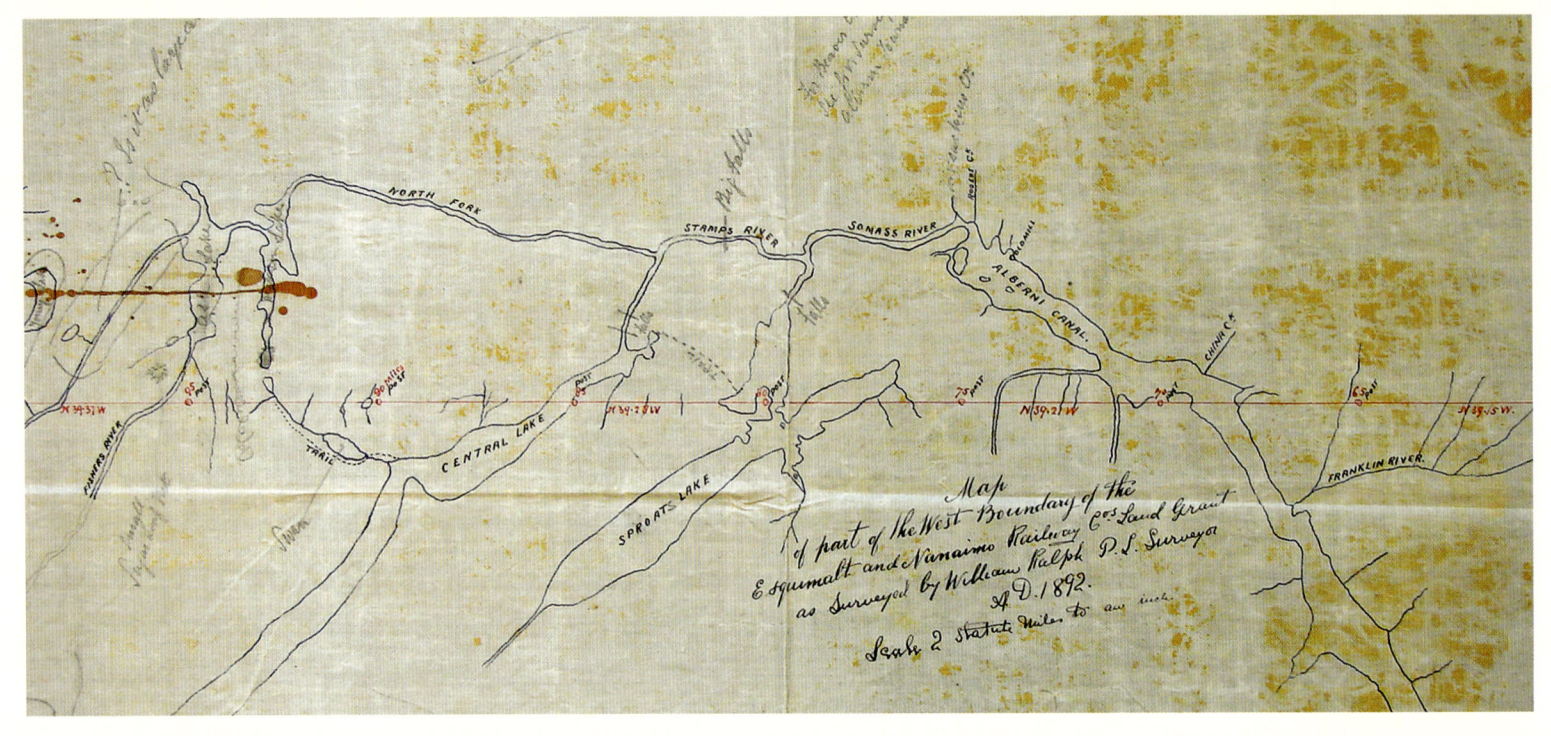

Fig. 103 William Ralph sketched the route of his three-season survey along the mountainous spine of Vancouver Island, marking the western boundary of the E&N land grant.

Ralph's three-season survey of the western boundary of the land grant was among the most noteworthy explorations of Vancouver Island. Surveying such a long, straight line presented technical and logistic challenges, and he planned and executed the project well. In addition, the work required extraordinary feats of mountaineering. In his annual report for 1892, Tom Kains, the new surveyor general, described Ralph's accomplishment as "a standing monument of scientific skill and physical endurance."

Ralph's sketch map of the sections of the line between about Mile 55 and Crown Mountain showed the topography on both sides of the line, reflecting his assessment of how the various streams and lakes he crossed continued and interconnected. It indicated that as well as cutting the line, he explored the country on both sides of it. Ralph and his party were the first to make a reliable sighting of that mysterious body of water called "Buttle's Lake," which had been named after, but almost certainly not seen by, John Buttle. (See Fig. 103)

The earlier depiction of Buttle's Lake (now Buttle Lake) was still used for a special printed map, *Southern Districts of Vancouver Island, B.C.*, published in 1892—"From the Latest Surveys"—by M.W. Waitt & Co. The map, configured to show the extent of the E&N land grant, emphasized the cadastral layout. (See Fig. 104) A series of maps published over the next two decades reflected the degree of the real-estate potential within the land grant.

When William Ralph died in Victoria in May 1905, aged seventy-three, the *Daily Colonist* provided an editorial tribute: "perhaps the best informed man on the topographic features of Vancouver Island."

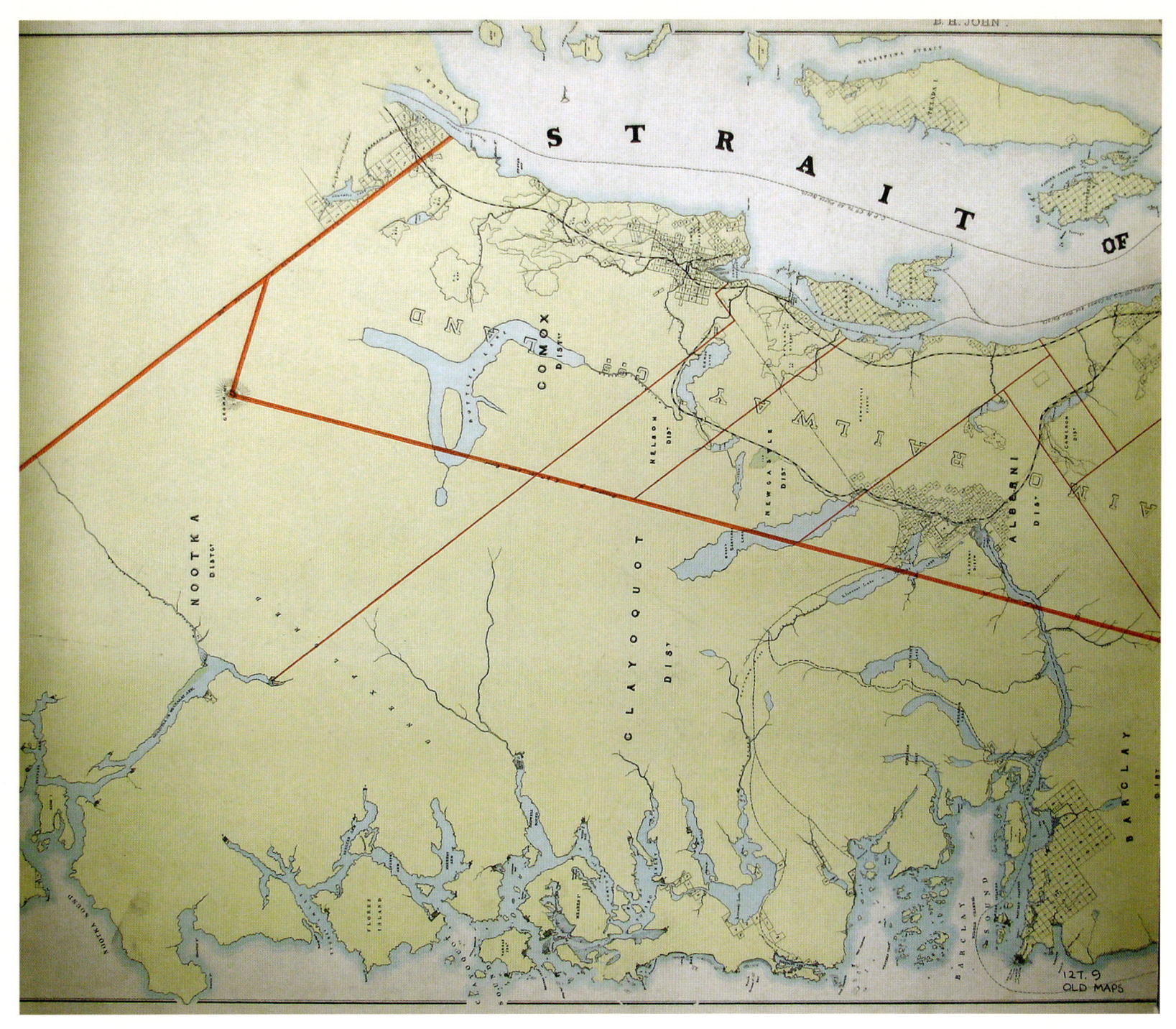

Fig. 104 The senior draftsman at Lands and Works, Eric "E.B." McKay, compiled the manuscript for this version of the E&N land grant and adjacent areas. Note that Ralph's discovery of the correct position and shape of Buttle's Lake had not yet registered with cartographers.

Fig. 105 Dr. George Dawson led a team from the Geological Survey of Canada to map the coal deposits of northern Vancouver Island and Queen Charlotte Sound.

CHAPTER TWENTY

"The Most Perfect Map": Tom Kains's Campaigns

ANOTHER OF THE 1871 TERMS of British Columbia's entry into Canada called for the Dominion to survey the geology of the province. Four years later, the Geological Survey of Canada (GSC) in Ottawa sent a team to comply with this commitment. After investigating the southern parts of the BC interior by the field season of 1878, the men had reached and mapped the Queen Charlotte Islands and had made a brief reconnaissance of the northern end of Vancouver Island. They returned for four months during the summer of 1885 to map the geology of both coasts of Queen Charlotte Sound, and also covered Quatsino Sound and Nimpkish, or Karmutzen, Lake. Their primary purpose this time was to investigate the extent and probable value of the coal deposits in the northern part of the island, but they also reported on natural history and anthropology.

The remarkable surveyor and scientific generalist Dr. George Mercer Dawson led the team. Despite a physical handicap, Dawson showed, throughout twenty years of arduous fieldwork, extraordinary dedication, fortitude, and endurance. A childhood illness had stunted his growth, leaving him with a distorted spine and the physique of a twelve-year-old. His mental capabilities, however, were unimpaired. He rose to the post of director of the GSC and was counted among Canada's most distinguished scientists.

Dawson's report on his 1885 season, published two years later, contained a lithographed *Geological Map of the Northern Part of Vancouver Island and Adjacent Coasts* at a scale of 7 nautical miles to 1 inch (1:506,880), based on a coastline taken from Admiralty charts, with many inland peaks added. (See Fig. 105) An inset map of Nimpkish Lake at 2 nautical miles to 1 inch (1:144,823) used hachures to represent landforms, a style that Dawson had pioneered. (See Fig. 106, page 174)

The year 1891 brought several significant changes to surveying in BC, as shortcomings in the pre-emption and land-registry systems needed correcting. Inaccuracies had occurred in surveys of isolated parcels or blocks of parcels, and since new surveys were often based upon marks previously

173

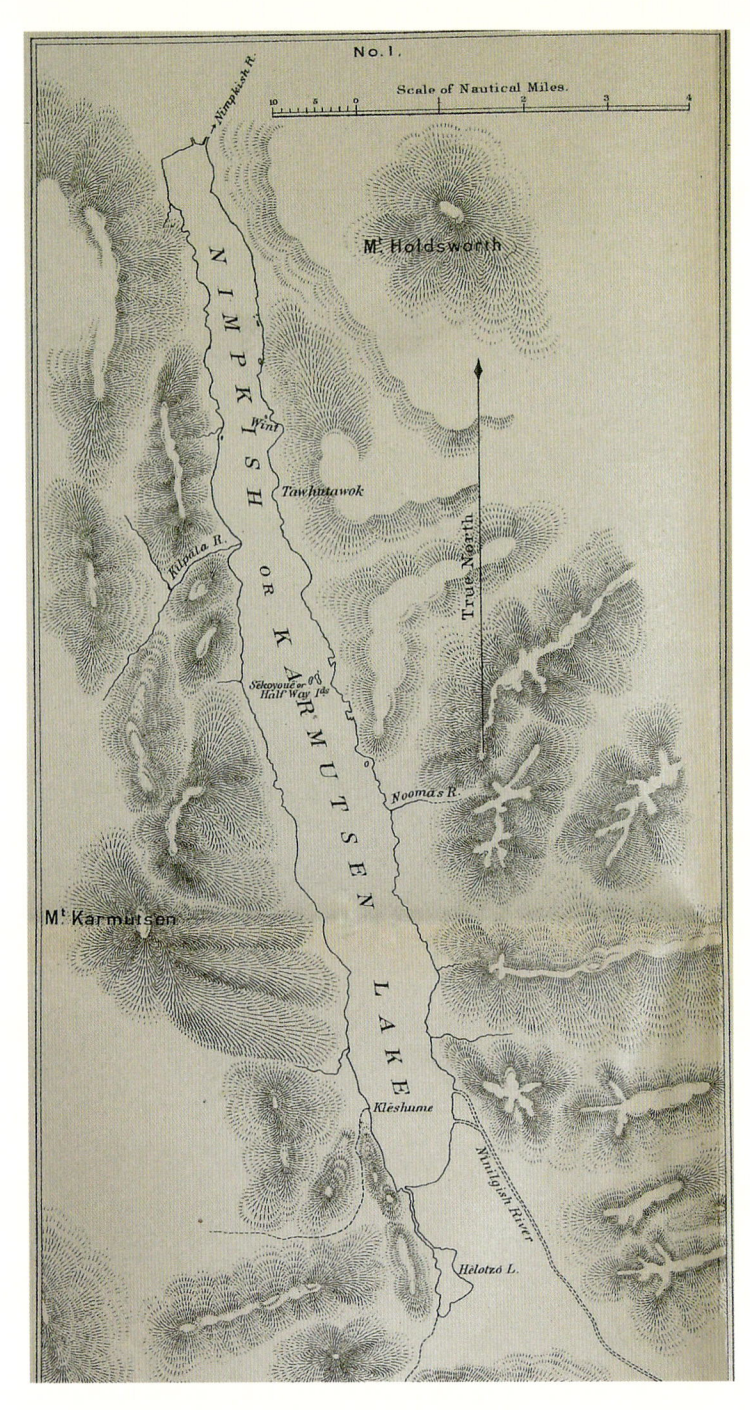

Fig. 106 Dawson's team of geologists explored the area of Nimpkish Lake. Their inset map pioneered the use of hachures to depict terrain relief.

established, any errors were cumulative. Ambiguity over property and mineral claims had become a serious problem.

Two factors caused these inaccuracies. The first was the technical difficulty of placing the first survey marks in their correct coordinates, which was partly the result of using the grid cadastral system. The grid consisted of rectangular parcels based upon either compass directions or a baseline related to an important topographical feature such as a river rather than coordinates derived from a triangulation network. However, not all surveyors practising at the time could achieve the necessary accuracy for this to work.

The second factor was a lack of rigorous checks on the competence of surveyors who had been granted licences to practise. In order to register a previously pre-empted parcel under the Act of 1871, a landowner had to support his application with a "properly authenticated map." In 1880 this was clarified to mean one made by a surveyor authorized by the chief commissioner of Lands and Works or the surveyor general. Often, however, this authorization was cursory.

One surveyor, Charles Busk, remembered that in 1883 "I established myself in a couple of rooms on Yates Street until I could look around and learn something of the country and opportunities in my profession. As a preliminary I called on Sir Jos. Trutch [the lieutenant-governor] and the Surveyor General [W.S. Gore], and from both learned that as I owned a theodolite and level and allied instruments it was to be presumed I knew how to use them, and accordingly no examination nor licence was necessary—all I had to do was to get the offer of some work and go and do it."[1]

The surveyors themselves, many of whom were qualified as civil engineers or Dominion Land Surveyors (DLS), diagnosed the problem and attempted to correct it. In December 1890 they called a meeting of all "authorised land surveyors" and formed the Association of Professional Land Surveyors of British Columbia. They elected Edward Mohun as president, with William Gore, the surveyor general, acting *ex officio*. Their primary mission was to petition the government to regulate the profession through admission by examination and to grant disciplinary powers to the association. The Provincial Land Surveyors' Act of 1891 rewarded their efforts. All eighty-two previously authorized surveyors still active at the time were grandfathered in.

Also in 1891, Tom Kains replaced the long-serving Gore as surveyor general, the latter being promoted to the newly established post of deputy commissioner of Lands and Works. Kains, a DLS with a degree in civil engineering from the University of Toronto, had a strategy for the first aspect of the inconsistency problem. In his first formal reports as surveyor general, he advocated a comprehensive change to the survey system for the province.

While the rectangular township system of cadastre had worked over the previous twenty years on the Prairies, in Australia, and in the flatter parts of BC, it was less practical or economic for mountainous, forested areas. This system entailed cutting and marking a grid of cutlines spaced 6 miles (9.7 kilometres) apart across the territory. On Vancouver Island, it divided the territory into districts and then superimposed a grid, with the parcels numbered in the order in which they were registered.

Kains recommended that a more appropriate example to follow would be that adopted in New Zealand: rigorous networks of triangulation. A specialized division of the Dominion government would need to undertake the primary, or geodetic, network, which would consist of triangles and geometric figures with 18.6- to 49.7-mile (30- to 80-kilometre) sides, measured with high precision. The primary net, mostly between points on prominent peaks, would provide control for secondary networks of shorter sides, with a lower degree of accuracy. These, in turn, would control a scheme of third-order points, designed to provide frameworks for cadastral surveys and topographic mapping. Kains's far-sighted strategy was gradually taken up and remained valid until the modern era with the advent of high-precision, satellite-based GPS (Geographic Positioning Systems). (See Fig. 107, page 176)

❃ ❃ ❃

Yet another event occurred in 1891 that held import for the charting history of Vancouver Island and the west coast, though it passed unremarked at the time: The newly commissioned Canadian Government's Steamship (CGS) *Quadra* arrived in Esquimalt Harbour, with John T. Walbran, master mariner, in command.

Captain Walbran devoted the next thirteen years to servicing lighthouses and buoys, and to fisheries protection. He also conducted some hydrographic research—charting remote harbours and reporting reefs and other hazards to navigation. CGS *Quadra*, the only government vessel on the Pacific coast other than British warships, searched for missing ships and carried police to deal with issues in isolated coastal communities. During his many years of sailing the intricate BC coastline and among its myriad islands, Walbran came to know every bay and inlet.

Around 1896, the origins of local place names and the stories behind those names started to fascinate Walbran. After he retired in 1904 to settle in Victoria, he continued to devote his time to this passion, assembling a rich collection of anecdotes, yarns, and vignettes about local maritime history and the characters who had made it. In 1909 his former employer, the Ministry of Marine and Fisheries in

Fig. 107   Primary (or geodetic) and secondary triangulation schemes superimposed upon a 1912 map illustrate the density of control points required for accurate mapping. Such networks were far beyond the resources available to Grant and his successors for the next eighty years.

Fig. 108 The anthropologist Franz Boas investigated the complex tribal territories surrounding Queen Charlotte Sound and the Strait of Georgia, producing a report with this map in 1869.

Ottawa, published his monumental book *British Columbia Coast Names: Their Origin and History.*

❖ ❖ ❖

Another work on the toponymy of Vancouver Island appeared in 1887 in Petermann's *Geographischer Mittheilungen*, the German journal that had published Robert Brown's *Memoir* and map of the island in 1869. Dr. Franz Boas, a noted German-American anthropologist, produced a new map, *Die Indianerstämme von Vancouver Id.* (The Indian Tribes of Vancouver Island). (See Fig. 108, page 177) It illustrated the distribution and territories of the First Nations around both sides of the "Salish Sea"—the Strait of Juan de Fuca, Puget Sound, and the Strait of Georgia—and of Desolation Sound, Johnstone Strait, the Broughton Archipelago, and Queen Charlotte Sound.

Starting in 1885 and for nearly sixty years, Boas studied various aspects of the ethnology of the Native people of the Pacific Northwest, in particular the "Kwakiutl" (Kwakwaka'wakw). (See Fig. 109) Boas's maps showed the clans' territories extending inland, generally to the mountains or major lakes. This reflected a far better appreciation of zones of occupation than the very restricted version used for the allocation of Indian Reserves by the provincial, Dominion, and imperial governments. (See Fig. 110) He showed the land along the entire east coast of the island, the corresponding coast of the mainland, and the islands lying between them as fully occupied by First Nations.

Nearly fifty years later, Boas published a book, *Geographical Names of the Kwakiutl Indians*, containing some thirty line maps of the coast from Cape Scott to Discovery Passage and the Broughton Archipelago, marked with the toponyms listed in phonetic notation.

Several of those maps dealt with the Nimpkish River and the trading trail to Tahsish Arm in Kyuquot Sound. In his introductory remarks, Boas explained: "The geographical terminology of the Kwakiutl is that of a sea-faring people to whom the forms of land and water and the dangers of the sea are all-important and who obtain their subsistence from both the sea and from the land."[2] (See Fig. 111, page 180, and Fig. 112, page 181)

❖ ❖ ❖

During his seven years as surveyor general, Tom Kains directed the production and publication of some fifty new maps of the province or parts of it, many printed in two or more colours. Of these maps, twenty covered, in whole or in part, Vancouver Island. Kains developed an excellent working arrangement with a local lithographer, The Colonist Printing and Publishing Company, which produced most of the maps. These printed maps were created in addition to the department's regular work of tracing older maps, drafting township cadastral diagrams and individual property plats, and preparing small maps to accompany official reports. This cartographic activity reflected Kains's policy of reviving the topographic side of his department rather than concentrating primarily on cadastral work.

By 1892 stocks of the Mohun map of the province had run out; besides, it was out of date because of recent surges in settlement and industrial development, particularly railways, roads, and mining. Moreover, results from exploration surveys had started to bring in important new or corrected topographic detail. It was time for a new map of BC. As Kains phrased it, "A reliable map speaks more to an intending settler and carries more weight generally than volumes of printed matter."[3]

He commissioned James Brownlee, DLS, to prepare

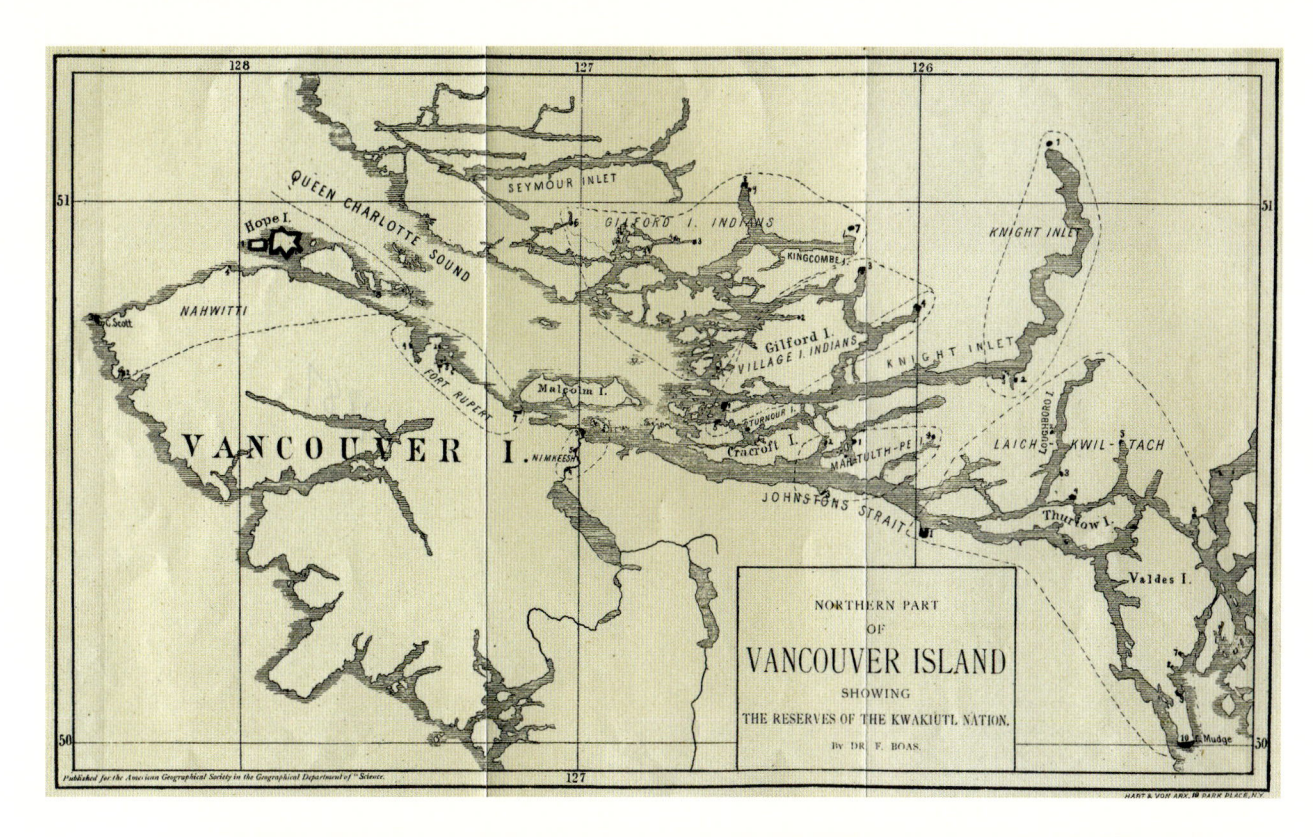

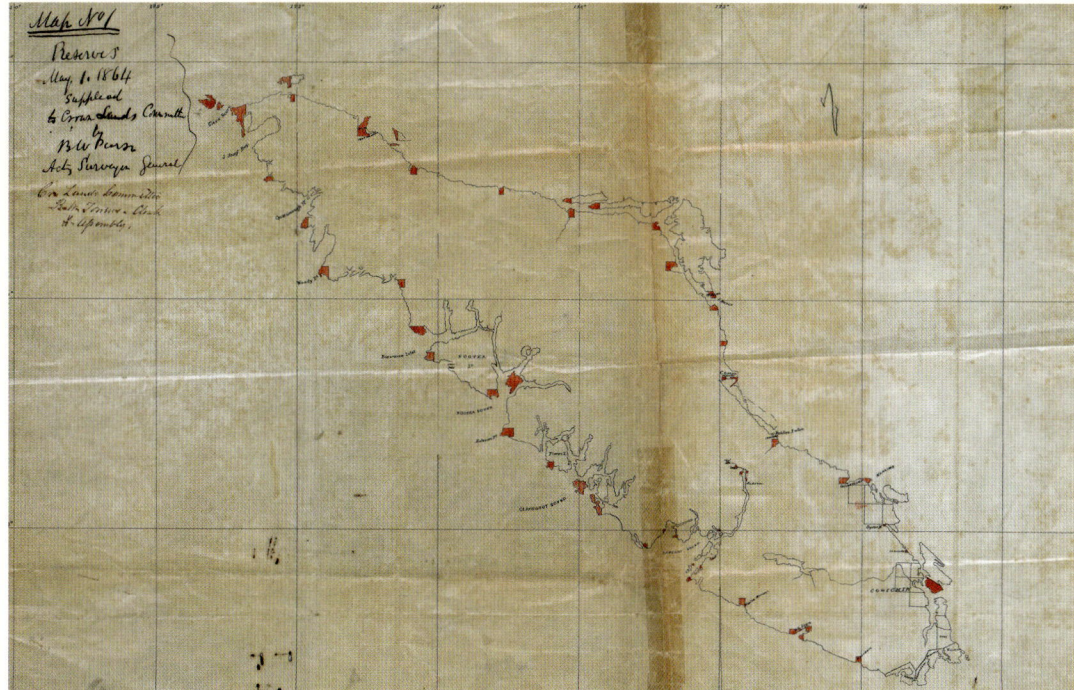

TOP

Fig. 109 In this map by Dr. Franz Boas of the Kwakiutl (now Kwakwaka'wakw) territories, he termed them "Reserves," but his interpretation of the word did not match that of the civil authorities.

RIGHT

Fig. 110 Pearse, acting surveyor general for the colony, prepared this tracing of the "official" Indian Reserves on Vancouver Island. It shows parcels significantly smaller than those identified by Boas. Note that they are all coastal.

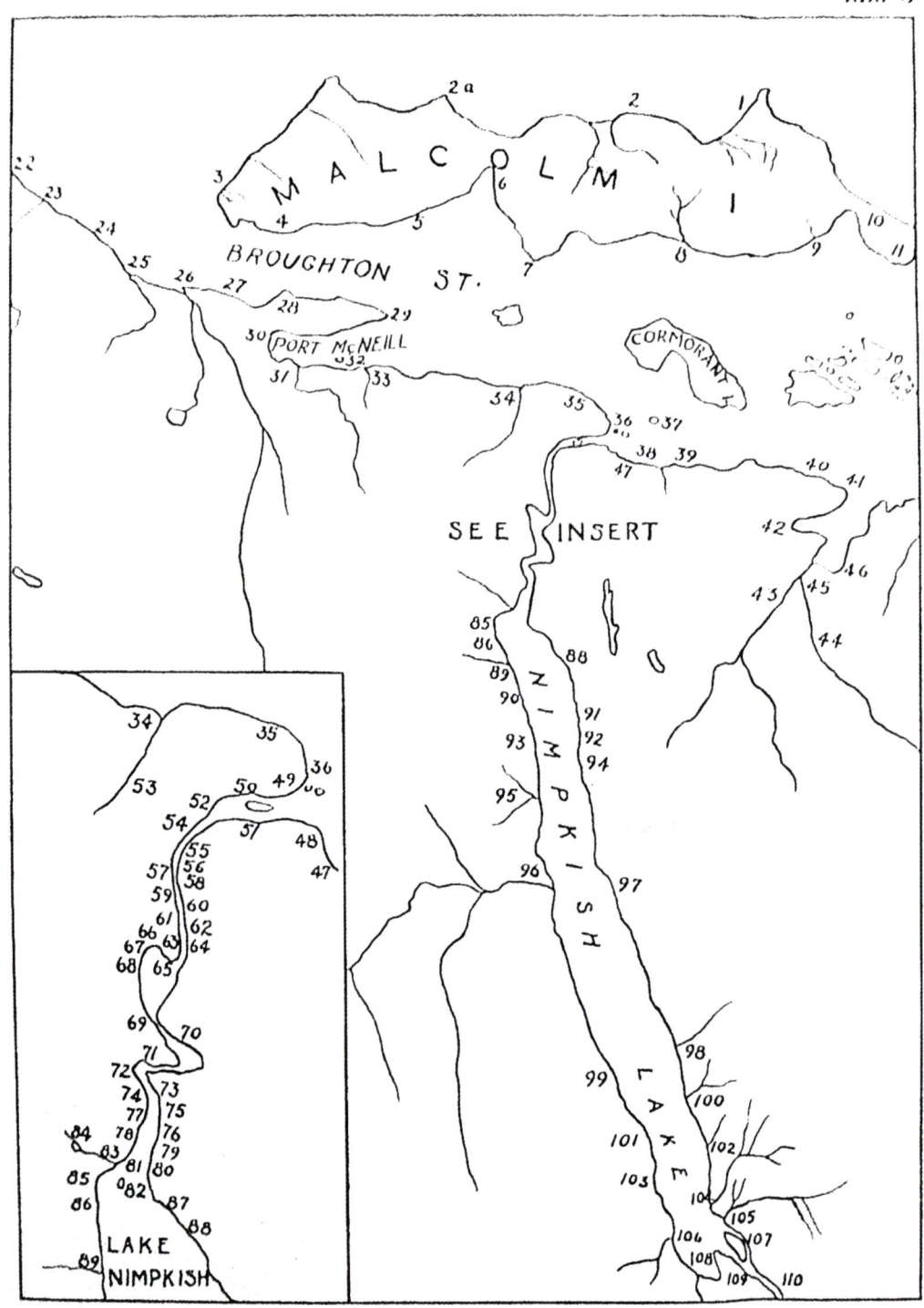

Fig. 111 Boas collected the place names used by the "Kwakiutl Indians," now known as Kwakwaka'wakw. His 1934 book clearly demonstrated the detailed knowledge of the coast held in the collective memory of the local First Nations.

1. maᵉlɛ'm two faces
2. ĕ'k·!aēlba high point
2a. ĕ'k·!aē ba high point
3. ōxsdeᵉli's beach at hind end
4. wā'gexʟēᵉ river on small of back
5. ʟ!ā'ʟ!ask·!ōdi's seaward opposite beaches
6. ᵉnā'ᵉnaʟaqekᵘ turned inside out (?) [out (?)
7. ᵉnā'ᵉnaʟaqekᵘ turned inside
8. q!āp!ēkᵘ gathered (stones?)
9. saᵉgwa's place of meat carving
10. ōxʟaᵉli's beach at hind end
11. ō'gŭmaᵉlis front beach
12. sē'gēg·ēᵉ dry behind
13. sɛ'ʟsɛlᵉyāg·iwēᵉ
14. ō'sgɛmēᵉ surface
15. ō'gwitɛmaᵉlis beach at head of body
16. ăwē'g·aᵉlis beach at back
17. wā'waʟexts!a trying to go aboard (?)
18. ōxsdeᵉli's beach at hind end
19. ōxʟaᵉli's beach at hind end
20. ᵉyilē's spreading leg beach, i. e., a bay bounded by two narrow points: Alert Bay
21. t!ā't!ᵉyɛ'm gravel
22. ʟexsᵉalis
23. saᵉgwa's place of meat carving
24. māxstâla striped eyes (raccoon)
25. tsɛx·â'ᵉyē tide made to run out
26. ʟɛx·si'wēᵉ clover root or bar on mouth of river
27. q!ɛdē's patch on beach
28. ē'g·isbalis sandy beach at point
29. ʟ!ā'sōtbēᵉ seaward opposite point
30. ᵉnā'ʟaxstala having mouth upstream
31. dɛx·dɛli'ldɛᵉmis place of owls on beach
32. pɛ'lq!exʟalis thin (flat rocky) beach at hind end
33. mɛdā'dēᵉ having horse clams
34. wāg·a'lis river behind on beach
35. xŭ'mdas land otter place
36. tsɛ'nsēdē having twitching, having dipping of vessel into water (?)
37. dā'g·ŭlkᵘ
38. dzaᵉwŭ'naᵉdē having cohoes salmon
39. tsā'ᵉmɛlq!wāla sound of dripping water
40. ᵉnɛ'lqɛmlis beach facing up river
41. gwa'k·!ōdɛxstēᵉ mouth on opposite side downstream
42. gwax·ʟāᵉlis downstream at head beach
43. lā'xstɛᵉwa clear colored (water) on rock
44. ʟ!ō'ladēᵉ having elks
45. ts!ō'ltō black colored
46. q!ŭg·i's notched beach
47. g·ildɛdzō'lis long flat beach
48. k·ō'xɛkᵘ
49. xŭlkᵘ (logs) placed crosswise
50. k·!ē'dɛxᵉŭnā'la body with grass
51. k·!ā'gēs logs laid crosswise foundation on ground
52. ʟ!ē'ts!ēᵉ (sunny place)
53. wāx·sɛᵉmakᵘ
54. mā'ts!a rock lengthwise against current; or striped rock
55. ʟ!ē'gelis clay inside beach (?)
56. q!ā'ᵉwa pond on rock
57. ga'xsɛmēᵉ straddling on surface
58. mā'smats!a rocks lengthwise against current
59. xŭts!exʟā'labaᵉlas place of fort at end on point
60. tɛᵉwē'sēᵉ attacking on beach (poling against strong tide?)
61. mɛ'nk·!a excrement (rusty color) on rock
62. k!wē'tk!ŭt!aakᵘ pried up on rock
63. wanā'la river on side
64. ā'siwēᵉ
65. tɛ'lk!waxʟēᵉ splashing behind
66. dē'qŭnxēᵉ pile driving at edge
67. lā'lălatsʟᵉ
68. ʟ!ē'xadēᵉ having sea lions
69. ĕk·!ɛgɛ'mlīlkᵘ caused to be face upward in house
70. ā'ʟɛk·!ɛnēᵉ inland body; i. e. inland from a spit
71. gwa'ᵉdzēᵉ
73. ōdzā'ᵉlas flat place
74. mā'k·!ɛs near ground
75. k·!ā'k·!axʟāla crossed logs on top
76. hayat!aᵉyo
77. ʟ!ɛsaᵉlilkᵘ
78. xŭtēᵉᵉ groove
79. sɛ'ldzadēᵉ having blueberries
80. k·!ō'gwis put up on edge on beach
81. ᵉmɛlxā'wēᵉ white neck, or twisted neck (of river)
82. ᵉmɛk!waxā'wēᵉ round thing at neck (of river)
83. ts!ᵉyi'mᵉyē intestines
84. q!ăwē's pond on beach
85. ō'baᵉlis beach at end, Knight Inlet
86. q!ō'dzadē having (crabs)
87. mā'dɛmxtála mā'dɛm on top
88. wŭ'lk·ɛmēᵉ wreath around head
89. wāx·ᵉwak·a bent (Koskimo)
90. wŭlk·ᵉwas place where ring comes off
91. ʟɛlʟɛlxdɛᵉma rocky site for canoe carrying
92. qā'qɛlᵉwaɛ'mdzɛgwis beach with scotch fir patches
93. dɛk!ɛbō'ᵉ grave on chest
94. ē'xɛlba
95. g·ō'xᵘdɛᵉmis house site on beach
96. g·i'ltbala long stretching point
97. sē'sɛq!axʟaᵉlis dry ones (i. e. stump) at hind end of beach
98. wŭnē'ᵉ
99. nō'mas old man i. e. sea monster; name of many dangerous points
100. wadzō' river on flat place
101. waɛ'lbalis river on point on beach
102. sē'goᵉyāᵉlis dry in middle on beach
104. lɛmxɛmsta nō'mas green waters old man
105. ᵉnɛnʟabɛkᵘ
106. ăxē'lba point
107. ʟ!ā'sɛmēᵉ alder on surface
108. hē'gɛms said to mean "facing outward"
109. ōxᵘsi'wēᵉ mouth of river
110. x·ɛlā's drying place or dentalia place

Fig. 112 List of Kwakwa̱ka'wakw toponyms for Map 8, Nimpkish River and Lake.

another complete map of the province. The steady arrival of new survey information delayed the work for a year, but by the spring of 1893, ten thousand copies had been printed. Kains was able to report for that year that "the High Commissioner for Canada in London now had a supply for distribution in Great Britain and the Continent where a demand was likely to arise. A large number have been sent to the World's Exposition in Chicago."[4] (See Fig. 113)

The Canadian Banknote Company of Montreal lithographed Brownlee's map in four colours, at a scale of 33 miles to 1 inch (1:2.1 million approximately). On Vancouver Island it showed, by a dashed line, the "Line of Ry. Belt"—the western boundary of the E&N lands. The shape and position of Buttle Lake, crossed by that line, were as shown on Brown's and Mohun's maps, not the correct configuration already discovered by Ralph, and Nitinat and Nimkish [sic] Lakes were still exaggerated in width. Woss Lake was shown, indicating that the cartographer had studied Fry's reconnaissance report.

No sooner had the Brownlee map been printed than Kains knew it was inadequate, and he made a successful case to a new chief commissioner, George B. Martin, that a wholly new map was essential. Not only would it better show the province's topography, it would also indicate the new electoral districts then being enacted. It would be at a larger scale than the Brownlee map and its forerunners, and be constructed on a new projection. It was called a "modified Lambert's conical orthomorphic projection," and it was better suited to the extent and latitudes of BC than any of those used in Canada or the US.

Kains, in his report for 1893, listed eleven sources for the detail to be incorporated in the new map, including "Reports from private explorations." By this he meant an expedition led by William Bolton, just about to embark for the northern end of Vancouver Island. Kains explained that the map would show detail previously not possible, such as smaller settlements, Native villages, schools, and missions.

The new map indicated, by means of conventional symbols, areas with agricultural potential and mineral locations. Included were the newly revealed details along the western boundary of the E&N land grant, as well as new settlements at the northern end of the island. The overall size of the map manuscript was 7 by 5.5 feet (2.1 by 1.7 metres). The printed version was reduced but still large, with a final scale of 20 miles to 1 inch (1:1.3 million). (See Fig. 114, page 184)

Biographical detail about the cartographer, Gotfred Jörgensen, is meagre, but according to his byline on the map, he was a qualified civil engineer. Since the three-colour map was to be printed by the latest technique of photolithography, Kains entrusted the Colonist company to subcontract the Sabiston Company of Montreal. In 1895, mounted copies of the map had been distributed to "various public institutions throughout the land." Kains affirmed, "[It] is certainly the most perfect map of British Columbia which has thus far been placed before the public."[5]

Kains's opinion was justified. The map recorded significant advances over its predecessors—Mohun's map of 1880 and Brownlee's of 1893—in geographical knowledge of both BC and Vancouver Island. It showed the findings of the reconnaissance explorations by Mohun, Fry, and Gray in the Sayward and Rupert Districts, and Ralph's detail along the western boundary of the E&N grant. As well as the track of the E&N, it showed the line of the newly opened Victoria & Sidney Railway (nicknamed "The Cordwood Limited"). Some names in the centre of the Saanich Peninsula—Garnham, Heal, Slugget, Young, Targoose, and Hagar—had symbols as post offices, but most are now forgotten.

Fig. 113   James Brownlee's four-colour, 1893 map of most of the province of BC was published in large quantities for distribution to potential settlers. While incorporating some new detail, it still contained major errors.

Fig. 114   This is part of a four-sheet wall map of the province drawn by Gotfred Jörgensen and printed in three colours in Montreal in 1895. This copy was later annotated with the electoral boundaries of the Provincial Elections Act of 1898.

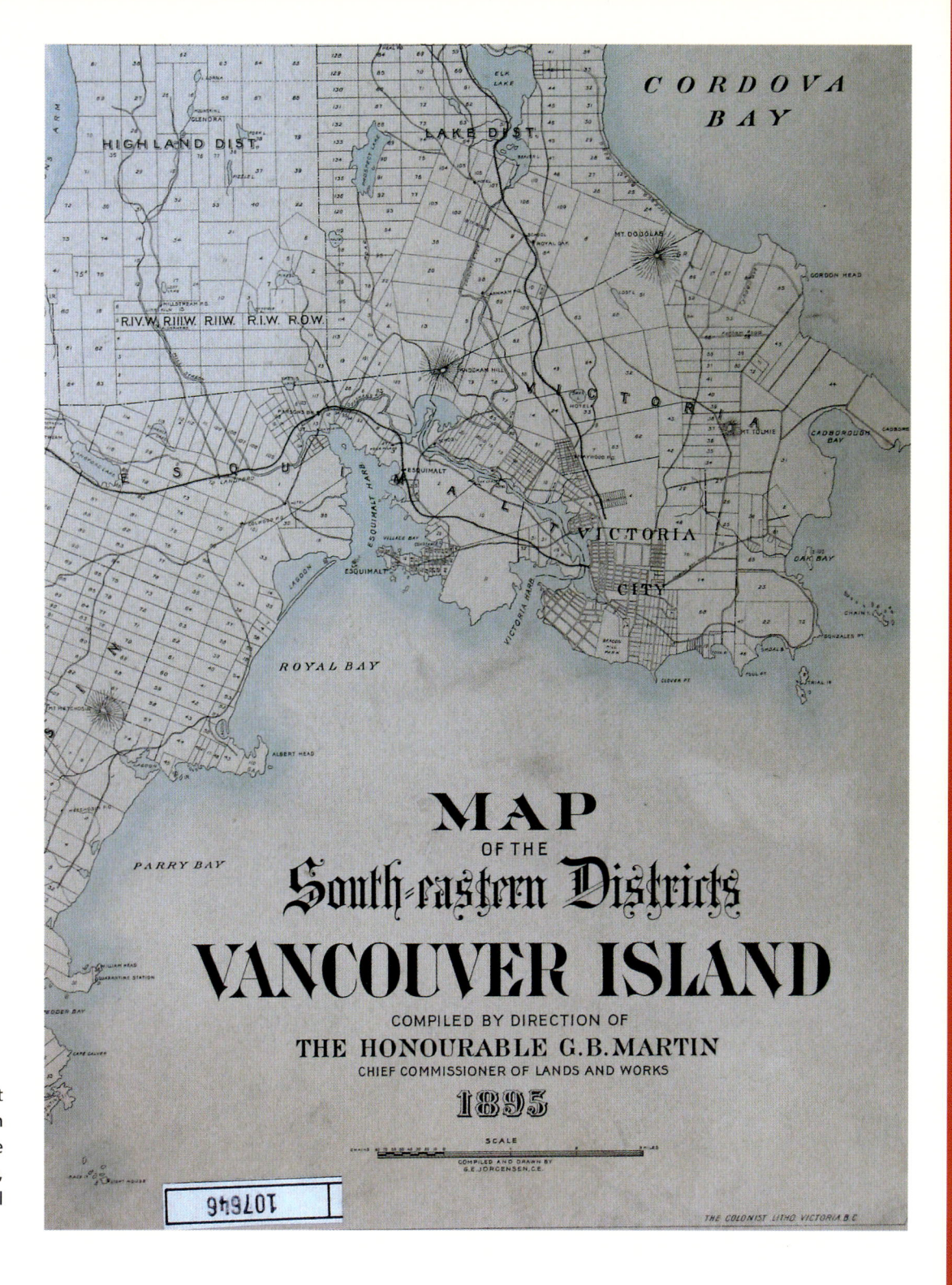

Fig. 115 The part of Vancouver Island most attractive for settlement was the southeastern districts. Civil engineer Jörgensen drew the manuscript for this fine example of cartography, showing cadastral and transportation detail for a growing greater Victoria.

Jörgensen used artistic hill shading effectively to portray mountainous terrain. A 6-mile (9.6-kilometre) grid of numbered "townships" covered the north end of the island—not actual centres of population, but a cadastral registry system. He showed most of the interior lakes more accurately than had Brownlee, but he still drew both Nimpkish and Nitinat Lakes, although well oriented, far wider than their real dimensions. He also still named Valdes Island as such, but showed the narrow waterways dividing it.

That same year, 1895, Kains also had the Colonist company print, in two colours, two thousand copies of a 1 mile to 1 inch map, *The South-eastern Districts of Vancouver Island*, also by Jörgensen and amply confirming his excellent cartographic skills. It covered Victoria, the Saanich Peninsula, Cowichan harbour, and as far west as Muir Creek. (See Fig. 115, page 185) Two years later, Kains commissioned the same printer to publish three thousand copies of a two-colour map, at 12 miles to 1 inch (1:760,320), *The South-western Part of British Columbia*. The detail shown for Vancouver Island differed little from that of the earlier wall map but omitted Jörgensen's hill shading. No draftsman received credit for the map.

Around the turn of the century, turbulence returned to BC politics. Between 1898 and 1903 there were no fewer than five changes of premier. In 1898 Kains resigned suddenly from his position as surveyor general for, as rumour had it, political reasons, although it could well have been because of his failing health. Gore returned in an acting capacity while retaining the title of deputy commissioner of Lands and Works. Kains died, aged only fifty, soon afterward.

His far-sighted advocacy of the superiority of triangulation over a linear grid for surveys in mountainous terrain was ignored for a generation but revived in 1914 for a huge irrigation project in the Okanagan Valley. Both of Kains's new maps—Brownlee's in 1893 and Jörgensen's finely executed one of two years later—contributed significantly to international awareness of the province's potential for immigrants. The first decade of the new century saw a mounting wave of settlers, not only from Britain but also from Scandinavia and other parts of Europe.

CHAPTER TWENTY-ONE

"Vancouver Island by Land and Water": Reverend William Bolton and *The Province* Expeditions

NOT EVERYONE WHO CONTRIBUTED NEW geographical data to the map of Vancouver Island was a professional hydrographer, surveyor, civil engineer, or social scientist; some amateur explorers and mountaineers helped as well.

The "private explorations" that Tom Kains listed as one of his sources for the Jörgensen map of 1895 originated in the offices of *The Province*, a new weekly magazine in Victoria. For publicity, as well as to generate interesting content, Arthur Scaife, the owner and managing editor, decided to sponsor an exploring expedition.

From discussions with Kains, Scaife knew that the northern half of the interior of Vancouver Island contained "forests and mountains heretofore unpenetrated by explorers," and he conceived a project for a longitudinal trek of the island from its northernmost point to Victoria. Aware of Ralph's marking of the western boundary of the E&N, Scaife felt that the concept might be matched for the rest of the island.

He sought suitable participants and in particular, an expedition leader. At just the right time, an excellent candidate arrived back in Victoria. The Reverend William W. Bolton, MA, was on a three-month leave of absence from his parish in San Francisco. He had been away from Vancouver Island for four years, but before that he had spent three years as rector of St. Paul's Church in Esquimalt. During that time he had acquired "an ardent admiration for the Island of Vancouver" and had returned in order to learn more of it. Born in London, Bolton was educated at Cambridge University. While there, he had proved himself a champion athlete and all-round sportsman; he had mountaineering experience and was a first-class shot. Now aged thirty-six, he remained in excellent physical shape.

At the end of June 1894, Scaife formally appointed Bolton to lead "The 'Province' Exploring Expedition, for the purpose of exploring certain parts of the western interior of Vancouver Island from Cape Commerell to the city of Victoria."[1] Four others with complementary skills—a photographer, an artist, a nutritionist (and mountaineer),

THE "PROVINCE" E

Fig. 116 The Reverend William W. Bolton, on his 1894 attempt to traverse the length of Vancouver Island, relied on this manuscript map, drawn by an anonymous hand at *The Province* magazine. Note the regions marked "Unexplored" on the northern part of the island.

and Jim Magee, a timber cruiser of vast experience and strength—would accompany him.

The intention was to keep to a planned route as closely as possible, on foot except for lakes and rivers, where rafting or paddling was more appropriate. The route ran from Cape Commerell, so named by Captain Richards (but later changed to its earlier, Spanish toponym of Cape Sutil), overland to the head of the western arm of Quatsino Sound. The group would then acquire canoes to convey them through the narrows and into and up the southeastern arm.

From its head, they would continue hiking southeast. After crossing the Gold River, they would attempt to find and verify Buttle's Lake and continue overland to the western end of Great Central Lake. From there, they would take canoes and paddle down the lake, into the Stamp River Valley and on to Alberni. Thence they would paddle halfway down the canal to the mouth of the Franklin River and then walk overland again southeast to the western end of Cowichan Lake. From there, a well-established route led to Victoria by way of Duncans (now Duncan).

The Province team assembled what maps they could, consulted with Kains, and read accounts of some previous explorers. Someone, perhaps on staff, prepared a manuscript map of the island from a variety of sources, some of dubious reliability. (See Fig. 116, pages 188–89) Several blank spaces were marked "Unexplored." Bolton carried this map, drawn on tracing linen, with him on the expedition. He also had copies of the Admiralty chart #1917 of 1865 and Kains's latest published map, the one drawn by Brownlee in 1893. Bolton had barely a few days in which to study those maps and reports, meet with the team, and prepare his plan.

The six-mile (ten-kilometre) cadastral grid for Rupert District at the northwestern end of Vancouver Island, shown on Jörgensen's 1895 map, was the work of three surveyors during the 1891, '92, and '93 seasons. While very little topographic detail was recorded in that region, the surveyors' written reports did describe some characteristics of the numbered "townships." Preliminary tracings of the Rupert District township network and those reports would have been available to Bolton prior to his setting out.

Bolton was disconcerted, later, to find errors in the map. He reported, "We have not had to retrace our steps, though maps have tried their utmost to entrap us . . . We could not tell that the chart was wrong, and came near to paying very dearly for our ignorance."[2] Evidently, neither he nor *The Province*'s cartographer knew of Fry and Gray's explorations of this area in 1887.

Given more time for preparation prior to embarking on his expedition, Bolton would have understood that very little accurate surveying had ever been carried out in this region. He would also have been able to study the reports of previous explorers such as Gooch, Hankin, Brown, Buttle, Meade, and Leech; their accounts would have better prepared him for the weather and the conditions that he would be facing, and warned him of the uncertainties in obtaining local logistical support.

Once they were under way, Bolton soon realized that he needed to change the plan. At Woss Lake, it became clear that it would not be possible to get all the way to Alberni before winter set in. He called a halt for the season and returned to Victoria by way of Tahsis, Friendly Cove, and Alberni, and went back to San Francisco. *The Province* published Bolton's account, rich in descriptive detail, in nineteen weekly instalments.

Nearly two years passed before Bolton could continue his longitudinal traverse of Vancouver Island. In San Francisco he had renewed a friendship from his university athletics days with John William Laing, a Fellow of the Royal Geographic Society (FRGS), an accomplished mountaineer, and a fellow member of the Alpine Club. Laing offered not only to participate in the expedition's continuation, but also to provide a reported twelve hundred dollars to fund it. Bolton's relationship with *The Province* remained good, although the magazine could no longer act as his financial sponsor. Nonetheless, Bolton granted Scaife first right to continue publishing his chronicle in weekly instalments.

The expedition was now called "Vancouver Island by Land and Water" and included Edgar Fleming, a member of a Victoria family of photographers. Bolton had had more time to study reports of earlier travellers on this route: Moffatt in 1852 and Gray and Fry in 1888. An additional advantage was the availability of the newly published Jörgensen map.

From the mouth of the Nimpkish River, the expedition moved inland to recommence its exploration at the southern end of Woss Lake. Well into their season's journey and just before descending to Buttle's Lake, Bolton and his small team skirted a prominent mountain he called Twin Peaks. This would later be called Rooster's Comb and measured as the highest point on Vancouver Island. Later still, it would be renamed Golden Hinde to commemorate Francis Drake's ship.

After covering 315 miles (507 kilometres) in forty-six days, the men reached Alberni, and Bolton threw down his pack in relief, content that "he had traversed Vancouver Island by land and water from end to end."[3] The total journey, by canoe, raft, and on foot, between Cape Commerell and Victoria had been 650 miles (1,046 kilometres), to cover a straight-line distance of 434. No one has yet repeated this arduous achievement.

In his summary, Bolton noted that the central portion he had visited that year "is nothing but a mass of glorious mountains, shining, sparkling glaciers, perpetual snow, torrents, waterfalls, with lakes of every size, some bound the year round in ice . . . It is a beautiful land but only available for the artist, the mountaineer and the sportsman . . . For its size there is no portion of the whole earth where there are more mountain peaks, ridges, rivers, creeks, waterfalls and lakes than on Vancouver Island."[4] He was describing the area that, fifteen years later, would be declared Strathcona Park.

An undated, neatly drawn *Corrected Map of Portion of Vancouver Island explored by Jno. W. Laing M.A. Oxon, FRGS and W.W. Bolton M.A. Cantab* indicated by a dotted red line the route taken by the 1896 team. Since no equivalent map appears to exist for Bolton's earlier expedition, it seems probable that Laing drew it. At a scale of 10 miles to 1 inch (1:633,600), it would have provided useful information for the provincial surveys branch. (See Fig. 117, page 192)

The year 1897 was an exciting one for the people in that branch. Not only was Victoria abuzz with the news of a new gold rush in the Klondike, the branch had a new identity and a new home. It had separated from the lands department and moved into comfortable quarters in the recently completed Parliament Buildings. Among the maps it published that year was one at a scale of 3 miles to 1 inch (1:190,080) "shewing portion of the west coast of Vancouver Island" that was lithographed at the Colonist press. (See Fig. 118, page 193) The map covered the island from Clayoquot Sound to Otter Point and from Alberni across to Nanoose and Nanaimo. The cadastral grid and the roads provided good indicators of the state of settlement at that date.

CHAPTER TWENTY-ONE 191

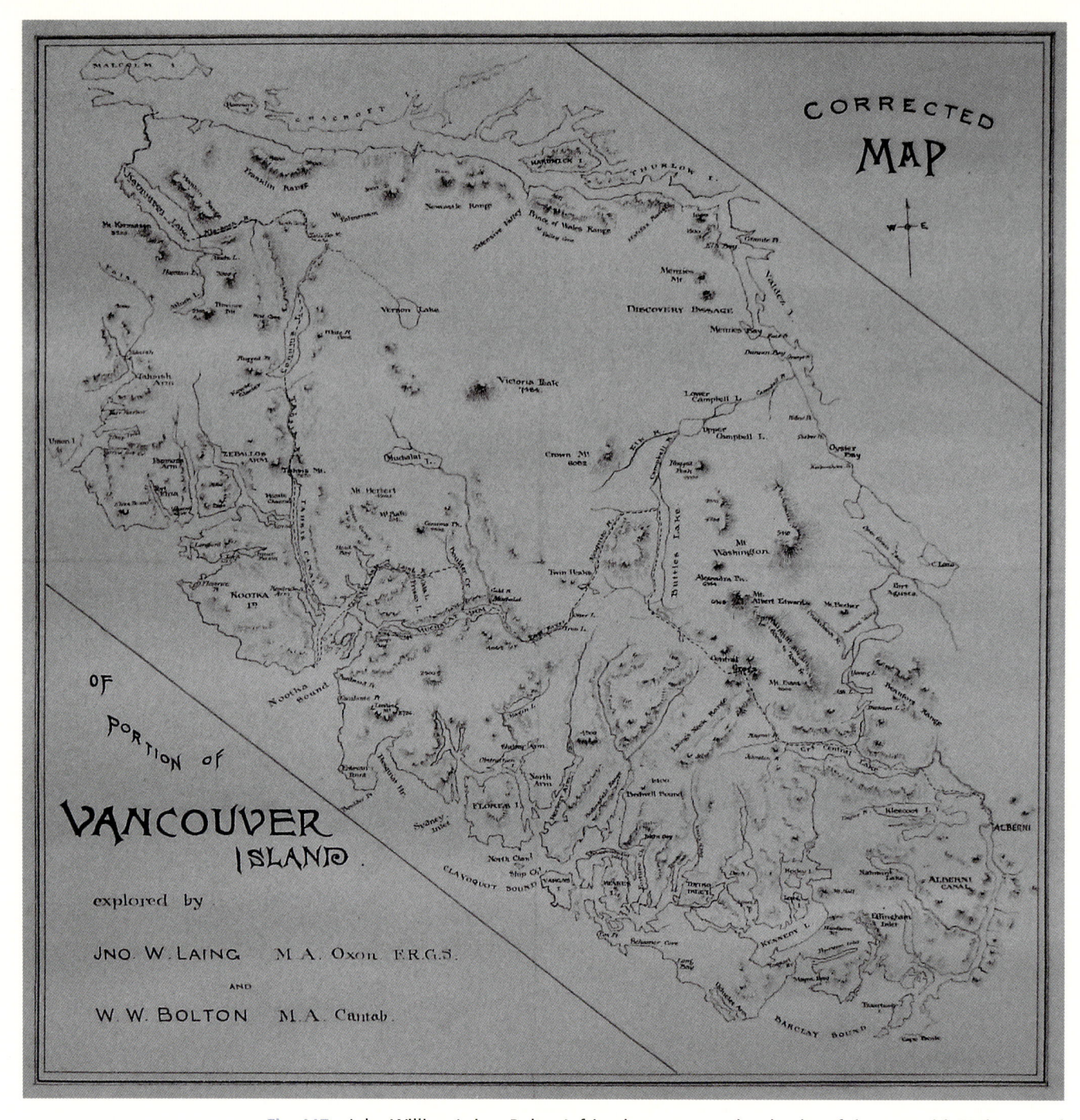

Fig. 117   John William Laing, Bolton's friend, sponsor, and co-leader of the second (1896) stage of the expedition, was the probable author of this map. It shows their route between the mouth of the Nimpkish River and Alberni, including a first traverse of what would become Strathcona Park.

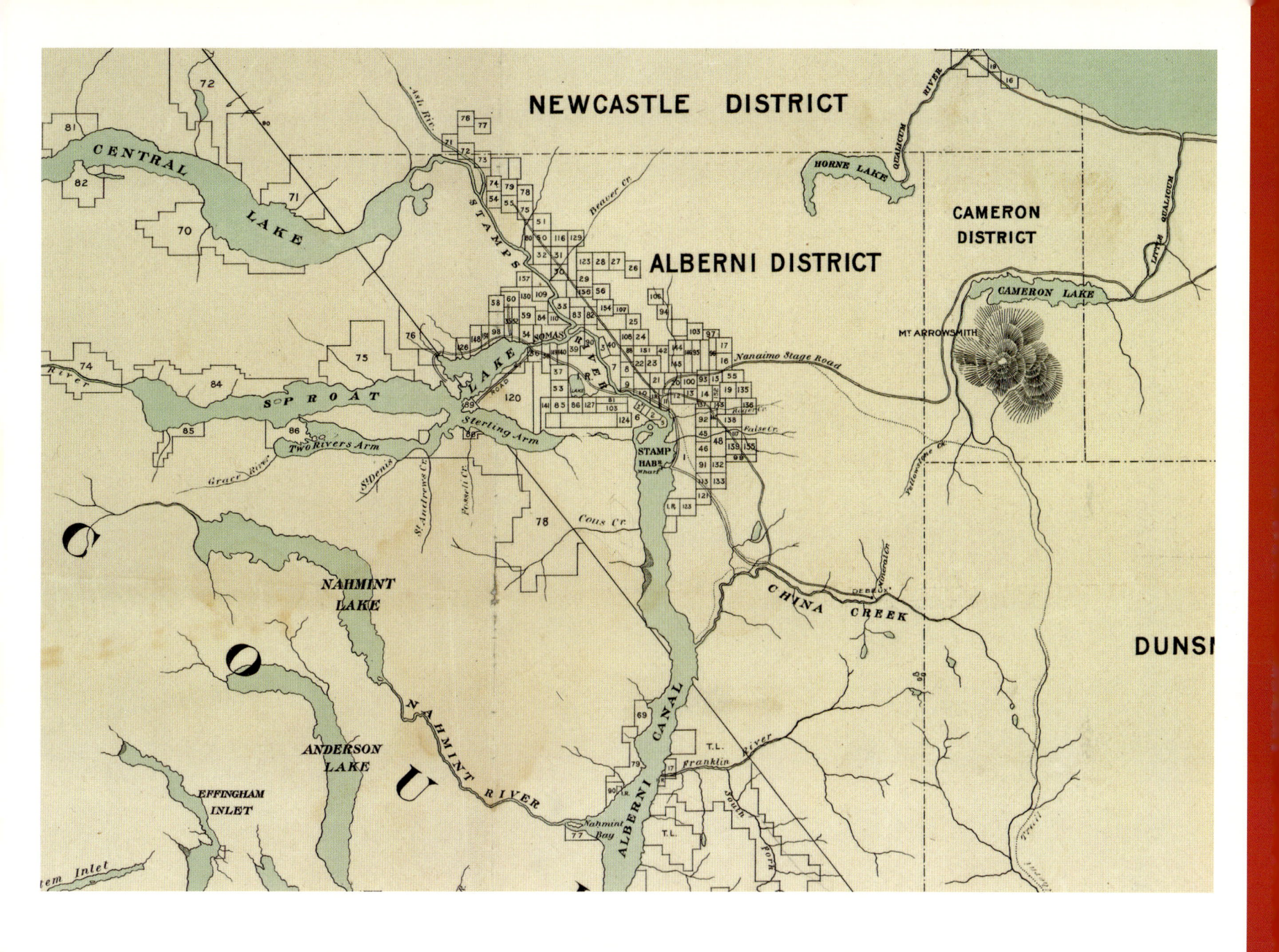

Fig. 118 One of the first maps generated by the newly independent surveys branch of the provincial government, this illustrates the spread of settlement into the Alberni–Sproat Lake area, with its wealth of timber resources and agricultural potential.

TOPOGRAPHY

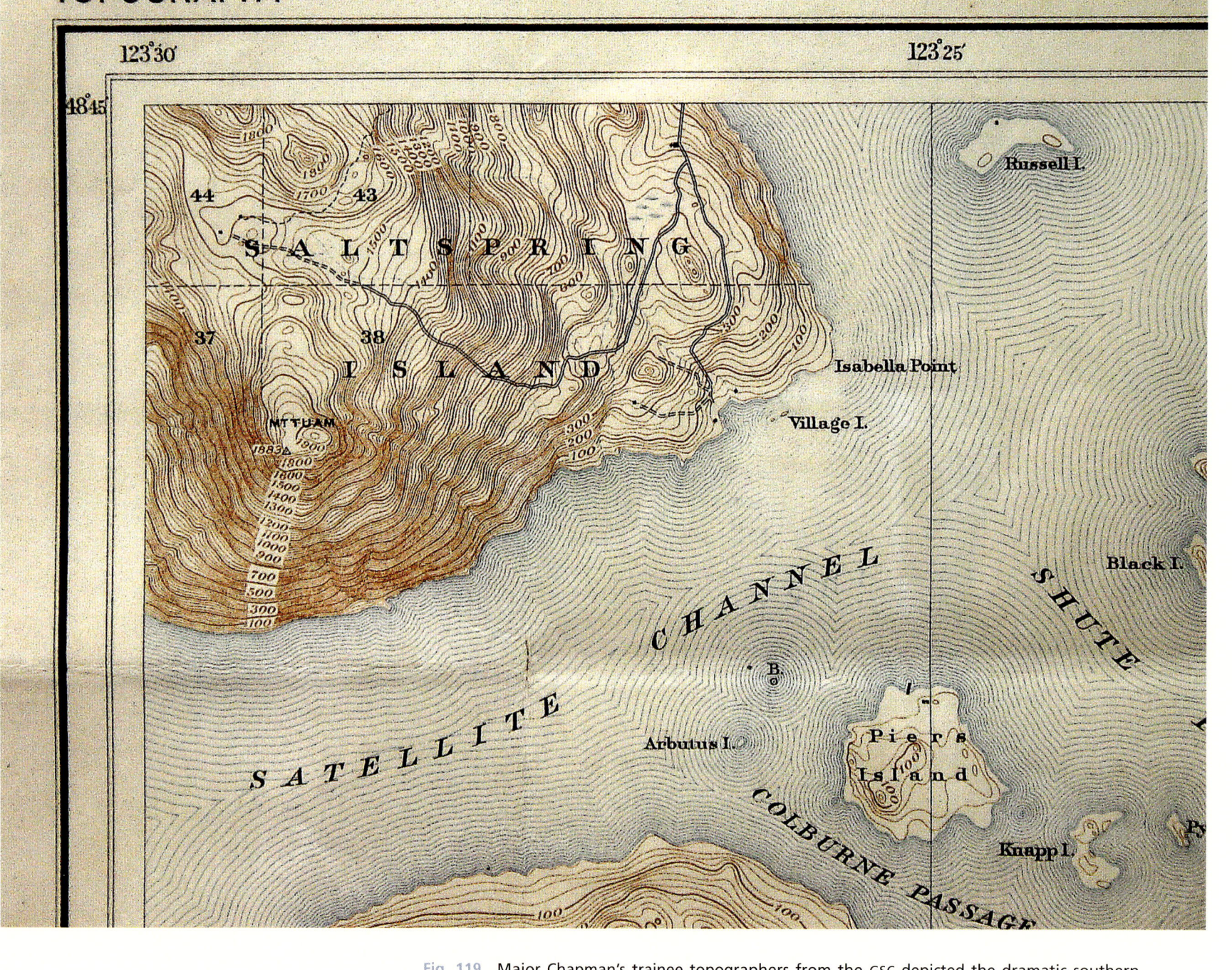

Fig. 119   Major Chapman's trainee topographers from the GSC depicted the dramatic southern ramparts of Mount Tuam, on Saltspring Island, by contours on one of their first map sheets.

CHAPTER TWENTY-TWO

The New Century: The Dominion Comes to the Rescue

THE FIRST DECADE OF THE new century brought about promising reversals to British Columbia's restricted fortunes. In 1903, Richard McBride became premier and managed to secure an annual grant of one hundred thousand dollars from the Dominion for ten years.

McBride championed three interrelated causes: railways, mining, and settlement. The proliferation of railways throughout the province supported the export not only of minerals, especially coal, but of canned salmon and lumber as well. Access by rail also stimulated immigration and settlement in rural areas.

The province's land surveyors finally achieved their Incorporation Act in 1905, and a growing real-estate market brought them increased business.

In 1908, the Geological Survey of Canada (GSC) started a reorganization that benefited BC, creating a new division based in Ottawa and dedicated to topographic mapping under the direction of Walter H. Boyd. He decided to follow the model provided by the US Geological Survey, and hired one of its most senior topographic technicians, Major Robert H. Chapman. He was given a three-year consulting contract to help build the GSC's topographic division.

Chapman advised Boyd on the selection and training of suitable recruits. They looked for reliability, responsibility, technical aptitude, and physical endurance—a scarce combination.

Major Chapman needed an area of terrain that would serve as a training ground for his cadre of topographers. Because it offered the longest field season anywhere in Canada, and because it needed both geological and topographic surveys, he selected the Saanich Peninsula, along with part of Saltspring Island and adjacent Gulf Islands. In June 1909, Chapman came out to Vancouver Island, bringing several parties of trainee topographers.

In Ottawa, the new director of the GSC, Reginald W. Brock, had recruited a second American, the geologist Charles H. Clapp, from the Massachusetts Institute of Technology. Clapp's first task was to reconnoitre the geology

ABOVE

Fig. 120 This shows part of the Cowichan Valley, one of the richest agricultural areas on Vancouver Island, as mapped by Major Chapman's trainee topographers from the GSC.

RIGHT

Fig. 121 This excellent, detailed topographic map, including the wetlands at the estuary of the Nanaimo River between the town and Duke Point, was made by Chapman's GSC trainees.

of southern Vancouver Island and then join Chapman's team of topographers. His three seasons of fieldwork covered the island south of the Alberni–Nanaimo road and east of the Alberni Canal, including Saltspring and other islands in Haro Strait. Between 1912 and 1917 the GSC published several reports and memoirs by Clapp on his reconnaissance, most of which included coloured, lithographed map sheets, both geological—bedrock and superficial—and topographical; the latter was the work of Chapman's teams, and served as base maps for the geologists.

By November they had completed work in the selected area. (See Fig. 119, page 194) The following year, despite the hindrance of forest fires and smoke, followed by periods of continuous, heavy rain, they completed another 1,000 square miles (2,591 square kilometres) of Vancouver Island in various locations. In Chapman's third and final season, 1911, they mapped 2,805 square miles (7,267 square kilometres) around the Alberni and Cowichan settlements, at various scales. The plane tabling method they used was found to be unreliable in densely forested areas such as Great Central Lake, Alberni, and Cowichan. Nonetheless, around settlements such as Victoria, Nanaimo, Duncan, and Sooke, the sheets set a new high standard for topographic maps in Canada. The director of the GSC believed that "these maps compare favourably with those produced anywhere."[1] (See Figs. 120 and 121)

The officer responsible for coordinating the production of all these maps, who had also drawn the Nanaimo sheet, was George G. Aitken. Born in 1885 in Scotland, Aitken had been trained as a cartographer at the Edinburgh Geographic Institute, run by the world-famous map and atlas publishing dynasty John Bartholomew & Son. He then immigrated, first to New York, where he worked with another well-known name in atlases, Hammond's Mapmaking Institute, and later to Ottawa in 1906 to join the GSC. Working under Boyd, Aitken prepared the final manuscripts from which the engraver produced the copper printing plates.

In 1912, the BC government asked the GSC to second someone who could help them establish and manage a provincial geographical or mapping—as opposed to mapmaking—division. When nominated, Aitken agreed, "with Scotch caution," to take three months' leave of absence to see if he might offer the skills needed.

The new BC surveyor general, G. Herbert Dawson (no relation to the late Dr. George M. Dawson), took Aitken to meet McBride, who was by this time Sir Richard. The premier outlined his urgent requirement for a large, detailed map of the province—a wall map—to help plan railways and settlements. Earlier, midway in his premiership, McBride had instructed then-surveyor general Eric "E.B." McKay to prepare a new, single-sheet map of the southern two-thirds of the province. The results so disappointed McBride that he ordered the entire print run destroyed. The overworked, understaffed McKay resigned.

McBride told Aitken that he wanted the new map within six months. Aitken accepted the challenge and the title of BC's chief geographer. His career in that office continued for the next thirty years, interrupted only by military service.

Although it took Aitken's team two months longer than McBride had wanted, their four-sheet wall map of 1912 was used for the next twenty-one years. The urgent need for the new map did not allow time for full depiction of the province's complex topography, so Aitken decided to limit this aspect to indicating just the principal peaks by name and the height of their summits. Dawson reported that the map, published at a scale of 17.75 miles to 1 inch (1:1.125 million), "met with a most flattering reception on the part of the public."² (See Fig. 122)

The following year, by photographic reduction, the Colonist company printed a single-sheet version, at a scale of 30 miles to 1 inch (1:1.9 million), showing planimetric detail and district boundaries only. (See Fig. 123)

Another interesting cartographic variant of the Vancouver Island section of Aitken's 1912 map appeared a year later. A Victoria realtor, Frederick Sturgess, sponsored the publication of a bird's-eye view of the island and the adjacent lower mainland entitled *Physical Map of Vancouver Island 1913*. A cartographic artist, J.H. Kennedy of Seattle, generated a perspective projection of the island and the adjacent coasts as though seen from high above the ocean to the west of the Olympic Peninsula.

Kennedy showed the island's mountains, lakes, rivers, and intricate coastlines in full colour. He also rendered railways, both actual and projected, steamship routes, and puffs of smoke from vessels, pulp mills, and unknown other sources. The title box claims that the view was "prepared from latest official records." More than 660 locations, physical features, and transportation links were numbered and indexed. The Seattle lithographer Stone Limited printed the map, and Sturgess distributed copies in Victoria. (See Fig. 124, pages 200–201)

During the compilation and production of the wall map, Aitken uncovered serious shortfalls in the province's mapping systems. For BC as a whole, geodetic control points were sparse and unsystematic. The only reliable work had resulted from a few sources: the Royal Engineers' Boundary Survey of 1858 to '62 and the various projects of the Columbia Detachment during the same period; hydrographic charting along the coast between 1857 and '70 by Captain Richards in HMS *Plumper*, then *Hecate*, followed by Commander Pender in HMS *Beaver*; the boundaries of the various railway land grants; and a scattering of unadjusted astronomical fixes. The situation on Vancouver Island, particularly the southeastern end, was better, with both coastlines surveyed; in addition, for the previous few years, the hydrographic vessel HMS *Egeria* had been resurveying the coastal waters. Added to these were Ralph's stations along the "spine" and the control points for the ongoing topographic surveying by Chapman's parties.

Aitken also noted that the toponymy of the province "was nearly all in confusion and dispute,"³ so he set about compiling the first official *Geographical Gazetteer of British Columbia*, a work that took him until 1930 to publish. He began by referring to an existing collection of three hundred index cards of the post offices throughout the province. Upon publication, the new listing contained some twenty-five thousand entries with their coordinates. He worked in accordance with rules established by the Geographical Board of Canada and the Royal Geographical Society, of which he was a Fellow.

Aitken's was not BC's first gazetteer. In 1909 a private company in Vancouver, Provincial Publishing, issued a list of forty-seven hundred names and brief descriptions for "Cities, Towns, Post Offices, Settlements, Islands, Rivers, Lakes, Capes, Bays and Mountains of the Province" but without providing coordinates for the places listed. As their source, the publishers claimed "the maps issued by the Information Bureau of the Provincial Government"—the inferior cartography that Aitken had been summoned to rectify. Also that year, the same company published a companion volume, the *Directory of Vancouver Island and Adjacent Islands for 1909*.

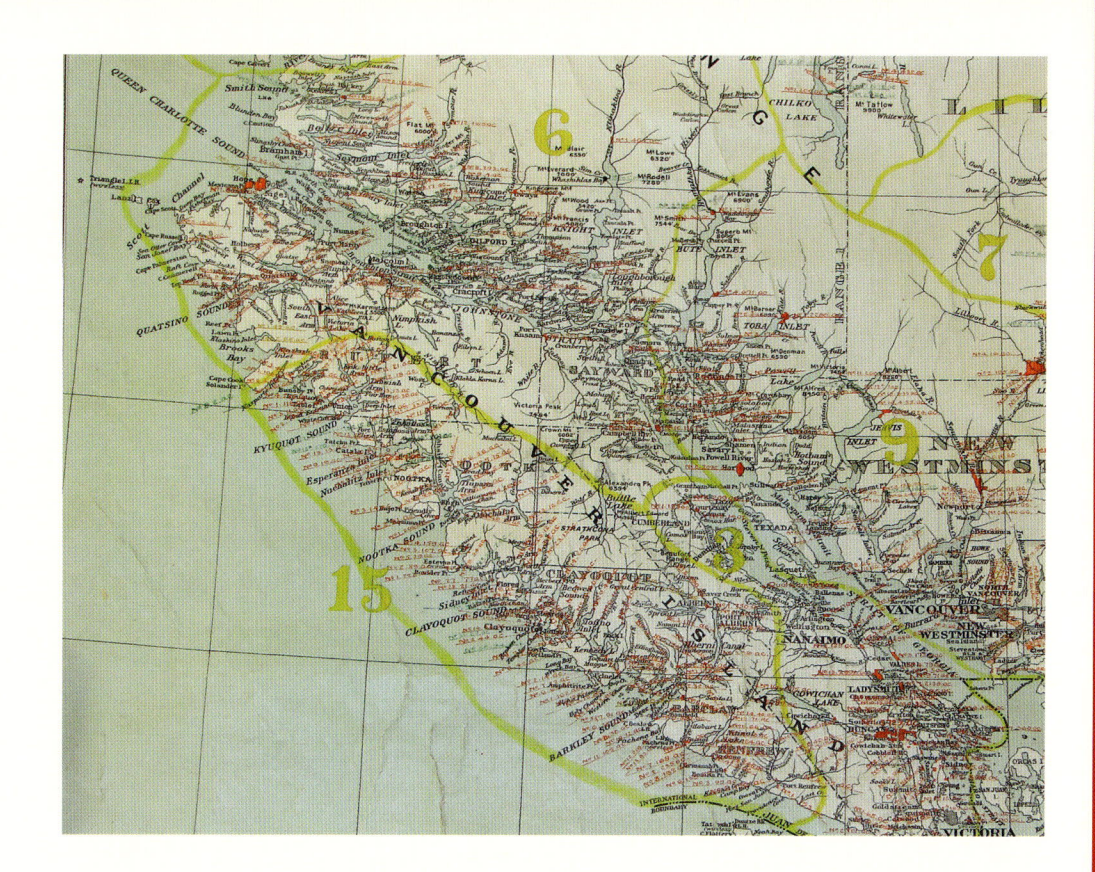

TOP

Fig. 122 Premier Richard McBride gave George Aitken six months to produce a completely new, four-sheet wall map. The tight schedule prevented the inclusion of full relief. This copy was later annotated with Indian Reserves.

RIGHT

Fig. 123 A single-sheet version of Aitken's wall map.

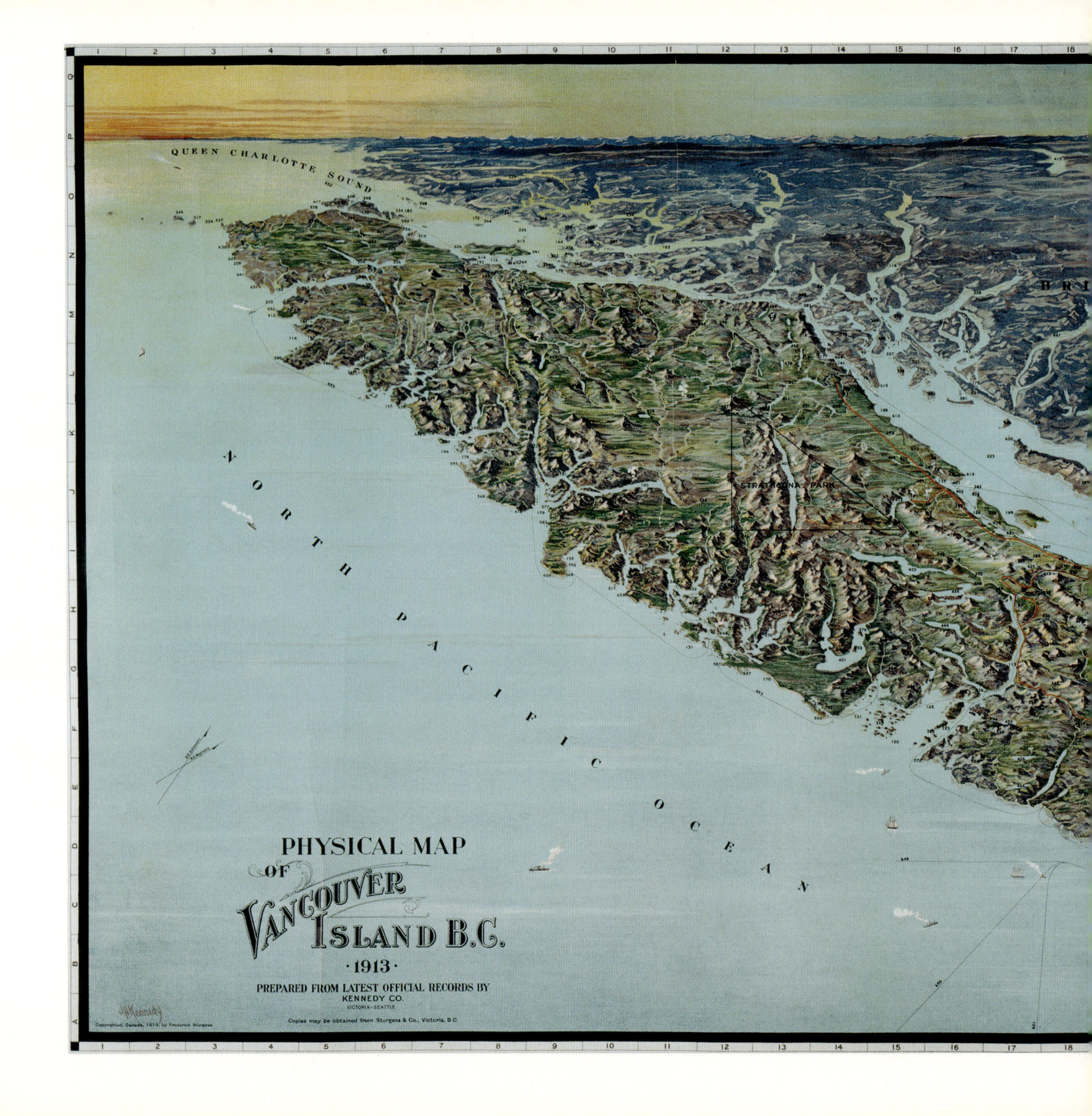

PHYSICAL MAP
OF
Vancouver
Island B.C.
·1913·

PREPARED FROM LATEST OFFICIAL RECORDS BY
KENNEDY CO.
VICTORIA-SEATTLE

Copies may be obtained from Sturgess & Co., Victoria, B.C.

Fig. 124 Kennedy's bird's-eye view of Vancouver Island was derived from part of the 1912 wall map, using perspective geometry. Reflecting popular interest in railways and tourism, the map shows six rail lines, constructed and proposed, and Strathcona Park.

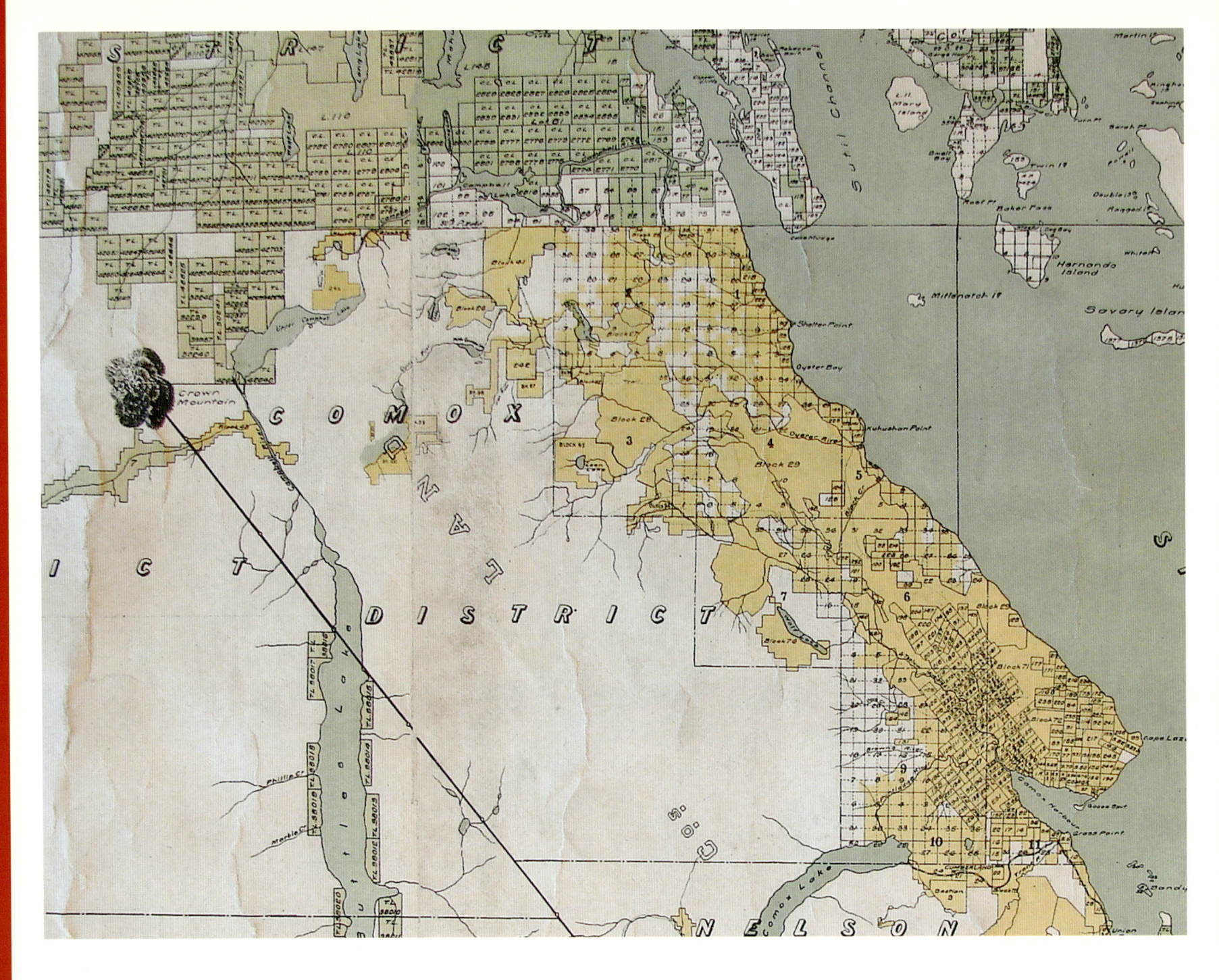

Fig. 125   In response to great demand from settlers, lumber interests, and speculators for maps showing land parcels available, Victoria stationers Hibben & Co. published a series of cadastral maps such as this one.

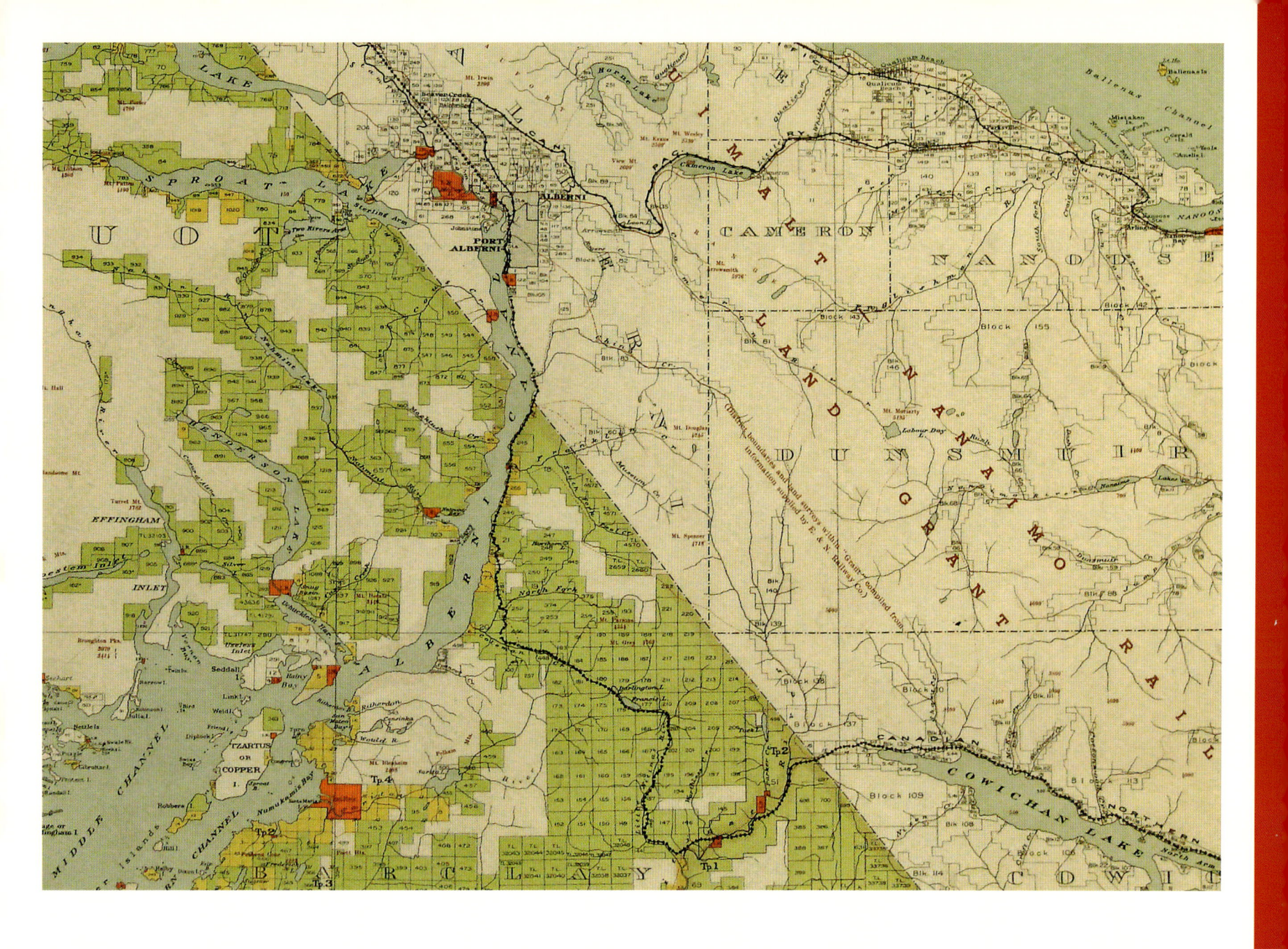

Fig. 126   Aitken adopted the style of Hibben's maps for the first of a two-sheet series covering the island. Only this, the southern sheet, saw publication before the First World War intervened.

At the time of Aitken's taking office, the real-estate boom had been swelling for several years, and there was a huge ongoing demand for maps showing the land available for claiming and for trading. This need had been met by republishing old, generally out-of-date maps. Victoria stationers Hibben & Co. published a series of maps showing the island's cadastral pattern, particularly within the E&N grant. (See Fig. 125, page 202) One version, issued in 1910 at a scale of 4 miles to 1 inch (1:253,440), measured 10 feet (3.04 metres) long. Another call was for maps that showed the roads, to meet the growing novelty of automobile tourism.

In 1913, Dawson and Aitken published the southern sheet of a two-sheet composite map of Vancouver Island that combined cadastral information and communications, and details of rivers and other water features. This map, complementary in style and scale to Hibben's four-mile (six-kilometre) map of the E&N land grant, was printed in four colours by the Colonist. (See Fig. 126, page 203) Publication of the northern sheet came later, delayed by the First World War.

The map recorded the booming economy: It showed dense Crown grants for agricultural settlements throughout the southeastern districts surrounding Victoria, and in the Gulf Islands; several railways both built and under construction, including three along the Saanich Peninsula; and the burgeoning interest in timber leases and licences west of the E&N grant, from Sooke to beyond Alberni. The previous year had seen the creation of the Forest Branch within the Department of Lands; it later became the BC Forest Service, with H.R. MacMillan as the first chief forester. Also, the map documented many Indian Reserves, mostly small, dotting the coasts, inlets, and lakes, but including a large block in the Cowichan Valley.

A flood of applications for pre-emptions, land sales, timber permits, and mineral claims, resulting from booms in settlement and resource speculation, had poured into the lands office in Victoria, and the increased workload swamped the surveyor general's fifteen-man team. "E.B." McKay, who had been chief draftsman for the previous fourteen years, replaced William Gore in 1905, but was unfairly over-burdened and resigned in 1911, McBride's rejection of the new provincial map adding the last straw. He agreed, however, to remain for a year to hand over to G. Herbert Dawson.

Among Dawson's early achievements as BC's surveyor general was a threefold increase in the size of the team. Prior to accepting the position, he had been commissioned to study ways to improve the department's handling of the increased workload, travelling to Ottawa and to Washington, DC. Aitken and his new Geographic Division formed part of that expansion.

Premier McBride not only appreciated the importance of maps for his pet policies fostering settlement, development, and transportation, he now had room in the budget for upgrading the capacity to produce them. The provincial expenditure on surveys in the year 1903–04 (the year McBride took office) was $5,191. By 1910–11 it had grown to $448,885—more than eighty-six times greater. To emphasize the status of this department, the surveyor general now reported directly to the minister of lands.

Dawson was able to bring back Kains's strategy of sending surveyors on reconnaissance surveys into "the unsettled portions of the Province" and publishing abstracts of their reports, which had lapsed during the previous decade. He also dispatched surveyors into areas where cadastral subdivision was needed. He agreed with Aitken (and the premier) about the poor state of mapping of BC, acknowledging that the maps then in use were "in reality sketch maps prepared from the best information available . . . intended for office use only."[4] Copies had been issued, reluctantly, to the public in response to demand.

During 1913 Aitken became concerned about how best to preserve the province's cartographic heritage. Previously, draftsmen at the lands office maintained a set of master maps as working documents, updating them whenever new information arrived. Tracings from these master maps were then issued to other government departments and occasionally to the public. The master maps were also available for consultation by the public. As they were handled, the original paper versions deteriorated to the point of illegibility. Aitken ordered his staff to prepare reference copies of the masters on more durable tracing linen, and he consulted with the British Museum about the preservation of the precious original manuscripts.

❋ ❋ ❋

In 1913, Dr. William King, the chief astronomer of Canada, sent a team of specialists to BC. Among the six first-order geodetic stations they established was one at Bamfield on the island's west coast. That same year, King selected Little Saanich Mountain, a few miles outside Victoria, as the site of the new Dominion Astrophysical Observatory. It would be equipped with the largest reflecting telescope in the world. Part of the observatory's work would be the precise measurement of time, and the related longitudinal position of the location, essential for the geodesy of Vancouver Island.

❋ ❋ ❋

The northern boundary of the E&N land grant had been left unsurveyed and unmarked until 1910, although the southern boundary had been established since 1885 and the western boundary by 1892. William Ralph had surveyed both of those lines. The reason for the delay was that the theoretical northern boundary had changed. The Settlement Act of 1884 described it as "a straight line drawn from Crown Mountain to Seymour Narrows." In 1905, to compensate for the lands that had already been alienated—sold, leased, or identified as reserves—the northern boundary was adjusted to a more complex description. It now ran from the shoreline at Discovery Passage, generally along the 50° parallel, with a dogleg to connect with Ralph's closing point on Crown Mountain.

Five years later, in 1910, the E&N, by then a subsidiary of the CPR, was allowed to select an additional 20,000 acres (8,100 hectares) of land, separate from the original grant; to incorporate the new areas, the northern boundary needed to be established on the ground. A joint survey team was assembled and in September travelled by steamer to Campbell River. Colonel William J. Holmes represented the CPR and Surveyor General McKay nominated Henry Fry to represent the provincial government. Holmes was a well-respected BC land surveyor who had served as secretary-treasurer of the surveyors' association. He and Fry traced the boundary from a previously established post on Discovery Passage, just south of Campbell River, to connect with Ralph's 135-mile (217-kilometre) post of the western boundary on the flank of Crown Mountain. The work took two seasons, with Holmes doing most of the surveying.

After Holmes had completed his traverse, the team turned back for Campbell River but had not yet arrived when a messenger from McKay brought a fresh commission, an expedition to be called The Strathcona Park Discovery Party.

Fig. 127 The first cartographic appearance of what would become Strathcona Park was depicted on this 1911 edition of *The South-western Part of British Columbia* as "Park Reserve."

CHAPTER TWENTY-THREE

"A Sea of Mountains": Strathcona Park

THE JUNE 2, 1910, EDITION of the *Daily Colonist* carried, buried on page four, a short official notice: "A triangle of Crown land, from the summit of Crown Mountain, due south and thence due east to meet the western boundary of the E&N land grant at milepost 100 from Muir Creek, is reserved for Government purposes." Premier McBride instructed his surveyor general, "E.B." McKay, to have the reserved triangle indicated on official maps. The 1911 version of *The South-western Part of British Columbia* was the first to show the new "Park Reserve." (See Fig. 127)

McBride, acutely aware that the real estate boom was deflating, identified tourism as a potential new source of revenue for the treasury, and discussed the concept with his chief commissioner of lands, Price Ellison. They agreed that Ellison should lead an exploratory mission to verify the potential for tourism in the vicinity of Buttle's Lake. Ellison quickly assembled a party of chums, relatives, and specialist advisers. McKay knew that the eminent, experienced surveyor William Holmes was already in the area; he would be the ideal man to guide them.

Ellison's 1911 party, twenty-three strong, was by far the largest Vancouver Island exploring expedition ever, well over twice the size of Robert Brown's in 1864. After achieving the first ascent of Crown Mountain, they made their way along Upper Campbell and Buttle's Lakes. They met the relief party as planned and continued on to Alberni, from there by a new motor road to Nanaimo, and finally, by E&N train to Victoria. Their adventure had lasted about six weeks.

In his official report to McBride, Ellison enthusiastically endorsed the potential for tourism in the area, and the formal declaration of BC's first provincial park, Strathcona, followed one year later. McBride named it for Donald Smith, Lord Strathcona, who had famously driven the last spike of the CPR, uniting Canada from the Atlantic to the Pacific.

The toponym "Strathcona Park" first appeared in the 1912 edition of *The South-western Part of British Columbia*. (See Fig. 128, page 209) That same map depicted McBride's ambitious program of railway construction—both actual and proposed—including an east–west spur line from the Canadian Northern Pacific and the E&N lines between Campbell River and Gold River, crossing the northern apex of the new park. No cartographer is indicated, but it was probably one of the last maps made before George Aitken took over cartographic responsibility from McKay. As new chief geographer, Aitken also included the triangular park in the four-sheet wall map published that same year, adding a few local and recently named peaks.

The location, size, and configuration of the new reserve's boundaries were based on scant information. Little consideration was given to factors other than the limit dictated by the E&N land grant; the initial boundaries did not represent natural factors such as watersheds, wildlife habitat, or even access corridors for the public. Thus, the important feature, Buttle's Lake, had its northern quarter excluded, and there was no provision for a road or rail link to Alberni from the southern end of the park.

Once the act establishing the park was passed, McBride announced the creation of the Strathcona Park Development Company, under the direction of Reginald H. Thomson, an American civil engineer. In 1912 he went to investigate the designated area and its surroundings.

As a result of Thomson's report on his reconnaissance, the official boundaries of the park were extended. The southern boundary was repositioned to Mile 92½ of Ralph's line, an increase of 7.5 miles (12 kilometres), and the western boundary was moved out by about 4 miles (6.4 kilometres). These additional areas ensured the inclusion of many significant peaks, including Tyee, Colonel Foster, Splendor, Lone Wolf, Big Interior, Nine Peaks, and Rosseau, all previously excluded. The expanded park also incorporated the pass between Price and Drinkwater Creeks and Della Falls, Donner and Volcano Lakes, and the upper valley of the Salmon River. Although the whole of Crown Mountain now fell within the park, the northern part of Buttle's Lake remained outside. The estimated area of Strathcona Park was just over 830 square miles (2,152 square kilometres).

Good access for visitors to the park was a priority, so while Thomson was reconnoitring, Holmes surveyed a wagon road from Duncan Bay, near the estuary of the Campbell River, along the south side of the lakes, to Buttle's Lake. The work took him two seasons, with construction crews following close behind.

Thomson prepared an album of snapshots—"A few glimpses of Strathcona Park"—as a gift for Lord Strathcona, the high commissioner for Canada in London, and included a well-executed sketch map of the new park by J.C. Weston, a draftsman in the survey office. By the time Weston drew his map, the northern, southern, and western boundaries of the park had been expanded, almost doubling the area described in the original act. (See Fig. 129, page 210) Thomson invited Strathcona to suggest names for any of the "various rivers, lakes and mountains" within the park, but the high commissioner does not seem to have taken up the offer.

During the summers of 1913 and '14 Thomson employed two American topographers, W.W. Urquhart and W.G. Warnick, to prepare a topographical map of the park. (See Figs. 130 and 131, page 211) A photographer, W.R. Kent, was another member of the team. The work required them to climb many of the peaks within the park to the west of Buttle's Lake. Urquhart's mapping technique, originally developed for the survey of Yellowstone Park, was based on photography.

Also during the 1913 field season, William Holmes surveyed the new northern and western boundaries of the

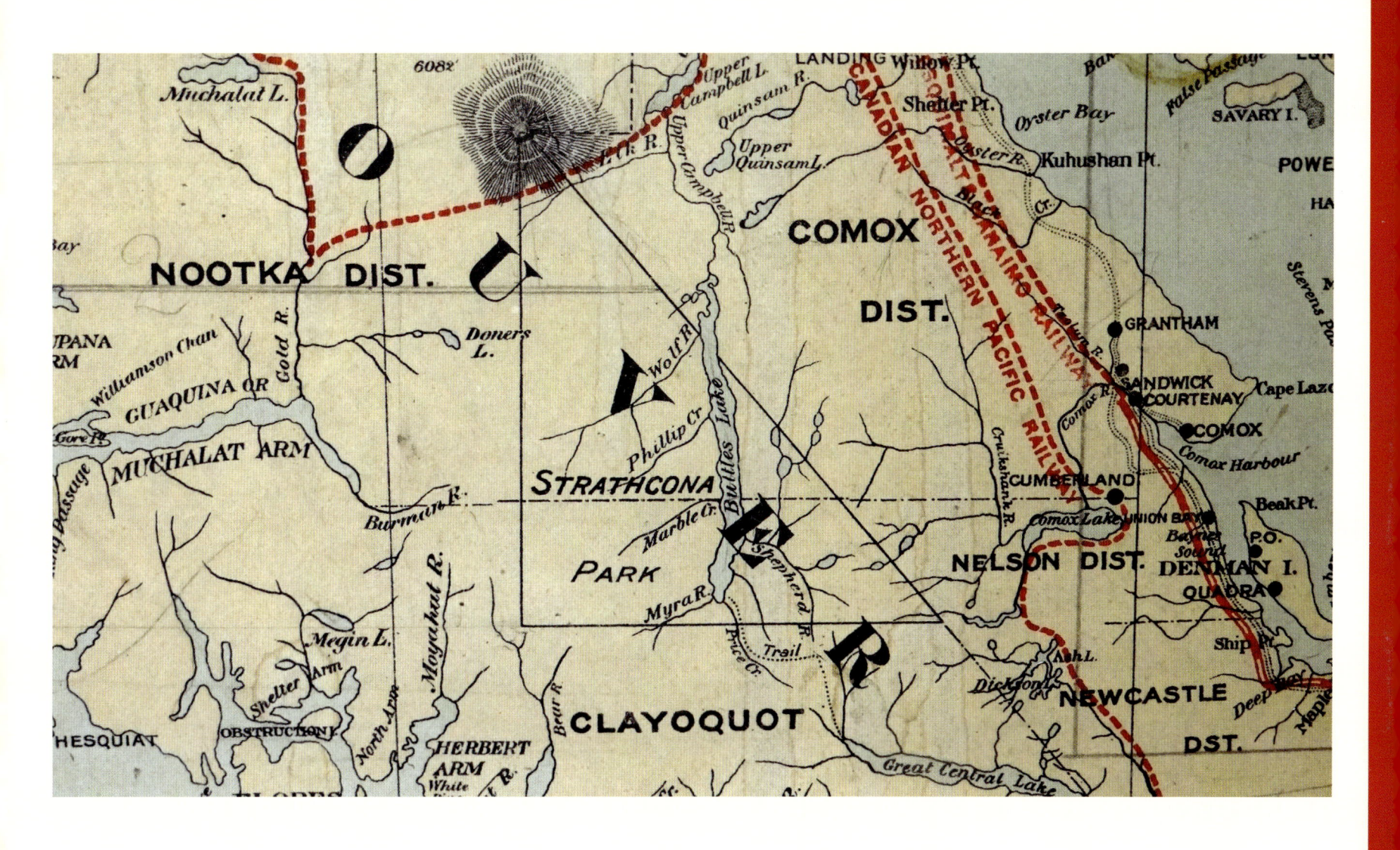

Fig. 128   This 1912 edition was the first published map to carry the new toponym Strathcona Park. The area is larger than that indicated a year earlier as "Park Reserve."

Fig. 129 This map accompanied an album of scenic photos presented to Lord Strathcona, the park's nominal patron, by Premier McBride in 1913. Note that the area has again been expanded to the north, west, and south.

park and the two neighbouring districts and established a triangulation network from which they surveyed and marked every second mile of the boundary with five-foot (two-metre) cedar posts.

The outbreak of the "European War," as it was called in the provincial press, halted the progress of Strathcona Park as well as other mapping operations. During the course of 1914 and '15, cartographic activity for Vancouver Island dropped drastically. The war brought surveying and mapping, province-wide, to a standstill. A significant portion of the technical staff, including George Aitken, and professional contractors had enlisted, and public funds available to the branch were severely curtailed. Although immigration had also diminished, reducing some of the workload, the scarce remaining resources focused on registering full title to earlier pre-emptions rather than on topographic mapping.

The state of geographical knowledge about the island and its surrounding waters was still incomplete. HMS *Egeria* had resurveyed Richards's hydrographic work using improved technology. While there was reasonable general chorography for the settled regions of the southern half, as shown on the 1913 composite map, only preliminary work had been completed on the corresponding northern sheet. Much remained to be done throughout the island once peace had been secured and economic prosperity could return.

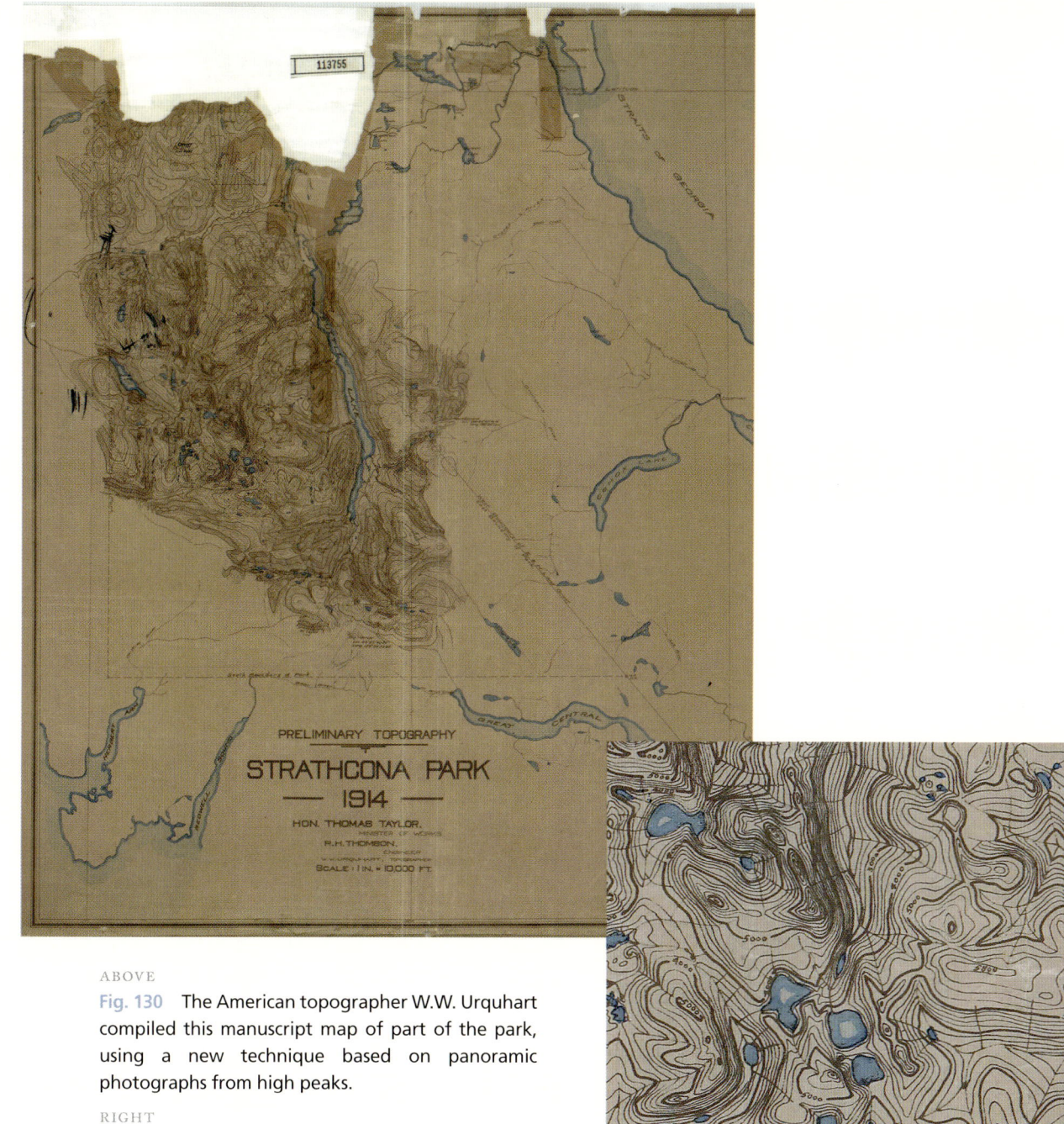

ABOVE
Fig. 130 The American topographer W.W. Urquhart compiled this manuscript map of part of the park, using a new technique based on panoramic photographs from high peaks.

RIGHT
Fig. 131 The triple peak to the north of the lakes, centre left, was called Rooster's Comb originally. The main peak was later measured to be the highest on the island and renamed Golden Hinde.

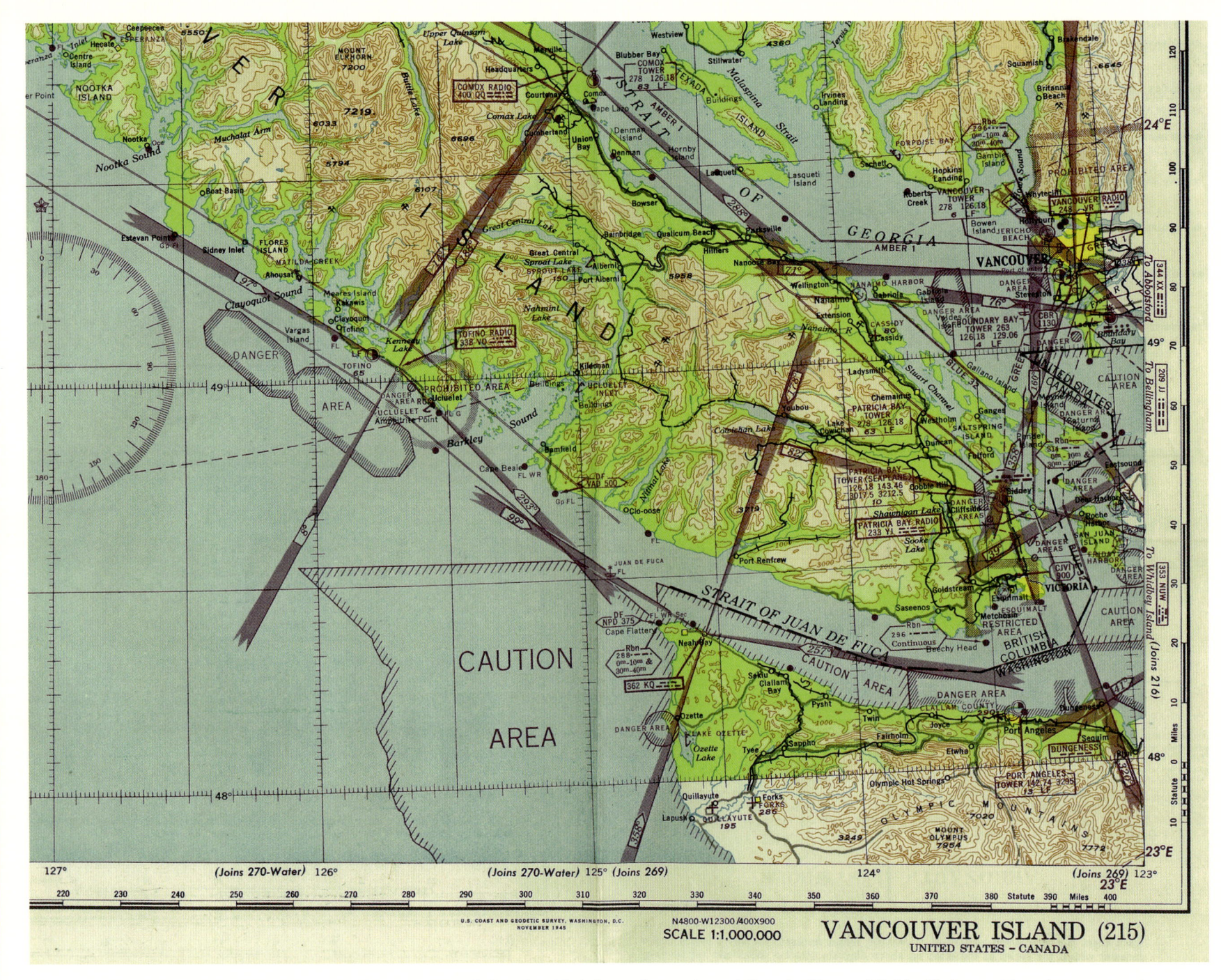

Fig. 132 Specialized charts to provide operators of aircraft with information such as civil and military airfields, flight corridors, beacons, and radio frequencies, as well as visible landmarks such as lighthouses, railway lines, lakes, and mountains, are vital to navigators reliant on their eyes to fix their location.

Afterword

THE EXPLORATION AND MAPPING OF Vancouver Island was not completed by 1915. Nor did this work cease. Following the First World War, despite tight economic times, surveyors still explored the forests and mountains and they continued to submit area reports for publication by the Department of Lands. They extended the triangulation network and made innovative use of panoramic horizon photography for triangulation and terrain mapping.

The Second World War brought enormous technological developments to the science and practice of making maps. Airborne cameras for taking vertical photography, precise instruments for the stereoscopic viewing of those photographs, and measuring and plotting the results onto maps, all saw huge advances due to the war effort. Photogrammetric technicians, trained and practised in the use of the instruments, came home when hostilities concluded, as did pilots, navigators, and interpreters of air photos. War-surplus aircraft fitted for photography, aerial cameras, and stereo-plotting instruments came onto the market.

Specialized air-survey firms set up in business offering their services to governments. In BC, the growing economic implications of the forest justified the establishment of the provincial government's own air-survey division within the Survey Branch, headed by the innovative forester and engineer Lieutenant-Colonel "Gerry" Andrews. The photographic output brought dual benefit: it enabled interpretation of the canopy of the forests, increasingly important to both the lumber industry and its regulators, and was used for topographic mapping by photogrammetry. In 1948 a helicopter was chartered for BC forest-survey work, the first time in Canada.

Lithographic printing made similar strides forward for military purposes, and these improvements were immediately used for producing civilian maps. The systematic production and publication of the BC *Regional Map Series* by the Geographic Branch, Department of Lands, had begun under George Aitken in 1911. It continued until 1970, when it became the Map Production Division.

Other map series were also published: *Geographic*, *Land*, and *Pre-emptors'*.

From 1904 on, maps for military purposes, especially with contours, became a priority. This need included Vancouver Island, since Esquimalt, the home port for the British fleet in the Pacific, continued as the western base for the new Naval Service of Canada. The topographical surveys branch of the Department of the Interior and the mapping branch of Military Intelligence each developed a separate series of maps, based on the British Ordnance Survey, at a scale of 1 inch to 1 mile (1:63,360).

In the 1920s, three federal agencies—Department of the Interior, Geological Survey of Canada, and Department of National Defence—agreed to cooperate in a single Canada-wide system for map sheets, which eventually became the National Topographic System (or Series). Within the NTS structure, topographic maps at scales of 1, 2, 4, 8, and 16 inches to 1 mile fitted, without gaps or overlaps, into a coherent reference system and to a standard cartographic design. In the 1950s, the NTS was converted to metric equivalents.

British Columbia, in contrast to many of the other provinces, maintained its own air-survey and cartographic capability for some decades after the creation of the topographic division of the Geological Survey of Canada. Thus, two systems of map sheets continued to be published until about 1970, when the NTS finally replaced BC's provincial map series. (See Fig. 133)

In 1910, after a short transition period with their Admiralty counterparts aboard HMS *Egeria*, the Canadian Hydrographic Service took over responsibility for local charting in the waters surrounding Vancouver Island. Developments in technology from wartime stimulus also benefited hydrographers by bringing great advances in depth finding by sonar and radar ranging, as well as radar and radio navigational beacons.

In the air, too, cartographic developments occurred during and after the Second World War. With the great increase in air traffic came the need for special aeronautical charts, the first of which, covering Vancouver Island, appeared in 1939, with revisions published in the early 1940s. In 1945, the Canadian system merged with the international World Aeronautical Chart system, and sheet #215, at a scale of 16 miles to 1 inch (1:1 million), covered Vancouver Island. After the first edition, it was updated twice a year. (See Fig. 132, page 212)

More recently, advances in computer-based digital mapping, now called "spatial data," have continued to radically alter the field of cartography. So have developments in satellite technology, both positional (GPS) and multispectral imagery, and the growth and use of Geographic Information Systems (GIS) such as Google Earth and more local terrain and real-estate databases.

To keep abreast of developments in demographics and land use, the mapping of Vancouver Island should continue to progress for the foreseeable future.

Fig. 133   The heavy blue lines on the NTS index map indicate maps at scale 1:250,000. For example, most of Strathcona Park is on sheet #92 F. The lighter lines show scale 1:50,000. For example, Sooke is on sheet #92 B/5.

Glossary

Cadastral: Pertaining to the system of documenting and registering real property boundaries. Also called legal mapping.

Careen (naut.): To turn a ship on its side for cleaning, caulking, or repairing.

Chorography: The geographical description or depiction of a region—includes mapping and natural-resource inventories.

Chronometer: An exceptionally precise clock, watch, or other timepiece.

Datum (Chart): The level below which depths are indicated on a marine chart and above which heights of the tide are expressed. It usually indicates the mean level of low water at ordinary spring tide.

DLS: Dominion Land Surveyor.

E&N: Esquimalt & Nanaimo Railway company.

Gazetteer: A geographical dictionary or index of place names.

Geodesy (n.; geodetic, adj.): The mathematical science of calculating or measuring the shape of the Earth or large areas of land. High-precision observation and spherical geometry are normally involved.

GIS: Geographical Information System. A digital database of terrain-related information.

GPS: Geographical Positioning System. A method of position finding from a network of specialized orbiting satellites and ground receivers.

GSC: Geological Survey of Canada. A federal government agency, earlier known as the Geological and Natural History Survey of Canada.

Hachure: A conventional sign on a topographic map depicting slopes.

Hydrography: Specialized mapping or charting of oceans, lakes, rivers, and other surface waters, emphasizing depths of water.

Latitude: The angle between a point on the Earth's surface and the equator, north or south. Since Vancouver Island and its vicinity are all within the northern hemisphere, either the qualifier, or the term latitude, have been omitted in this work as redundant.

Lee shore (naut.): The situation of a ship positioned or manoeuvring close to shore when the wind is blowing toward that shore. Perilous for vessels reliant on sails.

NTS: National Topographic Series, the reference system for Canadian mapping.

Oolichan, or grease, trail: Traditional overland trade route in the Pacific Northwest used to bring grease from oolichan ("candlefish"), harvested by coastal people, into the interior.

Photogrammetry: The science and practice of determining accurate 3D positions for cartographic detail and terrain data (such as contours) from stereoscopic pairs of vertical aerial photographs. There are also non-cartographic applications.

Pinnace (naut.): A ship's boat fitted with a mast and sails or rowed by up to sixteen oars. Used for inshore charting work prior to advent of inboard engines.

Plat: A type of map specifically showing cadastre or real-estate/legal boundaries. Used in registering property rights.

Prime meridian: The line of longitude designated as zero (or 180) degrees. Usually defined in conjunction with a fixed, terrestrial observatory, such as Greenwich, but most European maritime powers designated and used their own (sometimes multiple) prime meridians.

RE: The [Corps of the] Royal Engineers, a technical service of the British Army. Members of the corps are known, collectively and individually, as sappers.

RGS: The Royal Geographical Society. The London-based learned society founded in 1830, dedicated to worldwide geographical exploration, research, and education.

RN (naut.): Pertaining to the British Royal Navy. Added to the rank of officers and men—for example, Henry Richards, Captain, RN.

Running survey (naut.): A method of charting a coastline while remaining aboard ship and under way. Angles between identified points along the coastline are measured and recorded, as well as the vessel's course and estimated distance run.

Station pointer (naut.): A three-armed protractor used to chart a vessel's position from two simultaneous, horizontal, sextant angles taken between three fixed points ("stations") on shore.

Timber cruising: The field survey activity of assessing the value of standing timber by recording density, size, and condition of tree species in an area of forest. Ease of access is also considered.

Toponymy: The aspect of chorography (c.f.) associated with geographic place names.

Traverse: A survey technique to calculate the coordinates of a series of points on the ground by means of measuring the bearing and distance from one point to the next. The starting point and opening bearing are obtained from previous work, and the traverse "closes" on another known point or loops back on itself.

USGS: United States Geological Survey, the US federal geosciences and mapping agency.

Vigia (naut.): A suspected or reported hazard to shipping not yet surveyed accurately or depicted on charts, such as a rock, reef, or sandbank below the surface, of potential danger to passing vessels.

Voltigeurs: A lightly armed militia, formed by the HBC mainly from Métis and French Canadian employees, skilled in backwoodsmanship.

Endnotes

Dedication
1. Theroux, "Mapping the World," p. 278.

Chapter One: Maps of Speculation
1. Hodgins, *A Passion for Narrative*, p. 261.

Chapter Two: Maps of Mystery
1. Bishop, "Drake's Course in the Pacific."

Chapter Three: First European Contact
1. Beals, *Juan Pérez*, p. 28.
2. Beals, "The Juan Pérez-Josef De Cañizarez Map," pp. 46–56.
3. Ibid.
4. Barrington, "Maurelle's Journal."

Chapter Four: *Makook!*
1. Cook's secret orders from the Admiralty are #2/1343, reprinted in Harlow and Madden, eds., *British Colonial Developments, 1774–1834*, Oxford, UK: Clarendon Press, 1953, pp. 1–4.

Chapter Five: Soft Gold
1. Hill, with Converse, *Frances Barkley*, p. 53.

Chapter Six: Imperial Flashpoint
1. Meares, *Voyages*.
2. Dixon, *Remarks on the voyages of John Meares Esq.*, p. 22.

Chapter Seven: "Exploration Will Resolve the Doubts"
1. Wagner, *Spanish Explorations in the Strait of Juan de Fuca*, p. 206.
2. Doe, "Gabriola's Coastal Place Names," p. 30.
3. McDowell, *José Narváez*.
4. Jane, *A Spanish Voyage*, p. 89.

Chapter Eight: "No Place More Eligible"
1. Lamb, Kaye, *Voyage of George Vancouver*, pp. 42, 283–86.
2. Ibid., p. 672.
3. Seeman, *Narrative of the Voyage*, p. 110.
4. For a full biography of Bodega y Quadra, see Tovell, *At the Far Reaches of Empire*.
5. Lamb, Kaye, *Voyage of George Vancouver*, p. 1390 f.
6. Ibid.
7. Clayton, *Islands of Truth*.

Chapter Nine: "A Perfect 'Eden'"
1. Verner, "The Arrowsmith firm." See also Ruggles, *A Country So Interesting*, p. 118.
2. *The New Encyclopedia Britannica*, Volume 8, 15th Edition, 1993, under "Monroe Doctrine."
3. Cook, *Flood Tide of Empire*, p. 521.
4. Douglas to McLoughlin, Fort Vancouver, July 12, 1842, quoted in "Founding of Fort Victoria," *The Beaver*, March 1943, pp. 4–7.
5. Pelly to McLoughlin, December 31, 1839, HBC Archives A.6/25 fo. 54d.
6. Glazebrook, *The Hargrave Correspondence*, p. 420.
7. Begg, *The History of British Columbia*, p. 156.

Chapter Ten: Settling into Fort Victoria
1. Bancroft, "Memorial on the Canal de Haro," p. 14. Also HBC Governor & Committee to Board of Management, October 7, 1846, HBC Archives A.6/27 fo. 60.
2. Ms. annotation on map *Vancouvers Island*, 2nd edition, Wyld, James, National Archives, Kew, UK: FO 925–1479, 1861 [but refers to first edition, 1848].

Chapter Eleven: "In Free and Common Socage"
1. Barman, Jean, *The West Beyond the West* (revised edition), Toronto: University of Toronto Press, 1996, p. 56.
2. Cited in Bowsfield, *Fort Victoria Letters*, Barclay to Douglas, December 17, 1849, fo. 91, p. liii.
3. *London Correspondence Inward from Eden Colvile 1849-51*, London: The Champlain Society, Volume 19, p. 11.
4. *Statutes at Large* (37 volumes), "Administration of Justice (Vancouver's Island) 1849," art. IV, p. 284.
5. Duff, Wilson, "The Fort Victoria Treaties," pp. 3–57.
6. Douglas to Barclay, September 3, 1849, HBC Archives A-11/72.
7. Barclay to Douglas, February 8, 1850, cited in Ireland, Willard, "Captain Walter Colquhoun Grant," p. 102, note 49.
8. Bowsfield, *Fort Victoria Letters*, Douglas to Barclay, November 16, 1850.

Chapter Twelve: Pemberton and Pearse
The most thorough study to date of the maps of Pemberton's work with the HBC is Ruggles, *A Country So Interesting*, Chapter 12.
1. Barclay A. to Pemberton, London, February 1851, BC Archives A/C/15, p. 36.
2. Bowsfield, *Fort Victoria Letters*, Douglas to Barclay, October 6, 1851, p. 218.
3. *J.D.P.'s Correspondence*, Report, January 5, 1852, p. 27.
4. Bowsfield, *Fort Victoria Letters*, Douglas to Barclay, September 3, 1849, p. 47.
5. Ibid., p. 42.
6. Douglas, "Report of a Canoe Expedition."
7. Doe, "A Russian Map of Gabriola."
8. Ibid., p. 17.
9. Pemberton, *Facts and Figures*, p. 143.
10. Ibid., p. 148.

Chapter Thirteen: Explosive Growth
1. Douglas to Barclay, February 11, 1854, cited in Sampson, "My Father, J.D. Pemberton."
2. Barclay to Pemberton, July 28, 1854, BC Archives A/C/10, p. 36.
3. Smith to Pemberton, October 8, 1855, BC Archives A/C/15, p. 36.
4. Pemberton, *Facts and Figures*, p. 131.
5. The most detailed account to date of the RE Columbia Detachment is Woodward, "Influence of the Royal Engineers," pp. 3–51. See also an informative website created by a local group of "living history" enthusiasts, royalengineers.ca.
6. Imperial Statute, August 2, 1858, cited in Ireland, "Evolution of the Boundaries," p. 274.
7. Miller, Hunter, *The San Juan Archipelago*, Bellows Falls, Vt.: Wyndham Press, 1943, p. 46.

Chapter Fourteen: The San Juan Dispute
1. Duntz, Captain J.A., "Six Months in Puget Sound," *The Nautical Magazine*, May 21, 1852, p. 248.
2. Moody to Arthur Blackwood, February 1, 1859, cited in Ireland, "First Impressions," p. 106.
3. *Papers relating to The Treaty of Washington, Volume V.—Berlin Arbitration*, Washington: Government Printing Office, 1872. (Includes reproductions of thirty-seven maps.)

Chapter Fifteen: "Navigating this Boisterous Neighbourhood"
1. Washington, *Hydrographic Instructions for Capt. George Richards*.
2. Ibid., p. 6.
3. Mayne, *Four Years*, p. 220.
4. Richards to Douglas, June 20, 1862, printed in *British Colonist*, December 13, 1862, p. 3.
5. Biographies of Richards, Mayne, and Pender are in Dawson, *Memoirs of Hydrography*.

Chapter Sixteen: "The Back of the World"
1. Colonial Dispatches, June 10, 1858, Ref 7828 60/1.
2. Wells, Oliver, *General report on the Cowichan Valley*, Victoria: Colonial Secretary's Office, s.n. 1860?, University of Victoria Library Microforms CIHM 17246.

Chapter Seventeen: The Vancouver Island Exploring Expeditions
1. Rattray, *Vancouver Island*, p. 3.
2. Letter signed "Geographicus" to editors *Daily Chronicle*, May 4 (published May 8 and 10), 1864. See Hayman, *Robert Brown*, p. 34.
3. Brown, "First Journey," *Illustrated Travels*, I, p. 275.
4. Buttle, John, report to Colonial Secretary, July 26, 1865, BC Archives G V27 V27A.
5. Buttle, John, "Journal," August 2, 1865, BC Archives G V47 B97A, pp. 59–60.
6. Brown, "First Journey," *Illustrated Travels*.
7. Brown, *Memoir*.

Chapter Eighteen: Canada's New Province
1. Brown, *Memoir*.
2. Trutch, Joseph W., letter to Colonial Secretary, February 5, 1869, BC Archives B 0134, F 954-3; also Pearse to Walkem, July 17, 1872, BC Archives W185, 186, and 191a.
3. Andrews, G.S., *Sir Joseph William Trutch*, Victoria: BC Land Service in cooperation with Corporation of Land Surveyors of BC, 1972, p. 27.
4. *Daily Colonist*, March 14, 1878, p. 2, "Nanaimo."
5. Carr, Emily, *The Book of Small*, Toronto and London: Oxford University Press, 1942, p. 245.

Chapter Nineteen: The Two-Million-Acre Dowry
1. Manuscript report by Mohun, October 29, 1873, in BC Archives GR 0868, B16901-1-6, 1856/73.

2. Rowan, Andrew S., [secret] *Preliminary Report on Fortifications at Esquimalt, Victoria, BC*, Seattle WA, 1897. Copy held in library, Fort Rodd Hill National Historic Site.
3. *Abstracts from Reports on Vancouver Island Made by British Columbia Land Surveyors to the Department of Lands 1887–1928*, Victoria: Department of Lands, 1929.

Chapter Twenty: "The Most Perfect Map"
1. Andrews, G. S., "The Land Surveying Profession in British Columbia," *Proceedings of the Fiftieth AGM of the Corporation of Land Surveyors of the Province of British Columbia*, Victoria, 1955, pp. 62-63.
2. Boas, Franz, *Geographical Names of the Kwakiutl Indians*, New York: Columbia University Press, 1934, p. 9.
3. Surveyor General's Report for 1891, *Sessional Papers 1892*, p. 349.
4. Surveyor General's Report for 1893, *Sessional Papers 1894*, p. 954.
5. Surveyor General's Report for 1895, *Sessional Papers 1896*, p. 734.

Chapter Twenty-One: "Vancouver Island by Land and Water"
1. "The 'Province' Exploring Expedition," *The Province*, Victoria: June 16, 1894. Scrapbook of clippings, BC Archives MS-2777, Microfilm A 1682, p. 1.
2. Ibid., pp. 6, 24.
3. "Vancouver Island by Land and Water," *The Province*, Victoria, December 5, 1896, p. 850.
4. Ibid., August 22, 1896, p. 585.

Chapter Twenty-Two: The New Century
1. "Summary Report, Geological Survey of Canada," *Canadian Sessional Papers*, Ottawa, Number 26, 1911, p. 7.
2. Survey Branch, *Annual Report for 1913*, Victoria: Department of Lands, p. 9.
3. Aitken, G.G., "A few recollections of thirty years of maps and map makers in British Columbia," Association of BC Land Surveyors, *Proceedings*, *1939*, Victoria, p. 44.
4. Surveyor General's *Annual Report for 1911*, p. G10.

Bibliography

Bancroft, George, "Memorial on the Canal de Haro...," in Papers related to the Treaty of Washington, Washington: US Government Printing Office, 1872.

Barrington, Daines, "Maurelle's [sic] Journal of a Voyage from New Spain to Alaska," *Miscellanies*, London: 1781.

Beaglehole, John, ed., *The Journals of Captain Cook on his voyages of discovery*, Volume 3, *The Voyage of the 'Revolution' and 'Discovery' 1776-1780*, Cambridge, UK: The Hakluyt Society, 1967.

Beals, Herbert K., "The Juan Pérez-Josef De Cañizarez Map of the Northwest Coast," *Terrae Incognitae* (Journal of the Society for the History of Discoveries), Volume XXVII, 1995.

———, *Juan Pérez on the Northwest Coast*, Portland, OR: Oregon Historical Society, 1989.

Begg, Alexander, *The History of British Columbia from its earliest discovery to the present time*, Toronto: William Briggs, 1894.

Bishop, Richard, "Drake's Course in the Pacific," *BC Historical Quarterly*, Volume VIII, Number 8, 1939.

Bowsfield, Hartwell, ed., *Fort Victoria Letters 1846–1851*, Winnipeg: Hudson's Bay Record Society, 1979.

Brown, Robert, "The First Journey of Exploration Across Vancouver Island," a series of articles in *Illustrated Travels*, H.W. Bates, ed., 6 volumes, London, Paris and New York: Cassell, Petter & Gilpin, ND, c. 1880.

———, "Memoir on the Geography of the Colony of Vancouver Island," BC Archives MS–0749, Volume 1, File 10.

Clayton, Daniel W., *Islands of Truth: The Imperial Fashioning of Vancouver Island*, Vancouver: University of British Columbia Press, 2004.

Colonial Dispatches (online), bcgenesis.uvic.ca.

Cook, Warren L., *Flood Tide of Empire: Spain and the Pacific Northwest 1543-1819*. New Haven and London: Yale University Press, 1973.

Cotton, H. Barry, *The L.S. Group: BC's First Land Surveyors*, Victoria: The Association of BC Land Surveyors, 2007.

Cutter, Donald C., *Malaspina and Galiano: Spanish Voyages to the Northwest Coast 1791 & 1792*, Vancouver: Douglas & McIntyre, 1991.

Dalrymple, Alexander, *Plan for promoting the fur-trade, and securing it to this country, by uniting the operations of the East Indies and Hudson's Bay Companys*, London: George Bigg, 1789.

Dawson, L.S., *Memoirs of Hydrography*, Eastbourne: Henry W. Keay, 1885.

Delgado, James, *The Beaver: First Steamship on the West Coast*, Victoria: Horsdal & Schubart, 1993.

Dixon, George, *Remarks on the voyages of John Meares, Esq. in a letter to that Gentleman*, and *Further Remarks on the voyages of J. Meares*, London: Stockdale and Goulding, 1790, 1791.

Doe, Nick, "Gabriola's Coastal Place Names," *Shale*, Number 25, March 2011, Gabriola Island: Gabriola Historical & Museum Society.

———, "A Russian Map of Gabriola—1849," *Shale*, Number 3, January 2002, Gabriola Island: Gabriola Historical & Museum Society.

Dorricott, Linda, and Deidre Cullon, eds., *The Private Journal of Captain G.H. Richards: The Vancouver Island Survey (1860–1862)*, Vancouver: Ronsdale Press, 2012.

Douglas, James, "Report of a Canoe Expedition along the East Coast of Vancouver Island," communicated by the Colonial Office to the Royal Geographical Society and read at meeting, February 28, 1853.

Duff, Wilson, "The Fort Victoria Treaties," *BC Studies*, Number 3, Autumn 1969.

Elms, Lindsay, *Beyond Nootka: A Historical Perspective of Vancouver Island Mountains*, Courtenay, BC: Misthorn Press, 1996. See also members.shaw.ca/beyondnootka/articles/island6000.html.

Forbes, Charles, "Vancouver Island: Its resources and capabilities, as a colony," prize essay, Victoria: Colonial Government, 1862.

Glazebrook, George Parkin de Twenebroker, ed., *The Hargrave Correspondence, 1821–1843*, Toronto: The Champlain Society, 1938.

Gordon, George T., *Cormorant's Remarks Book*, September 22, 1846, Taunton: British Hydrographic Office, Misc. File Number 16, Folder 1, Item 3.

Gough, Barry, *Fortune's a River: The Collision of Empires in Northwest America*, Madeira Park, BC: Harbour Publishing, 2007.

———, *The Royal Navy and the Northwest Coast of North America, 1810–1914*, Vancouver: University of British Columbia Press, 1971.

Hayes, Derek, *British Columbia: A New Historical Atlas*, Vancouver, BC, and Toronto: Douglas & McIntyre, 2012.

———, *Historical Atlas of British Columbia and the Pacific Northwest: Maps of Exploration*, Vancouver, BC: Cavendish Books, 1999.

Hayman, John, ed., *Robert Brown and the Vancouver Island Exploring Expedition*, Vancouver: University of British Columbia Press, 1989.

Hendrickson, James E., ed., *Journals of the Colonial Legislature of the Colonies of Vancouver Island and British Columbia*, Victoria: Provincial Archives, 1980.

Hill, Beth, *Sappers: The Royal Engineers in British Columbia*, Ganges, BC: Horsdal & Schubart, 1987.

Hill, Beth, with Cathy Converse, *The Remarkable World of Frances Barkley 1769–1845*, Victoria: TouchWood Editions, 2003.

Hodgins, Jack, *A Passion for Narrative*, Toronto: McClelland & Stewart, 1993.

Howay, Frederick W., *The Work of the Royal Engineers in British Columbia 1858 to 1863*, Victoria: R. Wolfenden, King's Printer, 1910.

Inglis, Robin, *Historical Dictionary of the Discovery and Exploration of the Northwest Coast of America*, Lanham, MD: Scarecrow Press, 2008.

Ireland, Willard, "Captain Walter Colquhoun Grant: Vancouver Island's First Independent Settler," *BC Historical Quarterly*, Volume XVII, 1953.

———, "The Evolution of the Boundaries of British Columbia," *BC Historical Quarterly*, FC3801, October 1939.

———, "First Impressions," *BC Historical Quarterly*, Volume XV, 1951.

Jane, Cecil, translator, *A Spanish Voyage to Vancouver and the North-West Coast of America*, London: The Argonaut Press, 1930.

"J.D. Pemberton," *British Columbia: Pictorial and Biographical*, Winnipeg: S.J. Clarke, 1914, author unknown.

Lamb, W. Kaye, ed., *The Voyage of George Vancouver 1791–1795*, London: The Hakluyt Society, 1964.

Mackie, Richard, "J.D. Pemberton," *Dictionary of Canadian Biography Online*, National Archives of Canada, biographi.ca.

Manning, William Ray, *The Nootka Sound Controversy*, New York: The Argonaut Press, 1905, 1966.

Mayne, Richard C., *Four Years in British Columbia and Vancouver Island*, London: John Murray, 1862.

McCabe, James O., *The San Juan Water Boundary Question*, Toronto: University of Toronto Press, 1965.

McDowell, Jim, *José Narváez: The Forgotten Explorer*, Spokane, WA: Arthur Clark, 1998.

Meares, John, *Voyages made in the years 1788 and 1789 from China to the North West Coast of America*, London: Logographic Press, 1790.

Pearson, D.F., *A History of the British Columbia Lands Service*, Victoria: 1971, BC Archives Library NW 971.24 B866h.

Pemberton, J. Despard, *Facts and Figures relating to Vancouver Island and British Columbia Showing What to Expect and How to Get There*, London: Longman, Green, Longman, and Roberts, 1860. Pemberton's reports and correspondence are in the Archives of Manitoba, *J.D.P.'s Correspondence, 1851–1855*, location code A.6/120 and also A11/74, microfilm number 47.

Rattray, Alexander, *Vancouver Island and British Columbia: where they are; what they are; and what they may become*, London: Smith, Elder & Co., 1862.

Roberts, John E., *A Discovery Journal: George Vancouver's First Survey Season—1792*, Victoria: Trafford Publishing, 2005.

Ruggles, Richard I., *A Country So Interesting: The Hudson's Bay Company and Two Centuries of Mapping, 1670-1870*, Montreal and Kingston: McGill–Queen's University Press, 1991.

Sampson, Harriet Susan, "My Father, J.D. Pemberton: 1821-93," *BC Historical Quarterly*, Volume VIII, Number 2, 1944.

Sandilands, R.W., "The History of Hydrographic Surveying in British Columbia," unpublished transcript of a paper presented in Victoria, January 28, 1965. A bound copy is in the University of Victoria library, VK 597 C32 S2.

Seeman, Berthold, *Narrative of the Voyage of HMS Herald During the Years 1845–51*, London: Reeve & Co., Volume 1, 1853.

Sherwood, Jay, *Furrows in the Sky: The adventures of Gerry Andrews*, Victoria: Royal BC Museum Publishing, 2012.

Taylor, W.A., BCLS, *Crown Land Grants: A History of the Esquimalt and Nanaimo Railway Land Grants, the Railway Belt and the Peace River Block*, Victoria: Registries and Titles Department, Ministry of Sustainable Resource Management, 1975, 4th reprint 1997.

———, *Crown Lands: A History of Survey Systems*, Victoria: Registries and Titles Department, Ministry of Sustainable Resource Management, 1975, 4th reprint 1997.

———, "Early Cadastral Surveys," The Association of BC Land Surveyors, *The Link*, Victoria, Volume 10, Number 1, July 1987.

Theroux, Paul, "Mapping the World," essay in *Sunrise With Seamonsters*, Boston: Houghton Mifflin, 1985.

Tovell, Freeman M., *At the Far Reaches of Empire: The Life of Juan Francisco de la Bodega y Quadra*, Vancouver: University of British Columbia Press, 2008.

Vaughan, Thomas, and Bill Holm, *Soft Gold*, Portland, OR: Oregon Historical Society, 1990.

Verner, Coolie, "The Arrowsmith Firm and the Cartography of Canada," *Explorations in the History of Canadian Mapping: A Collection of Essays*, Farrell and Desbarats, eds., Ottawa: Association of Canadian Map Libraries, 1988.

Vouri, Michael, *The Pig War: Standoff at Griffin Bay*, Friday Harbor, WA: Griffin Bay Bookstore, 1999.

Wagner, Henry R., *Cartography of the Northwest Coast of America to the Year 1800*, Berkeley: University of California Press, 1937. Reprinted, Amsterdam: N. Israel, 1968.

———, "Confidential Instruction To Be Observed by the Teniente De Fragata of the Royal Navy Don Francisco Antonio Mourelle On His Voyage to the Coast of California in the Schooner *Mexicana*," *Spanish Explorations in the Strait of Juan de Fuca*, Santa Ana, CA: Fine Arts Press, 1933 (204–209).

Washington, John, *Hydrographic Instructions for Capt. George Richards about to proceed to Vancouver's Island*, letter, Taunton: British Hydrographic Office, Misc. File Number 2, Folder 3, Item 2, March 1857, BC Archives GR 284.

Woodward, Frances M., "The Influence of the Royal Engineers on the Development of British Columbia," *BC Studies*, Number 24, Winter 1974–75.

List of Illustrations

Please note that many of the images have been cropped to emphasize specific detail and digitally adjusted for legibility.

Fig. 1	Il Disegno del discoperto della nova Franza. Bolognini Zaltieri, 1566. (Association of Canadian Map Libraries and Archives, facsimile of an original held in Archives Canada)	page 4
Fig. 2	Quivirae Regnum cum aliī versus Boream. Cornelis de Jode, 1593. (Barry Lawrence Ruderman Antique Maps Inc., 23178)	page 6
Fig. 3	detail from Quivirae Regnum cum aliī versus Boream. Cornelis de Jode, 1593. (Barry Lawrence Ruderman Antique Maps Inc., 23178)	page 6
Fig. 4	Nuove Scoperte de' Russi al Nord del Mare del Sud sí nell' Asia, che nell' America. Antonio Zatta, 1776. (author's collection)	page 9
Fig. 5	A Chart for the better understanding of De Font's Letter. Edward Holding, 1748. (private collection)	page 10
Fig. 6	Carte Générale des Découvertes de l'Amiral de Fonte 1640. Robert de Vaugondy, 1755. (private collection)	page 11
Fig. 7	Vera Totius Expeditionis Nauticae. Jodocus Hondius, 1589. (RGS—London, CA15F-013 [003], image taken from a facsimile, not the original map)	page 12
Fig. 8	detail from Vera Totius Expeditionis Nauticae. Jodocus Hondius, 1589. (RGS—London, CA15F-013 [003], image taken from a facsimile, not the original map)	page 12
Fig. 9	Drake's Course in the North Pacific 1579. Richard Bishop, 1939. (University of Victoria Library, Special Collections, FC3801 B7, *British Columbia Historical Quarterly*, v.3, pp. 151–182)	page 15
Fig. 10	Carta particolare dello stretto di Iezo fra l'America è l'Isola Iezo. Robert Dudley, 1647. (author's collection)	page 16
Fig. 11	detail from Carta particolare dello stretto di Iezo fra l'America è l'Isola Iezo. Robert Dudley, 1647. (author's collection)	page 16
Fig. 12	Untitled. 2000. (author's collection, *Mercator's World* magazine, November 2000, p. 19)	page 17
Fig. 13	Carta Reducída del Oceano Asiatico ó Mar del Sur . . . Dn. Juan Perez. Josef de Cañizarez, 1774. (National Archives and Records Administration, NARA RG77 #67)	page 18
Fig. 14	detail from Carta Reducída del Oceano Asiatico ó Mar del Sur . . . Dn. Juan Perez. Josef de Cañizarez, 1774. (National Archives and Records Administration, NARA RG77 #67)	page 18
Fig. 15	Carta reducída de las Costas y Mares Septentrionales de California. Juan Francisco de la Bodega y Quadra and Francisco Antonio Mourelle, 1775. (Archivo General de Indias—Seville, Mexico, 381)	page 21
Fig. 16	Map of the northwest coast from the voyage of Juan Francisco de la Bodega y Quadra 1775. Francisco Antonio Mourelle, 1781. (private collection)	page 22
Fig. 17	A Chart of the North West Coast of America and the North East Coast of Asia, Explored in the Years 1778 & 1779. James Cook and James King, 1784. (author's collection)	page 24
Fig. 18	View of the Entrance of Nootka Sound when the N. point of the Entrance bore E. distant 4 Miles [Cook]. Lieutenant Henry Roberts, RN, 1778. (University of Victoria Library, Special Collections, G420 C6 1784)	pages 26–27
Fig. 19	Sketch of Nootka Sound. Lieutenant Henry Roberts, RN, 1778. (University of Victoria Library, Special Collections, G420 C6 1784)	page 28
Fig. 20	Track of the Snow Experiment in Company with the Captain Cook. S. Wedgbrough, 1789. (University of British Columbia Library, Rare Books and Special Collections, G3350 D34 1789)	page 30
Fig. 21	Plan of Port Effingham in Berkley's Sound. John Meares, 1790. (University of British Columbia Library, Rare Books and Special Collections, ARC 1677 MD1758E)	page 33
Fig. 22	Chart of Part of the NW Coast of America by Captain James Hanna in snow *Sea Otter*. James Hanna, 1786. (University of British Columbia Library, Rare Books and Special Collections, G3350 D34 1789)	page 34
Fig. 23	Sketch of the Entrance of the Strait of Juan de Fuca. Charles Duncan, 1788. (BC Archives, CM_A442)	page 37
Fig. 24	Carte de la Côte Ouest de l'Amérique du Nord, de Mt. St. Elias à Monterey, avec la trajectoire l'expédition de La Pérouse. Gérault-Sébastien Bernizet, 1797. (Archives Nationales—Paris)	page 38
Fig. 25	Plano del Estrecho de Fuca Reconocido y lebantado. Gonzalo López de Haro, 1790. (BC Archives, CM_A447)	page 41
Fig. 26	Carta general de quanto asta hoy se ha descubierto, y examinado por los Españoles en la Costa Septentrional de California. Juan Francisco de la Bodega y Quadra, 1791. (Museo Naval—Madrid)	page 42
Fig. 27	A Sketch of Port Cox in the District of Wicananish. John Meares, 1790. (private collection)	page 43

Fig. 28	A Chart of the Interior Part of North America, Demonstrating the very great probability of an Inland Navigation from Hudson's Bay to the West Coast. John Meares, 1790. (University of Victoria Library, Special Collections, F851.5 M47)	page 45
Fig. 29	Carta esférica . . . de sus canales navegables. Alejandro Malaspina and Moreno Tejada, 1795. (University of British Columbia Library, Rare Books and Special Collections, G3512.V3 1792 .A4)	page 46
Fig. 30	Carta que Comprehende los interiores y veril de la Costa desde los 48° de Latitud N. hasta los 50°. Juan Carrasco, José María Narváez, and Juan Pantoja, 1791. (Library of Congress, LC G3351.P5 1799.C)	page 50
Fig. 31	Plano del Estrecho de Juan de Fuca descuvierto el año 1592, reconocido en 1789 por Dn. José Narváez. Juan Francisco de la Bodega y Quadra, 1792. (Oregon Historical Society, G3512.V3 1792 .B62)	page 53
Fig. 32	A Chart showing part of the Western Coast of N. America. Joseph Baker, 1792. (United Kingdom Hydrographic Office, 228 ON 82)	page 56
Fig. 33	Friendly Cove, Nootka Sound. Henry Humphries, 1798. (Greater Victoria Public Library, Local History Collection, 910.9 VAN V223 VO)	page 59
Fig. 34	A Chart shewing part of the Coast of NW America with the tracks of His Majesty's Sloop Discovery and Armed Tender Chatham. Joseph Baker, 1798. (Greater Victoria Public Library, Local History Collection, LH 910.9 VAN)	page 60
Fig. 35	A Map Exhibiting all the New Discoveries in the Interior Parts of North America. Aaron Arrowsmith, 1795, with additions to 1824. (HBC Archives, Archives of Manitoba, G.4/31)	page 62
Fig. 36	Disputed Territory of Columbia or Oregon, showing its limits as settled by different treaties, and the boundaries proposed by England & America. W. & A.K. Johnston, 1846. (BC Archives, CM_A156)	page 65
Fig. 37	Archipelago of Arro, Gulf of Georgia. United States Exploring Expedition Atlas, *Charts of the Pacific NW coastal territory*, 1841. (BC Archives, CM_B878)	page 66
Fig. 38	Carta Esférica de las Costas del NO de la América, Que corren desde el Puerto y Archípielago de Bucareli. Felipe Bauza, 1791, with annotations in 1793. (Museo Naval—Madrid, 3-E-6)	page 67
Fig. 39	Ground Plan of Portion of Vancouvers Island selected for New Establishment. A. Lee Lewes, 1842. (HBC Archives, Archives of Manitoba, G.2/25)	page 68
Fig. 40	Ground Plan of Portion of Vancouvers Island selected for New Establishment. A. Lee Lewes, 1842. (HBC Archives, Archives of Manitoba, G.2/25)	page 68
Fig. 41	Ground Plan of Portion of Vancouvers Island selected for New Establishment, inset map. A. Lee Lewes, 1842. (HBC Archives, Archives of Manitoba, G.2/25)	page 69
Fig. 42	Victoria Harbour, surveyed by Captain Henry Kellett, RN, 1847. Lieutenant James Wood, Admiralty chart #1897, 1848. (author's collection)	page 70
Fig. 43	Vancouver Island and the Gulf of Georgia, from the surveys of Captain G. Vancouver, RN, 1793; Captains D. Galiano and C. Valdés, 1792; Captain H. Kellett, RN, 1847. Admiralty chart #1917, 1849. (author's collection)	page 73
Fig. 44	Vancouvers Island. James Wyld, 1848. (National Archives UK—Kew, FO 925-1864)	page 74
Fig. 45	The 1850–52 Fort Victoria Treaties. Grant Keddie, 2003. (BC Archives, NW 971.128 K42 2003, "Songhees Pictorial," p. 48)	page 79
Fig. 46	Map of the Victoria District, Vancouvers Island. Walter Colquhoun Grant, 1850. (HBC Archives, Archives of Manitoba, G.1/256 [R. #308A])	page 80
Fig. 47	Untitled. Anonymous, 1850. (HBC Archives, Archives of Manitoba, G.1/134 [R. #309A])	page 80
Fig. 48	Map of Vancouver Island, with the adjacent Coast, to illustrate a description of the Island, by Lieutenant Colonel W.C. Grant. John Arrowsmith, Journal of the Royal Geographical Society, 1857. (author's collection)	page 81
Fig. 49	A Plan of the Town of Victoria shewing proposed improvements. J.D. Pemberton, 1851. (Land Title and Survey Authority, 7L9 Victoria Town)	pages 84–85
Fig. 50	Untitled. J.D. Pemberton, 1852. (HBC Archives, Archives of Manitoba, G.1/130)	page 87
Fig. 51	Victoria District, Section I, Lot No. 2. J.D. Pemberton, 1851. (HBC Archives, Archives of Manitoba, H.1/1 fo. 6)	page 88
Fig. 52	Plan of Reserve of 1300 Acres at Fort Victoria. J.D. Pemberton, 1851. (HBC Archives, Archives of Manitoba, A.11/73 fo. 215B)	page 90
Fig. 53	[Chart of Quadra and Vancouver's Island]. Mikhail Dmitrievich Teben'kov, *Atlas of NW coast of America*, 1849. (Russian State Library, Δ 379/116)	page 93
Fig. 54	Sketch to illustrate Report of a Canoe Expedition along the East Coast of Vancouver Island, by James Douglas, Esquire, Governor. John Arrowsmith, *Journal* of the Royal Geographical Society, 1854. (RGS—London, Society proceedings for 1854)	page 94

Fig. 55	Vancouver Island and Gulf of Georgia. J.D. Pemberton and Edward Weller, 1860. (Greater Victoria Public Library, Local History Collection, 917.11 PEM)	page 96
Fig. 56	Diagram of Victoria and Esquimalt Harbours. J.D. Pemberton and Edward Weller, 1860. (Greater Victoria Public Library, Local History Collection, 917.11 PEM)	page 97
Fig. 57	Untitled. J.D. Pemberton, 1853. (HBC Archives, Archives of Manitoba, G.1/137 [R. #360A])	page 98
Fig. 58	Plan of Reserve . . . Cadboro Bay. J.D. Pemberton, 1852. (HBC Archives, Archives of Manitoba, G.1/258l)	page 100
Fig. 59	Victoria District Official Map. J.D. Pemberton and H.O. Tiedemann, 1858. (Land Title and Survey Authority, 37T2 East Coast VI 37 T2)	page 102
Fig. 59b	list of property owners shown on Victoria District Official Map. J.D. Pemberton and H.O. Tiedemann, 1858. (Land Title and Survey Authority, 37T2 East Coast VI 37 T2)	page 102
Fig. 60	The South-Eastern Districts of Vancouver Island, from a trigonometric Survey made by Order of the Honourable Hudson's Bay Company. J.D. Pemberton, 1855. (BC Archives, CM_W125 or CM_B1549)	page 103
Fig. 61	Vancouver Island. Edward Weller, *Weekly Dispatch Atlas*, 1858. (author's collection)	page 106
Fig. 62	British Columbia (New Caledonia). Edward Weller, *Weekly Dispatch Atlas*, 1858. (author's collection)	page 107
Fig. 63	Map of British Columbia and Vancouver's Island. Francis Young, *British Columbia and Vancouver's Island* (by William Carew Hazlitt), 1858. (BC Archives, NW 971K H431)	page 109
Fig. 64	"The New Gold Colonies." Cover of *British Columbia and Vancouver's Island*, by William Carew Hazlitt, 1858. (BC Archives, NW 971K H431)	page 109
Fig. 65	Sketch K, showing the progress of the survey in Section No. XI, from Tillamook Bay to the boundary, from 1850 to 1857. US Coast Survey, 1857. (author's collection)	page 110
Fig. 66	Vancouvers Island (Second Edition). James Wyld, 1861. (National Archives UK—Kew, FO 925-1479)	page 113
Fig. 67	detail from Admiralty chart #2840—Haro Strait and Middle Channel. Captain G.H. Richards and the officers of HMS *Plumper*, 1860. (Land Title and Survey Authority, 38 Tray 1 Land Reserves)	page 113
Fig. 68	Karte des San Juan od. Haro Archipels mit der neuen Grenze nach der schiedsrichterlichen Entscheidung des Deutschen Kaisers am 21 Oktober 1872. Augustus Petermann, *Geographischer Mittheilungen*, 1872. (author's collection)	page 114
Fig. 69	Sketch of the S.E. end Vancouver Island and Haro Strait . . . with a track of HMS *Virago*, Mr. G.H. Inskip, Acting Master. C.E. Stuart, 1853. (United Kingdom Hydrographic Office, Remarks Book, HMS *Virago* 1853)	page 116
Fig. 70	Haro and Rosario Strait . . . HMS *Plumper* 1858–59. Captain G.H. Richards, RN, Admiralty chart #2689, 1861. (BC Archives, CM_B892)	page 120
Fig. 71	Victoria Harbour Surveyed by Captain G.H. Richards & the officers of HMS *Plumper*, 1859; The Town & Interior from a Survey by J.D. Pemberton, Esquire, Surveyor General. Admiralty chart #1897b, 1861. (BC Archives, CM_C697)	page 121
Fig. 72	Vancouver Island, part of Barclay Sound [Pipestem Inlet], surveyed by HMS *Hecate*. Captain G.H. Richards, 1861. (Land Title and Survey Authority, 16 Tray 1 Charts)	page 123
Fig. 73	ms authentication by RE officer on Vancouver Island, part of Barclay Sound [Pipestem Inlet], surveyed by HMS *Hecate*. Captain G.H. Richards, 1861. (Land Title and Survey Authority, 16 Tray 1 Charts)	page 123
Fig. 74	Vancouver Island and Adjacent Shores of British Columbia. Admiralty Chart #1917, 1865, with corrections 1868. (BC Archives, CM_C2367)	page 124
Fig. 75	Discovery Passage Seymour Narrows [Surveyed Nov. 1866]. Lieutenant D. Pender, RN, 1866. (United Kingdom Hydrographic Office)	page 127
Fig. 76	Discovery Passage Seymour Narrows [Surveyed May 1867]. Lieutenant D. Pender, RN, 1867. (United Kingdom Hydrographic Office)	page 127
Fig. 77	Discovery Passage Seymour Narrows [Surveyed Sept. 1867]. Lieutenant D. Pender, RN, 1868. (United Kingdom Hydrographic Office)	page 127
Fig. 78	Map of the Nanaimo Country comprising four of the Eastern Districts, Vancouver Island. Rudolph d'Heureuse, 1860. (Land Title and Survey Authority, 10T3 Old Maps)	page 128
Fig. 79	Map of Victoria and part of Esquimalt Districts. Day & Son, 1861. (BC Archives, CM_B1523)	page 131
Fig. 80	Map of the City of Victoria, Vancouver Island. Alfred Waddington, 1861. (BC Archives, CM_A497)	page 132
Fig. 81	Map of the City of Victoria, Vancouver Island, numbered, revised and corrected from the Official Map and the best authorities. Alfred Waddington, 1863. (BC Archives, CM_B274)	page 133

Fig. 82	Map of the South-eastern of Districts of Vancouver Island. Rudolph d'Heureuse, 1858. (University of British Columbia Library, Rare Books and Special Collections, G3512.V357 1860 D4)	page 135
Fig. 83	Nanaimo District Official Map. Surveyor General, Vancouver Island, 1859. (Land Title and Survey Authority, 26T2 ECVI, also 12T1 Land Divs)	page 136
Fig. 84	Vancouver Island Colony Index Map. Topographical Depot, War Office, 1859. (Land Title and Survey Authority, 21T1 Land Divs, also 9T3 Old Maps)	page 137
Fig. 85	Plan of Victoria District, Lot 24, Section 18. 1862. (Land Title and Survey Authority, 12T2 Victoria Town)	page 139
Fig. 86	"The Victoria Incorporation Act" Schedule, Plan A. J.D. Pemberton, 1862. (Land Title and Survey Authority, 5T2 Victoria Town)	page 141
Fig. 87	Map of Vancouver Island to illustrate the Paper of Dr. C. Forbes, RN [middle section]. Edward Weller, *Journal* of the Royal Geographical Society, 1865. (author's collection)	page 142
Fig. 88	Vancouver Island Colony, Cowichan District. Rudolph d'Heureuse, 1859. (Land Title and Survey Authority, 33T1 Vancouver Island)	page 146
Fig. 89	British Columbia and Vancouver Island. Edward Weller, 1865. (BC Archives, NW 971M M144 Copy #5)	page 149
Fig. 90	Originalkarte von Vancouver Insel zur Übersicht der Aufnahmen und Forschugen im innern durch die officiellen Expeditionen unter dem Befehl von Robert Brown, 1863–1866. Engraved for Augustus Petermann's *Geographischer Mittheilungen*, 1869. (author's collection)	page 150
Fig. 91	Map of Vancouver Island and part of British Columbia to accompany the Paper by Robert Brown, Esquire. Edward Weller, *Journal* of the Royal Geographical Society, 1869. (author's collection)	page 152
Fig. 92	detail from Map of Vancouver Island and part of British Columbia to accompany the Paper by R. Brown, Esquire [showing Buttle Lake area]. Edward Weller, *Journal* of the Royal Geographical Society, 1869. (author's collection)	page 153
Fig. 93	Map of British Columbia to the 56th Parallel, North Latitude … additions to 1871. J.B. Launders, 1871. (Land Title and Survey Authority, 54T1 Orig. Maps)	page 156
Fig. 94	north point created by ex-Royal Engineers cartographic draftsman J.B. Launders. 1874. (Surveyor General)	page 158
Fig. 95	detail from north point created by ex-Royal Engineers cartographic draftsman J.B. Launders [centre inscribed with the Lord's Prayer]. 1874. (Surveyor General)	page 158
Fig. 96	Bird's-Eye View of Victoria, Vancouver Island, BC. Eli Glover, 1878. (author's collection)	page 159
Fig. 97	detail from Bird's-Eye View of Victoria, Vancouver Island, BC [showing Carr House]. Eli Glover, 1878. (author's collection)	page 159
Fig. 98	Map of the Pacific Ocean across the Rocky Mountain Zone to accompany Report on the Exploratory Survey. Sandford Fleming and Marcus Smith, Canadian Pacific Railway, 1874. (Land Title and Survey Authority, 52T1 Orig. Maps)	page 160
Fig. 99	Vancouver Island. *Encyclopedia Britannica*, ninth edition—vol. XXIV, plate III, 1889. (author's collection)	page 163
Fig. 100	Map of the Esquimalt & Nanaimo Railway Company's Land Grant, Vancouver Island, British Columbia. W.A. Owen, 1905. (courtesy Kilshaw's Auctioneers)	page 164
Fig. 101	"Frontier Survey" Vancouver Island, British Columbia. Lieutenant John I. Lang, RE, and Company Sergeant Major E. Hopkins, 1887. (University of British Columbia Library, Rare Books and Special Collections, G3512 V52 1888 Sheet IV)	page 167
Fig. 102	Map of the South-eastern Districts of Vancouver Island, BC. F.G. Richards, 1880. (BC Archives, CM_D81)	page 168
Fig. 103	Untitled. W. Ralph, 1892. (BC Archives, CM_C991)	page 170
Fig. 104	Map of the Southern Districts of Vancouver Island, BC. M.W. Waitt & Co., 1892. (Land Title and Survey Authority, 12T9 Old Maps)	page 171
Fig. 105	Geological Map of the Northern part of Vancouver Island and adjacent coasts. George M. Dawson, 1887. (Natural Resources Canada, originally published by the Geological and Natural History Survey of Canada)	page 172
Fig. 106	Inset No. 1 to Geological Map of the Northern part of Vancouver Island and adjacent coasts. George M. Dawson, 1887. (Natural Resources Canada, originally published by the Geological and Natural History Survey of Canada)	page 174
Fig. 107	South-Western Districts. BC Department of Lands, 1912. (Land Title and Survey Authority, 1 TR 8 Old Maps)	page 176
Fig. 108	Die Indianerstämme von Vancouver Island und an der Küste von Britisch-Columbia. Dr. Franz Boas, 1887. (University of British Columbia Library, Rare Books and Special Collections, G3512 V352 E3 1887 B6)	page 177

Fig. 109	Northern Part of Vancouver Island showing the reserves of the Kwakiutl Nation. Dr. Franz Boas, 1887. (author's collection)	page 179
Fig. 110	Map No. 1, Reserves May 1, 1864, supplied to Crown Lands Committee by B.W. Pearse, acting surveyor general. 1864. (Land Title and Survey Authority, 6A T1)	page 179
Fig. 111	Geographical Names of the Kwakiutl Indians—Map 8 [Nimpkish River and Lake]. Dr. Franz Boas, 1934. (Greater Victoria Public Library, Local History Collection, 970.3 B662G)	page 180
Fig. 112	list of of Kwakwaka'wakw toponyms for Geographical Names of the Kwakiutl Indians—Map 8. Dr. Franz Boas, 1934. (Greater Victoria Public Library, Local History Collection, 970.3 B662G)	page 181
Fig. 113	Brownlee's New Indexed Map of British Columbia south of 54° North Latitude [overprinted with mining and railway info 1898]. James Brownlee, DLS, 1893. (Land Title and Survey Authority, 16T5 Old Maps)	page 183
Fig. 114	Map of the province of British Columbia [annotated with new Provincial Electoral Boundaries 1898]. Gotfred Jörgensen, Department of Lands and Works, 1895. (Land Title and Survey Authority, 15 Locker I)	page 184
Fig. 115	Map of the South-eastern Districts, Vancouver Island. Gotfred Jörgensen, 1895. (Land Title and Survey Authority, 15T9 Old Maps)	page 185
Fig. 116	The "Province" Exploring Expedition. Anonymous, 1894. (BC Archives, MS-2777 CM_D130)	pages 188–189
Fig. 117	Corrected Map of portion of Vancouver Island explored by Jno. W. Laing and W.W. Bolton. Anonymous, (1896?). (BC Archives, CM_A914)	page 192
Fig. 118	Map showing Portion of West Coast of Vancouver Island. Tom Kains, 1897. (University of British Columbia Library, Rare Books and Special Collections, G3512 V34 G465 1897 B7)	page 193
Fig. 119	Topography—Saanich Sheet. R.H. Chapman and K.G. Chipman, 1909. (Natural Resources Canada, Mem. 36)	page 194
Fig. 120	Topography—Cowichan Sheet. R.H. Chapman and K.G. Chipman, 1909. (Natural Resources Canada, Mem. 96)	page 196
Fig. 121	Topography—Nanaimo Sheet. R.H. Chapman and K.G. Chipman, 1910. (Natural Resources Canada, Mem. 51)	page 196
Fig. 122	British Columbia [part of four-sheet wall-map, annotated with Indian Reserves]. G.G. Aitken, 1912. (Land Title and Survey Authority, 7 Locker T)	page 199
Fig. 123	British Columbia [part of single-sheet version]. G.G. Aitken, 1913. (University of Victoria Library, Special Collections, Drawer 4 Folder 2)	page 199
Fig. 124	Physical Map of Vancouver Island, BC. Kennedy Co. Seattle, 1913. (author's collection)	pages 200–201
Fig. 125	Map of Vancouver Island and Adjacent Islands. T.N. Hibben & Co., 1910. (University of Victoria Library, Special Collections)	page 202
Fig. 126	Southerly portion Vancouver Island. G.G. Aitken, 1913. (Land Title and Survey Authority, #3 and #10 T7 Old Maps)	page 203
Fig. 127	Map of the South-Western Part of British Columbia. Colonist Printing and Publishing Company, 1911. (Land Title and Survey Authority, 9T7 Old Maps)	page 206
Fig. 128	Map of the South-Western Part of British Columbia. Colonist Printing and Publishing Company, 1912. (Land Title and Survey Authority, 2T8 Old Maps, also 1 Tube 170)	page 209
Fig. 129	Sketch map of Strathcona Park, Vancouver Island, BC. S.C. Weston, 1913. (BC Archives, G-03974, 198206-018 [Album])	page 210
Fig. 130	Preliminary topography Strathcona Park. W.W. Urquhart, topographer, and R.H. Thomson, engineer, 1914. (Land Title and Survey Authority, 1 Tube 170)	page 211
Fig. 131	detail from Preliminary topography Strathcona Park. W.W. Urquhart, topographer, and R.H. Thomson, engineer, 1914. (Land Title and Survey Authority, 1 Tube 170)	page 211
Fig. 132	World Aeronautical Chart (215)—Vancouver Island. US Coast and Geodetic Survey, 1945. (National Archives and Records Administration, RG379, Old Series, #215 First Edition)	page 212
Fig. 133	British Columbia Index map of the National Topographic System. Centre for Topographic Information, 1998. (Natural Resources Canada, CTI-05)	page 215

Index

A
Admiralty Inlet, 51, 55, 111, 126
agricultural land, 88, 134, **137**, 138
Aitken, George G., 197–198, **199**, 204, 205, 208, 210
Alaska, 1, 27, 31, 34, 40, 125, 155
Alberni, Pedro, 48
Alberni District, 122, 140, 161, **193**, **203**
Alcalá Galiano, Dionisio, 51, 52, 55, **60**, 72, 118
D'America XXXIII (*Carta particolare*), 14, **16**, **17**
American explorers, 35, 36, 44, 63
Andrews, Gerry, 213
Antoine, Tomo, 145
Dell' Arcano del Mare (Dudley), 14, **16**, 17
Arrowsmith, Aaron
    colony map, **81**, 82, 108
    publishing, 64, 112, 155
    Victoria area, 101, **103**
    Wakash Nation map, **62**, 64
Atlas marítimo español of 1795, 52
Ayala, Juan de, 20, 23

B
Baker, Joseph, 55, **56**
Barkley, Charles, 32, 35, **37**
Barkley, Frances, 32
Barkley Sound, 32, **33**, 122, **123**, **142**
Barrington, Daines, **22**
Bauza, Felipe, 48
Bayly, William, 27
HMS *Beaver*, 64, 67, 125, 126
Beaver Harbour, 75, 91
Bishop, Richard, 14, **15**
Blanshard, Richard, 77, 82, **110**
Boas, Franz, **177**, 178, **179**, **180**, **181**
Bodega y Quadra, Juan Francisco de la
    1775 chart, **21**
    1781 variant map, **22**, 23
    1791 composite map, **42**, 43
    1792 composite chart, **53**
    and Eliza expedition, 47, 49
    and Nootka Convention, 51, 57–58
    and place names, 2, 72, 119
    reoccupation of Nootka, 40, 42–44
    voyage, 20, 23
Bolton, William W., 187, **189**, 190–191, **192**
Boyd, Walter H., 195
Breakers Point, 26, **28**
Britain
    exploration, 13–14, 51–52, **53**, 55
    fur traders, 31–37
    and Nootka, 49, 51, 54, 57, 59, 64
    and Spanish claims, 13, 23, 25, 44
    and US claims, 63–64
British Columbia
    Brownlee map, 182, **183**
    colony of, 104, **107**, 108
    Jörgensen map, 182, **184**, 186
    survey department, 166, 204–205, 213–214
    union with Canada, 155, 161, 173
    united colonies, 115, 134, 154
    and WWI, 210
British Columbia Land Surveyors (BCLS), 162
British explorers
    Drake's voyage, **12**, 13–14
    fur traders, 31–37
    sharing of charts, 51–52, **53**, 55
British–United States boundary
    forty-ninth parallel, 63–64
    map of alternatives, **65**
    San Juan dispute, **110**, 111–115
    water boundary, 72–75, 77, 104, 105, **106**, 108
Brooks Peninsula, 26
Broughton, William, 51, 55, 58, 59
Brown, Robert, **128**, **153**
    expedition, 144, 145, **146**, 147
    memoir, 148, **150**, 151, 155
Brownlee, James, 178, 182, **183**
Bucareli y Ursúa, Antonio, 19, 20, 23
Burrard Inlet, 51
Busk, Charles, 174
Buttle, John, 144, 147, 148, 151
Buttle Lake, **153**, 170, **171**, 182, 190, 208

C
Cadboro Bay, 69, **100**
Campbell River, 205, 208
Canada
    harbour defence, 165–166, **167**
    terms of union, 155, 161, 173
Canada–US boundary. *see* British–United States boundary
Canadian Pacific Railroad, 157, **160**, 161
Cañizarez, Josef de, **18**, 20
Cape Cook, 14
Cape Flattery, **24**, 25, 29
Cape Foulweather, **24**
Cape Lazo, 48
Cape Mudge, 48, 95
Cape Scott, **30**, 32
Cardero, José, 52
Carr, Emily, 158, **159**
Carrasco, Juan, 47, 48, **50**
Carta particolare, 14, **16**, **17**
Carta que comprehende, 49, **50**, 51
cartography. *see* mapmaking
Cavendish, Thomas, 14
Cerros de Santa Clara, **18**, 20
Chapman, Robert H., **194**, 195, 197
Cheslakees, 57, **67**, 92, 143
Chinese explorers, 3, 8
Classet (Neah Bay), 36
Clayoquot Sound, 42, 44, 148, **153**
Clayton, Daniel, 61
coal deposits, 48, 75, 91, **172**, 173
Colnett, James, **43**
colonial development. *see* settlement
Columbia River, 14, 47, **65**, 67
Colviletown, 92, 95, **136**. *see also* Nanaimo
Comox District, 147, **202**
Concepción, 40, 47
Cook, James, 1, **18**, 25–29, 31
Cook's Harbour 1778 (Nootka Sound), **22**, 23
HMS *Cormorant*, 71
Costa Septentrional de California 1791, 42, 43, 47
Courtenay, George, 75
Cowichan, 91
Cowichan District, 145, **146**
Cowichan Lake, 104, 105, **142**, 143
Cowichan Valley, **196**
    settlement, 91, 129, 134, **137**, 138
Cox, John Henry, 35, 36, 44
Crown Mountain, 205, 207

D
Dalrymple, Alexander, 32, 54
Dawson, G. Herbert, 197, 204
Dawson, George Mercer, **172**, 173
Desolation Sound, 51, 55
Dobbs, Arthur, 8
Dominion Astrophysical Observatory, 205
Douglas, James
    1852 canoe expedition, 48, 91, 92, **94**
    and boundary dispute, 108, 112
    career, 75, 76–79, 82, 105, 140
    and Fort Victoria, 67–69
    and gold mining, 104
    and need for survey work, 82, 83, 129–130
    on Pemberton's work, 86, 101
    and treaties, 78–79, 138
Drage, Theodore (T.S.), 8, **10**, 32
Drake, Francis
    latitude of landfall, **12**, 14
    subsequent mapmaking, **15**, **16**, 17
    voyage, **12**, 13–14

228

Dudley, Robert, 14, **16**, **17**
Duncan, 190, 197
Duncan, Charles, 35–36, **37**

E
East India Company, 31, 35, 36
HMS *Egeria*, 126, 198, 210, 214
Eliza, Francisco de, 40, 47, 48–49
Ellison, Price, 207
English Bay, 51, 55
Esquimalt & Nanaimo Railway, land grant, 161–162, **164**, 165–166, 169–170, **171**, **202**, 205
Esquimalt District, **98**
Esquimalt Harbour, 43, 48, 51, 71, 72, **97**, 165–166, **167**

F
Fidalgo, Salvador, 40, 92
First Nations
    Cowichan, 91, 104, 138
    ethnographic sources, 27, 49, 52, **177**, 178, **179**
    fur trade, 27, 29, 31–32, 35, 36, 64
    impact of disease, 63
    land allotments, 78–79, 204
    local geographic names, 51, 67, 92
    oolichan trail, 67, 89, 92, 95, 216
    pictographs, 5
    settlements, 69, **100**, 129
    Songhees, 78–79, 130
    and Spanish, 19–20, 23
    territories, **177**, 178, **179**
Fleming, Edgar, 191
Fleming, Sandford, **160**, 161
Flores, Manuel Antonio de, 39, 40
Fonte, Bartolome de, **11**
    hoax voyage, 8, 10, **21**
Forbes, Charles, **142**, 143, 147
Fort Langley, 64, 74, 119
Fort Rodd Hill, 166
Fort Rupert, 78–79
Fort Vancouver (Columbia River), 64, 75
Fort Victoria. *see also* Victoria (city); Victoria District
    1842 *Ground Plan*, 67, **68**, 69, 79, 82
    harbour, **70**, 72
    settlement, 85, 89, **90**, **121**
    site of, 67–69
    topography, **87**, **88**
France, 39, 59, 63
Fraser River, 51, 64, 119, 154
    gold rush, 104, 108, 111
Friendly Cove (Yuquot), **46**, **59**
    fur trade, 26, 31–32, 35–36
    Meares's property, 58, 59
    occupation, 39–44
    withdrawal from, 59, 63
Frontier Survey maps (1888), 165–166, **167**
Fry, Henry, 169, 182, 190, 205
Fuca, Juan de, 10, 17, 23, 25, 48
fur trade, 27, 29, 31–32, 35, 36, 64

G
Gabriola Island, 48, 118
Galiano Island, 48, 118, 119
Gálvez, José de, 23
Geological Survey of Canada (GSC), 172, 173, 194–197, 214, 216
Glover, Eli, 158, **159**
gold deposits, 145, 147, 148, **168**, 169
Golden Hinde, 13, 14, 191
Golden Hinde Mountain, 191, **211**
Goletas Channel, 51–52, 105, **106**
Gore, William, 165, 169, 175, 186, 204
Grant, Walter Colquhoun, 78, 79, **80**, **81**, 82, 83, **98**
Gray, John, 169, 182, 190
Gray, Robert, 35, 55
Gulf Islands, 48, **116**, 118

H
Haida, 19
Haida Gwaii. *see* Queen Charlotte Islands
Hakluyt, Richard, 13
Hankin, Philip, 122, **124**
Haro Strait, 43, 47, 72, 73, 118
    boundary, 104, 108, 115, 119, 157
Hazlitt, William Carew, 108, **109**
HMS *Hecate*, 122, 125, 126
d'Heureuse, Rudolph, **128**, 134, **135**
Hezeta, Bruno de, 20, **22**, 23
Hibben & Co., **202**, **203**
Hodgins, Jack, 7
Holmes, William J., 205, 207, 208
Hondius, Jodocus, **12**, 14
Hope Bay, 26, 29
Hopkins, E., 165, 166
Horne, Adam, 95, 104
Hudson's Bay Company (HBC)
    and boundary dispute, 73, 75
    fur trade, 35, 64, 67
    Letters Patent, 76–77, 89, 105
    maps of, **62**, 67, 74, 92
    properties, 82, 88, 130, 138, **139**
    treaties, 78–79
Hydrographer of the Navy, the, 35, 54, 117, 125
hydrographic
    charts, 14, **16**, **73**, **110**, **124**
    surveying, 111, 175, 198, 210

J
Jode, Cornelis de, **6**, 7–8
Jörgensen, Gotfred, 182, **184**, **185**, 186, 187
Juan de Fuca strait. *see* Strait of Juan de Fuca

K
Kains, Tom, 170, 175, 178, 182, 186
Keddie, Grant, 79
Kellett, Henry, **70**, 71, 72, 73, 91
Kendrick, John, 35, 40, 48
Kennedy, Arthur Edward, 140, 143, 144, 148, 154
Kennedy, J.H., 198, **201**
King, James, **24**, 29, 31
Kwakiutl, **177**, 178, **179**, **180**, **181**

L
La Pérouse, **38**, 39
Lady Washington, 35, 44, 55
Laing, John William, 191, **192**
land surveyors, 130, 174–175, 195
land title
    cadastral system, **80**, 82, 88, 89, 174
    inaccuracies, 173–175
    new system, **128**, 129–130
    surface rights, 165
Lang, John I., 165, **167**
Langford, 88, **98**
latitude, **17**, 216
    54°40' N, 1, **18**, 67
Launders, James Benjamin, 154, 155, **156**, 157, 158
Leech, Peter, 144, 145, 147
Leech River, 145, 147, 148, 169
Leechtown, 147, 148, **168**, 169
Lewes, Adolphus Lee, 67–69, 78, 79, 82
longitude, **17**, 27
López de Haro, Gonzalo, 40, **41**, 42, 43, 47, 55, 101

M
Macfie, Matthew, 145, 147, **149**
Mackay, John, 32
Makah Bay, 25
Makah nation, 35
Malaspina, Alejandro, **46**, 48, 49, 51, 52
mapmaking. *see also* place names; surveying methods
    cadastral system, **80**, 82, 88, 89, 174
    coastal view charts, **27**, 72
    correcting for longitude, **17**
    earliest, 3–5
    first coordinated point, 27
    hydrographic charts, **16**, 73, 119
    index map, **215**
    Mercator's projection, 14
    motives, 7–10

perspective views, 158, **159**, 198, **201**
and place names, 118, 175, 178, 198
specialized maps, **212**
technology, 3, 208, 213–214
terrain relief, **174**
topography, **87**, **194**, **196**
use of local printing press, 122, **123**
use of scale, 99
Maquinna, Chief, 32, 35, 36, 40, 58
and oolichan trail, **67**, 92
Martínez, Esteban, 39–40, 42
Maurelle Island, 119, 157. *see also* Valdes Island
Mayne, Richard, 117, 122, 138
Mayne Island, 48, 118
Mazarredo Island (Nookta Island), 40, 48, 58
McBride, Richard, 195, 197, 204, 207–208
McKay, Eric "E.B.", 171, 197, 204, 205, 207, 208
McNeill, William, 91
Meade, John, 144, 147, 151
Meares, John, **33**, 35, 36
"butter-pat" map, 44, **45**, 54, 55
Friendly Cove property, 44, 49, 57, 59
Port Cox map, **43**, 44
Meares Island, 44
Menzies, Archibald, 55
Moffatt, Hamilton, 92, 95, 140, 151
Mohun, Edward, 162, **163**, 169, 175
Mount Baker, 55, 158
Mount De Cosmos, **128**
Mount Douglas (Cedar Hill), 82, **87**, 118–119, **120**
Mount Newton, 101, 130
Mount Tolmie, 82, **87**, 119
Mourelle, Francisco, **21**, 23, 49, 119
Mowachaht, 23, 26–27, 32, 36

N
Nanaimo, **128**
coal deposit, 48, 91
Colviletown, 92, 95, **136**
harbour, 48, 92, **94**
treaties, 78–79
Nanaimo District, **136**, **196**
promotion, 134, **137**, 138
Narváez, José María, 47–48, 49, **50**
natural resources, 165, 169, 195
coal, 48, 75, 91, **172**, 173
copper, 74
timber cruising, 190, 204, 217
navigation hazards
charting of, 175
Ripple Rock, 119, 125, **127**
Newton, William, 99, 101

Nimpkish Lake, 92, 151, 162, 169, 173, **174**, **181**, 186
Nitinat Lake, 104, 105, **113**, 151, 186
Nitinat people, **94**, 104
Nootka Conventions, 49, 51, 54, 57, 59, 64
Nootka Island, **18**, 46
circumnavigation of, 40, 48, 58
Nootka Sound, **28**, 46
coastal view chart, **27**, 72
and Cook's voyage, 14, **18**, **22**, 23, **24**
Friendly Cove (Yuquot), **59**
fur trade, 26, 31–32, 35–36
Meares's property, 44, 49, 57, 59
naming of, 26–27
occupation, 39–44, 59, 63
and Spanish claims, 20, 39, 40, 42–44
Northwest America (schooner), 35, 59
Northwest Passage
myths, 8, **9**, **10**, **11**
search for, 8, 23, 25, 32, **45**
Strait of Anian, **4**, **6**, 17
Vancouver's expedition, 51, 54, 61

O
Olympic Peninsula, 67
Oregon Territory, 63–64, **65**, 67, 72, 76

P
Pacific Northwest coast, **38**, **42**
overview, 1–2, 3, 5, 7
place names (toponymy), **17**
Pantoja, Juan, 47, **50**
parks. *see* Strathcona Park
Pearse, Benjamin William
career, **85**, 86, 89, 92, 134, 138, 147
land of, 101, **102**, 105, 140
Pemberton, Joseph Despard, **90**, **121**
about, 83, 155
career, 83–92, 101–104, 134, 147
expeditions, 48, 91, 92, 95, 104
Facts and Figures, 95, **96**, **97**, 104
land of, 101, **102**, 105, 140
and land title system, 89, 99, 105, 129–130, 138
Pender, Daniel, 117, 118, 119, 125, **127**, 157
Pérez, Juan, 1, **18**, 19–20, 23, 26
place names (toponymy), 198
history, 118, 175, 178
Kwakiutl, **180**, **181**
Nootka Sound, 26–27
Pacific coast, **17**
Point Breakers, 26, **28**, 140
Point Roberts, 112, 117
Port Alberni, **193**, **203**

Port Cox, **43**
Princesa Real, 40, 42
The Province, expedition, 187, **189**, 190
Puget, Peter, 55, 57
Puget Sound, 7, 55, 67, 71, 75, **110**
Puget's Sound Agricultural Company (PSAC), 76, 88, 95, 99, 111, 112

Q
Quadra. *see* Bodega y Quadra, Juan Francisco de la
CGS *Quadra*, 175
Quadra and Vancouver's Island, 2, 54–62, **69**
Quadra Island, 119. *see also* Valdes Island
Quatsino Sound, 91, **124**, 173, 190
Queen Charlotte Islands, 1, 19
Queen Charlotte Sound, **10**, **30**, 32, **34**, 39, **172**
Quimper, Manuel, 40, **41**, 42, 43, 49
Quivirae Regnum, **6**, 7–8

R
railway construction, 155
E&N land grant, 161–162, **164**, 165–166, 169–170, **171**, **202**, 205
possible routes, **160**, 161, 182, 204, 207–208, **209**
Ralph, William, 165, 169, 170, 187, 198, 205
Rattray, Alexander, 143
Revillagigedo (Sooke Inlet), 42, 51
Revillagigedo, count of, 40, 47, 49
Richards, Francis G., **168**, 169
Richards, George Henry, 26, 117–127, 140
Ripple Rock, 119, 125, **127**
Roberts, Henry, **28**
Rogers, Henry, 29
Royal Engineers, 89, 105, 112, 122, **123**, 130, **137**, 138, 140, 144, 154, 165, 198, 217
Royal Geographical Society (RGS), 74, **81**, 82, 92, 122, 138, 143, 198
Royal Roads, 42
Rugged Mountain, **18**
Russia, 29, 63
Russian explorers, 1, 19
1849 chart, 92, **93**, 118

S
Saanich Peninsula
maps of, 134, **135**, 195
settlement, 78–79, 129
Salish Sea, 178
Saltspring Island, 92, **194**, 195
San Blas, 19, 20, 23, 39, 40, 49
San Carlos, 20, 23, 40, 47, 48
San Juan Archipelago, 55, **66**, 67, **73**, 104, **106**
boundary dispute, 75, 108, 111–115

San Juan Island, 119
    dispute, 111–112, 115
San Lorenzo, 20, 40
San Miguel (Nootka Sound entrance), 40, **46**
Santa Cruz de Nuca, 42, 43, 47, 48
Santiago, 19, 20, 23
Saturna Island, 48, 118
Scaife, Arthur, 187, 191
Scott, David, 32
settlement. *see also* land title
    agricultural land, 88, 134, **137**, 138
    civic infrastructure, 76
    and the E&N land grant, 162
    expansion of, 99, 169
    first settlers, 88, 99, 101, **102**
    and HBC, 76–77, 88–89, 105
    and land surveying, **85**, 89, **128**, 129–130
    road construction, 88, 89, **97**, 138
    Wakefield system, 76–77, 86, 99, 129
Seymour, George, 71
Seymour Narrows, 125, **127**
Sidney, 119
Sombrio River, 42
Songhees territories, 78–79, 130
Sonora, 20, **21**, 23, 119
Sonora Island, 119. *see also* Valdes Island
Sooke, harbour, **98**, 134, **135**
Sooke Inlet, 42, 51
Spain
    1791 mapping surveys, 47–53
    and Nootka, 39–44, 54, 57, 59
    territorial claim, 1, 19–20, 23, 25
    and US, 64
Spanish explorers, 1, 17, 19–23
    sharing of charts, 51–52, **53**, 55
Spanish-Portuguese Treaty, 13
Sproat, Gilbert, 157
Stanford, Edward, 155
Strait of Anian, **4**, **6**, 17. *see also* Northwest Passage
Strait of Georgia, 48, **50**, 51, **66**, 67, 69, 92, 118
    boundary dispute, 75, 104, 115, 155
Strait of Juan de Fuca
    charts, 36, **37**, **41**, 43
    exploration, 47, 54–55
    identification of, 10, 25, 35, 36
Strange, James, **30**, 32
Strathcona, Lord, 208, **210**
Strathcona Park, **201**, **206**, 207–211
surveying methods. *see also* mapmaking
    chaining, 89
    first coordinated point, 27

latitude, **17**, 216
longitude, **17**, 27
and technology, 3, 208, 213–214
triangulation networks, **110**, 175, **176**
surveyor general, role of, 134, 138, 166, 175
Swiftsure shoal, **38**, 39

T
Tahsis (village), 40, 58
Tahsis Inlet, **18**, 92, 151
Teben'kov, M.D., 92, **93**, **116**, 118
Tetacus, 51, 55
Tiedemann, Hermann Otto, 130, 134, **135**
Tolmie, William, 78, 88
toponymy. *see* place names
Trollope, Henry, 58
Trutch, John, 130
Trutch, Joseph, 151, 154–155, **156**, 157
Trutch Map, 151, **156**, 157
Twin Peaks Mountain, 191

U
United States
    and Esquimalts' defences, 166
    Oregon Territory, 63–64, **65**, 67, 72, 76
    San Juan dispute, **110**, 111–115
    water boundary, 72–75, 77, 104, 105, **106**
    Wilkes expedition, 64, **66**, 67
Urquhart, W.W., 208, **211**

V
Valdes Island, 48, 118, 119, 157, 161, 162, 186
Valdés y Flores, Caetano, 51, 52, 55, **60**, 72, 118
Valerianos, Apóstolos, 25, 48
Vancouver, George
    about, 5, 54, 61
    and Nootka Convention, 57–59
    sharing of charts, 51–52, **53**
    surveying of, **53**, 59, 61, 64
Vancouver Island
    1846 chart, 72, **73**
    1848 chart, 75, 112, **113**
    1856 map, **81**
    1884 map, **163**
    1911 map, **206**
    1912 wall map, 197–198, **199**
    books about, 143–144, 145, 147, **149**
    circumnavigation of, 52, **53**, 61
    colonial development, 76–82
    composite maps, **50**, **56**, **60**
    Drage chart, **10**
    Facts and Figures, 95, **96**, **97**, 104, 140
    flight corridors, **212**

HBC maps, **62**, **69**
interior, **96**, 122, **124**, 143–144, **170**, **171**, 187–192
Mohun's map, 162, **163**
naming of, 2, 54–62, **69**
perspective view, 198, **201**
Trutch Map, **156**
united colonies, 115, 134, 154
Vancouver Island Exploring Expedition, 144–148, 150–153
Victoria (city). *see also* Fort Victoria
    incorporation, 140, **141**
    Johnson Street bridge, 95, **97**
    legislative buildings, 130
    perspective view, 158, **159**
    statue of Vancouver, 61
    street maps, **121**, **132**, **133**, **159**, **185**
Victoria District
    1858 maps, **102**, **103**
    1860 harbour, 95, **97**
    hydrographic chart, **120**
    inland from, **98**
    maps of, **79**, **80**, **131**, **168**
    treaties, 78–79
Voltigeurs, 86, 217

W
Waddington, Alfred, 130, **132**, **133**, 134
Wagner, Henry, 49
Wakash Nation, **62**, 64
Wakefield, Edward Gibbon, 76, 77, 86, 99
Walbran, John T., 175–176
Wedgbrough, S., **30**, 32
Weller, Edward, 95, **96**, **97**, 104–105, **106**, **107**, **142**, 143, 147, **149**, **152**
Wells, Oliver, 134, 138, 145, **146**
Wentuhuysen (Nanaimo Harbour), 48, 92, **94**. *see also* Nanaimo
Whidbey, Joseph, 57
Whymper, Frederick, 145, 147
Wickaninnish, Chief, 32, 42
Wilkes, Charles, 64, 67, 73, 118
Wood, Charles, 122, **124**
Wood, James, **70**, 71–72
Woody Point, 26, 29, 42
world map, 1589, **12**
Wyld, James, 74–75, 112, **113**, 157

Y
Yuquot. *see* Friendly Cove (Yuquot)

Z
Zaltieri, Bolognini, **4**
Zatta, Antonio, 8, **9**

INDEX   **231**

Acknowledgments

I GRATEFULLY ACKNOWLEDGE THE CONSIDERABLE help I have had in preparing this work.

Derek Hayes, for having suggested the idea and for his knowledgeable and generous support as it came to fruition.

The British Columbia Arts Council, for a grant through their Project Assistance for Creative Writers.

Andrew Cook, Nick Doe, Barry Gough, Francis Herbert, Robin Inglis, Grant Keddie, Richard Mackie, Janet Mason, Leonard McCann, Christopher Petter, Ted Roberts, Sandy Sandilands, Bob Ward, and Fran Woodward for their knowledge, expertise, and assistance in locating material.

The archivists, librarians, and map-room staff at the BC Archives, the Land Title and Survey Authority, the University of British Columbia Special Collections, the University of Victoria Special Collections, the Archives of Manitoba, the Royal Geographical Society, the Vancouver Maritime Museum, the Hydrographic Office Taunton, and the Museo Naval, Madrid, for their help.

I have made extensive, and grateful, use of Lindsay Elms's researches into the mountaineering history of the island. His book and website provide much more detail. I thank Barry Cotton for his "The LS Group, British Columbia's First Land Surveyors" and John Whittaker for his "Early Land Surveyors of BC." I have frequently called upon the database "Index of Historical Victoria Newspapers," built by Leona Taylor and Dorothy Mindenhall.

My sincere thanks go to my editor, Marlyn Horsdal, and to my publishers, Pat and Rodger Touchie, and Ruth Linka, for their patience, consideration, and highly professional guidance during the book's long gestation.

And, above all, my thanks go to my wife Jean, for her encouragement, editorial skills, and so much more.